(New #4500)   Used- $22^{50}

D0895572

(New #4500)   Used- $22^{50}

ARCHEOLOGY
OF THE
FROBISHER
VOYAGES

With contributions by Réginald Auger,

Richard G. Cresswell, Robert M. Ehrenreich,

Garman Harbottle, Donald D. Hogarth,

Dosia Laeyendecker, Susan Rowley, Raymond W. Stoenner,

Henry Unglik, Wilcomb E. Washburn, and

Michael L. Wayman

ARCHEOLOGY OF THE FROBISHER VOYAGES

Edited by William W. Fitzhugh and Jacqueline S. Olin

SMITHSONIAN INSTITUTION PRESS
Washington   London

Copyright © 1993 by the Smithsonian Institution.
All rights reserved.

Editing and page layout by Nancy P. Dutro.

Cover design by Janice Wheeler. Cover depicts Frobisher's flagship, the *Ayde,* loaned to him by Queen Elizabeth I, as portrayed in battle in 1580. Detail from a chart (courtesy of London Public Record Office).

Title page: View west over Countess of Warwick Sound from Tikkoon. Kodlunarn Island in left foreground with Gull Rock (featured in John White's battle scene, fig. 1.2) at right. Fog partially obscures Cape Sarah, Newland Island, and Willows Island, right to left in distance.

Library of Congress Cataloging-in-Publication Data
Kodlunarn Island: Archeology of the Frobisher voyages /
edited by William W. Fitzhugh and Jacqueline S. Olin.
        p.   cm.
    Includes bibliographical references and index.
    ISBN 1-56098-171-7
    1. Frobisher Bay Region (N.W.T.)—Antiquities. 2.
Kodlunarn Island (N.W.T.)—Antiquities. 3. Frobisher,
Martin, Sir. ca 1536–1594. 4. America—Discovery and
exploration—English. I. Fitzhugh, William W., 1943–
II. Olin, Jacqueline S. F1105.F74A73 1992
    971.9'5—dc20   92-6561
                                        CIP

British Library Cataloging-in-Publication Data is available.

Manufactured in the United States of America.

∞ The paper used in this publication meets the minimum requirements of the American National Standard for Performance of Paper for Printed Library Materials Z39.48-1984.

For permission to reproduce illustrations appearing in this book, please correspond directly with the authors, or the owners of the works as listed in the individual captions. The Smithsonian Institution Press does not retain reproduction rights for these illustrations individually, or maintain a file of addresses for photo sources.

To the memory of Inuit historians who kept alive the traditions of the Frobisher voyages;

to Charles Francis Hall, explorer, ethnographer, and amateur archeologist, who connected these traditions with the Frobisher voyages and sought to preserve his collections of Frobisher relicts;

and to Walter A. Kenyon, the first professional archeologist to recognize the significance of the Frobisher sites.

Contents

Contributors   ix

List of Illustrations and Tables   xi

Introduction: WILLIAM W. FITZHUGH   1

HISTORY

1

Exploration History of Frobisher Bay:
WILLIAM W. FITZHUGH, DOSIA LAEYENDECKER,
AND DONALD D. HOGARTH   11

A Brief Narrative of the Frobisher Voyages: WILLIAM
W. FITZHUGH AND DOSIA LAEYENDECKER   11

The Ships' Company in the Frobisher Voyages:
DONALD D. HOGARTH   15

Exploration after Frobisher: WILLIAM W. FITZHUGH
16

2

Frobisher Miksanut: Inuit Accounts of the
Frobisher Voyages: SUSAN ROWLEY   27

3

The Frobisher Relics: A Museum History:
WILCOMB E. WASHBURN   41

4

History of Research on the Smithsonian Bloom:
JACQUELINE S. OLIN   49

FIELD STUDIES

5

Archeology of Kodlunarn Island: WILLIAM W.
FITZHUGH   59

6

Field Surveys in Outer Frobisher Bay:
WILLIAM W. FITZHUGH   99

7

Mining and Metallurgy of the Frobisher Ores:
DONALD D. HOGARTH   137

8

Sixteenth-Century Ceramics from Kodlunarn
Island: RÉGINALD AUGER   147

ANALYSIS

9

Wood and Charcoal Remains from Kodlunarn
Island: DOSIA LAEYENDECKER   155

10

Carbon-14 Dating of Iron Blooms from
Kodlunarn Island: GARMON HARBOTTLE,
RICHARD G. CRESSWELL, AND RAYMOND W.
STOENNER   173

11

Metallurgical Study of an Iron Bloom and
Associated Finds from Kodlunarn Island:
HENRY UNGLIK   181

12

Metallurgical Study of Small Iron Finds:
MICHAEL L. WAYMAN AND ROBERT M.
EHRENREICH   213

13

An Evaluation of the Frobisher Iron Blooms: A
Cautionary Tale: ROBERT M. EHRENREICH   221

TAKING STOCK

14

Questions remain: WILLIAM W. FITZHUGH   231

Epilogue   234

Appendices

1. Personnel, ship assignments, and duties in the
   three voyages of Martin Frobisher   241

2. Summary of ships and personnel of the three
   voyages of Martin Frobisher   251

3. 1981 Frobisher catalog of artifacts   252

4. 1981 Frobisher sample list   253

Glossary   255

Bibliography   257

Index   269

Contributors

Réginald Auger
CELAT—Faculté des Lettres
Université Laval
Quebec, PQ, Canada G1K 7P4

Richard G. Cresswell
IsoTrace Laboratory
University of Toronto
Toronto, Ontario, Canada M5S 1A7

Robert M. Ehrenreich
National Materials Advisory Board
National Research Council
2101 Constitution Avenue NW
Washington, D.C. 20418

William W. Fitzhugh
Arctic Studies Center
Department of Anthropology
Smithsonian Institution
Washington, D.C. 20560

Garman Harbottle
Chemistry Department
Brookhaven National Laboratory
Upton, New York 11973
and
Department of Anthropology
State University of New York
Stony Brook, New York 11792

Donald D. Hogarth
Department of Geology
University of Ottawa and Ottawa-Carleton
Geoscience Centre
Ottawa, Ontario, Canada, K1N 6N5

Dosia Laeyendecker
Arctic Studies Center
Department of Anthropology
Smithsonian Institution
Washington, D.C. 20560

Jacqueline S. Olin
Conservation Analytical Laboratory
Smithsonian Institution
Washington, D.C. 20560

Susan Rowley
6660 Forest Glen Road
Pittsburgh, Pennsylvania 15217

Raymond W. Stoenner
Chemistry Department
Brookhaven National Laboratory
Upton, New York 11973

Henry Unglik
Analytical Laboratory
Historic Resource Conservation
Canadian Parks Service
Environment Canada
Ottawa, Ontario, Canada K1A 0H3

Wilcomb Washburn
American Studies Program
Barney House
Smithsonian Institution
Washington, D.C. 20560

Michael L. Wayman
Department of Mining, Metallurgical, and
    Petroleum Engineering
University of Alberta
Edmonton, Alberta, Canada T6G 2G6

List of Illustrations and Tables

Illustrations

n.n.   View west over Countess of Warwick Sound from Tikkoon. Kodlunarn Island in left foreground with Gull Rock (featured in John White's battle scene, fig. 1.2) at right. Fog partially obscures Cape Sarah, Newland Island, and Willows Island, right to left in distance **ii–iii**

I.1   Title page of George Best's narrative of the Frobisher voyages, published in 1578 **xvi**

I.2   Index maps of Frobisher Bay, Baffin Island, and Countess of Warwick Sound **2**

I.3   Paintings by John White of Inuit man, Kalicho, and woman and child, Arnaq and Nutaaq **3**

I.4   Blooms 1, 2, 3 in a controlled atmosphere chamber after transfer to Ottawa, January 1982 **6**

n.n.   Kodlunarn Island from the hills above Tikkoon **8–9**

1.1   "Map of Frobisher Bay and Meta Incognita, with XVIth Century Place Names," from Stefansson and McCaskill 1938 **10**

1.2   "Encounter with Eskimos," depiction of an Inuit attack by the artist John White, and photo of the site of the encounter **12–13**

1.3   James Beare's schematic view of Martin Frobisher's discoveries **14**

1.4   Frobisher's flagship, the *Ayde* **14**

1.5   "A Chart of Frobisher Bay . . . showing the track and discoveries of C. F. Hall" **17**

1.6   "Contents of Box J," Hall's illustration of relics he sent to the Royal Geographical Society for deposit **18**

1.7   Pencil illustration from Hall's archives of two blooms **18**

1.8   "The Author and his Innuit Company . . . gathering Frobisher Relics" **19**

1.9   "Frobisher Relics in my old Stockings" **19**

1.10   Map of Countess of Warwick Sound by C. F. Hall **20**

1.11   "Kodlunarn—or White Man's—Island." Map of Frobisher finds and features prepared by C. F. Hall **20**

1.12   Donald MacMillan team excavating Fenton's house foundation on Kodlunarn Island, 1929 **21**

1.13   Smithsonian field team aboard Pauloosie Kilabuk's boat, August 1981 **24**

2.1   The *George Henry* in winter quarters **26**

2.2   "Esquimaux chart No. 1, drawn by Koojesse at Rescue Harbor, 1860" **28**

2.3   "Tookoolitoo, C. F. Hall, and Ebierbing" **30**

2.4   "Innuit Summer Village" **31**

2.5   "One of Frobisher's gold 'proofs.' (An iron relic of 1578)" **31**

2.6   Inuit models of the iron anvil **33**

2.7   "The discovery of Frobisher relics nearly three hundred years old, Sunday, August 11, 1861" at Niountelik Island **35**

2.8   Sketch map of Kodlunarn Island region showing locations and place names relating to the Frobisher story as told to Hall by Inuit in 1861–62 **35**

2.9   Sketch drawn for Hall by Ookijoxy Ninoo **37**

3.1   Title page to *Martin Frobisher* by Dionyse Settle, 1577 **41**

3.2   Martin Frobisher portrait by Cornelius Ketel **42**

3.3   World Map, attributed to James Beare **43**

3.4   Michael Lok's Map, 1582 **44**

4.1   An iron bloom in the collection of the Department of Naval History, National Museum of American History, Smithsonian Institution **48**

4.2   Smithsonian bloom base after sampling for conventional carbon-14 dating **51**

4.3   Graph showing weights of blooms produced by the bloomhearth during its period of use **52**

4.4   Change in phosphorus content of slag and metal, later Medieval Iron Age **53**

4.5   Diagram of a furnace at High Bishopley, Co. Durham, in the British Isles used for iron smelting in the 12–13th century **54**

4.6   Plan of excavation of the 12–13th-century iron smelting site at High Bishopley, Co. Durham **55**

n.n.   Excavation in progress at Kamaiyuk site **56–57**

5.1   Smithsonian team working at Frobisher's smithy on Kodlunarn Island **58**

5.2   "Ig-loos or Snow Village at Oopungnewing" **60**

5.3   Archeological features located in 1981 **62**

5.4   Map of Frobisher features, 1981 survey **64**

5.5   Southeast side of Kodlunarn Island, the major area of Elizabethan settlement, at low tide **65**

5.6   Dry pond west of smithy, view east **66**

5.7   James Blackman and Garman Harbottle excavating test pit at western edge of the Frobisher smithy **67**

5.8   Structure 1 (smithy) plan **67**

5.9   Structure 2 (assay shop), looking south **69**

5.10   Structure 2 (assay shop) plan **69**

5.11   Structure 3 (charcoal "store") **70**

5.12   Structure 3 (charcoal "store") plan **70**

5.13   Structure 4 ("dam") **70**

5.14   Structures 5 and 6 (cache pits) area, possibly with Hall's Inuit tentrings to right, view west **71**

5.15   Profile of Structure 6 cache **71**

5.16   Structure 5 cache, view northeast **71**

5.17   Structure 6 cache vandalized, view northwest **71**

5.18   Structure 7 (longhouse), view south **72**

5.19   Structure 7 (longhouse) plan **73**

5.20   Structure 8, "Watch Tower", a stone and mortar construction house built by William Fenton at the crest of Kodlunarn Island, as it appeared in 1990, view west **74**

5.21   Plan of Structure 8, Fenton's tower **74**

5.22   1990 survey team inspects Structure 9 cairn and commemorative plaque erected in 1966 **75**

5.23   Joshua Fitzhugh at Structure 10 (mine/ reservoir), view southeast **76**

5.24   Schematic profile of Structure 11, a buried pit near the cove edge south of the Structure 1 smithy **76**

5.25   Structure 12 (ship's trench), view north **77**

5.26   Bloom 2 excavation site in ship's trench **77**

5.27   Wilcomb Washburn at bloom 3 excavation site at lower end of ship's trench **78**

5.28   Wood remains associated with bloom 3 **78**

5.29   Best's Bulwark, with Inuit tentrings, view southeast **79**

5.30   Structure A5 tentring sketch map **80**

5.31   Structure A7, sketch map and photo **81**

5.32   Bloom 1 (KeDe-1:87) **83**

5.33   Bloom 2 (KeDe-1:87) **84**

5.34   Bloom 3 (KeDe-1:90) **85**

5.35   Lookout Island bloom **86**

5.36   Iron arrowhead found in A7 tentring **87**

5.37   Crucible fragments from Structure 2 **89**

5.38   Slag encrusted crucible rim sherds from Structure 1 pond area **89**

5.39   Crucible cross-sections showing fused paste of a slag-encrusted specimen, KeDe-1:18, and unfused paste of an unused specimen, KeDe-1:21 **89**

5.40   Pedestal base of broken and unused crucible fragment, KeDe-1:39 **89**

5.41   Crucible plates. KeDe-1:71, KeDe-1:83, and cross-section of KeDe-1:21 **89**

5.42   Crucible plate fragments, KeDe-1:26-27-28, with glazed edge **89**

5.43   Ceramic rooftile fragments, KeDe-1:74, and section of uncatalogued cross-section fragment **90**

5.44   Early 17th-century English rooftile (courtesy of Walter Kenyon and Royal Ontario Museum) **90**

5.45   Slag lumps with encrusted soil from test pit in Kodlunarn Island 1 smithy **92**

5.46   Nodules of English flint found in coal deposit at Denham's Mount mine **92**

6.1   Ancient Inuit camp at Kamaiyuk **98**

6.2   Inuit brought home to England by Martin Frobisher in 1577, from engraving in Dionyse Settle's *La Navigation . . .*, published in Geneva in 1578 **100**

6.3   Changes in Eastern Inuit dwelling styles in response to European contact ca. AD 1200–1900 **101**

6.4   RV *Pitsiulak* in Jackman Sound, August 1991 **102**

6.5   Archeological survey regions in outer Frobisher Bay and Cyrus Field Bay, 1990, 1991 **103**

6.6   20th century Inuit tentring **104**

6.7   Winter's Furnace mine on northeastern Newland Island   105

6.8   Donald Hogarth inspects "black ore" spoil pile at Countess of Sussex Mine   105

6.9   Archeological sites found in 1981, 1990, and 1991   106

6.10 Inspecting the coal deposit at Denham's Mount Mine (Kenyon's "Judy" Point), Victoria Bay   108

6.11 Lefferts Island black ore quarry on Beare Sound. View east   109

6.12 Quartz outcrop in inner reaches of Jackman Sound, probably Frobisher's "Smithes Island silver mine"   109

6.13 Anvil Cove 1 site, location of Inuit tent camps found above a remnant lens of Frobisher coal, eroding at the bank   110

6.14 South shore of Kodlunarn Island showing rapidly eroding banks at "Best's Bulwark" and smithy area sites   111

6.15 Late Dorset implements collected from eroding bank at Willows Island 1 (KeDe-2)   112

6.16 Willows Island 2 (KeDe-8) Late Dorset implements from eroding bank   112

6.17 Walrus mandibles nested tooth-side up in part of a 5-meter line at Willows Island 2   113

6.18 Nestled walrus mandibles at Anvil Cove 1, part of a sinuous 25-meter-long alignment in which all mandibles have been buried tooth-side down   114

6.19 Tikkoon Point west beaches, overlooking black ore outcrop on shore and Kodlunarn Island   115

6.20 Tar-encrusted hearth base with two kettle-bottom depressions at crest of Tikkoon beachpass   115

6.21 Remnants of one of several unusual rectangular stone pavements (S4) at Tikkoon, partially buried under slopewash   116

6.22 Cape Sarah Neck 1 (KeDe-3), Transitional Dorset, ca. 2500 B.P., ground and spalled burins and spalls   117

6.23 Early winter site, Hall Peninsula 1, visited by Hall in 1862 (Kussegeerarkjuan)   118

6.24 Kuyait site area (KfDf-2), view to south   118

6.25 Kuyait House 8, excavation in progress   119

6.26 European materials found in Kuyait House 8   119

6.27 Kamaiyuk site (Napoleon Bay 1, KfDe-5), view south   120

6.28 Kamaiyuk House 2 in process of excavation   121

6.29 Artifacts collected from eroding Kamaiyuk houses   121

6.30 Whalebone plaque with inset rim and perforations for mounting, found at base of House 2, Kamaiyuk   121

6.31 Minguktoo site at Brewster Point, Barrow Peninsula   122

6.32 Well-preserved house depressions at Imilik (Ward Inlet) which date to Dorset and Thule times   122

6.33 Modern Inuit dwelling in Waddell Bay with sod walls, carpeted roof, and hold-down rocks   123

6.34 York River entering York Sound and gravel bar on which Inuit were probably camped at time of the arrival of Frobisher's ships in 1577. View north   124

6.35 View south over York Sound 1 site   124

6.36 "Weasel Point" cache of ship's timber, dowel, and iron spikes   125

6.37 Eric Loring, Ned Searles, and Pauloosie Pishuktie at Late Dorset Itilikjuak site (KfDd-2), House 1, view east   126

6.38 Late Dorset finds from Itilikjuak   126

6.39 Eric Loring finding Hall's Lookout Island iron bloom at Cyrus Field Bay 1 (KfDc-1), one meter from the white bank of rocks marking the encroaching sea's high tide line. View to northeast   127

6.40 Surface finds from Cyrus Field Bay 1 (Lookout Island) site (KfDc-1)   127

6.41 Lookout Island finds   127

6.42 Lookout Island iron bloom in situ in bed of rust flakes   128

6.43 Island-95 lookout hill structure inspected by Skipper Perry Colbourne   128

6.44 Ned Searles and Eric Loring mapping George Henry Island 1 (KfDd-4) Thule/Recent Inuit site, Structure 20. View to west   129

6.45 Lead sheet, nail, and trigger guard, the latter found eroding into the sea from a small cache in Structure 1, KfDd-4, George Henry Island 1   129

6.46 Aerial view of Cape Haven whaling station, view east   130

6.47 Corner of main structure at Cape Haven showing large paving stones and sea-washed wood remains and driftwood   130

6.48 Anne Henshaw and Lynda Gullason inspecting Inuit tentrings at the Cape Haven station   131

6.49 Iron nauluk, based on traditional Inuit design, with a chunk of weathered and sawn ivory found eroding from the bank into the sea at the Cape Haven site   131

6.50 Kamaiyuk Houses 3 and 4 showing whalebone and collapsing walls   133

6.51 Recent Inuit tent ring near "Best's Bulwark" half-eroded into the sea   134

6.52 1990 field team   135

6.53 1991 field team   135

7.1   A fanciful depiction of a Frobisher mine in the third expedition   136

7.2   Location map showing established and probable mines, approximate position of other mines, and coal deposits   139

7.3   Countess of Warwick Mine, Kodlunarn Island
      140

7.4   16th-century mining tools, from Agricola (1561)
      143

7.5   Etching in the anonymous Mining Laws and
      Statutes of Bohemia (Anon. 1616), copied from
      an unidentified 16th-century woodcut, showing
      curved, single-tined picks, weighty sledges, and the
      combined pick and sledge operation of breaking
      rock in a European mine   **144**

7.6   16th-century assay laboratory in Ercker's
      Beschreibung Allerfürnemsten **145**

8.1   Coarse earthenware culinary vessels, rim sherds
      148

8.2   Utilitarian decorated sherd, green lead glaze on
      plastic decoration; crucible sherds; cupel sherds
      148

8.3   Scorifier, crucible and cupel, from Agricola (1950)
      149

8.4   Refractory ceramics; red tile fragments   **149**

8.5   Muffle, from Agricola (1950)   **150**

8.6   Bowl sherd, beige fabric, clear lead glaze; reddish
      brown coarse earthenware sherd   **151**

n.n. Willow (*Salix* sp.), radial section   **152–153**

9.1   Driftwood occurrence on Chapell Inlet beach
      154

9.2   Charcoal production in Elizabethan England,
      sequential illustrations   **156–157**

9.3   Microscopic features of hardwood (dicotyledonous
      wood)   **159**

9.4   Microscopic features of coniferous wood   **159**

9.5   Macroscopic features of wood   **159**

9.6   Major directions of ice drift and surface currents in
      the Arctic Ocean and Northeast Canada, showing
      treeline of the subarctic region and driftwood
      occurrences and origins   **164**

9.7   Radiocarbon dates (calibrated 1 σ range) from
      Kodlunarn Island (KeDe-1)   **166**

9.8   Oak (*Quercus* sp.), transverse section   **168**

9.9   Oak (*Quercus* sp.), radial section   **168**

9.10 Beech (*Fagus* sp.), transverse section   **168**

9.11 Beech (*Fagus* sp.), tangential section   **168**

9.12 Birch (*Betula* sp.), transverse section   **169**

9.13 Birch (*Betula* sp.), radial section   **169**

9.14 Willow (*Salix* sp.), transverse section   **169**

9.15 Willow (*Salix* sp.), radial section   **169**

9.16 Ash (*Fraxinus* sp.), transverse section   **170**

9.17 Ash (*Fraxinus* sp.), tangential section   **170**

9.18 Ash (*Fraxinus* sp.), radial section   **170**

9.19 Maple (*Acer* sp.), transverse section   **171**

9.20 Maple (*Acer* sp.), tangential section   **171**

9.21 Hazel (*Corylus* sp.), transverse section   **171**

9.22 Hazel (*Corylus* sp.), radial section   **171**

9.23 Coniferous sp. (*Picea-Larix* type), transverse
      section   **172**

9.24 Coniferous sp. (*Picea-Larix* type), tangential
      section   **172**

9.25 Coniferous sp. (*Picea-Larix* type), radial section
      172

10.1 Stuiver calibration curve for conventional
      radiocarbon dates   **177**

10.2 Portal detail in the stave church at Hylestad,
      Aust-Agder, Norway   **180**

11.1 Photogrammetric record of bloom 2, KeDe-
      1.87.981   **182**

11.2 Sketches of iron blooms   **183**

11.3 Location of macrosections in bloom 2   **183**

11.4 Iron blooms before and after sectioning   **184**

11.5 Structural phases in iron bloom 2: Part H
      (at widest end)   **186**

11.6 Structural phases in iron bloom 2: Part V
      (at smallest end)   **187**

11.7 Structure of metal in bloom (Part H)   **188**

11.8 Structure of metal in bloom (Part V)   **189**

11.9 Structure of slag in bloom   **192**

11.10 Constitution and melting point of slag in bloom 2
      196

11.11 Structure of lumps of slag and cinder   **199**

11.12 Constitution and melting points of lumps of slag,
      contaminated slag, and cinder   **202**

11.13 Constitution of slag from Kodlunarn Island in
      terms of $(FeO + MnO)$, SiO_2, and $(CaO + Al_2O_3 + MgO + P_2O_5)$ **203**

11.14 Structure of bloom fragments   **205**

12.1 Locations where samples were cut from original
      objects   **214**

12.2 Microstructure of transverse section of arrowhead,
      showing nonmetallic inclusions in metallic matrix
      215

12.3 Microstructure of transverse section of arrowhead,
      showing nonmetallic inclusions in equiaxed ferrite
      matrix   **215**

12.4 Microstructure of wedge, showing distribution of
      graphite flakes in metallic matrix   **216**

12.5 Microstructure of wedge, showing graphite flakes
      embedded in a background structure that consists
      of pearlite dendrites in a matrix of eutectic steadite
      217

12.6 Microstructure of wedge, showing details of the
      pearlite dendrites and the eutectic steadite   **217**

13.1 Summary of the iron production cycle for a basic
      hand-bellowed, charcoal-burning furnace system
      222

13.2 Illustration of the 16th century ore-roasting
      process (Agricola 1950:275)   **223**

13.3 Illustration of the 16th century procedure for
      crushing ore (Agricola 1950:272)   **224**

13.4 Cleaning of an iron bloom through repeated
      heating and hammering (Agricola 1950:422)
      224

n.n.   Polar bear photographed in Jackman Sound, 1991
       229
14.1   Dosia Laeyendecker mapping Structure A7
       tentring at Tikkoon   **230**

Tables
2.1   Questionnaire devised by Charles F. Hall   **32**
2.2   Number of Inuit observations of Frobisher relics at
       different places   **34**
5.1   Frobisher structures and features on Kodlunarn
       Island   **63**
5.2   Kodlunarn Island tent camps   **82**
5.3   Kodlunarn Island date list   **85**
6.1   Archeological sites recorded in 1981, 1990, and
       1991   **107**
7.1   Tonnages of ore shipped in the third voyage (1578)
       138
7.2   Miners' tools appearing in the bills of lading
       142
8.1   Ceramics inventory from Kodlunarn Island and
       two Inuit sites   **147**
9.1   Occurrences of identified charcoal in different
       structures   **162**
9.2   Radiocarbon dates from wood and charcoal
       samples from Kodlunarn Island   **167**
10.1   Radiocarbon dates of the iron blooms from
       Kodlunarn Island   **176**
11.1   Designation of iron blooms from Kodlunarn Island
       181
11.2   Microstructure of iron bloom 2   **185**

11.3   Microhardness of phases in iron bloom 2, HV_{50}
       189
11.4   Comparison of part H and part V of bloom 2
       190
11.5   Analysis of selected iron samples in bloom 2, wt.%
       191
11.6   Average composition of English and Irish blooms,
       wt.%   **191**
11.7   Microhardness of slag phases in bloom 2, HV_{50}
       192
11.8   Analysis of slag in bloom 2, wt.%   **193**
11.9   Average composition of ancient bloomery slags
       from various countries, wt.%   **194**
11.10 Constitution of slag in bloom 2, wt.%   **195**
11.11 Location and material of associated finds   **196**
11.12 Description of lumps of slag and associated
       material   **197**
11.13 Microstucture of lumps of slag   **198**
11.14 Microhardness of phases in slag lumps, HV_{50}
       198
11.15 Microhardness of phases in cinder lumps, HV_{50}
       200
11.16 Average composition of lumps of slag and cinder,
       wt.%   **200**
11.17 Constitution of lumps of slag, wt.%   **201**
11.18 Average content of microconstituents in lumps of
       slag and cinder, wt.%   **202**
11.19 Microstructure of bloom fragments   **204**
11.20 Microhardness of phases in bloom fragments,
       HV_{50} **204**
11.21 Analysis of bloom fragments, wt.%   **204**

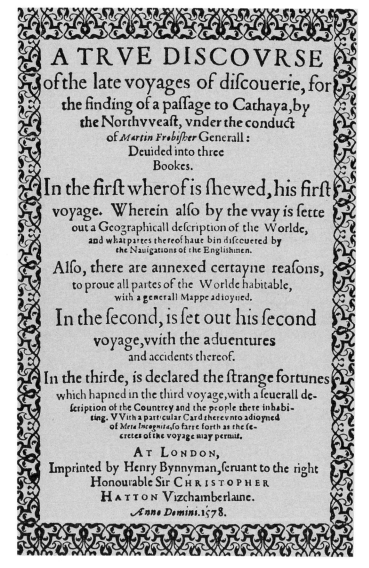

Fig. I.1. George Best's narrative of the Frobisher voyages appeared in print immediately after the third and final voyage in 1578 (title page shown above, from Stefansson and McCaskill 1938). Because his text is the only account to cover all three voyages and because Frobisher himself never learned to write, it has often been relied upon as the "official" account. Despite some biases and inaccuracies, it provides the best and most comprehensive first-hand description of the voyages. His informative commentary on arctic navigation and geography and his descriptions of Inuit life, material culture, and customs are among the first (following D. Settle) written records of Inuit ethnography. They also show concern for objectivity and descriptive accuracy at the dawn of the Elizabethan age.

Introduction

WILLIAM W. FITZHUGH

It sometimes happens that discovery of a single extraordinary, inexplicable artifact will touch off a whole train of archeological, literary-historical, or laboratory research, and such has been the impact of the Smithsonian Frobisher bloom (Harbottle et al., this volume).

The three voyages of Martin Frobisher hold a curious place in the history of New World exploration. Their failure to discover a quick and direct route to Cathay for England via the fabled Northwest Passage dampened European enthusiasm for arctic exploration and helped turn British interest in colonization and exploitation to southern regions of the New World. Few would recall this event further were it not for an indignant spouse who hurled her husband's "token of possession"—a chunk of black rock—from the first 1576 voyage into the fire in a fit of pique over the negative outcome of the voyage. When the rock was retrieved it sparkled "with a bright marquesset of golde," setting in motion the largest arctic exploration venture ever organized. But shortly after Frobisher's fifteen-ship armada returned in the fall of 1578, new assays revealed the "ore" to be worthless, and Frobisher and his chief financier, Michael Lok, were discredited, facing bankruptcy and legal proceedings. Despite disastrous consequences for the financiers, Frobisher was exonerated. His more lettered captains and "gentlemen adventurers" produced admirable accounts, many of which were published, making the Frobisher voyages among the best documented of the early exploration era.

For traditional historians, the story of the Frobisher expeditions is a sidebar among New World discovery sagas (McFee 1928). The voyages did not lead to new resources or markets, or settlement of new lands. In fact, the extensive historical documentation actually discouraged scholars from further study. As pundits noted, with so much already written, what was left to learn? Historians with a Western perspective found little reason to pursue further studies of the Frobisher archives.

In fact, the Frobisher voyages are a gold mine of scholarly information about the expanding European world at the beginning of the discovery era. The vast quantities of documents amassed by these voyages contain valuable information about Europe's—and particularly England's—attitude toward America (Taylor 1930). They reveal much about

1

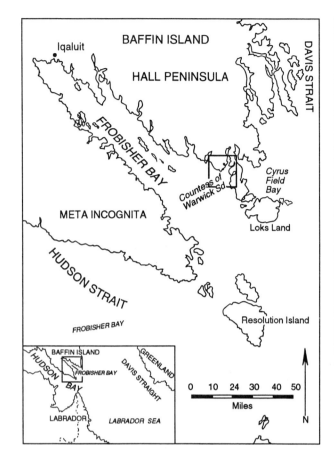

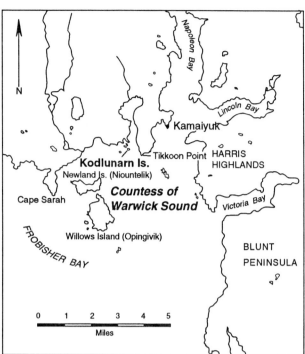

Fig. I.2. Index maps of Frobisher Bay, Baffin Island (left); Countess of Warwick Sound (above).

Elizabethan attitudes and conceptions of native peoples as geographic expansion and contacts with non-European societies revolutionized medieval European concepts of humanness and civilization. They tell us much about pioneering investment groups and financial practices that advanced 16th-century exploration and led the world into corporate and cultural renaissance. They also tell much about Inuit life and culture (Sturtevant and Quinn 1987). In fact, following fanciful folkloristic Norse accounts of Skraelings, the sober descriptions of the East Baffin Inuit by Frobisher's captains are refreshingly objective and ethnographic (cf. Boas 1888). Like John Davis, who explored Cumberland Sound (Quinn 1979:228–251) a decade later in 1585–87 and produced equally interesting accounts, the Frobisher reports provided Europe with its first detailed views of North American arctic peoples. These descriptions reveal a populous society whose complex social, religious, and political systems and wide-ranging contacts and economic exchanges flourished

in an environment harsher than any known to Europeans. To their great surprise, both Frobisher and Davis discovered that the Baffin Inuit had iron-tipped weapons, bars of iron, "fouresquare" iron needles, and buttons of copper worn on the forehead as ornaments. According to George Best, the Inuit "made signs" to them that they had seen gold and "bright plates of metal" among some people with whom they had commerce (Stefansson and Mc-Caskill 1938, 1:125–6). This information and the Oriental racial character of the Inuit he met led Frobisher to believe his self-styled title "High Admiral of Cathay." In short, the Frobisher and Davis descriptions hold considerable promise for new interpretation.

Frobisher's "failure" was especially important to history and ethnography because after these voyages Eastern Arctic Inuit slipped back into obscurity for 250 years, not to emerge again until the 19th-century contacts of Hall, Parry, Lyon, Ross, Rae, and Boas. In this expanded view, the Frobisher story is

Fig. I.3. Kidnapping and hostage-taking were practiced by both Frobisher and the Inuit in 1576. That year Frobisher captured an Inuk (described by Best as "this new prey"), whose Asiatic features convinced financiers that Cathay could be reached via "Frobisher's Streights." But the Inuk soon died and was buried in Saint Olaves Churchyard in London (Cheshire et al. 1980; Sturtevant and Quinn 1987:82). The next year Frobisher returned to London with three captives. The man, Kalicho, and the woman and child, Arnaq and Nutaaq, seen here, were painted by John White, most famous for his paintings of Virginia Natives (courtesy of the British Museum).

not only the account of an early English settlement in the Americas; it documents in written word and material remains one of the earliest episodes of European contact and offers a fascinating opportunity for scholarly inquiry at the interface of history, archeology, anthropology, and natural science.

For four centuries these voyages have been under

the purview, primarily, of traditional historians. In recent years this pattern has begun to change as researchers from other fields have sought data in the published histories and archival holdings. Increased attention to Frobisher research has been stimulated by the need to address new questions involving the history of science and technology, history of finance

(McDermott 1984), details of the Frobisher mine and ores (works of Hogarth and coauthors), ethnohistory (e.g., Cheshire et al. 1980; Sturtevant and Quinn 1987), and archeology (Kenyon 1975a,b; Fitzhugh 1985a). Whereas from a traditional historian's point of view the reams of unpublished archival documents including lading lists, personnel records, and financial accounts (figured to the penny for the bankruptcy proceedings, e.g., McDermott 1984: appendix) added little knowledge about court intrigues and the progress of nations, the quality of documentation of a pioneering commercial and discovery enterprise is an untapped treasure trove for historians and for other disciplines.

Yet, strangely, one of the most neglected areas of research has been study of the physical remains of the Frobisher settlements themselves. While the sites have been visited periodically by scientists and explorers, Charles F. Hall's discovery of the Frobisher mines, workshops, and artifact remains failed to excite scholarly interest for more than one hundred years, until stimulated by new research begun independently at the Royal Ontario Museum and the Smithsonian Institution in the 1970s. This delay is all the more surprising when one considers that the Kodlunarn Island sites are the earliest remains of English exploration in the New World. This fact somehow never seemed to cross the minds of arctic archeologists who since the 1930s were busy excavating Eskimo/Inuit archeological sites without pausing to consider the value of historical archeology at the Frobisher sites, apparently in the belief that these sites were sufficiently documented in historical records and had little intrinsic scientific value except as historical monuments. But recently the practice of historical archeology has begun to take root in the Arctic and has provided a new source of scholarly information about the history of arctic exploration and European-Inuit relationships and cultural development.

Whereas early interest in the Frobisher sites resulted from antiquarian curiosity, the new wave of research owed its origins to both commemorative and scholarly programs. Stimulated by the upcoming 400th anniversary of the Frobisher voyages, pioneer Canadian historical archeologist Walter Kenyon organized a Royal Ontario Museum excursion to Kodlunarn Island in 1974, returning with the first modern documentation from the site (Kenyon 1975b). Concurrently, research at the Smithsonian Institution began to focus on the Frobisher site in an attempt to determine the age of a curious iron artifact, known technically as an iron "bloom"—in effect a partially processed mass of smelted iron ore—that had remained unstudied since it had been deposited in the Smithsonian collections by Hall in 1863.

The Smithsonian Institution's involvement in Frobisher research began with Hall's donation of his records and half of his collection of artifacts to the institution. Further Smithsonian association with East Baffin came with publication of Franz Boas's *The Central Eskimo* by the Bureau of American Ethnology in 1888. Later, Henry Collins, the Smithsonian's pioneering arctic anthropologist, conducted excavations at Frobisher Bay at Crystal II Dorset and Thule culture sites (Collins 1950).

The studies reported here therefore result from a convergence of efforts and interests whose interdisciplinary, interinstitutional, and international nature reflect the history of the Frobisher voyages and subsequent research on the Kodlunarn Island sites and related documentation. This research has been directed at issues surrounding the Frobisher voyages, at studies of the Frobisher sites and remains, at its environmental context, and at an important aspect of history that has been as neglected as the archeology of Kodlunarn Island itself: the effects of Elizabethan and later European contact on the native Inuit population of southeast Baffin Island, whose post-A.D. 1500 development is largely unknown. These problems raised a series of questions that required consideration from historical, cultural, scientific, and other viewpoints by an international team of scholars and institutions.

The papers in this volume explore these questions in a variety of contexts. In the first section we have grouped a series of papers relating to history and ethnography. We begin with a chapter sketching the history of exploration on Kodlunarn Island. Discussion of the background and history of the Frobisher voyages includes Donald Hogarth's research into the ships' company. The story of Hall's 19th-century arctic explorations, contact with the Inuit and subsequent discovery of iron blooms and Frobisher artifacts leads into discussion of the expeditions of the 20th century, culminating in those reported in this volume. This is followed by Susan Rowley's analysis of Hall's records in the archives of the Smithsonian's Museum of American History with regard to Inuit oral history and ethnography relating to the Frobisher voyages. Wilcomb Washburn reviews the Elizabethan setting of the Frobisher voyages and the aftermath of Hall's deposit of collections at the Smithsonian and the Royal Geographic Society. Washburn, who relocated the "lost" Smithsonian bloom, studied the Smithsonian's connection with Frobisher and Hall and the context of Norse discoveries that resulted in the bloom being dated. A fourth contribution in this section is Jacqueline Olin's description of the analytical history of the Smithsonian bloom, the development of a small-volume counter at Brookhaven Laboratory, and the subsequent dating study. It was the Norse period results obtained from this work that stimulated plans for fieldwork at Kodlunarn Island in 1981.

The second section presents the results of archeological and geological studies in Frobisher Bay in 1981, 1990, and 1991. The first of two papers by Fitzhugh describes fieldwork conducted in 1981 at Kodlunarn Island and includes a history of site investigations, description of features and collections, and interpretations of subsequent analyses. The second paper describes "off-island" surveys in the Countess of Warwick Sound region in 1981 and preliminary results of a more widespread site survey conducted in 1990 and 1991. During the course of our work we developed increasingly closer ties with Donald Hogarth, a geologist at the University of Ottawa, whose knowledge about the Frobisher mines and ores (reported here) had been advancing on a parallel course with our archeological and archeometric studies and who had unsurpassed familiarity with the Frobisher archives in England. Finally, Réginald Auger provides us with a brief preliminary description of the Elizabethan ceramic materials from a test pit excavated in the assay shop in 1990, amplifying descriptions of ceramics recovered from the 1981 tests.

The third section reports the results of technical analyses of archeological materials, including the bloom, wood and charcoal remains, and metallurgical analyses. Many of these studies include the results of collaborative American and Canadian research efforts that began with the 1981 field program and have matured into a cooperative team effort during the past several years. Although much

of the information presented in this section is fairly technical, in assembling this volume we have tried to present both the technical information needed by specialists for evaluation purposes and sufficient overview and illustrative materials to make the results informative and interesting to a wider, nonspecialized audience. An interesting feature of the Frobisher research is that, like some other studies (such as the Vinland Map or Shroud of Turin), many of the answers to historical problems require solution by highly technical scientific studies.

Dosia Laeyendecker's study of species identification of charcoal and wood remains from Frobisher structures, features, and blooms serves as a basis for interpreting radiocarbon dates, bloom origins, and sources of materials.

The three new blooms, initially stored at the Smithsonian, were transferred to Parks Canada (Conservation) in Ottawa early in 1982 after they were discovered to be deteriorating from hydration. Collaboration with Parks led to the stabilization and eventual study of one of the three blooms. The task of dating the new bloom finds was orchestrated initially by Garman Harbottle (Brookhaven National Laboratory) in collaboration with Henry Unglik (Parks Canada) and Richard Cresswell (Isotrace Laboratory, University of Toronto). These studies are interpreted here by Harbottle, Cresswell, and Raymond Stoenner, who conclude that the Smithsonian bloom is a product of Viking industry during the period of their voyages to North America, thus advancing the conclusions of Sayre et al. (1982). These dates and those obtained from non-bloom Frobisher site features constitute the Frobisher project's most problematic set of data. This paper is followed by a detailed metallurgical study by Henry Unglik on bloom no. 2 from the 1981 survey. Unglik's work represents the first complete examination of a Frobisher bloom, and as such adds greatly to information obtained previously in the only other study of a Frobisher bloom, that done on the Smithsonian specimen by William Rostoker and J. R. Dvorak (1986). Unglik's study provides detail also on some slags and bloom fragments recovered from the Kodlunarn Island smithy in 1981 and compares the corpus of data with other known blooms and related materials from other early sites, including L'Anse aux Meadows. Michael Wayman and Robert Ehrenreich provide a metallurgical analysis and in-

Fig. I.4. 1981 finds, Blooms 1, 2, 3 (top to bottom rows), found in our 1981 project on Kodlunarn Island, have been kept in a controlled atmosphere chamber after they were transfered to Ottawa in January 1982 (courtesy Parks Canada—Conservation)

terpretation of two new iron finds—an arrowhead and a wedge-shaped chunk of iron that resembled a bloom fragment—found on Kodlunarn Island and a nearby site in 1990. It was partially in response to these technical studies and their authors' interpretations of results that Ehrenreich was inspired to propose some alternative views in a paper that takes an archeological perspective on the bloom problem.

Finally, we pose some questions that still remain, such as the function of some structures on Kodlunarn Island, the possible existence of a smelter, the dating and origin of the iron blooms, and the identity of the abandoned sailors in the Inuit oral history.

We also speculate on possible interim solutions and note the need for continued research on the Frobisher sites, records, and collections and on studies of European-Inuit contact.

The results of most of these studies were presented first in a number of academic meetings and research seminars. The 1981 fieldwork was first reported by William Fitzhugh to the Canadian Archaeological Association in 1982. A more complete presentation was given by the research team at a symposium at the Annual Meeting of the Society for Historical Archaeology annual meetings in Savannah, Georgia, in 1987. Revised versions of these papers and remaining questions were discussed at a workshop held at the Smithsonian Museum of Natural History in November 1989, at which time the research group decided to propose expanding the work into a new and more formal phase of field studies as a joint Canadian, American, and British program. The new research was to be part of a Quincentennial effort featuring North Atlantic exploration and European-Inuit contacts in arctic North America. Our proposals soon led to creation of a formal structure known as the Meta Incognita Committee whose role, under Canadian ministerial oversight, was to control and coordinate the many interests involved in the growing Frobisher/Inuit-European contact research program. An important goal of this prospective research should be to focus on the Frobisher site and remains not as an isolated event in the history of European arctic exploration but as one facet of a larger story of European expansion and New World intercultural contact. These pages represent a way station toward this goal.

HISTORY

Fig. 1.1. "Map of Frobisher Bay and Meta Incognita, with XVIth Century Place Names," from Stefansson and McCaskill 1938. Framing the map are the names of the ships used in Frobisher's expeditions.

PREVIOUS PAGES: Kodlunarn Island from the hills above Tikkoon, the vantage point from which Inuit observed Frobisher's activities on the island (view west). Gull Rock, the probable setting used for John White's battle scene, is to the right of Kodlunarn Island.

1

Exploration History of Frobisher Bay

WILLIAM W. FITZHUGH,
DOSIA LAEYENDECKER, AND
DONALD D. HOGARTH

A Brief Narrative of the Frobisher Voyages

WILLIAM W. FITZHUGH AND
DOSIA LAEYENDECKER

Three arctic voyages were undertaken by Martin (later "Sir" Martin) Frobisher during the years 1576–78. Originally the purpose was to find a Northwest Passage to the Orient to benefit English trade and commerce. Backing was provided by a team of private investors organized by financier Michael Lok, who was an avowed Northwest Passage enthusiast.

On the first voyage Frobisher set out with two ships and a pinnace. The *Michael* defected in mid-voyage and the pinnace sank in a storm losing all hands. With his remaining ship, *Gabriel,* he reached Frobisher Bay, thinking that he had found a strait that would lead him to China. He explored and found the land to be inhabited by native (Inuit) peoples who had access to iron and copper implements and ornaments. Frobisher nearly lost his life and small boat when he was ambushed by Inuit while exploring ashore, barely escaping with an arrow in his buttocks. After engaging in a variety of contacts—both friendly and hostile—with the natives, Frobisher sent five of his men and the ship's boat ashore. Despite admonishing them to use caution they strayed out of sight of the *Gabriel* and were never seen again. Lacking a means of getting to shore to search for them, Frobisher captured an Inuk by luring him with an offer of a trade bell and lifting both him and his kayak aboard. Bearing "this newe pray" (Best 1578 in Collinson 1867:74) and an unusual black rock as "tokens of possession" and proof of his discoveries, Frobisher returned to England.

Upon his return the Inuk died and Frobisher presented the rock to Lok who, after four attempts, found an assayer who assured him it was high-grade gold ore. Lok thereupon interested a group of wealthy patrons, including Queen Elizabeth, formed the Cathay Company, and raised capital to support a second and eventually a third voyage.

For the second expedition a third, larger ship, the *Ayde,* was loaned to Frobisher by the queen to transport ore. Frobisher was instructed to continue exploration for the Northwest Passage but not to

travel far afield, as the main objective was to return to England with as much ore as possible.

This year, 1577, the voyage to "Frobisher Strait" was uneventful and there were few problems with sea ice. Frobisher's men discovered large veins of black ore on a small island in eastern Frobisher Bay, which he named Countess of Warwick Island (later to become "Kodlunarn" Island) and decided to use as his basecamp. While mining proceeded, Frobisher's men searched the south side of Frobisher Bay for signs of the missing sailors. In York Sound they met Inuit who signed that the men were alive but were living too far away to be reached. But Frobisher's suspicions of foul play were confirmed later when his men found English shoes and clothes, some with arrow holes in them, in an Inuit camp. The Englishmen attacked and several Inuit were killed. Later, an Inuit man and a woman with a child were taken hostage following an English attack on an Inuit camp at Bloody Point (York Sound) and were brought back to England, but they, too, soon died.

These events and other observations about Inuit culture and behavior compiled by George Best are among the most interesting features of the detailed 1577 narratives. While on Kodlunarn Island, Best constructed a small defensive fort on a ledge projecting from the side of the island. When the ships returned to England the ore was landed in Bristol. In the succeeding months numerous delays were encountered in getting the ore assayed, with the result that the 1578 expedition was organized before this crucial information became available.

In 1578, fifteen vessels sailed from England with a separate contingent of 100 miners and marines who were to establish a mining colony on Kodlunarn Island over the coming winter. For this purpose lumber and mortar had been brought to construct a stone and timber dwelling. The outgoing vessels called for supplies and crew in the Orkneys and stopped also in Greenland, which they thought to be "Freesland" and renamed "West-England." Here they found abandoned dwellings and implements, including a

Fig. 1.2. "Encounter with Eskimos"—This painting more than any other image or record has inspired popular opinion about the Frobisher voyages. Its battle scene mixes a fanciful reconstruction of the loss of Frobishers's five sailors with accurate rendering of Inuit kayaks, dress, and weapons, icepans, and treeless landscape. White has even captured the vertical faulting characteristic of the islands in Countess of Warwick Sound. The features in the painting—Gull Rock, the hills north of Tikkoon, the Diana Bay hill forms, and the Inuit summer camp—fit the geography of the region perfectly when viewed (as in the photograph above) from the eastern end of Kodlunarn Island. Only the European-style tents are in error.

In reality, although a "John White" is on the 1577 manifest, the artist is not believed to have been present (Sturtevant and Quinn 1987). His paintings are probably based on sketches drawn by an unknown expedition artist. Furthermore, this particular scene—if it records the 1576 encounter as suggested by the title and presence of five sailors—probably did not occur in Countess of Warwick Sound but elsewhere in Frobisher Bay.

box of iron nails, an unusual find suggesting that the inhabitants had been in recent contact with Europe.

The year 1578 turned out to be difficult all around. In addition to problems funding and planning the expedition, the fleet was tormented by storms and bad ice conditions off the Baffin coast. Many vessels were damaged; the ship carrying most of the timber for the miners' dwelling sank and many provisions carried on other ships were lost or destroyed. While waiting for Frobisher Strait to clear, Frobisher sailed up Hudson Strait, realizing eventually that this must be the true route to the northwest, but as the season was advancing he had to turn back to his mining mission. A basecamp, including assaying facilities, was established on Kodlunarn Island. Mines were found and opened in various locations, and ships damaged by ice were repaired and loaded with hundreds of tons of ore. Although Inuit were frequently seen observing the European activities from Tikkoon and other vantage points, few contacts were reported, probably be-

cause the massive display of force was daunting to the small Inuit population.

Toward the end of summer it was decided that too many provisions and materials had been lost to leave a colony on Kodlunarn over the winter. However, as an experiment, a small stone and mortar house was constructed to test its survival under arctic conditions, and in a gesture intended to acquaint the natives with civilized life, trade goods and loaves of bread were left in the stone and wood house. Perhaps the most remarkable act of faith was the sowing of a test plot of peas, corn, and grains onto the Kodlunarn Island ground. Finally, timber, food, iron and other materials were buried in the belief that the expedition would return again in 1579.

The return to England proved as difficult as the earlier summer voyage had been. Just as the flotilla was about to depart a severe storm struck and many men and expedition pinnaces were lost. Food was also extremely scarce and many men died on the homeward voyage. When the fleet arrived in Eng-

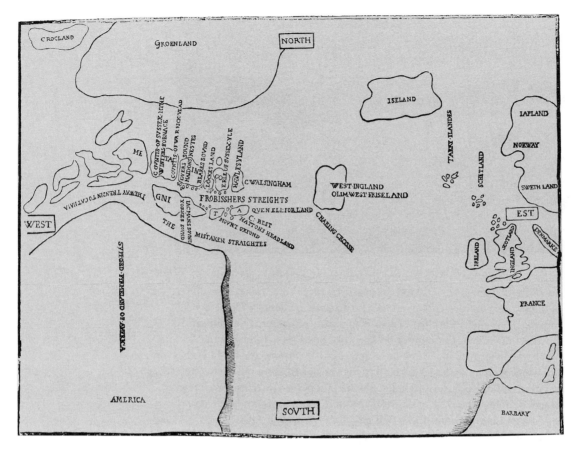

Fig. 1.3 (above). James Beare's schematic view reveals the North Atlantic world as seen from the perspective of the explorer charting new-found lands in relation to Europe and his projected destination, Cathay. The "explorer's eye view" accounts for exaggerated detail of "Frobissher Streights" and the supposed northwest passage route to Cathay which inspired English explorers for centuries. Baffin Island is here mistaken for Greenland, and southern Greenland for "West-Ingland/Friseland." The latter turned out to be completely mythical (courtesy of the Hakluyt Society).

Fig. 1.4 (right). Frobisher's flagship, *Ayde,* loaned to him by Queen Elizabeth I, as portrayed in battle in 1580, as seen in a detail on a nautical chart (courtesy London Public Record Office).

land it learned that the 1577 ore was essentially worthless. Shortly after, similar results were obtained from the 1578 ore. Soon the Cathay Company declared bankruptcy, and a cycle of investigations and recriminations broke out. Many of the investors, including Queen Elizabeth, lost money; Lok found his career ruined.

Martin Frobisher suffered financially but lost little time recovering from ill fortune and adverse public opinion. He returned to his former quasi-authorized activity as a pirate, primarily against Spain. After being reestablished in the Navy by Queen Elizabeth, he distinguished himself in battle against the Armada and was knighted in 1588. In these and subsequent years he never lost the protection or confidence of the queen and died a Knight and Admiral of the Seas in the battle of Brest in 1594. His three arctic voyages remained an interlude in his illustrious naval career. In Frobisher Bay he left his name as an early explorer of the Canadian Arctic.

The Ships' Company in the Frobisher Voyages

DONALD D. HOGARTH

The size of Martin Frobisher's arctic expeditions is impressive, by any standard. It increases progressively as emphasis shifts from exploration to mining. Paylist and other data (appendices 1, 2) give 36 names of officers and men in the first voyage, 145 names in the second, and 397 in the third voyage. As large as the numbers for the last voyage may seem, they are not complete: some of the ships, especially the *Beare Leicester* and noncommissioned ships, are obviously understaffed with mariners and the numbers cannot be made up with the 38 unplaced officers and men. Grouped together, the three voyages constitute one of the largest arctic maritime ventures to date, and for a single voyage, the third is unsurpassed.

By far the most useful data sources are the paylists, included in the testimonies of Michael Lok, Edward Sellman, and Martin Frobisher before the Exchequer (Lok 1578a; Lok et al. 1576–78, 1578–81). Additional data have been derived from Edward Fenton's journal (Fenton 1578) and from various manuscripts in the British Library and Public Record Office. In some cases, names have been taken from published sources (e.g., Stefansson and McCaskill 1938). In appendix 1, surnames are recorded in the most commonly appearing form but, where spellings differ appreciably, two (or even three) entries have been made.

For most of the company, the voyages heralded a brief moment of emergence from obscurity. Some reappear in Edward Fenton's "troublesome voyage" to Africa and South America in 1582–83 (Taylor 1959). Luke Ward, Edward Robinson and Esdras Draper received promotions; Christopher Hall, John Smithe, Christopher Jackson, Nicholas Chancelor, and David Evans got their old jobs back. Richard Fairweather, the younger, was master's mate, under Christopher Hall, in the *Galleon Leicester*. For Chancelor and Evans it was to be their last voyage: they died mid-1582. Fairweather left the company at Rio Plate, where he married and took up permanent residence.

James Aldaye is a rather special case. He had been a merchant and mariner since at least 1551. In 1575 he prayed that, should Michael Lok outfit a voyage for discovery of the northern route to Cathay, he would be considered for service, and "therein to adventure life to the uttermost point" (Hakluyt 1598–1600, 1:412–13; 2:319–20). Aldaye was duly included in the ships' company in the first voyage and paid £5 in advance, possibly at the top mariner's wage (25 s. per month). In 1579, Aldaye's experience in the first voyage gained him a commission from King Frederik II of Denmark, with an express purpose to strengthen the ties of Denmark with Greenland. That summer he took two vessels and coasted southern Greenland, but ice prevented his landing. He had failed to reassert Danish sovereignty over Greenland and to establish the state church (Lutheranism) on the island. In spite of this, the commission was renewed. In 1580, Aldaye was to lead a second expedition to Greenland, but when his ships were commandeered for defense in the Baltic, Aldaye was promised employment at the Danish court. He then fades from history (Gad 1971:194–95).

Some mariners' careers overlapped the military. Edward Fenton led a voyage of exploration to Africa and South America (1582–83), but he served with the army in Ireland (1566, 1579–80). He also commanded the *Mary Rose* against the Armada (1588). Likewise, Gilbert Yorke served in Ireland (with the navy 1579–80) against the Armada (1588), but sailed with Drake and Hawkins to Panama (1594). John Smithe of Bridgwater, the erstwhile master of the ill-fated *Emanuel,* commanded a bark of 70 tons against the Armada (1588). Luke Ward, Fenton's man in Baffin (1578) and Africa–South America (1582–83), commanded the small galleon *Tramontana* and seventy men against the Armada (1588). Thomas Courtenay and his *Armonell* were hired by the Lord Justice of Ireland to patrol the Kerry coast against rebel insurgents (1579) but he soon retired from active maritime and military life to manage a sizable estate in north Devon, inherited by his wife, Alice (Parker). Hugh Randall, who with his *Salomon*, had been pressed into service in the third voyage (1578), became vice-admiral of Dorset (1583) and was charged with fortifying the Dorset coast against possible invasion from sea (1587).

The list (appendix 1) is also interesting from the point of view of absentees. For example, George Best, who wrote *A True Discourse . . .* describing all three voyages (Stefansson and McCaskill 1938, 1:1–129), may have attended voyages 2 and 3 only. Certainly the first voyage is presented sketchily and there is no mention of him in the pertinent manuscripts. The sole evidence for his presence is in his opening paragraph (ibid. 1:5) where he states he wishes to "lay open . . . the plain truth . . . which I myself have tasted and found." This refers, generally, to all three voyages. There is also no hard evidence for the attendance of the notorious Dr. John Dee. The Exchequer papers (Lok 1578a; Lok et al. 1576–78, 1578–81) plainly list a John Lee in both second and third voyages (not John Dee as reported by Ward 1926). Likewise the suggestion that John White, the governor of the second Virginia colony (1587), attended the second Frobisher voyage (Hulton 1961) lacks foundation. John White is not recorded as a member of the ships' complement in 1577, in what appears to be a complete listing. Thomas Ellis, chronicler of the third voyage, who by his own testimony was "one of the [ship's] company" (Stefansson and McCaskill 1938, 2:29) does not appear in the paylist nor in other references to the voyage. Similarly, no confirmation could be found for the presence of Thomas Skevington who was said to have sailed with Frobisher (Taylor 1959: xxxv, 160).

Originally, in the second voyage, eleven convicts, some under a death penalty, were chosen to colonize "Friseland" or southern Greenland, as stipulated in the "instructions" to Frobisher at the outset of the second voyage (Ellis 1816). One convict refused to budge from jail and the others became so unruly that Frobisher was forced to set them free, thereby complying with another stipulation of the instructions, which stated that he should select an orderly and obedient crew. However, by turning them loose in Cornwall he left himself open to serious criticism (Lok ca.1581).

On the other hand, some of the company may have been poorly chosen. That Frobisher indulged in favoritism and nepotism is suggested by his recommendation of his old companion Andrew Dyer, who critics claimed was lame and incompetent, and his kinsman Alexander Creake, who was described as young, unskilled and rebellious (Lok ca.1581: 30–32). We also find Francis Brackenbury, probably the husband of his sister Jane, but perhaps their son who was also Francis, on all three voyages, and Thomas Frobisher, a kinsman from Wakefield and, like Martin, descended from John Frobisher, Sr. (ca. 1455–1513) of Altofts (Frobisher n.d.), on the third voyage.

Eight officers and men from the first voyage signed for the second, sixty-two from the second voyage signed for the third, and six signed for all three voyages. In addition, the third voyage carried one Thomas Welder, possibly the convict Thomas Welder who was slated to be a settler in Greenland in 1577, but was set free in Cornwall at the onset of the second voyage.

Appendix 2 summarizes information in appendix 1 and gives additional data for the ships. Tonnages (burdens) are intermediate and approximate values taken from manuscripts, some of which show a broad range. They reflect the weight of ore returned, which is normally toward the lighter side of the range. The *Armonell* of Exeter, alias *Emanuel* of Exeter in Stefansson and McCaskill (1938), has been equated with the *Armonell* of Exmouth (100 tons, Anon. 1577, 104 tons, Anon. 1576).

The thesis of James McDermott (1984) has been useful in transcribing the accounts of the Cathay Company.

Exploration after Frobisher

WILLIAM W. FITZHUGH

Charles Francis Hall

Like many enthusiasts and adventure seekers, Charles F. Hall was enthralled with the mystery of the lost Sir John Franklin expedition (1845–48) and decided to make his own explorations. When he was unable to reach the Central Arctic regions where he supposed survivors of the Franklin expedition were living among the Inuit, he turned his attention to explorations in eastern Baffin Island. During the winter of 1861–62 he found himself frozen in aboard the whaler *George Henry* in Cyrus Field Bay, just north of Frobisher Bay. Here he befriended local Inuit and established a different style of arctic exploration from that used by official expeditions that preceded him. Instead of relying on ships to provide

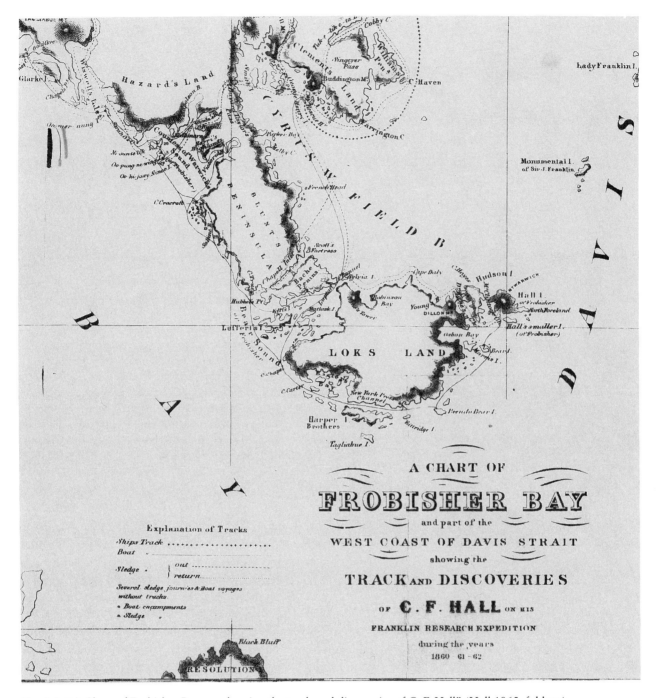

Fig. 1.5. "A Chart of Frobisher Bay . . . showing the track and discoveries of C. F. Hall" (Hall 1865, foldout).

a "civilized" European environment as other explorers—including Franklin—had done, Hall emulated Inuit methods of arctic travel and survival. He learned to speak Inuktitut, to eat Inuit food, and he lived and traveled with Eskimos for extended periods.

As he got to know the local Inuit, he heard nothing from them about Franklin's demise, but instead was surprised to discover stories about other Europeans who visited the area in much more ancient times. During the summer and fall of 1861, Hall traveled with Inuit to the main site of these events,

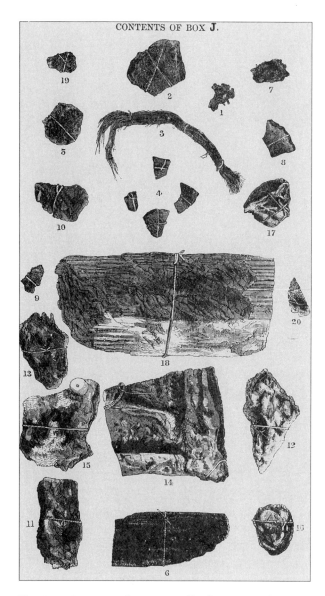

Fig. 1.6. "Contents of Box J," Hall's illustration of relics he sent to the Royal Geographical Society for deposit. Entrusted to the Greenwich Hospital Museum and later shifted to the British Museum, the collection has since been mislaid. Materials include fragments of tile (*1, 10*), cordage (*3*), glass (*4*), iron (*5*), wood (*6, 18*), ceramic (*2, 8, 16*), ceramic crucible (*9*), coal (*7, 11*), flint (*13, 17, 19*), the corner of a green-glazed stove tile (*14*), stone with lime cement (*15*), and charcoal (*20*) (Hall 1864, 2:294).

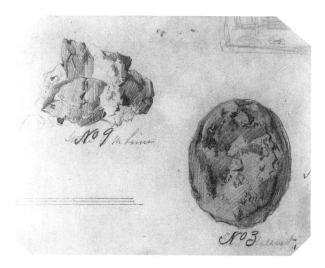

Fig. 1.7. This pencil illustration from Hall's archives shows two blooms. The drawing does not indicate locations. Presumably, No. 3 is the ship's trench find from Kodlunarn Island because No. 9 must be the bloom Hall found at Tikkoon and described as "time-eaten, with ragged teeth." Since only two blooms are drawn we suspect that Hall, despite statements to the contrary, did not collect the bloom he found at Cyrus Field Bay (see p. 86–87). Following this reasoning, Hall must have given No. 3 to the Smithsonian and No. 9 to the Royal Geographic Society. (Naval History Archives, Division of Military History, National Museum of American History, Smithsonian Institution.)

an island called "Kodlunarn" (from the Inuktitut word "kadlunat" or "white man"). There he found relics, including pottery fragments, flint-tempered mortar, slag, brick, tile, and a "proof" (actually an iron/slag mass resulting from direct reduction of iron ore in a bloomery furnace) of iron scattered among the ruins of a small settlement. Inuit tales in-

cluded information about "heavy stones" like the iron bloom Hall had found, and he was led to the discovery of a bloom at Tikkoon and found another in Cyrus Field Bay (Hall 1865b:132). Inuit made Hall models of a larger iron mass "red with rust" (probably a Frobisher anvil; see Rowley, this volume) that had been taken by dogsled from Kodlunarn to Oopungnewing (Opingivik; now Willows) Island where it was later thrown out onto the mud flat (ibid.:451–52).

Hall visited Kodlunarn and nearby islands several times during his explorations in 1861–62, and after examining the physical evidence—coal, flint, iron, wood, and ceramics as well as the remains of structures and pits—and comparing it with Inuit contemporary sites and European historical sources, concluded that many of the structures and associated finds were of European and not Inuit origin. On one occasion he camped near a feature he named the "Ship's Trench," said by Inuit to have been where a group of abandoned "kadlunat" had built a boat,

Fig. 1.8. "The Author and his Innuit Company . . . gathering Frobisher Relics" (Hall 1864, 2:292).

and made a detailed inspection of the island, mapping the locations of foundations and stone structures and noting the presence of European artifacts and remains in nearby Inuit tent sites. Most importantly, he kept detailed records, carefully tagged his finds (packing them in his dirty socks), and published a complete report with maps, illustrations,

Fig. 1.9. "Frobisher Relics in my old Stockings" (Hall 1864, 2:162).

and artifact inventories (Collinson 1867:366–374). His reports include detailed accounts of Inuit stories about these early European visitors.

Inuit also had been interested in the sites on Kodlunarn Island—the stone house, the ship's trench, a reservoir, and other features—where their ancestors used to go to hunt for materials to make tools, grindstones, metal polishers, and pigment (Hall 1865b:543). Hall discovered that the early Inuit had used abandoned coal from Kodlunarn Island for fuel and knew of the locations of other coal dumps on Niountelik (Newland Island) and in Victoria Bay (ibid.:432).

The congruence of his finds and Inuit oral history accounts (Rowley, this volume) convinced Hall that this site could be no other than the remains of Martin Frobisher's 16th-century mines and basecamp. Because the relics were not readily identifiable and could not, in Hall's time, be dated or positively linked to the Frobisher voyages, Hall's strongest arguments were the site's demonstrable age, Inuit oral history, and correspondence of site location, geography, and site features with the historical record.

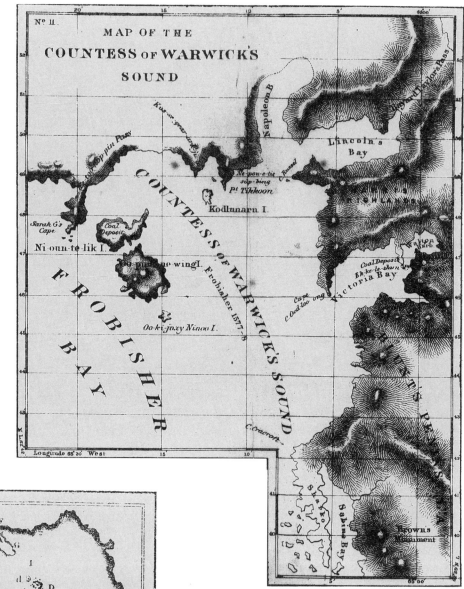

Fig. 1.10 (above). Map of Countess of Warwick Sound by C. F. Hall (1865, foldout).

Fig. 1.11 (left). "Kodlunarn—or White Man's—Island." Map of Frobisher finds and features prepared by C. F. Hall. Hall's accuracy can be assessed by comparing his map with the aerial photo base for figure 5.3. Hall's map key states: "Ships Trench" or Mine (A), Ruins of "House" (B), "Reservoir" or Mine (C), Ruins of Shop (Dd), Best's Bulwark (E), Iron Ballast (?) found (F), "Ship's Banks" or Mine (G), Oxide of Iron found (H), Glass found (I); No 1 to Ships Trench, and 2 to 3, and 4 to 5, represent Cliffs 25 to 35 feet high (Hall 1865, foldout).

Fig. 1.12. Donald MacMillan team excavating Fenton's house foundation on Kodlunarn Island, 1929 (Peary-MacMillan Arctic Museum, Bowdoin College).

Returning south, Hall found general acceptance for his discoveries, which he published, in several editions, in 1864 and 1865 in *Life with the Eskimaux*. In this work he gives a credible "site report" complete with a map of features and finds, artifact illustrations, and a sketch showing him posed like the early British archeologist, General Pitt-Rivers, directing the collecting activities of his sharp-eyed Inuit fieldhands. Later, as recounted elsewhere (Washburn, this volume), most of these collections, except for the iron bloom entrusted to the Smithsonian, disappeared—either lost, misplaced, or destroyed by careless or overzealous museum keepers.

In hindsight, Hall deserves great credit for his pioneering research, as much for his discoveries as for his methods of investigation. Not only did he map and publish finds, he also sought to preserve them for posterity, and his conclusions have been largely confirmed. In addition to his maps and notes on the Kodlunarn finds, he conducted many interviews, recording verbatim accounts of Inuit oral traditions about the early kadlunat who visited Frobisher Bay, and noted the disposition of some Frobisher artifacts used by the Inuit, including stories of blooms and anvils ("heavy stones"), tales of lost sailors, building of vessels on Kodlunarn Island, and many others. In fact, Hall's research was far ahead of his time. His methods anticipated a style of anthropological investigation that was not to become common practice

for another hundred years. But unfortunately, while Hall pioneered an excellent model for future research, scientists and explorers who followed viewed the Frobisher sites as a historical curiosity rather than as a resource for further research, and through their excavations and unrecorded collecting squandered its precious resources for little scientific gain.

Pre-1960: MacMillan and Strong

The Frobisher voyages received much attention from historians, but when Hall's discovery ended speculation about where Frobisher had actually gone, historians saw little benefit in pursuing further research at "Frobisher's mines." After all, as reported by Hall they were small and lacked archeologically glamorous remains. Remote and lacking controversy, Kodlunarn Island fell into a limbo of benign neglect and escaped scrutiny by Franz Boas when he worked among the East Baffin Inuit in 1883–84. Years passed before the site received scrutiny from 1927 Rawson-MacMillan Subarctic Expedition members William Duncan Strong and Sharat Roy, who spent a few hours unsystematically collecting surface finds and digging in the ruins of the Frobisher house, as Hall and Inuit had done previously. Although Strong had no great familiarity with early English artifacts, he agreed with Hall's conclusions and published confirming notes (Strong 1927–29, 1927, 1929;

comment in Stefansson and McCaskill 1938, 1:245), and Roy published a detailed report on the "Frobisher ore" (Roy 1937). Strong's collections of eighteen fragments of brick, ceramic vessels, and stone are in the Field Museum of Natural History (pers. comm. James VanStone, 1989); his diary notes are in the Smithsonian's National Anthropological Archives. Donald MacMillan returned to Kodlunarn at least two more times in later years, in 1929 and 1937, while voyaging along the East Baffin coast and spent a few hours continuing the destructive pattern of digging and collecting curiosities. No maps were made, but MacMillan's photographs show the Frobisher house in an advanced state of pillage in 1929. The site is documented also in an aerial photograph taken by Alexander Forbes in 1943 when the Frobisher Bay airbase was being constructed at the present town of Iqaluit (Forbes 1953:126).

1960s and 1970s: Pearson and Kenyon

In the 1960s a series of events unfolded that began to rectify past neglect. Among the new developments were discovery of the Norse settlement at L'anse aux Meadows, Newfoundland (Ingstad 1977) and publication of the Vinland Map (Skelton et al. 1965) and Chauncey Loomis's biography of C. F. Hall (1971).

In October 1964 the National Historic Sites and Monuments Board of Canada recognized the importance of the Frobisher sites on what was then called "Countess of Warwick Island." The official motion of the board noted that "the Frobisher site is of national historic importance, that the site should be preserved as far as possible by restricting fishing permits on the island, that a photographic record be obtained as soon as possible, and that archaeological investigations be made at the discretion of the Department." As it happened, however, this motion had little practical effect beyond official recognition, either in terms of site protection measures or photographic or archeological documentation.

In June 1965, five Iqaluit residents sponsored by Canada's first Inuit corporation, Inook Limited, explored Kodlunarn Island and vicinity to evaluate its potential as a tourist recreation area. The group included Simonie Michel, John Rae, Ioola, Bryan Pearson, and Fred Bruemmer. One day was spent exploring and photographing on Kodlunarn Island; some shovel testing was done and Frobisher ceramics were found. Breummer's photographs show the mine/

reservoir and the Frobisher house essentially as we found them in 1981. Pearson's interesting, breezy account, published in *Nord* in May 1966, was the first popular article on the site and the first to note that from a tourist's point of view, Kodlunarn "should be acknowledged and at least bear a permanent cairn and plaque" (Pearson 1966:1). That observation probably accounts for the erection of a cairn with a bronze plaque next to the Frobisher house, dated to 7 November 1966, a few months after the publication of Pearson's article. Installed by Lt. A. Brockley, Dr. R. West, and Mr. V. Brockley, the cairn was later dismantled by Robert McGhee and an archeological team from the Canadian Museum of Civilization in August of 1991. The plaque is now stored at the Prince of Wales Northern Heritage Centre in Yellowknife, NWT, Canada. Today, a plaque in the town of Iqaluit serves as the only public recognition of the Frobisher voyages and camps.

In 1974 historical archeologist Walter Kenyon visited Countess of Warwick Sound and Kodlunarn Island to provide photographic documentation and samples for a celebration of the 400th anniversary of the Frobisher voyages planned by the Royal Ontario Museum. Kenyon was specially interested in locating and inspecting Frobisher's mines. He and his team measured and photographed some structures and dug test pits into the south wall of the smithy and at the edge of the cove east of "Best's Bulwark," where Kenyon noted a buried lens of charcoal. And like others before him, he excavated in the ill-treated Frobisher house, clearing part of its foundation (Kenyon 1975b:148). No radiocarbon dating or ceramic analysis was done. Kenyon's reports and photos provide general documentation of the site. He noted the paucity of surface finds, the disturbed state of the stone house, and the presence of a cairn (Kenyon 1975a, 1975b:148; Royal Ontario Museum collections). Although Kenyon's visit was brief and did not result in much new scientific detail, he was the first archeologist to visit the site who was technically capable of confirming its Elizabethan dating and Frobisher attribution.

This review would not be complete without mention of archeological research on Inuit culture history that began with Henry Collins's work at Dorset and early Thule sites on the Sylvia Grinnell River (Collins 1950). In more recent years this work has been expanded to cover a variety of archeological, anthropological, geographical, and historical studies in Frobisher Bay, South Baffin, and Cumberland

Sound (Maxwell 1976, 1985, 1988; Schledermann 1975; Sabo 1981, 1991; Jacobs and Sabo 1978; Jacobs 1985; Jacobs et al. 1985; Jacobs and Stenton 1985; Stenton 1987, 1991; Eber 1989). Yet in spite of this gradual acceleration of research, the remote outer coast of southeast Baffin Island still remains archeologicaly one of the most poorly known regions of the Eastern Arctic.

Thus, after more than a century of sporadic and mostly unscientific effort, little had been learned about the archeology of the Frobisher voyages beyond what was reported first by Hall in 1865, except about mines and ores. Paralleling this rather depressing history of investigation is the much more serious loss of archeological resources from five centuries of continuous erosion of site deposits, including some meters of shoreline retreat; from systematic scavenging by 16th-century Inuit groups for whom the site was a treasure trove of valuable and useful European materials; and from post-16th-century visitation, collection, and vandalism. In more recent times this included losses at the hands of explorers, amateurs, and professional archeologists and museum curators who mostly failed to document or publish their work and allowed collections to be lost or misplaced.

The casual and antiquarian approach of these early Kodlunarn Island investigators and their lack of concern for scientific documentation or collection preservation is also reflected in the lack of analysis and reporting of artifact finds. Walter Kenyon felt confident that the bits of tile and brick found on Kodlunarn Island were the remains of the Frobisher expeditions, but his collections, like those of so many of his predecessors at the site, were so few in number and relatively undiagnostic that he never illustrated or published them. As a result, with the loss or misplacement of the materials Hall sent via the Royal Geographical Society to the Greenwich Hospital Museum (Hall 1865b:551; Collinson 1867:366–374) and of the Smithsonian collections (except for its Hall bloom), the sole extant source of information available on Kodlunarn Island artifact collections has been Hall's brief account and his illustrated plate of finds (Hall 1865b:552–53). Most of these specimens are small pieces of wood, slag, metal, and tile that could date to almost any period. Nevertheless, the historical archeologist Eric Klingelhofer (1976), studying Hall's illustrated finds, tentatively identified a ceramic sherd as a fragment of a glazed cast stove tile. Finding such an article in a

mining basecamp seemed a bit unusual and suggested to Klingelhofer that Kodlunarn might not have been entirely lacking in habitation amenities. With this observation Klingelhofer suggested that the Kodlunarn sites were more than "mines" and had archeological value in their own right apart from the historical record.

1981–1991: Hogarth and the Smithsonian Research

Except for the Smithsonian work reported in this volume, the only other recent documented research on Frobisher materials and sites was a study of local geology, ores, and mines initiated by Donald Hogarth and pursued by him and others through the 1980s. Hogarth and Gibbins (1984) made a geological map of the island, collected samples of "ore," and came to the conclusion that most of the mines previously identified by Hall and Kenyon were natural sea caves or erosional features. More recently, Hogarth has continued his search for and study of the mine sites, with the result that as of 1991 most of those utilized in the Countess of Warwick Sound region (about half of the mines known to have been worked) have been identified and documented. Analytical studies of the ores amplify Roy's conclusions (1937) on mineralogy and have been followed by studies related to the much more fascinating story of what happened to the ore once it arrived in Ireland and England (Hogarth and Loop 1986, Hogarth 1989a,b). Collectively these works lay to rest the oft-repeated but erroneous notion that the Frobisher "gold rush" resulted from the misidentification of iron pyrites; it seems that the appearance of the elusive "marquesset of gold" resulted from the oxidation of small flecks of biotite mica interspersed among black hornblende crystals when the rock was heated. They also document the fact that while these ores were not high-grade, they do in fact contain gold, but less than the country rock in which they occur. In fact, the gold identified by Lok's assayers came from the additives they introduced in the assay process (Hogarth, pers. comm.).

Prior to the present report the only other study conducted on Frobisher archeological materials was the analysis of the Smithsonian bloom, a project whose history is described elsewhere in this volume and which led directly to our 1981 fieldwork. At first the major issue concerning the bloom was its early radiocarbon date: two different samples gave

Fig. 1.13. Smithsonian field team aboard Pauloosie Kilabuk's boat, August 1981. In back, Garman Harbottle; left to right: Richard Linington, Jacqueline Olin, James Blackman, Joshua Fitzhugh holding dog, Wilcomb Washburn standing behind Thomas Dugan, Caroline Phillips, Robert Anderson. Inuit relative of our skipper Pauloosie Kilabuk beside Joshua. William Fitzhugh, behind camera.

calibrated radiocarbon ages of A.D. 1240–1400 and A.D. 1160–1280. These dates had stimulated considerable interest in the bloom and the possibility of the Kodlunarn Island site being Norse or having a Norse component. Further support for a Norse or some other European medieval association came from the bloom's weight—17 pounds—which was typical of 12th–15th-century iron blooms and out of place among larger 16th-century blooms produced after the introduction of water-powered bellows (Tylecote 1986). Inventory lists from the Frobisher voyages (Stefansson and McCaskill 1938, 2; McDermott 1984) indicate that "osmundes" (small highly refined Swedish blooms; Fenton, in Kenyon 1980/81:185) and iron bar stock were carried by Frobisher's ships for making and repairing tools in portable blacksmith forges. In a discussion of these problems (Sayre et al. 1982:449) the present author raised the possibility that the early date and small size of the Smithsonian bloom might have resulted from a local smelting operation on Kodlunarn Island using charcoal prepared from centuries-old arctic driftwood. It is well known that charcoal from prehistoric Eskimo sites in the Eastern Arctic and Greenland often dates several hundred years older than a site's actual occupation (Blake 1975). Alternatively, small sizes and early dates might be explained if the iron was smelted on Kodlunarn or in England in antiquated or "back-yard" British iron-

works using charcoal from old English heartwood (for further comment, see Laeyendecker and Ehrenreich papers, this volume).

As nothing was known about its original context, or even exactly where the bloom had been found, none of these questions could be resolved without new fieldwork. Consequently, in 1981 the Smithsonian's Department of Anthropology, Conservation Analytical Laboratory, and American Studies Program, together with a Parks Canada archeological associate, organized an expedition to Kodlunarn. The team was interdisciplinary and included Robert Anderson (engineer, San Jose State University), James Blackman (geochemist, Smithsonian), Thomas Dugan (ret. admiral, US Navy), Garman Harbottle (chemist, Brookhaven National Laboratory), William Fitzhugh (anthropologist, Smithsonian, assisted by Joshua Fitzhugh), Richard Linington (geophysicist, Lerici Foundation; deceased, 1984), Carolyn Phillips (historical archeologist, Parks Canada), Jacqueline Olin (chemist, Smithsonian), and Wilcomb Washburn (historian, Smithsonian). In addition to Smithsonian assistance, private funds were contributed by Robert Anderson, Frank Augsbury Jr., John Boreta, Landon Clay, Thomas Dugan, and Robert H. Power. The goals of the project included (1) investigation of the Frobisher remains for existence of local smelting activity (for this purpose magnetometer and metal detector surveys were to be conducted); (2) collection of archeometric dating and analytical samples from surface and subsurface contexts (aided by an electronic metal detector); (3) identification, testing, and mapping of all extant European structures; (4) survey of Kodlunarn Island and adjacent regions for Inuit sites occupied at or shortly after the time of the Frobisher visit to assist studies of Elizabethan-Inuit contact and culture change; and (5) assessment of the conservation status and physical condition of the Frobisher sites for future research, management, conservation, and development activities.

We spent a week at Kodlunarn in 1981, assisted by Pauloosie Kilabuk, who provided boat transportation and introduction to the Inuit summer camp near Kodlunarn Island at the western entrance of Diana Bay. Aided by excellent weather, in one intensive week we recovered a great amount of information. Our most important find was the discovery of three new iron blooms buried in situ in Elizabethan contexts. Two were found in Hall's "ship's trench" and another near the two caches (fig. 5.4: S5, S6) of probable Frobisher origin. We also mapped all the structures noted by Hall and identified several previously unknown ones, including an "assay shop," a "charcoal store," a "dam," a "longhouse," and a "pit." Associated with these structures were fragments of European tile, ceramic crucibles, brick, wood, charcoal, slag, cinder, flint, mortar, and other materials.

We also found evidence of numerous small tent camp sites situated around the margin of Kodlunarn Island, some of which were probably occupied by Hall and his companions during their 1861–62 survey. Other camps containing fragments of Elizabethan ceramics and tile appear to have been occupied by Inuit groups who came to the island after Frobisher's departure to scavenge European materials, while some may have been tent sites used by some of the Frobisher party who slept ashore. Un-

doubtledly, Inuit interest in scavenging from the Frobisher sites was intense in the years immediately following 1578. According to Hall, Inuit continued to mine the Frobisher sites for coal, tile, and brick as late as the early 19th century. Today, few Frobisher relics are found on the barren surface of Kodlunarn Island, and some of the Frobisher structures are noticeably disturbed. One of the two caches and Fenton's sentry house or "watchtower" show signs near destruction by amateur excavation, while others, including the smithy, assay shop, and ship's trench, appear intact.

In addition to surveys on Kodlunarn Island, the 1981 project surveyed the Countess of Warwick Sound region. This area is a popular hunting and fishing location and is used by Inuit from the Iqaluit/Frobisher Bay area today. Apparently it was an important settlement area in the past, for we found numerous Inuit sites dating to the 19th and 20th centuries and traces of prehistoric Thule and Dorset Eskimo groups.

Following the 1981 field project, fieldnotes, artifact catalogues (appendices 3, 4), photographic inventories, and maps were prepared, and a variety of research programs were planned. Principal targets of research were description of the Frobisher sites and features and analysis of the many archeological samples obtained from surface collections and test pits. Among the finds were charcoal, wood, coal, ceramics, iron, slab, mortar, and flint. Materials were parceled out to specialists in Canada and the United States, who gathered occasionally to review findings and compare results in workshops and symposia throughout the 1980s. Eventually, as reported in the Introduction, this work led to a new cycle of fieldwork beginning in 1990 directed both at continued study of the Kodlunarn Island sites and at questions of European-Inuit contact and interaction from the Frobisher period to the present day. Details are provided in Chapter 6.

Fig. 2.1. The *George Henry* in winter quarters (Hall 1864, 1:186).

2

Frobisher Miksanut: Inuit Accounts of the Frobisher Voyages

In 1860 Charles Francis Hall boarded the whaling ship *George Henry* bound for the Arctic. Hall, a journalist and self-made man from Cincinnati,[1] believed that some members of Sir John Franklin's Northwest Passage expedition (1845–48) could still be alive. This was despite the 15 years that had passed since the ill-fated expedition had set sail from Britain and the discovery of numerous bodies by McClintock's Franklin search expedition (1857–59).

Hall had two reasons for his belief. First, the only written record recovered reported that Franklin had died and Captain Crozier was now in charge of the expedition. Crozier was no greenhorn, rather, he was an old Arctic hand who had accompanied Captains Parry and Lyon on their 1821–23 Northwest Passage expedition. Unlike previous British expeditions, Parry and Lyon wintered twice in locations with large Inuit populations. During these winters there was much interaction between the two groups. As a result, Crozier could speak a little Inuktitut (the language of the Inuit) and had some understanding of Inuit customs.

Second, a few individuals, especially John Rae, a Hudson's Bay Company (HBC) employee, had proven that Europeans could survive in the Arctic with relative ease if they adopted an Inuit lifestyle. Not only could they travel in the same way as Inuit and wear Inuit clothing but they could eat the same food without suffering any ill effects.

This information, combined with the prevalent stereotype of the Inuit as a happy, kindly people, suggested to Hall that they might have adopted any survivors. However, no one had questioned the Inuit inhabitants of King William Island, the last known location of the Franklin expedition, on the fate of the British.

Hall put forward a bold plan to travel to King William Island with an Inuk interpreter and learn from the Inuit the history of the Franklin expedition. He also intended to bring home any survivors. Hall spent several years raising money for his enterprise and managed to persuade the influential American businessman Henry Grinnell to become one of his backers. He received corporate sponsorship from various companies including American Express, who paid for the shipment of his goods from Cincinnati to New York City. Hall never managed to raise all the funds for his journey, but he grew tired of wait-

---

1. Anyone wishing to read further about Charles Francis Hall is referred to his biography by Chauncey C. Loomis (1971).

SUSAN ROWLEY

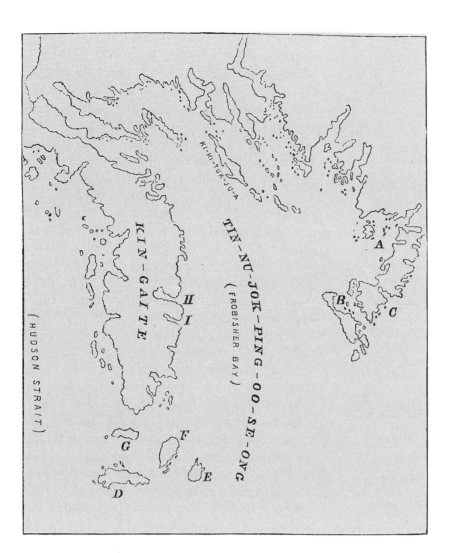

Fig. 2.2. "Esquimaux chart No. 1, drawn by Koojesse at Rescue Harbor, 1860" (Hall 1864, 1:127).

ing and so accepted a proffered passage to the Arctic with the whaling firm, Williams and Haven of New London, Connecticut, on the *George Henry*. Unfortunately for Hall, the *George Henry*, captained by Sidney Buddington, was not heading for the west coast of Hudson Bay but for the waters of Cyrus Field Bay (located between Cumberland Sound and Frobisher Bay).

Hall intended to cover the remaining distance using a small boat with an Inuit crew. By the time Hall arrived at Cyrus Field Bay it was too late in the season to set sail for King William Island. Later, in the fall, a tremendous storm blew up and Hall's boat was wrecked. Without it, his chances of reaching King William Island disappeared. Hall, however, had a lively mind and determined to make the best of his situation. He decided to spend the time honing the skills he would need when he finally reached

King William Island. These included learning to communicate and travel with the Inuit, and mapping their domain.

Hall not only mapped the region himself, but he also had Inuit draw charts for him. Hall was quite surprised when a chart drawn for him by Koojesse, one of the Inuit whaling captains,[2] showed the area called by the whalers Frobisher's Strait as a bay. His first reaction was that this bay could not be the area visited by Frobisher. He also ignored Inuit traditions of a place near Tikkoon where a mast was raised on a ship and an island, called Kodlunarn, pointed out

2. By 1860 it was common practice for both British and American whalers to hire Inuit crews for whaling. These crews would be under the leadership of an Inuit whaling captain. On this voyage Buddington hired two Inuit crews, one led by Koojesse, the other by Ugarng.

to him by Koojesse, where white men had once built a ship. Hall dismissed these stories because his grasp of the language was poor and he did not understand what the Inuit were trying to tell him.

It was not until the spring of 1861 that Hall's thoughts turned to Sir Martin Frobisher and his arctic voyages. Hall wrote in his published account:

> The idea of a vessel having been built in those regions seemed too improbable to be entertained for a moment. So unreasonable did the story appear of constructing a ship in such a perfectly woodless country, that I thought it a waste of time and paper to make record of it; therefore what transpired in the first two or three interviews with the Esquimaux Koojesse, in relation to this subject, is not in my original notes. Finally, in a few days, I began in my reflections to connect the Esquimaux report with the time when Martin Frobisher made his discoveries, and simultaneously commenced to make record of whatever was stated to be in subsequent interviews. (Hall 1864, 1:271–272)

Hall immediately determined to visit Kodlunarn Island to search for evidence that would substantiate the Inuit oral accounts.

Before he had the opportunity to realize this plan, Hall met the oldest inhabitant of the region, a woman by the name of Ookijoxy-Ninoo.[3] He took advantage of her presence to ask about the qallunat[4] who visited Frobisher Bay. She related that many, many, many years ago qallunat came to the area by ship. These qallunat came to Frobisher Bay several times:

> "First two, then two or three, then many—very many vessels."
>
> This was clear; and I immediately took up the only book I then had with me bearing upon the subject, "Barrow's Chronological History of Arctic Discovery," and, turning to the account of Frobisher's voyages, I read what had been given to the world by means of writing and printing, and compared it with what was now given to me by means of oral tradition. *Written* history tells me that Frobisher made three voyages to the arctic regions as follows:—

> First voyage in 1576, with *two* vessels.[5]
> Second voyage in 1577, three vessels.
> Third voyage in 1578, fifteen vessels.
> *Traditionary* history informs me that a 'great many, many years ago the vessels of white men visited the bay (Frobisher's) three successive years:—
> First, in *two* vessels.
> Second, in three vessels.
> Third, in many vessels (Hall 1864, 1:303).

Ookijoxy Ninoo also related how five white men were captured. She then added that on the east coast of Frobisher Bay five Inuit were killed while on the other side of the bay two women were captured (Hall 1864, 1:303–5). This provided further confirmation for Hall that she was recounting information about Frobisher. He was amazed by how closely her story mirrored that in Barrow. Barrow contained the following accounts of these two incidents. The first occurred on the first voyage and the second on the second voyage.

> They [the Inuit] approached the ships with some hesitation, and one of the natives presently went on board in the ship's boat; and Frobisher, having given him a bell and a knife, sent him back in the boat with five of the crew, directing them to land him on a rock and not to trust themselves where numbers of his countrymen were assembled on the shore; but they disobeyed his orders and were seized by the natives, together with the boat, and none of them heard of more. (Barrow 1818:82–3)

> In endeavouring to seize a party of natives in Yorke Sound, a skirmish ensued in which five or six of the savages were unfortunately put to death, and two women seized, "whereof the one being old and ugly, our men thought she had been a devil or some witch, and therefore let her goe; the other being young and incumbered with a sucking child" (ibid.:89).

While Hall was intrigued by how accurately Ookijoxy Ninoo's account reflected that of Barrow, it was the continuation of her story that captivated him.

The greatest mystery surrounding the Frobisher voyages was the resolution of the fate of the five men captured by the Inuit on the first expedition.

---

3. Hall's transcriptions of Inuit words are problematic. Therefore, his original spellings have been maintained in this paper. Ookijoxy-Ninoo's name was most likely Uqitjuasi Nanuk.

4. "Qallunat" is the Inuktitut word used to refer to Europeans and Americans. Hall generally spells this word "Kodlunars."

5. Barrow does not relate that one of the ships turned around before reaching Frobisher Bay, hence Hall's inaccuracy in this statement.

On Frobisher's second voyage: "It is stated that they found here sundry articles of the apparel of the five unfortunate men who had been seized by the natives the preceding year, which is the only apology offered for the cruel attack on these people" (Barrow 1818:89). It was generally believed that the sailors had been killed. Ookijoxy Ninoo, however, recounted a very different ending. She told how the captured qallunat wintered with the Inuit for at least one winter; "that they afterward built an oomien (large boat), and put a mast into her, and had sails; that early in the season, before much water appeared, they endeavoured to depart; that, in the effort, some froze their hands; but that finally they succeeded in getting into open water, and away they went, which was the last seen or heard of them"

(Hall 1864, 1:303). To Hall this was a great discovery, and he believed that the mystery of the fate of Frobisher's lost men was finally solved.

Hall's interpreter during this interview was Tookoolitoo, a woman who had traveled to England with the Hull whaler, Captain Parker, in 1854–55 and had met Queen Victoria. Hall could not have collected most of his data on Frobisher without the assistance of Tookoolitoo and her husband, Ebierbing. Not only was her knowledge of English extensive but she also had an interest in Inuit history. In fact, Tookoolitoo often interviewed people on her own and later relayed the information to Hall.

As a seasoned journalist and naturally inquisitive person, Hall was not satisfied with just one account and slowly began to interview all the elders he met.

Fig. 2.4. "Innuit Summer Village"
(Hall 1864, 2:92).

At first he was sometimes forgetful. In one instance, he was leaving an Inuit summer camp when he suddenly remembered not having asked an elder, Artarkpara, about Frobisher. He immediately turned his boat around and returned to the shore in order to conduct the interview (Hall 1864, 2:93).

Hall was among the earliest to collect oral history testimony in a structured manner. For his time, Hall's research was remarkable. He avidly sought out individuals and even created a list of 36 questions to ask each informant (see table 2.1). Some of these questions would be considered leading questions today. For example: Question 8. "Did some ships a great many years ago, come into Tu-nuk-jok-ping-oo-sy-ong and carry away some Innuits?". Anthropologists and oral historians avoid this type of question as they fear people will give the answer they think is wanted. In the case of Question 8 the obvious answer is "yes." Interestingly, Hall's informants were not prepared to provide the answer Hall wanted to hear. When Hall's informants did not know something they simply replied they "never heard of it." Hall repeatedly questioned people about the Inuit who were taken away to England. He was always told, "Never heard of it." This was

despite his interviewing several people who had visited the U.S and England and who therefore, could have made up plausible stories.

Hall checked and double checked answers that were unusual or he did not understand and often held a second interview at a later date. The following is an example of his tenacity in following up evidence and checking all leads. Ookijoxy Ninoo had referred to three items brought by the qallunat: coal, brick/tile, and "heavy stones." It quickly became obvious that these "heavy stones" were lumps of iron. Later, after Hall recovered the first bloom, he realized that people were telling him about two

Fig. 2.5. "One of Frobisher's gold 'proofs.' (An iron relic of 1578.)" (Hall 1864, 2:161)

TABLE 2.1. Questionnaire devised by Charles F. Hall

1. Have you ever seen Kod-loo-narn and been onto it?

2. Why do Innuits call that Island, *"Kod-lu-narn"*?

3. How many Kod-lu-narns lived there?

4. Did they build a ship or a boat there?

5. How did the Kod-lu-narns get there?

6. Where did those Kod-lu-narns get wood and iron to build a ship?

7. What did they make their ropes of?

8. Did some ships a great many years ago, come into Tu-nuk-jok-ping-oo-sy-ong and carry away some Innuits?

9. How many? and Did they ever come back again?

10. Did the Kod-lu-narns who came in the ships kill any of the Innuits?

11. Where did the bricks, coal and iron you have seen come from?

12. Did the Innuits ever find any *wood* that Kod-lu-narns left on Kod-lu-narn or on any of the other places about there?

13. *When* did Kod-lu-narns bring coal, wood, brick and iron here?

14. Did the ships that came here go away and come back again next year?

15. Are there any Innuits living who ever saw the Kod-lu-narns who built the ship?

16. Did the Kod-lu-narns who lived on the Island "Kod-lu-narn" live in snow houses in winter?

17. When they went away in the ship which they made, did they ever come back again?

18. Was it *cold* or *warm* when they went away in the ship?

19. How long did Kod-lu-narns live on the Island where they built the ship?

20. Were the Innuits kind to the them and did they give Kod-lu-narns seals and other food to eat?

21. Did Innuits help the Kod-lu-narns build Igloos and Tupiks?

22. Did Innuits help them dig out the stone where they built the ship?

23. Could the Kod-lu-narns talk *Innuit* with the Innuits?

24. Did the Kod-lu-narns have Innuit wives?

25. Did Innuits help Kod-lu-narns build the ship?

26. When the Kod-lu-narns went away, where did they say they were going to?

27. Where did the Kod-lu-narns who built the ship come from—*England* or *America?*

28. Did the Kod-lu-narns ever build stone houses and live in them on Kod-lu-narn?

29. Did any of the old Innuits ever see amasuadlo [many] ships in the Bay wh__ Oo-pung-ne-wing, Ni-oun-te-lik, Toor-pik-ju-a, Kod-lu-narn, Tik-koun and King-ge-geer-ark-ju-in area?

30. Who told you about Kod-lu-narns building a ship on Kod-lu-narn?

31. Was there ever a time when there were a great many more Innuits than now?

32. Did the Innuits then fight sometimes and kill one another?

33. Why do not the Innuits now live on the land beyond the channel Ik-er-ki-suk-ju-a?

34. How did the Kod-lu-narns who built the ship get from that land away beyond Ik-er-ki-suk-ju-a to the Island of Kod-lu-narn?

35. Why did the Innuits who lived *a great many years ago* on that land beyond Ik-er-ki-suk-ju-a take the 5 kod-lu-narns with their boat and keep them so that they could not go back to the ship?

36. Did the Innuits, or any one of them, ever get a paper ("all the same as this") from a ship that came into Tin-nu-jok-ping-oo-se-ing great many years ago and carry it to the Kod-lu-narns who lived on Kod-lu-narn?

UGARNG'S WOOD MODEL OF THE IRON RELIC.   ARTARKPARU'S WOOD MODEL OF THE IRON RELIC.   KOO-OU-LE-ARNG'S TOOD-NOO MODEL OF THE IRON RELIC.

Fig. 2.6. Inuit models of the iron anvil (Hall 1864, 2:179, 180).

different types of "heavy stone." The first referred to the blooms and the second to something larger. Hall first heard of this second "heavy stone" in August of 1861. He learned that this object was on the island of Oopungnewing (Willow's Island) and that the Inuit used it as a trial of strength. In fact, a very strong Inuk could just lift it. Sometimes, Annawa and Oulekirn told Hall, they had even used it in their tent as a seat for visitors (October 8, 1861).[6] Unlike the blooms, it was said to be smooth and soft. By this time Hall was mystified, and so asked several people to draw it and also had them make models of it. Well aware that people were influenced by the words and actions of others, he noted in his diary: "I have taken all precaution that neither Innuit should see or know of anyone's making any other" (October 10, 1861).

In fact, the resolution of this mystery was simply a matter of asking the right person the right question.

"... I got Ugarng to cut out with his knife its representation in wood. When he finished it I held it out, asking 'Ki-su?'—that is, what was the heavy iron at Oopungnewing formerly used for? His answer was an intelligible one, and *one that determines the nature of this important relic beyond all question.* . . . This Innuit had been in the States. . . . While there he desired to and did visit various manufacturing establishments. . . . I will now give his answer on stating to my question that, holding the index finger of his left hand on the little carved block as I held it up, with his other hand angled into

fist and raised above finger to represent hammer, he said, '*All the same as blacksmith.*' This expression . . . settles the matter satisfactorily to my mind that this relic of Frobisher on Oopungnewing is an anvil" (Hall 1864, 2:179–180).

As final confirmation of this identification, several Inuit told Hall that they had seen similarly shaped anvils on English whaling vessels.

Hall decided that this was an extremely important relic and was determined to try and find it. None of the Inuit had seen it recently and they were of the opinion that it had either fallen off the edge of Oopungnewing or been pushed into the sea (Hall 1864, 2:233). Hall therefore correlated his visit to the island with the lowest tides of the year. However, his search was to no avail. The anvil had probably been rafted away by the ice. (For modern surveys at this site see Chapter 6, this volume, and Fitzhugh 1991.)[7]

Hall was unusual for his time in that he recognized when an informant was feeling tired or preoccupied and would reschedule the interview.

This P.M. I suggested to Tuk-oo-li-too that I wanted to have a talk with old Oo-ki-jox-y-ni-noo. She thought I had better delay until my return as the old lady is sadly bemoaning over her sick great grand child, a little one eyed boy, who is indeed quite sick in her Tu-pik [tent]. I must acquiesce in this as T. informs me no use to try to talk with the old woman unless she feels just right. I have found that there is a right time and a wrong time for a person to make attempts to gain information of these old Innuits.

6. Dates in parentheses are for entries in Hall's unpublished diaries. These diaries are located in the Naval History Archives, Division of Military History, National Museum of American History, Smithsonian Institution, Washington, D.C.

7. Research by P. Goldring of Parks Canada indicates that the anvil may have been recovered after Hall's visit and transported to the United States by Peary (Goldring 1985–88:4.45).

My last interview with old Petato showed that she was all out of humor for a good "talk." My first conversation with her was carried out in excellent spirit on her part. Her whole soul entered into the great subject of our conversation—the history of Frobisher's Expeditions here (June 8, 1862).

He also paid his informants an honorarium—"After getting through my interviews with the various Innuits I make them presents—a "hand of tobacco"—pipe—or needles—or supunyers (beads)" (October 2, 1861).

In Hall's diaries there are records of interviews with 25 people—some more complete than others. In addition, there is evidence that he spoke to many others. When Hall traveled among the Inuit he tried to converse with the oldest people he could find—considering them the best source of traditional knowledge.

The information collected by Hall can be separated into two groups based on our ability to verify it. The first type is information that can be verified. It is based on tangible objects Hall was told about and could then see himself. Table 2.2 contains a list of these objects, where Inuit saw them, and the number of people who referred to objects at each of these locations. Hall was told about three deposits of coal each of which contained flints. The Inuit occasionally used the coal for fires, but they were more interested in the flints which they used as strike-a-lights (Hall 1864, 2:164). On one occasion, during a collecting trip, Hall noticed that people were pocketing the flints for future use. He therefore bribed them with percussion caps for the men and beads for the women. "My strategy worked like a charm; the relics came in by scores, each bringing me a quantity that surprised me, for I had not thought my company so largely deceitful" (ibid.:165).

TABLE 2.2. Number of Inuit observations of Frobisher relics at different places

Location	Wood	Iron	Tile	Coal
Niountelik	2	3	3	6
Kodlunarn	1	4	10	4
Ekeluzhern[a]				4
Oopungnewing		16[b]		
Tikkoon		3		
Kussegeerarkjuan[c]		6		
Look Out Island			1[d]	

a. Point of land in Victoria Bay
b. Transported from Kodlunarn Island
c. South point at the entrance to Diana Bay
d. Transported from Kussegeerarkjuan

The iron blooms and anvil that fascinated Hall had complicated histories, and he was careful to obtain as much information about them as possible. For example, the iron bloom he located at Look Out Island (in Cyrus Field Bay) was the same bloom that several Inuit had seen at Kussegeerarkjuan (southwest of the entrance to Diana Bay). Shevekko told Hall the bloom had been brought to Look Out Island in 1859 by Annawa and Manabing (December 24, 1861). Unfortunately, although Hall later interviewed Annawa, he did not ask this man why he had carried the bloom from Countess of Warwick Sound to Cyrus Field Bay. [In 1990, a Smithsonian team found this bloom at the Lookout Island site; see Chapter 6, this volume. –WWF] Similarly, Artarkpara informed Hall that the anvil had first been found on Kodlunarn Island and transported by sledge to Oopungnewing "many years ago" (October 12, 1861).

It is interesting to note that people rarely mentioned wood to Hall. Only when he specifically asked about it did they say that they had seen wood chips both at Niountelik and at Kodlunarn Island. Nooeler told Hall she had never seen wood on Kodlunarn Island but had heard Inuit tell that a long time ago a great deal of wood was left on Kodlunarn by the whites (October 2, 1861). Likewise, Karping, an Inuk from Cumberland Sound, said that good wood had been left behind by the whites (December 10, 1861). Apparently, all usable wood had long since been taken by the Inuit.[8] This is in contrast to the bricks and tiles Hall recovered. These relics were still in use to polish the brass hair ornaments of the women. Particles were scraped off the brick and then the powder was used as a polish (June 3, 1862). Although the fragments of brick and tile were fairly rare commodities they were widely traded. Ebierbing told Hall that many of his Cumberland Sound acquaintances had pieces of the tile (May 28, 1861). This use of the tiles as a polishing agent appears to have been a fairly recent development as brass ornaments would have been rare before the advent of British and American whaling in

8. In 1585 John Davis came across two Inuit sleds at Cape Mercy, the southeasternmost point of Cumberland Sound. One of the sleds was constructed entirely of whale bone. The other was made from fir, spruce, and sawn oaken boards (Markham 1880:12). These oaken boards most likely came from the cache of materials left on Kodlunarn Island at the end of Frobisher's third voyage.

Cumberland Sound in 1840.[9] Also, Ookijoxy Ninoo remembered having seen fragments of tile 10 to 12 inches long and 5 to 6 inches wide when she was young (June 10, 1862); the largest piece of tile Hall recovered, however, was less than 3 inches long by 2 inches wide. Her testimony and Hall's finds suggest this particular resource was being depleted rapidly owing to increased demand.

All the information Hall received concerning relics of the Frobisher voyage and their locations that he could check proved to be completely accurate. Occasionally, he learned, people had been asked not to tell him certain facts (October 2, 1861), but he was never told any untruths. This suggests that the Inuit were unlikely to have fabricated the information we cannot verify. Certainly, the Inuit believed they were transmitting factual information to Hall—information they had received from their parents who in turn had received it from their parents (Hall 1864, 2:171–72).

Hall was both shown and told of features that the Inuit said were left by or commemorated the qallu-

Fig. 2.7. "The discovery of Frobisher relics nearly three hundred years old, Sunday, August 11, 1861" at Niounte-lik Island (Hall 1864, 2:77).

nat. These included several archeological features and two place names. The archeological features included the so-called ship's trench, a smaller trench, and house remains on Kodlunarn Island as well as a stone monument at Kim-mook-tou-ju-a. These are more problematic than the relics. While there is no

9. Apparently some form of metal hair ornament was in use during Frobisher's time as it is remarked upon by Best in his journal: "certayne buttons of copper, whiche they use to weare uppon their forheads for ornament, as our ladyes in the Court of England do use great pearle" (Best, in Stefansson and McCaskill 1938, 1:126). The source of the copper for these ornaments is unknown.

Fig. 2.8. Sketch map (north is toward left) of Kodlunarn Island region showing locations and place names relating to the Frobisher story as told to Hall by Inuit in 1861–62 (Naval History Archives, Division of Military History, National Museum of American History, Smithsonian Institution).

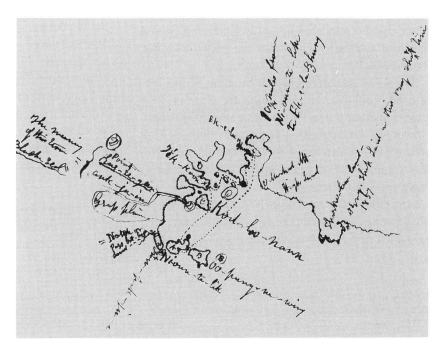

question of these features having been built by Inuit and there is every reason to believe they were built by Frobisher's men, there is a question about Inuit interpretations of these features. Do Inuit traditions refer to the use of the features or are they simply stories made up to explain unusual features on the landscape? Let us examine the Inuit claims for each feature one at a time.

The least controversial is the remains of the house. When Hall queried Inuit about it they simply told him "Have seen on Kod-lu-narn stone that was once an igloo—Innuits did not make it so" (October 16, 1861 interview with Artarkpara and Adlooloo). Petato, a female elder, indicated that a substance was used to bind the stones together in the house by using snow in a model she was building (Hall 1864, 2:207). Only Ookijoxy Ninoo mentioned the qallunat using the stone house. She said that it was too cold and so the qallunat moved into snow houses (June 10, 1862)!

There are two trenches on Kodlunarn Island: the ship's trench and a smaller trench. Later researchers have argued that the smaller trench is a mine and is possibly a continuation of the ship's trench (see, for example, Hogarth, this volume). Inuit oral testimony, as collected by Hall, is very definite that this trench was for fresh water. There is no good source of fresh water on Kodlunarn and so the qallunat had to create one. Old Ookijoxy Ninoo stated that "all the Innuits said that the water was always very cold in that dug out place" (June 10, 1862). There might have been a residual use for the trench. It is possible that later Inuit, camping on the island, made use of water that accumulated naturally in the trench and therefore assumed it had been constructed as a water reservoir.[10]

The so-called ship's trench is the most visible feature on Kodlunarn Island. Inuit are clear in their statements that this is where a ship was constructed. However, there have been suggestions both by Hall and by later researchers (see, for example, Hogarth, this volume) that this trench was actually a mine. From the Inuit testimony, I believe that a ship was constructed in this trench. In fact, the two explanations are not exclusive. The trench could have been excavated first as a mine and then used for building

a ship. The only problem with this solution is that it does not fit the known chronology of the Frobisher expeditions. The five men were lost on the first voyage and no mines were excavated until the second voyage.[11] Further archeological investigations of the ship's trench would elucidate the situation.

On June 10, 1862, only a few months before he left the north, Hall learned of a monument erected by the qallunat and visited by the Inuit whenever they passed by. Ookijoxy Ninoo described the monument and explained:

> The Kod-lu-nars in the two ships landed and made or erected this monument. It is not on very high land—the Innuits have always paid great respect to it for it gives them plenty took-too (reindeer)![12] Every year many Innuits go to it—give it powder, caps, balls, young took-too meat etc. In old times the Innuits going there and wishing success in killing many took-too would give it bows and arrows placing the same on the top or hanging the same from top of it. Give plenty and an Innuit would always kill plenty. This stone marker of Kod-lu-nars great help to Innuits—Always makes took-too plenty there. Every Innuit knows all about this. Ebierbing says that he has seen it. Recollects his father visiting it and giving it young Took-too (June 2, 1862).[13]

Later, Ookijoxy Ninoo drew a sketch of the monument for Hall. Hall was unable to visit the monument in the short time before he departed for the south. So far, no non-native researcher has visited this site located, according to Hall's informants, at Kim-mook-tou-ju-a (June 15, 1862).

Inuit state that two places were named because of the visit of the qallunat. The first, and most obvious, was Kodlunarn Island. Whenever Hall asked people his question 2: "Why do Innuits call that Island, *Kod-lu-narn*?" they always replied ". . . because qallunat lived there and built a ship" (example taken from interview with Shevekko and Ooshootar, October 2, 1861). The Inuit never separated these two pieces of information—the qallunat being on the island and the building of the ship were part of the

10. Some of these references to water may refer to the small well excavated at a seep below a ledge in the west side of the island—WWF.

11. There is a possibility that a boatload of sailors was lost on the third Frobisher voyage. For a discussion of this, see Chapter 14, this volume.

12. Hall's reference to reindeer should be read as caribou, as "reindeer" refers only to the domesticated Old World subspecies.

13. Comparisons of this journal entry with the published account (Hall 1864, 2:285) illustrate some of the problems in accepting Hall's published version verbatim.

Fig. 2.9. Sketch drawn for Hall by Ookijoxy Ninoo showing herself "performing devotions" to the Frobisher monument "in the bay called by the Innuits *Ker-nuk-too-joo-a*, and by me Newton's Fiord" (Wiswell Inlet). The outline in the foreground represents a freshwater lake near the monument. Pendant lines around the top of the monument are strings to which the natives hang their donations (Hall 1864, 2:285). Inuit today note the presence of a stone monument near the top of a high hill east of Wiswell Inlet rather than at the head of the fjord.

mast was set into a ship and Hall was told so very forcefully by several Inuit.

> Soon after Kooksmith had gone I called Tweroong into the cabin, and asked her, in Innuit, if she knew the story of the white people taking the ship to Tikkoon from Kodlunarn. Tweroong comprehended my question at once. She immediately took my pen and a tobacco-pipe, then bade me hold a book down by the table's edge, and placed on the book and table, at one end of the former, the pen, and at the other the pipe, both inclining against the table's edge, . . . She next raised one of the mimic masts to a perpendicular position, I still holding the book, and then the other (Hall 1864, 2:211–12).

But what of the intangibles and particularly the accounts of Frobisher's lost men? The five who disappeared on the 1576 voyage were never seen again. Only their clothing was spied on the second voyage, laid out, the English believed, as a trap. First, what is the story the Inuit tell of the qallunat who came to Kodlunarn Island, built a ship and then departed? As Hall notes after an extensive interview: "Some of the answers do not agree with numerous Innuits that I have before communicated with . . . But I do not expect all will agree in their statements" (October 2, 1861). It is impossible to put together a story of the qallunat who built the ship on Kodlunarn by simply adding all the information together. Some of the testimony is contradictory, while some comes from people who are less well informed than others. For example, Hall collected information from all the people he met. My research indicates that some of these people were Nugumiut, the inhabitants of Frobisher Bay, while others were Kinggamiut, inhabitants of Cumberland Sound. Fortunately, Hall's data are so complete that it is possible to reconstruct the group affiliation of each informant. All of Hall's information from the Nugumiut is remarkably consistent, while that from the Kinggamiut is less so—a fact which is unremarkable, but which indicates the importance of knowing the background of the informant when analyzing the oral history.

It is possible to reconstruct many different stories from the oral testimony. I have included two here. The first is the bare bones story. It includes the information that all informants agree upon. The second story is a fuller version drawing upon added details from selected informants to create a fuller picture.

The short version: Many, many, many years ago qallunat came to Frobisher Bay by ship. Some of them spent a winter on Kodlunarn Island and built a

same incident. The second place name is more intriguing. It is the bluff at Tikkoon which was named Nepouetiesupbing meaning place "to set up a mast" (Hall 1864, 2:212). Kodlunarn Island could have been named later; enough material was left on the island by Frobisher and his men that the Inuit would have noticed it. However, there is nothing at the site of Nepouetiesupbing to suggest the qallunat were there. The name certainly refers to a place where a ship in the ship's trench. At break-up they took the ship to the bluff at Tikkoon called Nepouetiesupbing where they put the mast into the ship. They then sailed away.

The extended version: A great while ago, all the Inuit who were alive then are dead, qallunat came to Frobisher Bay in a ship. They sailed up the Kingait (west) coast of the bay and stopped at Oulokerbing. There was a big storm and their ship was damaged. They built a ship on Kodlunarn Island. Some of the Inuit helped excavate the ship's trench. They received iron in payment which they turned into arrowheads and knives. During the summer the qallunat lived with the Inuit in tents and in winter they lived in snow houses. Eloudjouarng, one of the Inuit leaders, made the people be nice to the qallunat. The Inuit brought the qallunat food all winter—they preferred caribou and rabbits to seal. The women avoided the strangers because they were afraid of them. Very early in the season, when the ice first broke up, the qallunat put the mast in their ship at Nepouetiesupbing and sailed away. Eloudjouarng made a song for their good journey. However, they soon returned driven back by the ice; they could not get out of the bay. It had been very cold and the qallunat had frozen their hands and feet. The Inuit built the qallunat snow houses on Kodlunarn Island but they all died.

Is it possible that Inuit oral traditions could extend back 285 years? and do they refer to Frobisher? There are several problems to contend with when studying oral history testimony. One of these is conflation. Conflation refers to the collation of two events, sometimes separated in time, into one. In the case of the oral testimony of the Frobisher voyages, it is possible that later encounters with Europeans were added to the original accounts. This would make it very difficult to determine the events that occurred during the Frobisher voyages. However, as discussed below, there are very few later European-Inuit encounters in Frobisher Bay to cause such confusion.

Another major problem with oral history research is the collapsing and telescoping of time that occurs in oral societies. The former means events that occurred in the far distant past are brought forward in time while the latter refers to events that occurred in the recent past and are put into the distant past. Hall did collect some time indicators from the Inuit, but they only add confusion to the picture. These in-

dicators are: (1) All Inuit who saw the white men were dead a long time ago. (2) It happened many, many, many years ago—Petato in an attempt to indicate how many "years ago that a great many ships came into this bay . . . was truly eloquent. When pronouncing the word 'wich-ou,' and repeating it, which she did the several times indicated, she lifted her hands to each side of her head, raising in them handfuls of her gray locks" (Hall 1864,2:206). Petato was trying to show Hall that it was as many years ago as the hairs on her head. (3) The event occurred prior to the disappearance of the Loks Land people (at the latest sometime in the late 1700s—Rowley 1985:85–87). (4) Petato tells Hall that her mother's grandmother's grandfather knew a lot about them. (5) Ookijoxy Ninoo says that her father's grandfather was born before the qallunat built the ship. Points 4 and 5 are the only ones that can be used to figure out a date. Unfortunately, the results are conflicting dates, as Petato suggested the event occurred more than five generations before Hall while Ookijoxy Ninoo believed that it occurred three generations before Hall. In his eagerness to accept all data as referring to Frobisher, Hall overlooked these time problems.

Are there any later voyages to which these accounts could refer? The only other early voyages in the area are the 1602 voyage of Weymouth, the 1610–11 voyage of Hudson, and Munk's 1619–20 voyage. As far as we know, neither Weymouth nor Hudson made a landfall in Frobisher Bay. In 1611 Hudson, his young son, and five others were put into a small boat and left to perish in the cold waters of Hudson Strait. Given the tides and weather conditions in the strait it is unlikely they would have crossed the strait in order to reach land. They are more likely to have drifted onto the southern coast. Jens Munk entered Frobisher Bay by accident, but he did not land.

In the late 1600s the Hudson's Bay Company established several trading posts in James Bay and southern Hudson Bay. HBC ships taking supplies to these posts often traded with Inuit on the Savage Islands in Hudson Strait. However, these were supply voyages, not exploration voyages, and the HBC studiously avoided any possible exploration. It is unlikely that any of their ships entered Frobisher Bay.

The next Europeans to visit the area were Parry and Lyon in 1821. They did not enter Frobisher Bay and could not have been responsible for the Inuit oral history collected by Hall. In fact, Hall collected traditions that refer to Parry and Lyon from visiting Sikosuilarmiut (inhabitants of the Cape Dorset area).

> Ookgooalloo then told me "that ships did not come in sight of Sekoselar, nor at Noo-ook-ju-a, but his father, Koo-ook-jun, had said that many years ago *two* ships came close to Noo-ook-ju-a (King's Cape) and Sekoselar, and that he, Koo-ook-jun, with many other Innuits, went out to the ships in kias and oomiens, and went on board" (Hall 1864, 1:323).

This information, as Hall himself notes, complements the written accounts of both Parry and Lyon.

Other than the HBC supply voyages there were no other visitors except the whalers with whom the Inuit were well acquainted. Therefore, the only possibilites beside Frobisher are a stray HBC supply vessel or the abandoned Hudson party. Although either of these is possible they appear at present highly unlikely.[14]

Are the traditions historically accurate or is the history of the five white men building a ship and setting off only to die from the cold an attempt to show that no blame could be put on the Inuit? In effect, was there a conspiracy on the part of the Inuit to cover up the truth? There is no reason to believe that they would have made it up. By 1860, the Inuit had been dealing with British and American whalers for a generation and were well aware that the whalers had no interest in anything other than whales and the occasional woman to warm their beds. While there is some confusion in the accounts, slightly different accounts are to be expected in oral history. The basic story is so consistent that it must be factual. Whether it refers to the missing Frobisher men or some other qallunat remains to be determined.

How well does Hall's data correlate to the known chronology of the Frobisher expeditions? As already discussed, the problems of telescoping and collapsing time as well as conflation make it extremely difficult if not impossible to establish a chronology of events as recorded in the oral history. These problems are compounded by the fact that Hall was seemingly uninterested in the chronology. He rarely

---

14. There are two other possibilities: Dutch whalers and Bristol pirates. Both these groups kept their destinations secret and it is therefore very difficult to know if they ever entered this region of the Arctic.

questioned people about whether the qallunat built the ship first or lived on the island first. Nor did he ask if the people who lived on the island were the same people who built the ship. Finally, he never, ever questioned anyone about Frobisher's mining activities and how they were related to the occupation of Kodlunarn Island and the construction of the ship. These questions are now of great concern to researchers.

Hall's disinterest in the chronology probably derived from his unquestioning acceptance of the testimony of Ookijoxy Ninoo. She was the oldest person, and therefore the closest to the Frobisher events and she was very definite in her first interview with Hall. Hall measured all later informants against her testimony. More than a year after his first interview with Ookijoxy Ninoo, the opportunity arose to interview her again. This time her testimony was quite different. From his journal entry Hall was quite shaken by her information.

> It requires a vast deal of patience in one to pursue attempts to glean out information possessed by Innuits. *One is often baffled.* A most difficult work to get what I do relative to old Frobisher's visit here. . . . [Of course it requires one to do much "sifting" in coming to conclusions relative to the Great Facts at the bottom of the whole matter] . . . [I certainly felt some relief when the old lady brought to her recollection *facts that she had stated to me last year, that is that* there was a time when two ships came here one year] . . . (June 10, 1862).

Hall does not cope well with contradictory information. In the case of this interview with Ookijoxy Ninoo he ignored the new, contradictory information and omitted it from the published version. For this reason it is important to check data from the published journal against the unpublished material.

Do the Inuit traditions refer to the Frobisher voyages, and how might we test this information? One way is through archeological research. Several archeologists have excavated on Kodlunarn Island. Fitzhugh in 1981 and McGhee and Tuck in 1991 are only the most recent. Unfortunately, none of these researchers has been able to confirm or disprove the use of the ship's trench to construct a ship. However, all the material culture recovered in excavations of the ship's trench and other features on Kodlunarn Island is clearly Elizabethan and corresponds with materials brought over by Frobisher. Therefore, it is highly unlikely that other Europeans are the source of the Inuit oral traditions centered so strongly on Kodlunarn Island. Another way to verify the Inuit accounts is through a detailed comparison of the traditions collected by Hall with the published and unpublished accounts of Frobisher's voyages. Through such an analysis it would be possible to see if Hall collected any information not in Barrow, the only published account of Frobisher to which he had access. It would also allow one to determine if Hall altered any of the information he received. This analysis is currently underway.

The oral history Hall collected concerned the first contact that the Inuit had with Europeans. My research suggests that first contact stories continue in a way later traditions, when contact was commonplace, do not. It is therefore most likely that the oral history accounts collected by Hall refer to the Frobisher voyages. However, the nature of oral testimony mitigates against the possibility of constructing a simple diachronic account similar to those presented in the journals of Best and Settles.

Finally, when judging the oral accounts it is important to remember that correct transmission of information about environmental conditions and social patterns from one generation to another was crucial to ensure Inuit survival. Therefore, we would expect the same attention to detail to be applied to oral history, another vital component of Inuit culture. Hall wrote that Ebierbing

recollects hearing his father tell of these white men, and how they built a ship. The kodlunas had brought brick, coal, and "heavy stone," and left them on Niountelik and at other places about there. His father did not see them, but the *first* Innuits, who saw them, told other Innuits so, and so it continued to his day. Old Innuits tell young Innuits; and when *they* get to be old, they in turn tell it to the young. "When our baby boy," said he, "gets old enough, we tell him all about you, and about all those kodlunas who brought brick, iron, and coal to where you have been, and of the kodlunas who built a ship on Kodlunarn Island. When boy gets to be an old Innuit he tell it to other Innuits, and so all Innuits will know what we now know" (Hall 1864, 2:171).

Acknowledgments

I would like to thank Bill Fitzhugh who has always encouraged my interest in Charles Francis Hall. Phil Goldring of Parks Canada has been extremely gracious in sharing his south Baffin historical research with me. Bob McGhee reminded me of John Davis and the wooden sled he found in Cumberland Sound. Finally, I would like to thank Harold Ellis of the Division of Military History of the National Museum of American History, Smithsonian Institution, for his assistance.

3

The Frobisher Relics: A Museum History

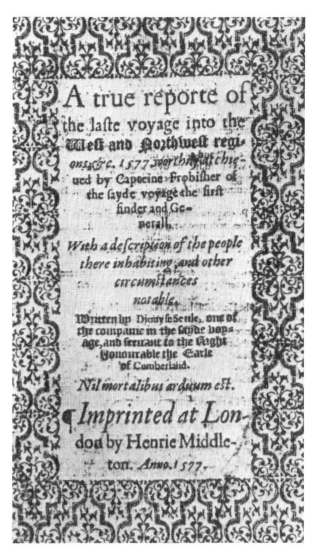

Fig. 3.1. Title page to *Martin Frobisher* by Dionyse Settle, 1577. Settle's account of the 1577 expedition was the first written report on Frobisher's explorations to appear in print. In it he provides the first published "eye-witness" description in English of Canadian Inuit life and customs. Settle's and Best's publications were extremely popular with the English public.

WILCOMB E. WASHBURN

The three voyages of Martin Frobisher, 1576–1578, are probably the best documented voyages in the entire period of European exploration and discovery. We know precisely what the explorers took, and we have a detailed account of what happened to them. The three voyages also turned out to be probably the most disappointing of all the great voyages of exploration and discovery. Not only did the gallant ships and crews not reach their hoped for destination—Asia—but their secondary objective of finding

Fig. 3.2. Martin Frobisher portrait by Cornelius Ketel (courtesy of Bodliean Library, Oxford).

mitments: in short, in utter and total failure. It is because of this failure that the expedition is so well documented in the legal documents that sought to assess blame and determine responsibility. This chapter will attempt to sketch the outlines of that history. It will also touch on the rediscovery of the material remains of those voyages by the 19th-century American explorer, Charles Francis Hall, and will provide a background to the 20th-century expedition undertaken by the Smithsonian Institution to reclaim the tattered remains of both Frobisher's and Hall's work from the careless handling to which they were subject in the past century.

The expansion of Europe was, at the time of the Frobisher voyages, largely a product of Spanish and Portuguese explorers, conquerors, traders, and settlers. In the years following the voyages of Columbus across the Western Ocean, and Dias and Da Gama around the southern tip of Africa to India, England and the other countries of northern Europe had not been entirely inactive, but their own voyages of exploration and discovery had not gained for them the vast overseas empires that had fallen into the hands of the Spanish and Portuguese. In England, particularly, the lack of a highly centralized and bureaucratized central governing authority made such explorations more a matter of private rather than of public enterprise. No overseas venture of a significant sort could be undertaken without royal approval; but English kings and queens made it clear that financial support for such undertakings should come from private purses rather than the royal treasury.

The joint-stock company was an English and capitalist improvisation to obtain the large sums of money needed to underwrite voyages of trade and exploration, but which allowed individuals to be protected in case of failure by limiting their liability for the financial consequences of failure. The 16th century saw the rise of such companies though their full development had to await the 17th century. Enterprises in the late 16th century depended upon the largesse and interest of powerful men, such as Sir Walter Raleigh, who risked their fortunes and sometimes their necks to promote English overseas ventures. The queen's permission was always necessary before a subject could engage in such activities, but a fickle or frightened monarch had the option of disowning her subjects if they endangered her relationships with foreign powers such as Spain. In the case of Sir Francis Drake in the same period, that great

wealth and establishing a way station on the way to Asia ended in a series of cruel delusions and frustrations. It cannot even be said that their mistakes led nevertheless to the settlement of a new continent or the discovery of an unexpected route. Rather the glorious expedition, England's challenge to the Spanish and Portuguese achievements in other quarters of the globe, ended in bitter recriminations, lawsuits, accusations, and evasion of financial com-

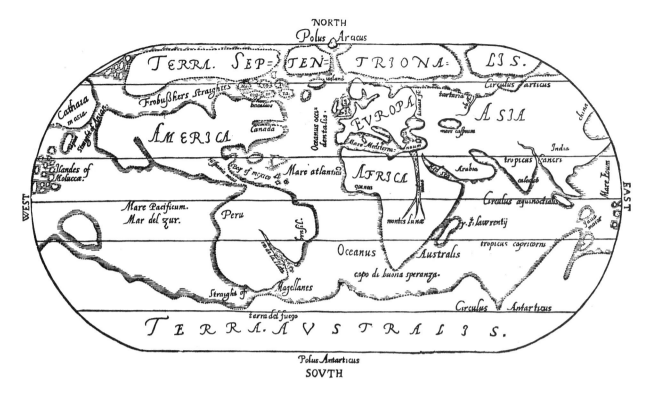

Fig. 3.3. World Map, attributed to James Beare, principal surveyor of the Frobisher expeditions, from Best (1578) (courtesy of the Hakluyt Society).

seaman's brilliant successes emboldened the queen to acknowledge his deeds despite the howls of the Spanish ambassador. The queen was also vitally interested in Frobisher's voyages, and, with some of her leading ministers, took shares in the enterprise, but let the principal financial burden fall on private investors. All three enterprises—those of Frobisher, Drake, and Raleigh—established claims to lands in the New World and, in the case of Frobisher and Raleigh, contemplated or attempted to create permanent colonies. All were doomed to failure. The activity of the English in intruding upon what had been an Iberian preserve was sufficient to generate not only diplomatic protests but armed clashes "beyond the line" where violence was condoned since it was not taken as threatening the European peace.

The expedition under consideration is known by the name of the great seaman who commanded the several fleets on the three voyages. Yet it could have been known by the name of the commercial company—the Cathay Company—that sponsored it, the great queen—Elizabeth I—who supported it, or the principal commercial backer—Michael Lok—who promoted it. That it should be known for the cap-

tain who commanded the ships is entirely appropriate for, as the historian Samuel Eliot Morison has put it, "I conclude that Frobisher was a very great seaman indeed, that his courage and resource enabled him and his ships to survive adversities of ice and weather which would have ruined anyone else, and that he fully deserves his reputation as one of the English mariners who paved the way for England's greatness" (Morison 1971:550). Frobisher was a proud and (to some) an intemperate man who, according to depositions made after the event, occasionally threatened subordinates with a drawn dagger (Stefansson and McCaskill 1938, 2:210).

Like Columbus, Frobisher did not really know where he was and did not succeed in doing what he intended to do. But, like Columbus, he is nevertheless deserving of the praise heaped upon him. The geographical conceptions of Frobisher and his backers, including the queen and most of the "great men" at court, can be illustrated in the accompanying maps. The achievements of Columbus for Spain and of various pilots for Portugal had established a prior claim to the routes they had discovered and jealously guarded. The two Iberian kingdoms had

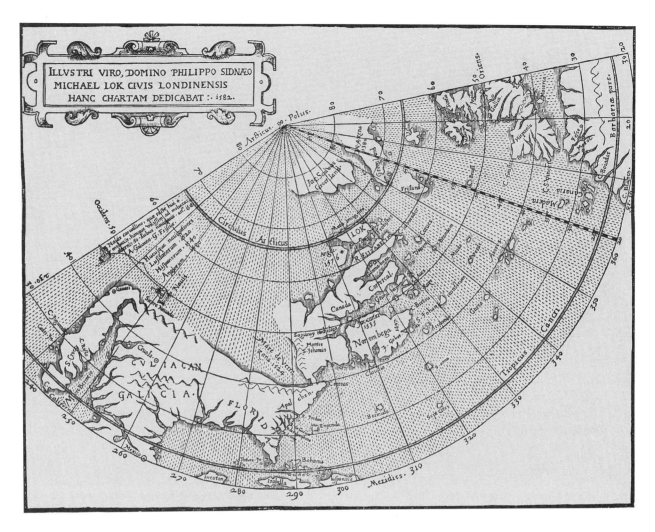

Fig. 3.4. Michael Lok's Map, 1582, from Best (1578).

resolved any early conflict between themselves by the Treaty of Tordesillas of 1494, which redefined the line of division of the world made by the pope within which they were given authority to explore, settle and missionize. But what of the less favored nations of northern Europe who had neither papal sanction nor sufficient military might to challenge Portugal and Spain directly? Their immediate alternative was to search for a different route to the common objective of China and the East. The late 16th century thus saw voyages by English and Dutch to the northwest and to the northeast searching for an elusive ice-free passage to the East that would allow Protestant ships to avoid the necessity to run the gauntlet of Spanish and Portuguese military power. Memories—vague and uncertain as they might be— of Norse voyages by a northern route to mysterious lands in the West may also have pointed the English

in the northern direction. Even the belated recognition of Frobisher's failure to find a true passage to Asia did not dampen the enthusiasm of the map-makers who continued to imagine easily passed straits through the Canadian Arctic to the fabled Orient.

Frobisher led three expeditions in as many successive years—1576, 1577, and 1578—the first two containing two, then three, and the last containing 15 ships, to the bay we now know as Frobisher's Bay and to the island named by Inuit as Kodlunarn Island (White Man's Island). The initial goal was to reach China through a postulated northwest passage. After fighting his way through countless icebergs on his first voyage (as the Smithsonian expedition was to do in reversing the course of Frobisher's route from the head of the bay to Kodlunarn Island), Frobisher decided that it was too late in the season to continue, and turned back. He concluded that he was in the middle of a passage to China, with an Asian promontory on his starboard side and America on his port side. He took with him on his return to England some "tokens of possession," as he put it, to prove that he had been in new and strange lands (Kenyon 1980/81:172). Among these tokens was a "strange man of Cataye" (Stefansson and McCaskill 1938, 2:185) and his kayak, and a piece of black rock picked up by one of Frobisher's men on a small island. (Michael Lok had asked to receive the first object picked up by the expedition.) The native was to inspire intense curiosity among Frobisher's countrymen, not least because of his "Asiatic" appearance. The rock, brought as a curiosity, was, when shown to the eager Lok, to stimulate the tragicomedy that quickly developed. Unwilling to accept the judgment of the first assayers to whom he took the rock, Lok was eventually assured by another assayer, the obliging John Baptista Agnello, that the rock contained a significant quantity of gold. When the faintly skeptical Lok asked how he could have gotten such results when other assayers failed to find any gold, Agnello answered "Bisogna sapere adulare la natura" (It is necessary to know how to coax nature) (ibid. 2:83). This cryptic remark evidently satisfied Lok and was enough to stimulate a rush to return and find more of the precious stuff. Two hundred tons of ore were packed into the holds of Frobisher's ships on the second expedition.

Frobisher's fame, in his now styled title "High Admiral of Cathay," was at its peak and the stockholders of the Cathay Company, now granted a royal charter as "The Adventurers to the Northwest for the Discovery of a Northwest Passage," looked ahead to even greater profits on the huge fleet assembled for the third voyage. But the hopes of finding the Northwest Passage to China, and vast riches in precious minerals in the areas already reached, were cruelly frustrated by geography, weather, and science. The cartographically insignificant bay which we see on today's maps was neither to reveal the long-sought passage to the Orient (a strait that Englishmen would continue to seek in succeeding centuries) nor to provide precious metals to English miners. Hope expired where the bay terminates at the Inuit village known today as Iqaluit. The minerals laboriously mined in the lands adjacent to Kodlunarn Island—the island headquarters for the expedition—ended up at the bottom of Bristol harbor or as material for paving roads in the Bristol area. It

may surprise modern-day sophisticates that Michael Lok could have been fooled by false assay reports on the minerals brought back by Frobisher, but the fact that human hope springs eternal and is often blind to reason can be illustrated by many other historical events. The fact that science and technology as we know them today were in their infancy and geography and history were informed by speculation and imagination as much as by fact may also help to explain why credulity rather than skepticism was elicited by Frobisher's precious ore.

The Frobisher story finishes on a bizarre note when the admiral's masons built a house of lime and stone on the highest eminence of Kodlunarn Island intending to "prove againste the nexte yere, whether the snowe could overwhelme it, the frosts breake uppe, or the people dismember the same." "And the better to allure those brutish & uncivill people to courtesie, against other times of oure comming, we left therein dyvers of oure countrie toyes, as belles, and knives, wherein they specially delight, one for the necessarie use, and the other for the great pleasure thereof. Also pictures of men & women in lead, men a horsebacke, lookinglasses, whistles, and pipes. Also in the house was made an oven, and breade lefte baked therein, for them to see and taste." Grain and peas were also planted "to prove the fruitfulnesse of the soyle against the next yeare," perhaps the most unrealistic hope of all (Morison 1971:542; Stefansson and McCaskill 1938, 1:116).

When the products of the mining operations were finally recognized as worthless, further expeditions were called off, but the material evidence of Frobisher's intermittent occupation of the island remained both in the memory of the Inuit of the area and in the ground. Because of the extensive documentary record of the voyages, including detailed inventories of the material culture carried on the ships, the present-day historian and archeologist are able to work in tandem to provide a detailed record of just what happened.

The Smithsonian Bloom

The Smithsonian involvement begins shortly after the founding of the institution in 1846. In 1861–62, the American explorer Captain Charles Francis Hall heard from local Inuit of earlier European occupation in the area. He visited Kodlunarn Island and the surrounding area to discover many traces of Frobisher's occupation, including "iron time-eaten, with ragged teeth, weighing from fifteen to twenty pounds, on the top of a granite rock, just within reach of high tide at full change of moon" and also "a piece of iron, semi-spherical in shape, weighing twenty pounds . . . under the stone that had been excavated for the 'ship's way'." The "ship's way" was a long narrow excavation used probably first as a mine and later as a ramp to launch or retrieve Frobisher's ships. It was in this trench that members of the Smithsonian's 1981 expedition discovered, like Hall, other iron blooms described in this volume.

Our historical survey now must incorporate a bit of museum history that will be painful to those who regard museums as the incorruptible and omniscient guardians of our national heritage. The keen interest of the Smithsonian in Hall's arctic materials was shown in the letter sent by the Secretary of the Smithsonian, Joseph Henry, to Hall on November 24, 1863, in response to a letter of Hall dated March 12 asking for a magnetic apparatus for his northern expedition:

> For the offer of the specimens of natural history, we are much obliged to you, and will gladly receive whatever you can send us. We are especially interested in the Natural History of the Arctic Regions, possessing already, in the results of Mr. Kennicott's explorations, and contributions of officers of the Hudson's Bay Company, very complete series for the regions adjacent to the lower Mackenzie, and about its mouth. We have, however, had but little from North Eastern America, and anything you can send us will be very welcome. The Frobisher relics too we will be much pleased to place on exhibition in our Hall, side by side with a gun formerly used by Sir John Franklin, in his second journey, and a short sword, relic of his last fatal expedition, obtained on the lower Mackenzie through an Esquimaux.

> Will it not be in your power to make some further collections, of objects of Natural History during your new expedition; among such may be especially mentioned a series of the different kinds of lemmings, mice, shrews & marmots, with skins of small land birds, white falcons, & the smaller gulls, one species with dark head, black ring round the neck & wedge-shaped tail (Ross's rosy gull) is particularly desired (SI Acc. 2157, Cat. 77831, W32).

Hall divided the relics he had recovered between the Smithsonian Institution in Washington and the Royal Geographical Society in London. Both organizations totally lost or mislaid their Frobisher collections. When Vilhjalmur Stefansson, the Arctic explorer, was working on his book *The Three Voyages of Martin Frobisher,* he wrote both institutions in an attempt to learn about the relics. Both institutions failed him. The first response from the Smithsonian to his inquiry (August 12, 1935) asserted that "a very careful search has been made of our records but we find no evidence that any relics of this gallant explorer were ever deposited here." Since this response did not agree with the known facts, prominently reported in the press at the time the objects were presented to the Smithsonian, Stefansson wrote again. This time (August 28, 1935), the reply came that

> a very thorough and careful search has been made of our records and of the specimens received by us from the Polaris [the name of Hall's ship] Expedition but unfortunately without any success so far as Frobisher relics are concerned. On one list there is mention of a single specimen as follows: "Iron bloom, obtained from Countess of Warwick Sound where it was made by Frobisher in 1578, searching for gold." A careful examination of the specimens, however, fails to reveal any object answering to this description. (SI Acc. 2157)

In fact the accession record of the U.S. National Museum (#2157) contains a full listing of the Hall objects both as accessioned in 1874 (they were received in 1871) and as they were returned from loan status at the 1876 International Exhibition held at Philadelphia to celebrate the centennial of American independence. Why they could not be located in 1935 is unknown, but in 1950, in gathering data for Remington Kellogg, director of the U.S. National Museum, for a response to Mrs. H. S. Marlett who had raised the same questions Stefansson had earlier broached, the curator of the Division of Ethnology, H. W. Krieger, in a memo to Frank M. Setzler, head curator, Department of Anthropology, dated March 17, 1950, reported that the "Iron Bloom" (Cat. #10,291) "was recently located by Mr. R. Sirlouis in the Gallery storage of the Department of History" and "respectfully requested" that permission be given to transfer the catalog card describing it to the Department of History. As for the "Relics of Frobisher's Voyage" (Cat. #14,247) Krieger opined that it offered "a problem not readily solved. . . . If the pieces of coal, fragments of iron, glass and pottery were not numbered individually," he went on "it is unlikely that they will be found." Krieger concluded his memo by noting that "practically all mistakes that a museum could make in accessioning, cataloguing, preservation, recording, classification, and correspondence are illustrated in our connection with the Charles F. Hall collections."

Unfortunately, Krieger, in a memo of January 26, 1953, to Dr. Kellogg through Mr. Setzler (correspondence File 197929) requested a condemnation committee to dispose of objects "fragmentary or broken beyond repair; in part, undocumented and unidentifiable." He noted that "a considerable number of these specimens were collected by exploring expeditions to the Arctic. Although the expeditions are historical, the relics submitted for disposal consist of driftwood fragments, stone pebbles, shells and animal bones. On inquiry, it was found that these items are not wanted either by History, Geology, Zoology or Anthropology." A condemnation committee chaired by Mr. Setzler, with Krieger and David H. Dunkle as members, recommended disposal of a variety of objects in a memo of March 27, 1953, to Dr. Kellogg, who approved the condemnation on March 30. Among the items discarded from the Hall collection were "minerals," "shot," "cross bar?," "quartzite," "iron pyrites," and "quartz rock," as well as "pebbles," "sand stone rock," "one lot sea shells," "drift wood," "plumbago used by natives," and "rib of spotted seal."

I came to the Smithsonian in 1958 as curator of the Division of Political History. This division had inherited some of the collections of the old Department of History, which in turn had broken off from the Division of Ethnology. In 1964 I "discovered" the iron bloom (earlier located by Mr. Sirlouis during the 1950 search) in a remote part of the history storage area in the Arts and Industries Building of the Smithsonian. The object was not catalogued in the Division of Political History, but I filed a request through the Division of Naval History, which had responsibility for the Hall materials, to the newly established analytical and conservation laboratory to analyze the metal and determine its age. I hoped to be able to get the answer to incorporate in a paper on "The Oriental Purpose of the Arctic Navigations" that I was scheduled to deliver in August 1970 in Moscow at a meeting of the International Commission of Maritime History during the XIII International Congress of Historical Sciences.

Unfortunately, as the next chapter will indicate, there were many problems facing the new laboratory, and I was unable to obtain the information prior to leaving for Moscow.

In today's sophisticated age, one can smile at the foul-ups and failures that marked both the Frobisher voyages themselves and the actions of distinguished institutions that sought to preserve the record of those voyages. But perhaps the lesson to be learned is that such difficulties are burdens inevitably carried by both the actors in history and those who seek to record and preserve the record of those actors.

Fig. 4.1. An iron bloom in the collection of the Department of Naval History, National Museum of American History, Smithsonian Institution (Cat. No. 49459). The bloom weighs approximately 17 pounds after sampling and is approximately 18 cm in diameter on the base as shown (Smithsonian Institution negative No. 74836). Attempts to date this bloom provided the stimulus for the research reported in this volume and led to the current interest in the Frobisher voyages and Meta Incognita Program.

4

History of Research on the Smithsonian Bloom

JACQUELINE S. OLIN

The events leading up to the dating of the Smithsonian bloom parallel the development of the laboratory study of museum artifacts at the Institution. The Conservation Analytical Laboratory was established in 1963, just one year before the project on the bloom began. The research, which now also involves a group of iron artifacts from Kodlunarn Island, has taken place over many years and has ranged from the study of an object in the Smithsonian Institution's collections to an excavation at the site of Martin Frobisher's basecamp on Kodlunarn Island. During the course of the research, discussions between scientists at the Smithsonian and at Brookhaven National Laboratory led to an improvement in dating technology. Brookhaven scientists who were involved in measuring low levels of radioactivity worked on the development of small-volume counters for carbon-14 dating. The dating of the Smithsonian iron bloom played an important role in this process and in so doing became the stimulus for further research on the Frobisher sites and voyages.

Work on the Smithsonian bloom began in 1964 when Wilcomb Washburn submitted the newly located iron object to the Smithsonian's Conservation Analytical Laboratory for analysis. It was then described as a "20-lb. lump of ore presumably made by Martin Frobisher in the Arctic, 1578. Deposited after being found by Capt. C. F. Hall in the mid-nineteenth century, in the S.I." The significance of the object was in no way apparent except for the known history of where it had come from and how it had arrived at the Smithsonian (Washburn, this volume). Curiosity was aroused, however, and ways of finding out more about it were considered and explored. Fortunately, an institution like the Smithsonian has specialists in many areas of scientific inquiry. In early December 1965, the object was delivered to Roy Clarke, a chemist in the Division of Meteorites, to determine whether or not it was meteoritic. This was a valuable step, and the ensuing report set the stage for addressing not where the object came from but by whom it had been made and who carried it to the Arctic. The report states:

> The Frobisher Sound sample has been examined by us and found to be a slaggy piece of artifical [sic] iron. The small piece that was removed for chemical and metallographic examination contained numerous silicate inclusions. Behavior of the sample on solution in hydrochloric acid indicated that it contains a significant (from a metallographic point of view) quantity of carbon. The sample contains a minor

amount of manganese and essentially no nickel. Indications are that the metal phase is essentially iron. Metallographic examination of an etched surface showed structures typical of an impure iron or carbon steel.

The presence of carbon established that the object was a manufactured specimen that had been made by direct reduction of iron ore and was in a stage of production known as an iron "bloom." Technically, bloomery iron is an alloy of carbon with an inhomogeneous carbon content which may vary from nearly zero to 0.8%. It was possible that the artifact had been smelted by Frobisher's men on Kodlunarn Island, but this was considered unlikely because of the limited time Frobisher's men spent on the island during any of the three voyages. Perhaps the object was not a Frobisher artifact at all. As of this time the Kodlunarn Island sites had been inspected only by Hall, who was not a trained archeologist. Perhaps the site was not Frobisher's, but the remains of a Norse settlement. It seemed likely that determining the age of the bloom might help answer this question. As the bloom contained carbon, radiocarbon dating might be possible. But how much carbon was also important because at that time, standard radiocarbon dating laboratories required a large carbon sample to obtain a date. An additional problem that had to be solved was the matter of extracting the carbon from the iron.

In October 1965, Nikolaas J. van der Merwe, then Assistant in Research in the Department of Anthropology at Yale University, published a paper in *Current Anthropology* describing his research involving the dating of iron samples. Van der Merwe agreed to include a sample from the Smithsonian bloom in his studies, and in May he was sent a sample of 339 grams of iron. At that time the object had not yet been analyzed for carbon concentration. Most of the samples that van der Merwe had dated were of cast iron and had a carbon concentration of about 5%, so it had to be determined whether or not the Smithsonian sample contained a concentration high enough to carry out the carbon-14 dating. At that time the preferred sample size for dating was one gram of carbon. This would require that our iron bloom contain approximately 0.5% carbon for the 339 grams to be adequate. Unfortunately, up until this time we had no method available to us at the Smithsonian to analyze the carbon concentration.

In March 1967, interest in dating the Frobisher object was renewed by Chauncey C. Loomis, a Research Associate in the Division of Naval History. Loomis and Wilcomb Washburn of the Department of American Studies submitted requests to the Radiocarbon Dating Section of the Smithsonian's Radiation Biology Laboratory. Both Loomis and Washburn were eager to learn whether or not the bloom would date to the 16th century, confirming the association with Martin Frobisher, or some earlier date. However, the Smithsonian did not have the capability for combusting an iron sample to prepare the carbon for analysis. About the same time it was learned that van der Merwe's lab had not been able to proceed either, and the sample was returned.

By this time it became apparent that we might have to develop our own procedure for carbon extraction. In the meantime, the Smithsonian had procured equipment for microcarbon analysis, and obtained a result of carbon concentration ranging from 0.4 to 2.0%. Apparently, carbon was heterogeneously distributed in the bloom iron, a conclusion that was confirmed when later analyses varied markedly from these early data (Rostoker and Dvorak, 1986). However, with the concentration data in hand, it was possible to move to the problem of developing a procedure for carbon extraction. Lacking facilities at the Smithsonian, we began collaboration with the Naval Research Laboratory, where Walter Hopwood of the Smithsonian CAL staff prepared the samples for carbon-14 dating. The sample preparation system we developed involved combusting the iron to produce carbon dioxide, which we then collected as barium carbonate by bubbling the carbon dioxide into barium hydroxide. The barium carbonate was filtered inside a glove box using glass fiber filter paper in an atmosphere of nitrogen, dried under reduced pressure, and then transferred to leakproof polyethylene containers for mailing to a commercial carbon-14 dating laboratory. Arrangements for dating our samples were also being made with Teledyne Isotopes of Westwood, New Jersey.

The procedure was first tested using a sample of modern cast iron, NBS 4j, to determine that we were successfully preparing a sample uncontaminated with atmospheric carbon dioxide. Modern cast iron is prepared using coke rather than charcoal and therefore should be almost depleted of carbon-14.

Fig. 4.2. Smithsonian bloom base after sampling for conventional carbon-14 dating.

The dating report received from Teledyne Isotopes showed that our carbon dioxide sample from modern cast iron contained 1.7% of the amount of carbon-14 contained in the .950 NBS oxalic acid standard. Theoretically a sample of modern cast iron should contain no carbon-14 except for undetermined amounts of modern carbon either added at the foundry or adsorbed from the atmosphere. This result was consistent with other samples of modern, coke-smelted cast iron (van der Merwe, 1969).

By 1970 we had prepared samples for dating from two samples of known date: a stoveplate from the Redding Furnace, Pennsylvania, dated to 1761 and a sample of cast iron from the Saugus Ironworks, Massachusetts, dated to between 1648 and 1678. The dates we obtained from Teledyne Isotopes in 1971 for both samples were earlier than the known dates. For the Redding Furnace sample we obtained a date of A.D. 1385 ± 105 and for the Saugus Ironworks sample, a date of A.D. 1445 ± 85.

The date for the Redding Furnace sample falls out of the range of the carbon-14 date even at two standard deviations, suggesting that another sample should be run. The date for the Saugus Ironworks sample does fall within the two standard deviation range; it also agrees with a date obtained later at Brookhaven National Laboratory for that sample (Sayre et al., 1982).

There was some urgency developing to obtain a date for the Smithsonian bloom. We knew by that time that the carbon concentration of the bloom was less than 0.5% and closer to 0.1%. This would require at least 1000 grams of sample—more than two pounds—for the one gram of carbon needed for conventional carbon-14 dating. At that time, however, this was the only possible way of dating the bloom, and a sample was removed for that purpose even though it was not certain that a date would be immediately forthcoming. Commercial carbon-14 dating laboratories were not prepared to date iron

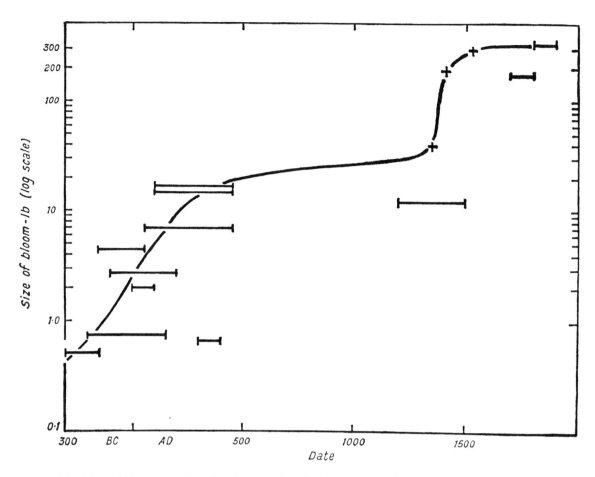

Fig. 4.3. Weights of blooms produced by the bloomhearth during its period of use (Tylecote 1962:296). The curve shows the increase in the weight of iron blooms as new techniques, such as introduction of forced air draft and other processes, were developed to increase production.

objects, and work was still proceeding in establishing satisfactory procedures at the Naval Research Laboratory. We had in the meantime begun conversations with Edward Sayre and Garman Harbottle at Brookhaven National Laboratory on the use of small-volume counters for carbon-14 dating of milligram samples of carbon. This certainly seemed the way to proceed, and in June 1975 the Conservation Analytical Laboratory contracted with the Chemistry Department at Brookhaven to develop small-volume counters for carbon-14 dating. This work proceeded over the next few years with the projection of dating the Frobisher bloom after the methods were developed. In March 1980, Brookhaven reported two dates for the Frobisher bloom: A.D. 1158 ± 107 and 1271 ± 133. By using the small-volume counter, only part of the sample was needed for dating. The remainder is available for other purposes.

The dates obtained did not match those of the Frobisher expeditions and raised new questions of the origin of the Smithsonian bloom. They were, however, consistent with other information regarding the sizes of blooms and the concentration of phosphorus in blooms. Tylecote (1962) presented evidence that blooms of the 16th century in England, produced using waterpower, weighed about 200 pounds. The Smithsonian's bloom weighed only about twenty pounds. Also our determination showed the phosphorus concentration in the Frobisher bloom was about 0.4%. During the 16th century, ores containing low phosphorus concentrations were sought in order to improve the properties of the iron. A concentration of 0.4% was not consistent with 16th-century iron from England, according to analyses of 16th-century blooms given by Tylecote.

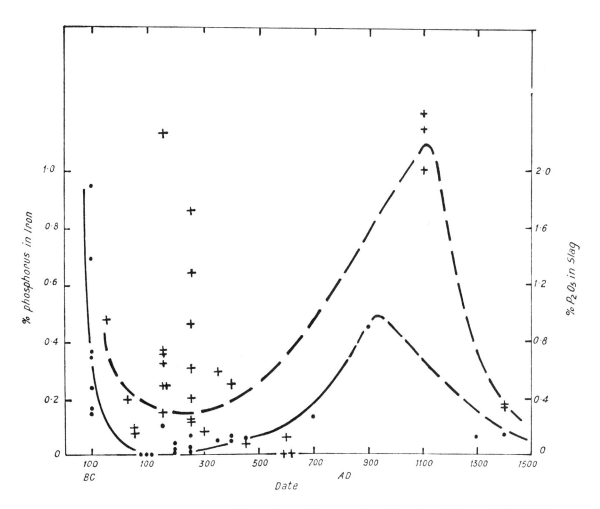

Fig. 4.4. Change in phosphorus content of slag and metal, later Medieval Iron Age (Tylecote 1962:297); circles: % P in metal (left-hand scale, bottom curve); crosses: % P_2O_5 in slag (right-hand scale, top curve).

We were now convinced that we needed to learn more about the site on Kodlunarn Island. Was it conceivable for Frobisher's men to have been smelting iron from local rock or bog ore (as done by the Norse at L'Anse aux Meadows in Newfoundland), perhaps using centuries-old arctic driftwood? If so, this might explain the early radiocarbon dates from the Smithsonian bloom, and it might also explain the bloom's small size compared with blooms currently being produced in English furnaces of the day.

The question of 16th-century smelting procedures and the requirements for the construction of a smelting furnace have to be considered in suggesting that Frobisher's group actually carried out smelting operations on Kodlunarn Island. Tylecote (1962) describes an iron smelting operation from the 14th–15th century in England as follows: "The construction of the mill race, which is about 100 yards long,

took four or five people thirty days. A forge house was constructed by a carpenter so it was timber framed, probably with wattle and daub walls. Two hearths were made, a bloom hearth and a string hearth, both made with the assistance of a bloomer from another bloomery. The string hearth would be used for working and cutting up the bloom after smelting. The carpenter constructed a waterwheel (by the 14th century in England water-power was being used as a source of power for the bellows) which could have had a diameter of about 15 feet. . . . The wheel had sufficient power to blow the bellows for the bloom hearth and perhaps for both hearths for most of the year."

It might be imagined that a more primitive smelting operation not involving a waterwheel could have been set up on Kodlunarn Island by Frobisher's group, but if so this is not noted in the records,

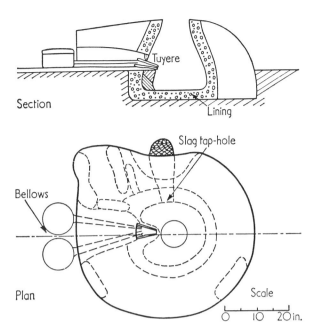

Fig. 4.5. An example of a furnace at High Bishopley, Co. Durham, in the British Isles used for iron smelting in the 12–13th century which might be like that used to produce the Smithsonian bloom and might be expected on Kodlunarn if Frobisher's party was engaged in smelting there. The bottom of this furnace was found only 20 inches below the present surface level. It was blown with a forced draught involving the use of bellows and tuyere (Tylecote 1962:269).

which do account for the presence of smithing and forging facilities and materials. Tylecote (1962) also describes a smelting furnace dating to the 12th–13th century which contained two bowl hearths with slag-tapping capabilities. The bowls were approximately three feet in diameter and eight inches deep and were filled with cinder. A nearby slag heap contained tap slag but no cinder or furnace bottoms. Simple furnaces of this type would have been of more use on Kodlunarn Island. Could it be that such methods were employed by Frobisher's men if they found themselves under duress in their exposed field site? If so, this might account for the unusually small size of the bloom and its high phosphorus content, both of which are anomalous in terms of 16th-century industrial iron production.

Among the new research relevant to the archeology of smelting is the work of Irmelin Martens in the Telemark region of Norway. Martens's excavations have over the past twenty years produced evidence of many iron production sites dating from the 5th to the 11th century A.D. In addition to evidence of changing technology of simple bloomery furnaces, first of non-slag tapping and later of slag-tapping varieties with chimneys, associated structures, slag heaps, slag studies (based on Anna Rosenquist's analyses), and settlement and geographical features are noted. Martens's studies reveal a type of iron production that seems close to that expected to have produced the Kodlunarn blooms, although the latter lack the split morphology seen in these early Norwegian blooms (Martens 1988:110). But this is getting ahead of our story.

At that point, in 1980, discussions began with Bill Fitzhugh about an expedition to learn more about the Frobisher sites on Kodlunarn Island than could be gleaned from Charles Francis Hall's field work in the 1860s. From an archeometric perspective, the purpose of such a trip was to determine whether or not iron smelting had taken place on Kodlunarn Island. The expedition took place in August 1981. In order to investigate the area where smelting may have been carried out, a proton magnetometer survey was made, and the results were essentially negative. Using a metal detector, however, three more iron blooms were found buried near and in the ship's trench. The subsequent dating and metallographic study of one of these blooms, described elsewhere in this volume, produced evidence that the material remains from Kodlunarn Island represent two different time periods. Some are clearly 16th-century English. The blooms, however, date from several centuries earlier. Based on earlier metallographic studies of the Smithsonian bloom, it was concluded that it was not possible to designate the origin of the bloom on the basis of the metallurgical evidence (Rostoker and Dvorak 1986).

The significance of this research has yet to be determined. We hope the data presented in these papers will contribute to defining future research goals in the archeology of Kodlunarn Island. All of the chapters contain information which should stimulate readers to develop their own conclusions. The archeological survey based on the 1981 expedition and the analytical and dating information from the wood, charcoal, and metal artifacts are always subject to reinterpretation. The historical material regarding the Inuit oral history of Frobisher's voyages and the known history of Frobisher's mining activities provides a context for interpreting that informa-

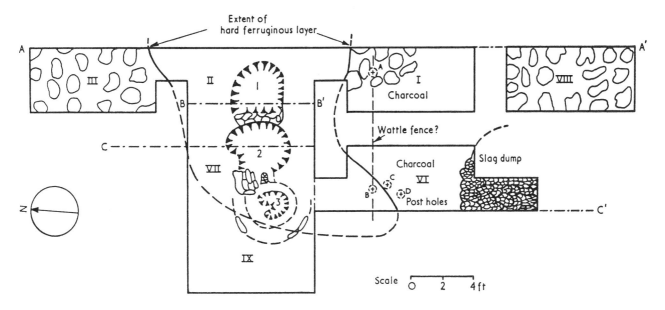

Fig. 4.6. Plan of excavation of the 12–13th-century iron smelting site at High Bishopley, Co. Durham, showing the furnace (3) and two bowl hearths (1 and 2). The bowl hearths would have been used prior to the construction of the furnace and are examples of a technology that dates back to the Roman period in the British Isles and produced blooms of only a few killograms in size. Thus they cannot be exact examples of what we could expect to have been used in producing the Smithsonian bloom (Tylecote 1962:267).

tion. Another context is suggested by the fact that there were Norse settlers in Greenland from A.D. 1000 to 1500 with a network that supplied iron to the Thule Eskimos (McCartney and Mack 1973). The Smithsonian bloom certainly dates to exactly this period. For the reader who likes to be challenged to investigate unresolved problems, this book will be a rewarding experience. It will certainly suggest new approaches to some. Already, there is discussion of collecting comparative material for both the blooms and the coal. The analysis of reference material for the blooms might lead to exploration of a new analytical approach involving the use of lead-isotope ratios in studying the provenance of iron artifacts. Some work has been done in this area (Mabuchi, pers. comm.). This volume should serve not only as a reference source for future investigators, but also to demonstrate why analytical, historical, and archeological information must be used collectively.

Acknowledgments

In the course of this research many individuals and institutions have participated. These include the staff of the Museum of American History who have been helpful in making the Smithsonian bloom available for study. Robert Organ as Chief of the Conservation Analytical Laboratory was supportive and provided the contract for the work carried out at Brookhaven National Laboratory. Martha Goodway carried out a number of metallurgical studies on samples from the bloom and contributed to Anonymous (1983). There have been numerous contributions of comparative samples such as the Redding Stoveplate from the Mercer Museum and the Saugus samples of cast iron provided to us by the late Cyril Stanley Smith. Smith also provided many useful comments on the work and supported the importance of this research to the developing Conservation Analytical Laboratory.

FIELD STUDIES

Fig. 5.1. Smithsonian team taking magnetometer readings and excavating test pits at Frobisher's smithy on Kodlunarn Island in August 1981. The Frobisher party erected a small fort on "Best's Bulwark" (center rear) to defend themselves against possible Inuit attack. Blunt Peninsula and Victoria Bay, the location of one of the Frobisher mines, are seen in the distance across Countess of Warwick Sound.

PREVIOUS PAGES: Excavation in progress at House 3 (right) and House 4 (left) at Kamaiyuk during the 1992 season. Generations of Inuit, Thule, and Dorset people have left traces at this site whose most recent occupation dates to shortly after the Frobisher voyages. These houses contain Native artifacts together with European materials scavenged primarily from Frobisher's Kodlunarn Island caches and workshops.

5

Archeology of Kodlunarn Island

WILLIAM W. FITZHUGH

The story of Martin Frobisher's pioneering explorations and mining enterprises in Frobisher Bay is one of the best known chapters of arctic exploration and has inspired a huge body of historical research. First-hand accounts fill volumes (e.g., Settle 1577; Best 1578; Ellis 1578; Fenton, in Kenyon 1980/81; Collinson 1867; Stefansson and McCaskill 1938), and unpublished archive resources continue to promote new contributions (e.g., Cheshire et al. 1980; works of Hogarth and coauthors). As detailed as these sources are, however, they do not indicate the precise location of the Frobisher sites and mines, nor do they tell much about the day-to-day activities of Frobisher's men who lived and worked on Kodlunarn Island in the summers of 1577 and 1578. And while these accounts provide some of the most objective 16th-century ethnographic accounts of Inuit peoples, the reports are not sufficient to judge the extent of European material, social, and economic interaction with native groups or, of course, to determine the consequences of that interaction on subsequent cultural development. In fact, the historical record of the Frobisher voyages has been so dominant that even the discovery of Frobisher's mines and shops by C. F. Hall in 1862 and his demonstration of their archeological potential did little to entice scholars to seek to augment or question this documentation through the material record. It has taken an additional 130 years for these historic sites to become the object of serious scientific attention.

Geography and Ethnography

As a geographic region Frobisher Bay offers excellent potential both for traditional Inuit settlement and for seasonal early European visitors (Hall 1865b; Boas 1888; Jacobs and Stenton 1985; Stenton 1987, 1991). Over 60 km wide at its mouth and 200 km from its mouth to head, Frobisher Bay has a variety of productive habitats ranging from a strongly arctic maritime outer coast zone in which seals, walrus, sea birds, and polar bears are abundant, to a heavily islanded inner bay zone frequented by large numbers of seals, large whales, and large runs of char. Caribou is the most important terrestrial resource in both areas. Less bold in physiography than other regions of the East Baffin coast, Frobisher Bay offers considerable protection for human settlement and hunting activity. Its winter sea ice surfaces are relatively stable and yet provide excellent potential

Fig. 5.2. "Ig-loos or Snow Village at Oopungnewing" (Hall 1864, 1:293), a late winter walrus-hunting camp at the south end of Willows Island, visited by Hall in 1862. Shows the return of hunters with walrus and seals, and a row of walrus heads on top of an igloo.

for ice edge marine mammal hunting, while the orientation of its highlands protects the bay from the most violent storms and less agreeable climatic conditions of the outer coast. In fact, Frobisher Bay has a relatively warm microclimate, more stable and calm and with less fog and permafrost than other regions of the Eastern Arctic at this latitude.

The large size of the bay and presence of two distinct ecological regions resulted at least during the past thousand years in the existence of two centers of Inuit concentration in the inner and outer bay regions. Although the antiquity of settlement in Iqaluit is attested by sites dating from early and late Paleoeskimo times (Pre-Dorset, 4000–2500 B.P.; Dorset, 2500–1000 B.P.) and a sequence of Neoeskimo settlements dating from at least the 12th century, this area was not occupied in the 19th century during C. F. Hall's visit. At that time the Inuit population was centered in the outer bay regions around Countess of Warwick Sound and Cyrus Field Bay where they were in contact with European whalers. It is not yet clear whether the abandonment of Iqaluit and concentration of settlement in the outer bay was motivated by ecological reasons or a desire for greater accesss to European resources (Jacobs and Stenton 1985; Eber 1989).

In Countess of Warwick Sound Hall found a large Inuit population whose elders were acquainted with stories about Kodlunarn Island and early "kadlunat." This area has a number of physical and biological resources making it an attractive settlement region. The local economy was strongly maritime-oriented and involved an annual cycle that included fall occupations in Cyrus Field Bay, winter quarters on Opingivik (today's Willows, Hall's Oopungnewing) Island in Countess of Warwick Sound, spring walrus hunting camps on islands in the middle reaches of Frobisher Bay, and summer caribou and seal hunting camps in the Countess of Warwick Sound (Hall 1865b; Boas 1888:14). Part of the attractiveness of the region was and continues to be its ease of access to marine mammals of outer Frobisher Bay and Davis Strait while at the same time providing hunters with protected waters for summer travel and a stable winter ice platform for hunting seals, walrus, and polar bear. From the point of view of early European mariners, either Norse or Elizabethan, Countess of Warwick Sound was an ideal summer base, with numerous protected boat anchorages and a plentiful supply of caribou, seal, fish, and birds, all within less than a day's travel from the outer coast.

Physically, Kodlunarn Island is a barren, flat-topped island less than 300 m in diameter and 20 m high. Besides its small size and barren landscape, its most prominent physiographic feature is its 10-m-high sea cliffs, which surround the island margins and prevent easy access to its upper surface, except at two locations: at the mine (ship's trench) on the north side of the island and at the opposite side of the island near the smithy. The eastern half of the island is covered with a thin mantle of sand and gravel washed down from eroding outcrops, while its western half is strewn with boulders and outcropping ledges. All surficial deposits are the result of marine sedimentation and beach formation processes associated with geological emergence during the mid-Holocene period. Much of this surface is completely barren of vegetation. Patches of grass and tundra shrubs survive only in protected, better-watered locales, such as in the 200-m-long swale (our "Elizabethan Alley") where most of the Frobisher sites are found. This trough harbors several intermittent ponds fed by meltwater and rain runoff.

Our 1981 fieldwork was conducted during the first week of August. The team was transported to Countess of Warwick Sound from Iqaluit through the broken pack ice of Frobisher Bay on a longliner owned by Palousie Kilabuk. Once there, we established a field camp on the west side of the entrance to Diana Bay a few hundred meters north of a busy Inuit seal and caribou hunting camp. Excellent weather permitted five days' work at Kodlunarn Island. In addition brief visits were made to Tikkoon Point, Cape Sarah, Opingivik (Willows) Island, and along four kilometers of shoreline west of the Diana Bay entrance. Results of these surveys are presented in the following chapter together with preliminary data from reconnaissance in the outer reaches of Frobisher Bay and Cyrus Field Bay in August 1990 and 1991. The purpose of this 1990–1991 work was to conduct preliminary regional surveys, primarily for Inuit and other sites, in preparation for a more intensive research program on the Frobisher sites and early European-Inuit contact (Fitzhugh 1990).

Methods

Our brief period of fieldwork in 1981 permitted only a general reconnaissance of Kodlunarn and nearby regions. The Kodlunarn survey concentrated on the eastern end of the island where most of the Frobisher sites are located. Most of these structures were easily identified because their turf-covered wall foundations, trenches, pits, or boulder arrangements stand out clearly against the barren gravel surface of the island. All features were plotted on base maps and were mapped with line and tape. Representative samples of artifacts, slag, coal, and other materials were collected and plotted when encountered as surface finds. Small test pits (generally ca. 50 cm^2) were excavated in the major structures to determine depth of deposit and to recover representative artifacts and archeometric samples. All sites were photographed in color, black and white, and Polaroid.

In addition to these standard methods, several remote sensing techniques were used to assist in locating buried metal, pits, furnaces, smelters, and new sites. Richard Linington, an Italian physicist who specialized in magnetometer prospection, surveyed the entire Elizabethan Alley area to locate potential subsurface smelter or furnace features, but we soon discovered that the threshold of any subsurface cultural features that might exist was masked by an overpowering bedrock signal. Linington died in 1984 before completing his field report, but his conclusions in any case were negative. The second technique was survey by a portable metal detector (D-Tex Electronics SK-60). This instrument provided excellent service and allowed us to cover most of the Elizabethan Alley region and parts of the island's coastal margin. This device led directly to discovery of three buried iron blooms that were the major finds of the field season; it also located metallic sources (not excavated) in the smithy (S1). In addition to these methods, we were able to conduct a brief aerial survey and make photographs of the region courtesy of the pilot H. King Cummings (deceased). Two possible cairns or pinnacles were noted on Blunt Peninsula summit east of Kodlunarn Island.

Results

Hall's notes in the Division of Naval History Archives, National Museum of American History, Smithsonian Institution, record the following details on his survey of Kodlunarn Island in September 1862:

[Distance from] ruins of 1st Stone House to head of Ship's Trench, 132 feet.

Reservoir: Distance between the extreme of outside of embankments, 102 [feet]. Top of excavated part,

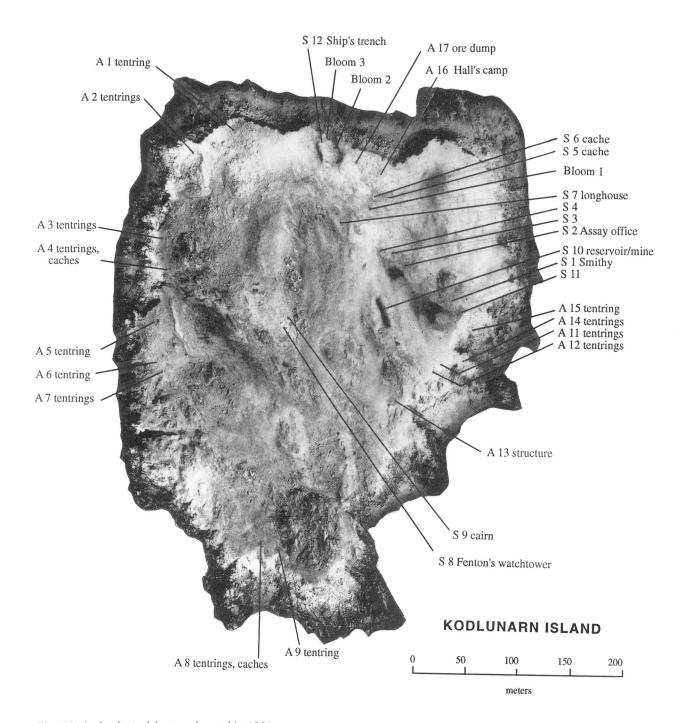

A 1 tentring

A 2 tentrings

A 3 tentrings

A 4 tentrings, caches

A 5 tentring

A 6 tentring

A 7 tentrings

A 8 tentrings, caches

A 9 tentring

S 12 Ship's trench

Bloom 3

Bloom 2

A 17 ore dump

A 16 Hall's camp

S 6 cache

S 5 cache

Bloom 1

S 7 longhouse

S 4

S 3

S 2 Assay office

S 10 reservoir/mine

S 1 Smithy

S 11

A 15 tentring

A 14 tentrings

A 11 tentrings

A 12 tentrings

A 13 structure

S 9 cairn

S 8 Fenton's watchtower

KODLUNARN ISLAND

| 0 | 50 | 100 | 150 | 200 |

meters

Fig. 5.3. Archeological features located in 1981.

89. Bottom part of all, 65. Water in it, 18 in. [wide?], and 1 foot deep. Greatest width between extreme outside of embankments, 58. Center and top of one bank to the other, 36. From one side to the other of commencement of excavating the stone, 20. From this it slopes down to almost an edge, from bottom to top of bank, 8. Average depth, 7.

Big black block of nearly pure mica [hornblende ore] about 50 feet from the south end. No water re-ceived from the slope of the east side of the hill on which the Reservoir is. The reservoir is dug out of stone. Stone is fragmentary. Willows and moss and wood of the country growing on its East bank, on the slope to the water, of the Reservoir. Distance from Ship's Trench, 367 feet. Between the two there is a slight rise of land (near the head of the latter) which shuts out the view of one from the other. Dis-tance to ruins of Stone House, 261.

Ruins of Stone House: It is of oval shape, after examination and excavation. Largest diameter from outside to outside walls, 20 feet. Shortest diameter from outside to outside walls, 17. Foundation from 3 to 3 1/2 feet thick. Stone laid in sand white lime cement. The cement exposed to air, hard as rock; but that under ground, friable. Digging down two feet could not find bottom of the foundation. Floor of stone and laid in iron cement. View from here, extensive and interesting, and commands all the approaches to the Island, embracing Twerpukjua, Niountelik, Opungnewing and as far as Sharko. Distance to Ship's Trench, 446 feet.

Ship's Trench: Sept. 17, 1862. Excavated part, in length, 110 feet. Depth of Solid rock at bluff, 13. The trench was considerably deeper. rocks have tumbled in from the banks that were thrown out of the excavated material. Width across bottom at opening to sea water, 20 feet. Width across top of excavated rock part, 30 feet. Middle or Apex of banks, one to the other 60 feet. From outer edge of one bank to outer edge of other, 87 feet. The view from Ship's Trench is more limited than that from the House on center of Island.

Sept. 22, 1962. The Island covered nearly all over with shingle. On the north side these small stones are very compact and of even surface.

Sept. 25, 1862. Sketch of Isl., Ship's Trench.

A major result of our 1981 fieldwork is the clarification and expansion of Hall's map of archeological finds (see fig. 1.11). Our preliminary site map of Kodlunarn Island (KeDe-1) shows the structures and features (S series) that we attribute to Frobisher and another set of data (A series) consisting mostly of tentrings of probable Inuit origin. Upon further investigation some of these may turn out to be tent sites of Frobisher's men, some of whom Fenton reported camped on the island. The latter series probably also includes the remains of Hall's encampment. Figure 5.21 is a map of the remains of Fenton's "watchtower" surveyed by Caroline Phillips. With a few exceptions (e.g., error in location of the blacksmith shop), our research corroborated Hall's map as far as it went, but we also identified several new Frobisher structures and plotted Inuit camps which he did not identify.

In addition to Hall's identification of four Frobisher structures, we located nine new structures or features, eight of which are provisionally attributed to the Frobisher occupation. The Frobisher structures and find locales as now known are listed in table 5.1.

Most of these remains are concentrated in a low swale that extends about 100 m across the island from the ship's trench on its northern shore to the

TABLE 5.1. Frobisher structures and features on Kodlunarn Island

S1	Rectangular foundation, probably a blacksmith shop, containing black earth deposits with crucible sherds, roof tile, brick, slag, charcoal, and iron bloom fragments
S2	Rectangular foundation, probably Fenton's assay shop, containing charcoal, slag, crucible fragments, tile, and brick
S3	Unidentified structure containing a large charcoal deposit
S4	Sod and rock earthwork built across the drainage, possibly functioning as a dam to hold runoff water for assay and smithy shops; alternatively a workshop
S5,6	Two boulder cache pits, probably Frobisher period, vandalized in recent years
S7	22 × 4 m longhouse structure excavated into gravel, containing tile and ceramic fragments
S8	Rectangular foundation of Fenton's hilltop "watchtower" built in 1578; disturbed by early diggings; contains tile, brick, ceramics, flint, mortar
S9	Commemorative cairn and plaque erected by Lt. Brockley, Dr. R. West, and Mr. V. Brockley in 1966
S10	25 × 6 m trench identified by Hall as a reservoir or mine; probably used first as a mine and later for water catchment
S11	Subsurface slab construction and traces of fire; possible smelter or furnace site
S12	"Ship's trench" identified in Inuit oral history and by Hall as a ship ways for repairing or rebuilding a boat; find location of three iron blooms and other Elizabethan materials
S13	"Best's Bulwark," site of George Best's defensive fortification
S14	Possible mine pit in black rock outcrop, 1 × 2 m diameter, at bank 100 m west of ship's trench
S15	Black ore spoil pile several meters east of ship's trench
S16	Two possible graves marked by upright slabs (noted by James Tuck in 1990)
S17	A well, the only freshwater source on Kodlunarn (noted by McGhee and Tuck in 1990 survey); protected from pollution by Frobisher decree

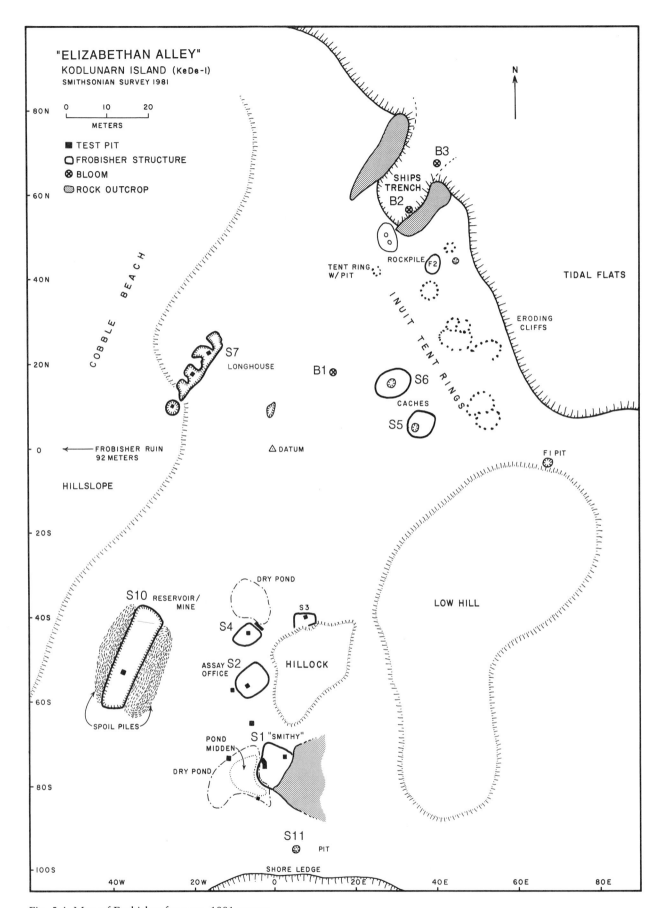

Fig. 5.4. Map of Frobisher features, 1981 survey.

Fig. 5.5. Southeast side of Kodlunarn Island, the major area of Elizabethan settlement, at low tide. Fenton's "watch tower" is seen as a light-colored disturbance area at lower right. Above and diagonally to the right are, respectively, the mine/reservoir (S10), dam (S4), assay shop (S2), and blacksmith shop (S1), and Best's Bulwark, a narrow tongue of rock extending toward the shore.

small rocky promontory identified by Hall as "Best's Bulwark" on its southeastern shore. Between the two lies a broad declivity draining eastward through a series of shallow basins and intermittent stream channels to the shore. This area, which we informally referred to as "Elizabethan Alley," is the principal area of Elizabethan activity on Kodlunarn Island, apart from the stone watchtower and possible campsites. Several thousand years ago this area was a marine channel; in more recent years its sediments have been mantled by surficial deposits of frost-riven shingle and detritus.

Among the peculiarities associated with Frobisher's selection of Kodlunarn Island as a basecamp is its lack of fresh water. The island's soils are essentially mineral and well drained; consequently, water is available only during early summer before the frost leaves the ground; otherwise it is available in summer only for brief periods after rainstorms. The island has no permanent ponds, although two shallow basins provide temporary catchment. No potable water was present during our two August visits, and vegetation is almost nonexistent except for lichens and small patches of grass in the moister soils bordering the pond basins and seeps. The only other source of water is in a small pit (S17) below ledges on the north side of the island, noted by McGhee and Tuck in 1990. This may be the source of drinking water referred to in a Frobisher edict promising stern treatment of polluters. Better water sources are available nearby on Tikkoon Point, less than a kilometer from Kodlunarn.

This absence of water has impressed most European visitors, beginning with Hall, who identified a deep cut across the hillslope as a mine that he thought Frobisher had probably later used as a

Fig. 5.6. Dry pond west of smithy, view east.

reservoir. Given these conditions, it is probably signficant that the smithy and assay shop, both of which required fresh water on a regular basis, are associated with the island's only drainage system. This system was dry during our three early August visits, but may have been better watered in the Little Ice Age climate of the 1570s.

We may ask why Frobisher selected this small, barren, almost waterless island as his principal expeditionary basecamp. The answer seems to lie in a combination of factors, including the presence here of two major mines (ship's trench and reservoir), safe access for small boats along its protected northern shore, defensive capabilities resulting from the high, steep-walled shore and excellent lookout position at the island's crest, and proximity to protected anchorages.

DESCRIPTION OF ELIZABETHAN STRUCTURES

STRUCTURE 1 (SMITHY)

Thirty five meters southeast of the most prominent human construction on the island, the mine/reservoir (S10), is a rectangular structure whose grass and willow vegetation, sod wall foundation, and internal rock piles mark it prominently as a cultural feature. This is probably the location identified by

Hall as a blacksmith shop, where he excavated (Collinson 1867:371) and collected a chunk of charcoal "of thrifty growth" (Hall 1865b:553.20) from under the stones and sods; it was probably also tested by Strong. Kenyon (1975b:148) excavated a pit outside its southern wall, which in 1974 was 67 feet from the edge of the eroding cove edge north of Best's Bulwark. The structure lies between the edge of a shallow intermittent pond to the west and a 2-m-high rock outcrop that formed part of the structure's eastern wall. When the pond is dry, as it was during our 1981 visit, we collected fragments of slag-encrusted crucibles and other earthenware here.

This pond is the only area on Kodlunarn Island where European artifacts are readily noticeable on the surface today, and the adjacent structure is probably Hall's feature "D" ("ruins of a shop"). If so, Hall has mismapped this structure in the middle of the island rather than near its eastern shore, below the reservoir. Alternatively, although it seems improbable, Hall may have failed to notice S1, and in that case his feature "D" corresponds in location to our S4.

Structure 1 is a rectangular structure measuring 8 × 7 m inside a low sod and rock foundation whose walls are 1.5–2.0 m wide and about 20 cm high. The northern and western portions of this foundation are clearly traced on the surface. The southern

Fig. 5.7. James Blackman and Garman Harbottle excavating testpit at western edge of the Frobisher smithy. The rock-strewn interior is contained within an arcing wall of mounded earth and rock. Artifacts, slag, coal, and other materials associated with the smithy are found in the adjacent dried-up pond. The presence of water, more prevalent probably during the wetter climate of the Little Ice Age, would have been a factor in choosing this location for the smithy.

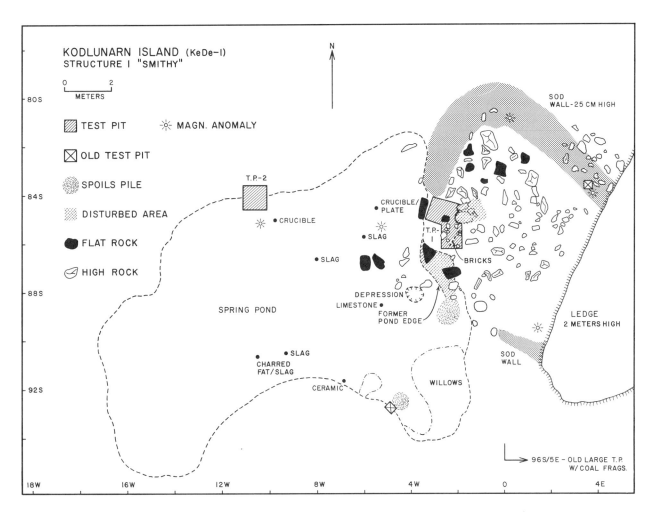

Fig. 5.8. Structure 1 (smithy) plan.

wall seems to have been partly destroyed by pond erosion or by previous excavations and relic collecting. No eastern wall exists; the vertical face of the rock outcrop seems to have served this function. All but the southeast corner of the structure is sodded over, and except for a few rocks overturned by recent curio hunters, the structure appears to have suffered little major disturbance. The interior contains a scatter of rocks and a possible hearth foundation. Evidence of such an internal structure was revealed in test pit 1: an alignment of stone slabs and a row of bricks, end-up, paralleling the wall about 50 cm inside. Gaps in the southern wall and the eastern end of the north wall may be remnants of a doorway or may result from previous excavations. Magnetic anomalies were recorded at the eastern and western ends of this wall.

Our test consisted of a "dogleg" 0.5 × 1.0-m pit just inside the gap in the western wall. The soil profile here was shallow and simple: a 5-cm-thick layer of undisturbed sod overlying a 5-cm level of yellow sandy soil, which in turn overlay a 5–10-cm layer of dark charcoal-stained deposit rich in cultural remains. The deposit seemed relatively intact, that is, hardly any Frobisher material was found in the sod level, so it may be that previous excavations by Hall and others have not disturbed the structure greatly. Among the finds recorded were small fragments of orange rooftile (some burned and cinder/slag encrusted); fragments of glazed earthenware crucibles bearing vitreous deposits on their surfaces; two types of brick, a yellow variety (fire brick?) and reddish building brick, some slag-encrusted and burned; chert nodules; glazed earthenware fragments; a wire lunchmeat can key (upper sod); a slag-encrusted iron nail; a fragment of an iron bloom (see Unglik, this volume); and quantities of cinder, slag, coal, clay, and charcoal. No wood or bone remains were found. The charcoal recovered (Laeyendecker, this volume) included oak, willow, ash, and beech, as well as coniferous and birch species. A sample of oak (i.e., non-local, non-arctic driftwood) charcoal produced a modern radiocarbon age: −20 ± 65 B.P. (see table 5.3); a second sample, also of oak, produced a calibrated age of A.D. 1322–1340 and 1392–1446. Remains of a rock pile construction in the center of the structure suggest the presence of a kiln or furnace foundation. Four crucible fragments were collected from the surface of the adjacent dry pond.

These finds tend to corroborate Hall's initial conclusion that this is the remains of a blacksmith shop. In addition to the direct evidence of slag and bloom fragments, charred and fire-cracked ceramics, brick, and crucibles, the structure's cramped location between the pond edge and the ledge seems more appropriate for an industrial site than for a domestic one, for in wet weather the structure would probably be flooded. On the other hand, if any site on Kodlunarn was used for domestic activities, such as during winter when floods could not occur, this structure has a solid wall foundation and the deepest deposits of artifacts and ashes, such as one might expect of an overwintering encampment, and should be investigated as a possible site of the 1578 overwintering group noted in Inuit stories.

STRUCTURE 2 (ASSAY OFFICE)

A second sod foundation 15 m north of S1 seems to contain the superimposed remains of two different rectangular structures, the larger of which measures 5 × 6 m inside its low sod walls, while the smaller and probably more recently constructed one measures 3 × 4 m, inside dimension. The western wall of the smaller structure lies along the western wall of the larger one. Both structures are entirely turfed over, but numerous small rocks protrude through the sod. There is a slight depression along the southwestern wall. This structure lies a few meters east of the drainage seep that runs down the middle of Elizabethan Alley and is probably purposefully associated with this drainage.

Three test pits were excavated in 1981. The pit in the external depression produced no artifacts or signs of disturbance; possibly it was excavated originally as a well. The 1981 test in the center of the structure produced 62 fragments of slag-encrusted ceramics, and samples of charcoal, brick, rooftile, and firebrick. Unlike the testpit in S1, the S2 finds did not include coal, slag, or cinder. Most of the slag-encrusted ceramics have been identified provisionally as crucible fragments. Several varieties were found: thin and thick-walled conical forms, and flat dish-shaped ones. Slag encrustation was found on all types of crucibles, but some of the thin-walled crucible forms appear not to have been used, perhaps having been broken in shipment or during pre-heating. The large numbers of crucible fragments and absence of smithing remains such as coal, slag, and

Fig. 5.9. Structure 2 (assay shop), looking south.

cinder suggests S2 functioned as a charcoal-fired assay workshop rather than as a coal-fired iron-working smithy or forge. As in the case of S1, access to water seems to have been important in the placement of S2. A third test pit excavated in 1981 between S1 and S2 was sterile. Finally, in 1990 a small test pit was excavated, again in the center of the structure. The ceramic sample from this pit (Auger, this volume) resembled that of the earlier collection but has some larger vessel forms (see figs. 8.2, 8.4, 8.6). It seems likely that this structure is the remains of Edward Fenton's assay shop (Fenton, in Kenyon 1980/81:190, 194, 196). A sample of oak charcoal (Beta 42659) produced a calibrated age of A.D. 1453–1657.

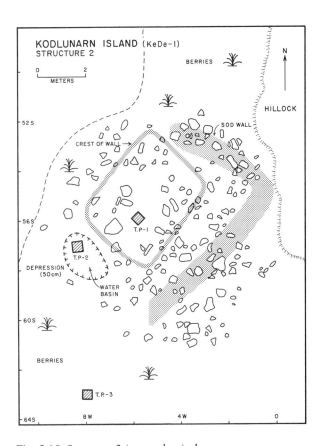

Fig. 5.10. Structure 2 (assay shop) plan.

Fig. 5.11. Structure 3 (charcoal "store").

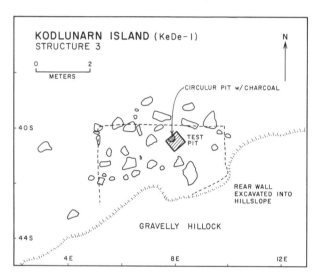

Fig. 5.12. Structure 3 (charcoal "store") plan.

Fig. 5.13. Structure 4 ("dam"), with mine seen at upper left.

STRUCTURE 3 (CHARCOAL STORE)

Structure 3 is located on the northwest side of the hillock 30 m north of S2. This small, rectangular, 3 × 5-m structure is covered in turf and has low sod and rock walls. The structure appears to have been excavated into the hillside, or alternatively has been partially inundated by erosional sediments. A test pit inside the north wall produced large amounts of charcoal of European wood species (beech, willow, oak, birch, hazel, and maple) and some cinder. Unlike the other structures, no ceramics or slag materials were recovered. Considering the species present, this structure probably was used for charcoal storage for the nearby assay and smithy shops; had it served as a charcoal production facility one would expect the charcoal to have been of local coniferous driftwood.

STRUCTURE 4 (DAM?)

This sod and rock construction consists of an oval arrangement of apparently undisturbed sod-covered rocks without any evidence of walls. It is located along the lower (south) side of the shallow basin in the center of Elizabethan Alley in the general area of feature "D" ("shop") on Hall's map. If this is Hall's feature "D" we would expect it to contain smithing materials like those found in S1. Our test pits in the center and eastern section of the structure, however, were sterile. If further excavation confirms the absence of a foundation and artifact-rich working surfaces, the possibility should be considered that S4 may have been constructed as a dam to retain water for the Elizabethan workshops below.

Fig. 5.14. Structures 5 and 6 (cache pits) area, possibly with Hall's Inuit tentrings to right, view west.

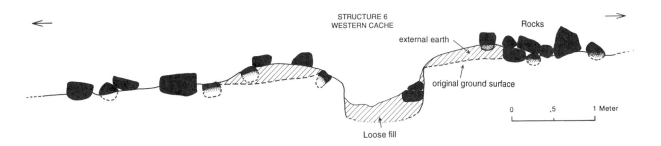

Fig. 5.15. Profile of Structure 6 cache.

Fig. 5.16. Structure 5 cache, view northeast.

Fig. 5.17. Structure 6 cache vandalized, view northwest. In background, J. Olin begins a test pit where bloom 1 was found.

STRUCTURES 5 AND 6 (CACHE PITS)

Two circular boulder piles, probably having functioned as cache pits, are situated prominently on an open gravel expanse east of the ship's trench a short distance from the remains of a group of tentrings (A16, A17) that may mark the remains of Hall's encampment with the Inuit in 1862. S6, the western cache, appears to have been excavated recently, per-haps within the past 10–20 years, judging from the preservation of a one-meter-deep pit in its center. Surrounding this pit is a ring of boulders eight meters in diameter whose circular arrangement suggests they were once part of a large stone pile securing a subsurface cache. S5 is less obviously disturbed and consists of a six-meter concentration of boulders with a central depression. This structure appears to have been opened also, but in earlier times.

Archeology of Kodlunarn Island   71

Fig. 5.18. Structure 7 (longhouse), view south.

Lacking artifacts and distinctive typology, it is difficult to determine the origin and function of these caches. These almost certainly are remains of caches constructed by Frobisher's men at the end of the 1578 season to store equipment and materials for their projected return in 1579 (Stefansson and McCaskill 1938, 1:116; Kenyon 1980/81:197, 200). We may also surmise that they were early targets of Inuit enterprise soon after Frobisher's departure and may have been probed repeatedly since then by Inuit and European visitors.

Bloom 1 was found buried beneath 10 cm of loose gravel a few meters west of S6. Possibly the bloom might have been associated with one of the caches, but there is no evidence for this. The isolated nature of the find suggests the bloom was left exposed on the surface and was later buried by natural agencies.

STRUCTURE 7 (LONGHOUSE)

West of the caches and about 60 m southwest of the ship's trench is a 22 × 4-m depression on the eastern side of the hill slope. At first this depression appears natural, but upon closer inspection we determined it was excavated into the gravel and cobble beach deposits. The structure consists of five rooms or spaces connected by a depression/corridor along its north side. Ridges of unexcavated beach deposits separate the rooms, whose floors are vegetated with *empetrum*. Exposed soil surfaces surrounding the structure show no artifacts or signs of occupation; but test pits in three of the depressions produced small amounts of rooftile, brick, coal, cinder, charcoal, and wood extending 3–8 cm below the vegetation level to sterile soil. A radiocarbon date run on oak charcoal from test pit 1 produced an age of 210 ± 60 B.P. (A.D. 1645–1683; 1739–1805; 1934–1955).

Although more investigation is needed, the presence of a linear structure with partially excavated interior rooms and cultural deposits raises the possibility that S7 is the remains of some type of shed or shelter. Its location at the head of the ship's trench would be useful for an equipment store or workshop where an eye could be kept on repair activities while also providing security for boats, equipment, and workers.

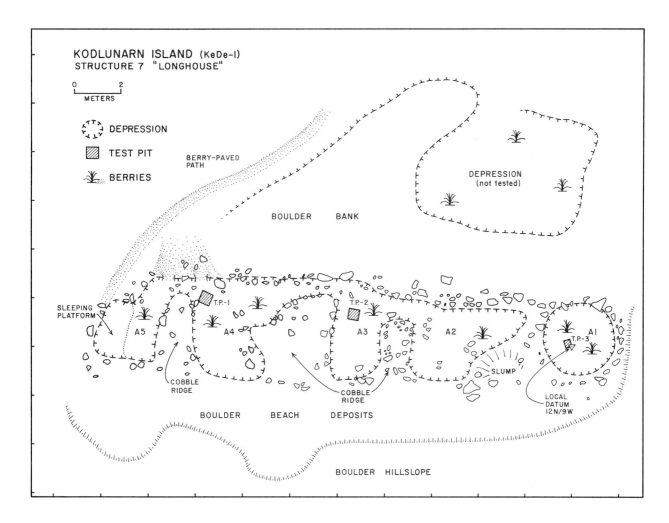

KODLUNARN ISLAND (KeDe-I)
STRUCTURE 7 "LONGHOUSE"

0   2
╵────────╵
METERS

DEPRESSION

TEST PIT

BERRIES

BERRY-PAVED
PATH

BOULDER   BANK

DEPRESSION
(not tested)

SLEEPING
PLATFORM

A5   A4   A3   A2   A1

T.P-1   T.P-2   T.P-3

COBBLE
RIDGE   COBBLE
RIDGE   SLUMP

LOCAL
DATUM
12N/9W

BOULDER   BEACH   DEPOSITS

BOULDER   HILLSLOPE

Fig. 5.19. Structure 7 (longhouse) plan.

STRUCTURE 8 (FENTON'S WATCHTOWER)

Located at the crest of the island 57 feet above sea level are the remains of a structure that is the most obvious, explored, and damaged of Frobisher's Kodlunarn constructions. It is unique not only in occupying an eminent vantage point apart from the center of the industrial activities in Elizabethan Alley, but also in being the only Frobisher structure built with a mortared stone foundation and the earliest permanent structure built by the English in the New World. This house was originally planned as the residence of the 100-man colony of miners and soldiers whom Frobisher had planned to leave here for the winter of 1578–79 and was to have been quite large.

However, with the loss of building supplies and food in the stormy crossing, plans were revised and a smaller house, measuring 14 by 8 feet, Fenton's "Watch Tower" (Fenton, in Kenyon 1980/81:198), was built with rock and mortar walls and a plank roof as an experiment to see how this type of construction would fare under arctic conditions. Unfortunately there is little documentation on its function or form, and little now is preserved for excavation.

Hall (1865b:429) describes this structure as the ruins of a house twelve feet "in diameter" built of stone cemented with lime and sand, with its foundation largely intact except that some stones appeared to have been turned over by "treasure seekers." He also noted a stone "breastwork" nearby such as used by the Inuit for a caribou hunting barricade,

Fig. 5.20. Structure 8, "Watch Tower", a stone and mortar construction house built by William Fenton at the crest of Kodlunarn Island, as it appeared in 1990, view west.

and a pile of rocks, like a cache, a few feet east of the house (see below). Our inspection revealed no cairn nor breastwork constructions east of the house although a natural ledge outcrop may answer Hall's description.

Today what remains of Fenton's watchhouse is a cleared rectangular area approximately 8 × 12 m wide and 0.5 m deep. Duncan Strong writes of digging here with the Rawson-MacMillan crew in 1927, and photographs show another MacMillan crew excavating in 1929; it is likely that Hall also excavated here. Backdirt and overturned rocks from these excavations, if not from post-Frobisher Inuit activities, surround the pit, creating a scar visible in aerial photographs of Kodlunarn Island taken by

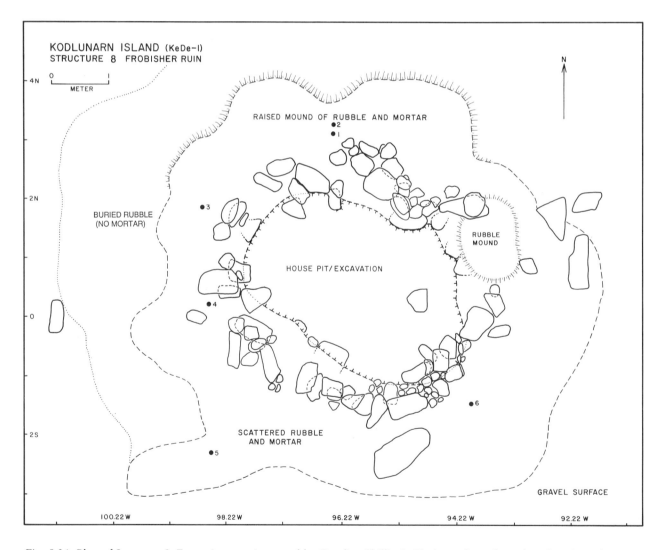

Fig. 5.21. Plan of Structure 8, Fenton's tower (prepared by Caroline Phillips). Circles and numbers show location of samples: tile (*1, 4*), mortar (*2, 5*), ivory fragment (*3*), tile and mortar (*6*).

Fig. 5.22. 1990 survey team (Chuck Arnold, James A. Tuck, Jr. (hidden), Robert McGhee, and Réginald Auger) inspects Structure 9 cairn and commemorative plaque erected in 1966 by servicemen to honor the Frobisher discoveries.

Alexander Forbes in 1942 (Forbes 1953:126). Some intact rubble masonry foundation sections seem to remain in place, but most of the structure and its deposits have been destroyed. Among the spoil dirt are found quantities of sandy mortar tempered with crushed brown European flint and bits of tile and ceramics. We mapped the structure but did not make any test excavations.

STRUCTURE 9 (CAIRN)

In 1981 we found a boulder cairn standing five meters north of Fenton's tower, 2.0 m wide at its base and 1.36 m high. A 27.3 × 27.2-cm copper or brass plaque was wired to a rectangular rock in the cairn and bore the following inscription:

THIS CAIRN WAS ERECTED

IN MEMORY OF

SIR MARTIN FROBISHER

AS A CENTENNIAL PROJECT BY

LT. A. BROCKLEY

DR. R. WEST

MR. V. BROCKLEY

FROBISHER BAY   11.7.66

This cairn may have been constructed from rocks taken from the Frobisher house foundation distributed by MacMillan's team in 1928–29. A small rub-ble pile west of the cairn may also be remains of a spoil pile from previous diggings here. However, Hall in 1861 noted "a pile of stones, which might have been made, as I thought, by Frobisher's men, to cover some memorial left by them when trying to escape in their ship" (Hall 1865b:428). We noted a human skull lodged in the center of the cairn. In 1991 this cairn was dismantled by an archeological team from the Canadian Museum of Civilization in the belief that it was an unofficial monument erected by amateurs.

STRUCTURE 10 (RESERVOIR/MINE)

The large trench, 25 m long and 6 m wide, excavated into the hill on the west side of Elizabethan Alley has been noted by all visitors to Kodlunarn from Hall's time on. Today it is about 1.5 m deep, but it must have been somewhat deeper in Frobisher's day before sand and gravel began to wash in. Surrounding the trench itself are slightly mounded walls created by backdirt from the original excavation. The trench cuts through the surficial deposits into the fissured basement rock below. A huge rectangular block of black hornblende similar to that found at other Frobisher mines rests on the surface a few meters south of the trench. Our test pit in the center of the trench floor produced small fragments of brick or rooftile.

Fig. 5.23. Joshua Fitzhugh at Structure 10 (mine/reservoir), view southeast.

Hall (1865b:427) called this structure the "reservoir/mine," reflecting both the Inuit view of its purpose (reservoir) and his own view (mine); Kenyon also felt it was a mine. This feature is the largest man-made structure on Kodlunarn, with the possible exception of the ship's trench, and its excavation would have taken a toll in energy and time on its miners. The basement rock and spoils along the edge of this trench do not show much sign of the black hornblende ore, but its alignment (exactly following the strike of the bedrock) with the ship's trench, which probably also originated as a mine, is viewed by Donald Hogarth as strong evidence for its mining origin. At a later point it may also have been used as a reservoir, although such use is not documented in the accounts. We found tile fragments and charcoal in a test pit excavated into the bottom of the trench.

STRUCTURE 11 (FURNACE PIT)

North of Best's Bulwark and east of the smithy, Walter Kenyon noted a buried coal horizon along the eroding bank of the island and excavated a test pit, between the cove edge and the hill behind. In 1981 we noted extensive erosion of cultural deposits in the same location and excavated a pit in a shallow surface depression (Kenyon's test pit) a few meters north of the bank. Our test pit produced evidence of rock slab constructions, ceramics, cinder, coal, and charcoal buried under 50 cm of slope wash. This feature merits further testing as a possible smelter or some other pyrotechnic activity. Similar conclusions were reached when this pit was briefly reopened for inspection in 1990.

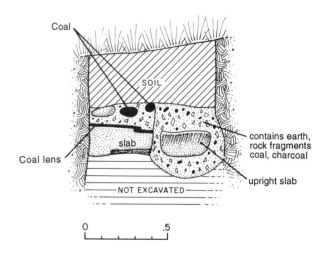

Fig. 5.24. Schematic profile of Structure 11, a buried pit near the cove edge south of the Structure 1 smithy.

Fig. 5.25. Structure 12 (ship's trench), view north.

STRUCTURE 12 (SHIP'S TRENCH/MINE)

The only break in the 10-m-high vertical sea cliff along the northern side of Kodlunarn Island is a 50-m-long ramp-like cut that extends from the low tide line to the island surface above. This cut is located in the most protected part of the island's shore, facing the nearby mainland and a shallow, well-protected small boat anchorage. The location is not subjected to heavy waves or ice pressure because shallow waters and reefs protect the area from strong tidal action. Hall (1865b:427) concluded that this feature was man-made and had been cut through the steep cliff face of the island. In fact, the trench would appear to be suitable for stranding a small vessel on a high tide for repairs, or for launching a newly made vessel, which is what Inuit told Hall it had been used for. However, Hall supposed the feature might have been excavated first as a mine and so marked it on his map, and later Kenyon and Hogarth came to the same conclusion. Frobisher used this area to cache expedition lumber and other supplies in the fall of 1578 (Best, in Stefansson and McCaskill 1938, 1:116; Fenton, in Kenyon 1980/81:199).

There seems to be no reason to doubt Inuit accounts that this feature was used for boat work, and it may be where some of Frobisher's vessels were grounded to effect emergency repairs (Best, in Stefansson and McCaskill 1938, 1:116). And it is here too that most of the major finds recovered at the is-

land over the years have been made. Hall's Kodlunarn bloom was found buried in the excavated earth of the trench, near where Inuit had also found the wood, tile, and a lead musket ball that they gave to Hall (Hall 1865b:542). Donald Hogarth (pers. comm.) reports having seen an iron spike in the rub-

Fig. 5.26. Bloom 2 excavation site in ship's trench. Pick marks in the rocks above show where the black ore seam was quarried from the bedrock.

Fig. 5.27. Wilcomb Washburn at bloom 3 excavation site at lower end of ship's trench.

ble of the trench during one of his early visits to the island. During 1981, using a metal detector, we located and excavated two more blooms here (blooms 2, 3) from beneath 15–20 cm of rubble overburden along the eastern wall of the trench. After clearing away the sterile rubble and reaching the upper surface of these blooms, we encountered masses of charcoal, wood, bark, ceramics, brick, and coal resting on the original working surface of the trench. Both blooms were found in direct association with these materials. Our tests indicate the deposits in this trench are relatively intact and contain a wide variety of Elizabethan remains. The presence of wood at this shoreside ramp, not found in other Frobisher structures on the island except in small fragments in S7, tends to corroborate the Inuit's and Hall's identification of this structure as a ship repair facility and/or one of Fenton's 1578 caches. Nevertheless, the steepness of the ramp and its narrow walls preclude the building or hauling of large ships. Our discussion of the blooms themselves notes that most of these artifacts have been found in or near the ship's trench, where they may possibly have been used as "dollies" (Ehrenreich, this volume), counter-

Fig. 5.28. Wood remains associated with bloom 3.

Fig. 5.29. Best's Bulwark, with Inuit tentrings, view southeast.

weight hammers used in spiking and nailing ship timbers.

In addition to the structures described above, which we investigated, the following locations or features, which we did not test, deserve note since they are mentioned in the accounts or appear to result from Elizabethan activities.

STRUCTURE 13 (BEST'S BULWARK)

A small flat promontory extending seaward from the south end of Elizabethan Alley served as the location for a fort with rock and sod walls constructed by Best in 1577 to defend Kodlunarn from the increasingly aggressive Inuit (Stefansson and McCaskill 1938, 1:72). Today this promontory has no visible traces of a fort and only exhibits the remains of partially eroded tentrings (A13); it is too small for any type of defensive structure or garrison, and its remaining surface area is being rapidly destroyed by sea cliff retreat. The Forbes photograph shows the feature as larger in 1942 than today (Forbes 1953:126). Probably this promontory is much reduced in size from what it was in the 1570s.

STRUCTURE 14 (MINE PIT?)

A depression approximately 1 × 2 m in diameter adjacent to an outcrop of black rock is found on the gravel surface about 100 m west of the ship's trench. No cultural materials were noted. This pit may be the remains of a small mining test pit.

STRUCTURE 15 (BLACK ORE SPOIL)

A circular concentration of small chunks of black hornblende ore lies a few meters east of the upper end of the ship's trench. This material may represent waste material or rejected ore, part of an ore sample tested at the Kodlunarn assay shop, or the remainder of an ore cache. Hall noticed and plotted this feature as well.

STRUCTURE 16 (GRAVESTONE?)

During his visit to Kodlunarn Island in 1990, James A. Tuck noticed two thick stone slabs standing upright in a level gravel area in the northeastern part of Elizabethan Alley. Standing slabs do not occur naturally in this area of the island. These slabs, which resemble early European grave markers, should be investigated since the Frobisher accounts document the burial of several crew members, although not specifically on Countess of Warwick (Kodlunarn) Island.

STRUCTURE 17 (WELL?)

In 1990 Robert McGhee and James Tuck found a small water-filled depression at the foot of the prominent ridge on the northeast side of Kodlunarn Island. This small (and rather unappetizing) pool seems to be the only source of fresh water on the island and is probably the well Frobisher sought to protect by promising severe penalties for polluters

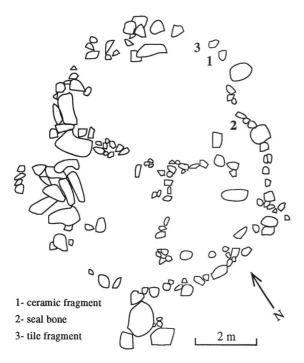

1- ceramic fragment
2- seal bone
3- tile fragment

2 m

Fig. 5.30. Structure A5 tentring sketch map.

(Best, in Stefansson and McCaskill 1938, 1:103). On one of his early visits to Kodlunarn, Donald Hogarth found a fragment of a ceramic vessel here. This specimen is in the collections of the Prince of Wales Northern Heritage Centre.

While the foregoing discussion presents evidence that is clearly related to the Frobisher occupation of Kodlunarn Island, it is likely that remains of other Elizabethan sites will be found here and elsewhere in Frobisher Bay. In addition to mines and activities associated with them, it seems likely some of Frobisher's shore party camps will be identified.

KODLUNARN ISLAND TENT CAMPS

Historical commentary by Frobisher's captains indicates considerable contact with Inuits residing in the Frobisher Bay region. At times these contacts were violent, resulting in loss of life and property, beginning with the loss of the pinnace and its crew in 1576 and numerous skirmishes and even a battle in 1577; at other times, peaceful contacts prevailed, permitting trade and social activity. The presence of a large number of European vessels whose men engaged in trade and mining and had a penchant for

caching supplies ensured that a large amount of European materials must have entered Inuit society, not only during the three years of active contact, but also later, as Inuit returned to scavenge materials from Kodlunarn and other Frobisher sites. Hall's accounts from the Inuit indicate that social contact was extensive enough to result in mutual friendships between the Inuit and the abandoned Frobisher crew. One of his informants even knew the names of the two Inuit, one a chief (E-loud-ju-arng [Ooleet-ua?]; Rowley, this volume), who had most dealings with the Englishmen during the period before they tried to escape (Hall 1865b:544). In addition to being a source of European goods, these contacts and materials may also have stimulated changes in Inuit social and economic behavior (Fitzhugh 1985a). As these issues are central to understanding Frobisher-Inuit interaction, part of the 1981 survey was devoted to a search of Kodlunarn and the surrounding region for Inuit sites that might be contemporary with the Frobisher voyages.

Kodlunarn Island lies east of the major walrus and seal hunting grounds of outer Frobisher Bay, and for this reason its waters are not especially productive from an Inuit hunter's point of view. Inuit occasionally hunt seals in the vicinity but find better hunting and fishing territory around Cape Sarah and Opingivik Island and more seaward islands to the south. Caribou, an important summer resource, are not attracted to Kodlunarn because it lacks vegetation. Nevertheless the surrounding region is an important area for late summer caribou hunting, which is often staged from one of several camp locations at the west side of the entrance to Diana Bay, at Tikkoon Point, or at the Kamaiyuk peninsula at the western entrance to Napoleon Bay a short distance from Kodlunarn Island. Lacking game, water, and shelter, Kodlunarn itself rarely receives Inuit visitors, and no signs of recent Inuit camps were noted there during our visits, quite in contrast to the situation at Tikkoon and on Newland and Opingivik (Willows) islands. Nevertheless, despite the island's relatively inhospitable nature, our 1981 surveys revealed a number of probable Inuit tent sites (table 5.2), all located around the periphery of the island within a few meters of its cliff-like shores. These sites were inspected and plotted; no test pits were dug, nor were collections made. In 1990 the sites were resurveyed; a few were mapped, and a few isolated finds were collected. The most notable of these was an iron arrow point.

Fig. 5.31. Structure A7, sketch map and photo (view northeast). One of many tentrings on Kodlunarn Island, this structure on the west shore of the island contained an iron arrowhead and an ivory pin.

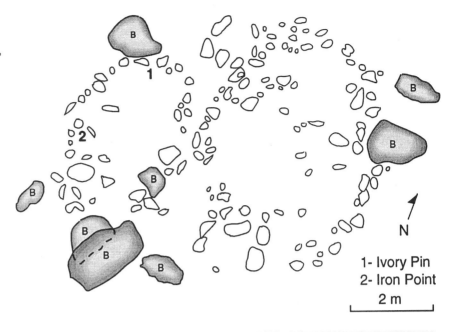

1- Ivory Pin
2- Iron Point
2 m

N

Our survey indicates that Kodlunarn has been used as an occasional camp site for many years. Many of these sites are found on exposed gravel surfaces that offer limited opportunity for excavation and in most cases seem to contain few, if any, artifacts. Others, especially those with sod cover, offer some archeological potential. In general, Kodlunarn does not appear to have been intensively occupied or settled for long periods of time. The existence of vaguely defined axial structures and flakes of chert suggest a few small Dorset sites may once have been present but have since been mostly lost to sea cliff retreat along the eroding edge of the island. The major occupations noted probably belong to the later period of Neoeskimo (i.e., Inuit) culture. No sites were found to contain artifacts dating to the Thule or Developed Thule period ca. A.D. 1000–1500. Most of the structures seem to date to A.D.

TABLE 5.2. Kodlunarn Island tent camps

A1	Possible axial (mid-passage) structure, 5 × 6 m, on an exposed gravel point 200 m west of ship's trench; flake of patinated brown chert of possible Paleoeskimo origin. No European materials
A2	In situ Neoeskimo double tentring in low swale; tile or brick fragments present
A3	Caches and tentring in small cove; flaked lithic core
A4	Across cove from A3, a bilobed 4 × 8 m subrectangular tent ring with axial feature
A5	30 m east of A4, large Neoeskimo tentring with sleeping platform and lateral hearth features; 1990 collections include Frobisher rooftile and ceramic vessel fragments, seal bone; small tentrings below toward shore
A6	Two small oval/rectangular boulder pavement features in shallow swale 20 m above A5
A7	Double tent ring at south end of boulder field; ivory or bone pin and iron arrowhead recovered in 1990. Caches upslope east of ridge (fig. 5.30)
A8	Two sod-covered tentrings at southwest point of island
A9	Oval tentring and stone cache on bluff at southwest extremity of island; brick fragments; remains of 50-cm (Kenyon?) test pit in north wall; fragment of perforated rooftile or brick, and tan painted ceramic in sod at eroding bank; sod cover provides good excavation potential for this rapidly eroding site
A10	Slab structure and disarranged boulder structures on a low point on south end of island; ice and tide damage evident
A11	Group of four or five large circular Neoeskimo tent rings, some 7–8 m diameter; some rings eroding into the sea; probable 18th–19th century date
A12	Large subrectangular tentring 50 m north of shore; rifle shell casing; black ore outcrop at east side of site
A13	Sod-covered structure uphill from A11 below ridge
A14	Inuit tentrings on Best's Bulwark, truncated by seacliff retreat
A15	Group of three or four recent tentrings on grassy slope in cove east of Best's Bulwark 15–20 m south of S1 smithy
A16	Large double bilobed tentrings of probable 19th-century age with sleeping platform borders. North and east of S5,6 caches between ship's trench and rock ridge. Remnants of other tentrings along rapidly eroding bank edge, including probably C.F. Hall's camp of 1862
A17	Small oval 2 × 1 m diameter rock ring at head of ship's trench on east side

1500–1900. Several of these contain considerable amounts of tile and brick (A2, A5, A7, A8, A9). The most recently occupied group of structures (e.g., A16) is probably the remains of Hall's camp of July 14–17, 1862 (Hall 1865b:551).

Surface indications suggest that many of the sites on Kodlunarn Island contain tile and brick remains acquired from the Elizabethan sites. In some cases these remains have been modified by grinding, either for use as polishers (Hall 1865b:543) or perhaps to produce ocher-colored pigment. Thus one attraction of the Kodlunarn Elizabethan sites to Inuit people may have been as a source of grindstones and polishing paste from hematite-rich ceramics. Some of these tile and brick remains found their way to Neoeskimo sites as far away as Peale Point, more than one hundred miles up Frobisher Bay (Stenton 1987).

The Frobisher records note that some of his crews slept ashore in tents on Kodlunarn and elsewhere in Frobisher Bay. These tents probably were rectangular, as depicted in the John White battle drawing (see fig. 1.2; Sturtevant and Quinn 1987) rather than the oval or round types found at most Inuit camps. Although none of the tent camps noted here had square configuration, it may be that some of them are Elizabethan, but this may be verified only by excavation.

In addition to documenting the Kodlunarn Island sites in 1981 we were able to briefly survey a few other locations in Countess of Warwick Sound, finding sites at Hall Peninsula (Paksakha), Tikkoon Point, Opingivik Island, and Cape Sarah Neck. The results of these surveys are included in the next chapter, which also presents preliminary survey data on several of the Frobisher mines encountered during the 1990 survey.

COLLECTION DESCRIPTION

Ninety-one artifacts and 93 samples were recovered in 1981 from the Frobisher sites described in the previous section of this chapter. These artifacts and samples are described by category of object in the following sections. Most of these objects were recovered from test pits, but a few were surface finds. Except for the blooms, most artifacts were ceramic finds, all of which are highly fragmented and rarely larger than a centimeter. The largest body of material came from the test pits in S1 (smithy) and S2 (assay shop). A breakdown of finds and samples by structure is given in appendices 3 and 4. As a general rule the collections consisted of only a few categories of artifact types and material remains. Artifact classes include iron blooms, nails, rooftiles, bricks, and crucibles. No obvious culinary wares or organic artifacts were recovered although they were noted in the 1990 collections (see Auger, this volume). Material samples consisted of mortar, European flint, charcoal, wood, slag, coal, and cinder. Most of the ceramic vessels have not been identified and dated as they are relatively rare, fragmented, undecorated industrial wares which are little known and poorly described in the literature. The process of specific identification awaits larger samples and detailed technical and compositional analysis. The ceramic descriptions offered here and in Auger (this volume) are preliminary and are offered here primarily to facilitate study and discussion. However, detailed studies of some Frobisher materials have been completed, including descriptive and metallurgical analysis of the Smithsonian bloom (Rostoker and Dvorak 1986), bloom 2 and the S1 bloom fragments (Unglik, this volume), radiocarbon dating of the Smithsonian bloom and blooms 1 and 2 (Harbottle et al., this volume), x-ray fluorescence analysis of some crucible fragments (inconclusive results, J. Olin, pers. comm.), and identification of wood and charcoal samples (Laeyendecker, this volume).

BLOOMS

Three raw or partially processed iron blooms were located and excavated in 1981 with the aid of a metal detector. A fourth bloom, known as the "Lookout Island" bloom, was found in 1990 at an Inuit site in Cyrus Field Bay (Hall 1865b:132). The Kodlunarn Island blooms certainly would not have been found without a metal detector, for they were recovered in or near the ship's trench (S12) buried under 10–30 cm of soil. No surface indications of their presence existed, and it is clear that accidental burial rather than caching was the reason they had escaped previous notice. All four of these blooms conform to a single basic type—a round loaf-like lump with flat-

tened top and bottom. Bloom 1 was the best preserved and was completely free of rust, while blooms 2 and 3 and the Lookout Island bloom were more deteriorated owing to their closer proximity to saltwater (see descriptions in Unglik, this volume). Bloom 1 and the tops of blooms 2 and 3 retained a smooth, almost glossy finish imparted by hammering to expel slag during the finishing process. The sides and bottoms of blooms 2 and 3 were found encased in beds of rust spalled from the parent artifact. None of these blooms or the Lookout Island bloom exhibited checking or cracking on their surfaces at time of recovery. These blooms may be the objects referred to by Fenton (Kenyon 1980/81:185, 188) as "osmundes."

BLOOM 1 (KeDe-1:91). The largest and most intact of the 1981 finds was buried by 15 cm of well-drained sandy soil 14 m west of the S6 cache pit and 35 m southwest of of the top of the ship's trench (see fig. 5.4). It was an isolated find, not associated with any other obvious cultural feature, and no oth-

Fig. 5.32. Bloom 1 (KeDe-1:87) had been partially processed, as indicated by its smooth surface, symmetrical shape, and hammer impressions. Partially processed bloomery iron cannot be forged or hammered into useful tools because it contains slag and is brittle. A small chunk of conifer charcoal was found encrusted into its surface.

er artifacts or signs of disturbance were noted in the subsoil. Originally, the bloom had probably been left on the surface and had become buried through natural agencies. The soil here is sandy and well drained, which seems to account for the specimen's excellent preservation; only a small amount of rust was noted. The bloom weighs 12.6 kg and measures 22 × 22 × 10 cm. One side is slightly convex while the other, probably the top of the bloom when originally smelted, is markedly concave; in cross-section, the bloom is completely symmetrical. The surface is smooth but slightly dimpled with scalloped depressions 1 cm in diameter, perhaps the result of hammer blows (or corrosion pits?) imparted during the finishing process. At the time of excavation a fragile chunk of charcoal was found embedded in a small declivity in the surface of the iron. This charcoal was extracted and identified as conifer (spruce or larch); later it was dated in the Brookhaven small-sample radiocarbon counter to A.D. 1250–1440 (calib.; table 5.3).

BLOOM 2 (KeDe-1:87). The second bloom, also located with the metal detector, came from TP1, halfway up the ship's trench (S12) near its east wall, and was found in a mass of amorphous carbon (decayed charcoal) beneath 15 cm of rock rubble, gravel, and sand (see fig. 5.26). This bloom, the smallest of those found, is slightly oblong (17 × 16 × 9 cm) and weighs 5.4 kg. Its slag-encrusted bottom is considerably eroded by rust, giving it a trapezoidal cross-section. Wood fragments (probably oak) were found immediately above and below the bloom, together with oak, beech, and hazel (probably) charcoal, charcoal powder, and a brick fragment. Like the others, bloom 2 was completely intact and lacked surface checking, despite a scaly, rust-eroded surface. Small flecks of charcoal were noted embedded in its surface upon excavation.

This bloom was selected for metallurgical analysis by Parks Canada Conservation and is reported in this volume by Henry Unglik. During the course of inspection and sectioning, a charcoal inclusion, later identified as alder/birch, was found embedded in the matrix of the iron. AMS dates run by IsoTrace Laboratory of the University of Toronto dated this charcoal to A.D. 1006–1060 (calib.). Three AMS dates were also obtained on interstitial carbon contained in the iron itself at A.D. 640–717 (calib.), A.D. 1307–55 (calib.), and A.D. 1400–42 (calib.) (table 5.3). A cinder lump found near the bloom was dated

Fig. 5.33. Bloom 2 (KeDe-1:87). The irregular surface is typical of an unprocessed "raw" bloom. Parks Canada Conservation photo, October 1982.

to 25,640 B.P. Three wood samples found immediately beneath the bloom were dated by the "standard" carbon-14 method: a charcoal (probably oak) sample dated A.D. 1477–1665; an oak sample, A.D. 1459–1529; and a beech sample, 103.7% modern.

BLOOM 3 (KeDe-1:90). The third complete iron bloom recovered in 1981 also was discovered from a metal detector signal, this time from the lower east wall of the ship's trench (S12, TP2) where it was buried 30 cm beneath sand, gravel, and rock slabs. This bloom (see fig. 5.27) was only a meter above normal high-tide line and within reach of salt spray and storm tide. Intermediate in size between the other two bloom finds, it measured 21.5 × 21.5 × 9 cm, had a trapezoidal section like bloom 2, and weighed 10.9 kg. The bloom was embedded in a mass of rust flakes and iron-stained sand with its widest diameter toward the surface. Like bloom 2, its trapezoidal shape resulted from attrition of its lower margins by rust, 500 g of which were collected from a deposit reaching to 45 cm below the surface. This was underlain by a 2-cm layer of wood mush that, when exposed, extended west under the rubble to become a 10-cm-thick band of wood chips and mush toward the center of the trench, while to the east it rose up in a thin band toward the rock wall. Brick fragments, ceramic chips, and a wood dowel were found

TABLE 5.3. Kodlunarn Island date list

Sample #[a]	Cat. #	Provenience	Material dated	Method	Age B.P.	Calib. age, A.D.[b]	Remarks
B-42660	81-49	smithy, S1	oak charcoal	std	510 ± 80	1322–1340, 1392–1446	
SI-5521	81-61	smithy, S1	oak, beech char.	std	−20 ± 65	modern	
B-42659	81-22	assay, S2	oak charcoal	std	320 ± 90	1453–1657	
SI-5522	81-22	assay, S2	beech charcoal	std	65 ± 60	modern	
SI-5523	81-19A/B	store, S3	beech, oak, birch charcoal	std	500 ± 35	1407–1436	
Brook.	KeDe-1:91	S12, TP1 (B1)	spruce/larch char.	10 mg	628 ±150	1250–1440	adhering char.
TO-347	KeDe-1:87	S12, TP1 (B2)	birch/alder char. in iron	AMS	970 ± 60	1006–1060, 1077–1125, 1136–1157	sample V2-2/7
TO-712	KeDe-1:87	S12, TP1 (B2)	iron (carbon), 0[c]	AMS	1340 ± 70	640–717, 742–760	sample V2-1B
TO-712-2	KeDe-1:87	S12, TP1 (B2)	iron (carbon), 2[c]	AMS	550 ± 60	1307–1355	sample V2-1A
TO-712-3a	KeDe-1:87	S12, TP1 (B2)	iron (carbon), 5[c]	AMS	500 ± 60	1400–1442	sample H1-2A
TO-2609	81-24	S7, TP1	oak charcoal	AMS	210 ± 60	1645–1683, 1739–1805, 1934–1955	
SI-5525	81-71	S12, TP1	wood, prob. oak	std	290 ± 85	1477–1665	assoc. bloom 2
SI-5526	81-68A	S12, TP1	beech charcoal	std	103.7%	modern	assoc. bloom 2
SI-5527	81-68B	S12, TP1	oak charcoal	std	355 ± 45	1459–1529	assoc. bloom 2
SI-5528	81-76	S12, TP2	wood, undeterm. species	std	415 ± 50	1435–1484	assoc. bloom 3
Brook.	49459	SI Bloom	carbon in iron	10 mg	679 ± 133	1240–1400	SI bloom
Brook.	49459	SI Bloom	carbon in iron	10 mg	792 ± 107	1160–1280	SI bloom
TO-348	53-16	smithy, S1	arbon in cinder	AMS	25,640 ± 220		30 mg

a. Laboratory identifications: B, Beta Analytic; SI, Smithsonian; Brook., Brookhaven National Laboratory; TO, IsoTrace Laboratory, University of Toronto.
b. One sigma ranges, Stuiver and Pearson calibrations.
c. Numbers indicate depth below surface of bloom 2, in cm.

Fig. 5.34. Bloom 3 (KeDe-1:90), like blooms 1 and 2, is in a partially processed state; photographed in the field.

in this level, which marks the working surface of the trench. The presence of a dowel, considerable volumes of wood remains (most of which resembled oak in macro samples but could not be positively identified microscopically due to advanced cell decomposition), and the shoreside venue support both claims—ship carpentry and wood caching—cited for this location. Frobisher's written history and Inuit accounts provide similar testimony. This bloom has not been dated directly or studied metallurgically, but an underlying wood sample (species not determinable) was dated at A.D. 1435–1484 (calib.).

Some months after these blooms arrived at the Smithsonian for cataloguing and study, changes began to be noticed in their physical condition. The blooms began to swell and their surfaces began checking and spalling. After consultation with conservators and Canadian authorities, the blooms were sent to Parks Canada Conservation for stabilization, documentation, and analysis (see fig. I.4; Unglik, this volume).

Fig. 5.35. Lookout Island bloom.

LOOKOUT ISLAND BLOOM. The Lookout Island bloom has not been analyzed or dated at the time of this writing. This bloom was found by Eric Loring in 1990 while our field team was surveying with the *Pitsiulak* in Cyrus Field Bay, the bay east of Countess of Warwick Sound across Blunt Peninsula, and was taken to Yellowknife by Charles Arnold a few days after its discovery. Notes on this site (Cyrus Field Bay 1) are included in the next chapter.

This bloom was recovered from a historic (primarily 19th century) Inuit site on the easternmost large seaward island two kilometers southwest of Mt. Budington. This island forms the southwest side of Hall's "Rescue Harbor." Hall reports visiting this site on September 5, 1860, and finding a remarkable "iron mineral weighing 19 pounds, and in shape and appearance resembling a round loaf of burned bread" (Hall 1865b:132). At the time Hall did not understand this specimen's connection with the Martin Frobisher sites in Countess of Warwick Sound, and it is not clear from this account whether he collected the piece or not. But in his journal for that day the situation is clearer. While his shipmates and the Inuit butchered a whale, "I took a tramp around on the island. I was fortunate in discovering a 'whale' of a piece of iron-mineral weighing 25 lbs. This I made 'fast' to for the benefit of the Scientific World. It is almost pure iron having in it but a very

small proportion of foreign substance." In the adjacent margin to this text is Hall's later notation: "*Vide* my private journal of Tuesday, Dec. 24, 1861, when I learned the history of this Whale of a piece of Iron Mineral" (Hall Archives, WO3 file, National Museum of American History). Later, in reference (Hall 1865b:437) to finding a similar specimen on Kodlunarn Island, after having learned of their Frobisher connection, he notes that he "obtained" a similar specimen on Lookout Island, "a half mile south of the ship." This is almost certainly the very bloom that Hall learned from later interviews had been carried by Annawa and Manabing from Kussegeerakjuan, the summer site traditionally occupied by Inuit at the southwest entrance of Diana Bay (named by Kenyon; see fig. 1.10), to Lookout Island in 1859, two years before his arrival (Rowley, this volume).

Given these statements, it is difficult to see how Hall's and our find can be the same specimen, unless his claims of collection are in error. It seems unlikely that two blooms would have been present at this location, and yet this is the conclusion one would reach from the notes. The problem is further complicated by the fact that Hall never mentioned the ultimate disposition of his Lookout Island or Tikkoon blooms and that his maps and descriptions do not precisely place the location of his "Lookout Island." The former resembled the "semisphere" of iron from the Kodlunarn Island ship's trench that he donated to the Royal Geographical Society in London (Collinson 1867:368) (which also resembles the bloom in the Smithsonian collection), while the latter he described as "time-eaten, with ragged teeth," a description matching a bloom illustration in Hall's unpublished papers (see fig. 1.7). Neither in Hall's papers, museum records, or published accounts do we learn about the disposition of the Tikkoon bloom. This leads to the possibility that the Smithsonian bloom may actually be Hall's Lookout Island find and that the 1990 "Lookout Island" bloom is a new find from an Inuit site on a neighboring island.

My field notes indicate that the Lookout Island bloom is 19.5 cm long, 16.0 cm wide, and 9.0 cm in maximum thickness; has the shape of a slouch hat in cross-section; and weighs ca. 8 kg (17.6 lb), intermediate in weight between the three Kodlunarn blooms described previously and close to Hall's 19-pound figure. Its surface is pock-marked and uneven and is perforated with small holes that may be degassing ducts created by the smelting process. No adhering charcoal chunks were noted. The surface is considerably rusted, especially the pointed end that had been buried in the soil. Depressions and angular features suggest the bloom has been battered, probably during processing but perhaps by Inuit who attempted to remove chunks from its surface. In fact, in addition to a rust spall, a small chunk of iron ca. 1 × 2 cm was found next to the bloom, apparently after having become detached either by hammering or natural weathering.

HALL'S BLOOMS.   Two blooms were recovered by C. F. Hall during his work at Kodlunarn Island and vicinity. One was discovered partially buried under excavated fill in the ship's trench; this is the bloom Hall gave to Greenwich Hospital Museum via the Royal Geographical Society in 1863 (Hall 1865b: 437, but note discrepancy in Hall text pointed out in footnote 1, Tikkoon Point section of Chapter 6). The other came from Tikkoon, where one of Hall's Inuit companions had found it on top of a rock just beyond the reach of high tide (ibid.:429); this specimen was given to the Smithsonian (ibid.:437). Probably the bloom from the ship's trench was found where it had been left by Frobisher's men, but the conspicuous location of the Tikkoon specimen suggests it may have been removed from Kodlunarn by Inuit, as seems likely in the case of the Kussegeerakjuan/Lookout Island bloom and for those seen on Newland Island/Winter's Furnace by Fenton in 1578. Description and analysis of the Smithsonian's "Hall" bloom is provided in Sayre et al. (1982) and Rostoker and Dvorak (1986). As noted above, Hall (1865b:132, 437) also reports finding a third bloom at Lookout Island. The only other major iron object known to have been found at Kodlunarn Island is the iron "anvil" which Inuit later moved to Opingivik Island. Hall (1865b:451, 498–99) searched for this piece but was unable to find it, and we had similar results in 1981 and 1991.

OTHER METAL

Other than blooms and bloom fragments (see Unglik, this volume), little metal has been recovered at Frobisher sites on Kodlunarn Island (see Wayman and Ehrenreich, this volume). A single slag-encrusted iron nail with a 1.3-cm-wide head was recovered in S1 (test pit 1) with other Elizabethan materials.

This test pit also produced a 20th-century metal lunch can key found in the sod, obviously unrelated to the main component. And, as noted previously, Donald Hogarth saw a 20–30-cm-long iron spike in the ship's trench on one of his visits to Kodlunarn Island in the 1980s.

In 1990 we recovered two iron finds in what appear to be Inuit contexts, an arrowhead (found with a bone or ivory pin of probable Inuit origin) in tentring A7 at the west end of Kodlunarn Island and a large chunk of iron in Structure 7 at Tikkoon Point. The former (fig. 5.36) is a well-shaped isosceles triangular point about 2 cm wide at the base and 4.5 cm long. Its thickness is a fairly even 2.0 mm. Wayman and Ehrenreich's analysis of this point (this volume) indicates that it is made from smelted rather

Fig. 5.36. Iron arrowhead found in A7 tentring. This piece probably has a Frobisher origin and is made of high-phosphorus iron similar to that used in the blooms (Prince of Wales Northern Heritage Centre photo).

than meteoric iron and shows no trace of cold-hammering, which should be indicated had it been made from European iron reworked by Inuit. As Frobisher's men were equipped with bows and arrows as well as muskets for hunting and defense, this may be an Elizabethan arrowhead and could have been left here by Frobisher's men, who also utilized temporary shore camps; but its context in a tentring structure containing a bone or ivory pin suggests that its more likely history is as an Elizabethan trade item obtained by Inuit (e.g., Best, in Stefansson and McCaskill 1938, 1:49, 58, 95). Analysis also indicates the arrowhead to be made of high-phosphorus iron similar to iron in the Frobisher blooms. This fact has led Wayman and Ehrenreich to suggest a possible common source for the iron in bloom 2 and the iron point; it also points toward an earlier rather than a later date, for high-phosphorus iron, common in the Elizabethan period, has not been used in recent centuries owing to its brittleness. More cannot be said without further metallurgical and typological study.

The Tikkoon piece is an angular chunk of iron ca. 3 × 4 × 1.5 cm that seems to be an unmodified piece of a larger object. Wayman and Ehrenreich's analysis shows this specimen to be a typical grey cast iron with high phosphorus and sulfur content. As in the case of the arrowhead, a post-Elizabethan date cannot be ruled out, but there is nothing inconsistent with the notion that this specimen could be Elizabethan cast iron. Lack of slag inclusions and indications of melting indicate it is not a bloom fragment. Both the arrowhead and the Tikkoon iron were found inside tentrings that appear to be the remains of Inuit summer camps.

CERAMICS

The ceramic materials described below originated largely from test pits in S1 (smithy) and S2 (assay shop). To date it has not been possible to analyze these remains in detail (see Auger, this volume) or to compare them with 16th-century ceramics from Basque sites in Red Bay, Labrador, or industrial sites in England. It seems quite likely that compositional and textural analysis of ceramics and slag encrustations would help identify manufacturing source locations of the ceramics and reveal information on aspects of 16th-century "gold fining" as practiced by the Frobisher assay specialists.

CRUCIBLES. Small broken crucible fragments were the most common ceramic found in S2, leading to the tentative interpretation of this structure as Frobisher's assay shop. Crucible fragments were also found, though to a lesser extent, in S1, the smithy, and in collections from the dry pond bottom adjoining S1 and S2. Assignment to the crucible category is based on paste, vessel shape, and presence of slag encrustation. But because the specimens recovered are so fragmentary, it is possible to define crucible vessel types only within broad limits. Frobisher crucible wares tend to have a grey, vitreous lustre with a texture like course, gritty stoneware. Sometimes the paste is sandy and homogeneous and has a porcelain-like structure; in others, especially heavily slagged specimens, it is platey and poorly consolidated. Some vessels have walls as thin as 0.3–0.4 cm. The vessels are generally unglazed although a greenish or yellow-orange glaze may be present.

The wide variation seen in these crucible wares may result from differences between the original unheated ware and its appearance after high-temperature assay use (fig. 5.40). Such use may also produce a false glaze (i.e., slag). For this reason analysis of specimens broken in shipment or before assay use is necesssary. A few such specimens are represented in our sample (figs. 5.40, 5.41). However, most crucible specimens are heavily encrusted with dark-green slaggy deposits whose analysis might provide information on assay technology (temperatures, fluxes, etc.) and ore sources. The highly fragmentary condition of these crucibles suggests that assay use generally resulted in crucible destruction.

Crucible cups. The collection includes a few examples of small, pedestaled crucible cups (KeDe-1:37, 39; fig. 5.37f,h) that are heavily slag-encrusted. Rims and bases indicate great variety in crucible sizes, with mouth diameters ranging from 4 cm to 16 cm in diameter (KeDe-1:51, 72; figs. 5.37b, 5.38a). Bases are also variable, with examples of pedestals 4 cm and 2 cm in diameter. Paste ranges from tan color and gritty sand to the fine porcelain-like texture described above for unused crucibles, to a grey-white vitreous fused appearance with interstitial air bubbles in heavily slagged sherds. Even large cups (KeDe-1:72) may have a wall thickness as thin as 0.3 cm, although 0.7–0.8 cm is more common for slag-encrusted sherds.

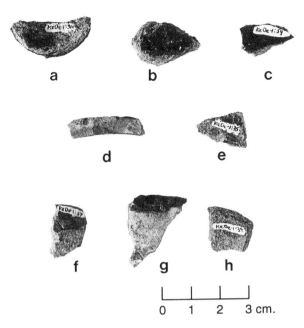

Fig. 5.37. Crucible fragments from Structure 2. Cat. nos. (left to right): top row, KeDe-1:36 (base), 51, 54; middle row, 49 (section view), 35; bottom row, 37, 18, 39 (base).

Fig. 5.38. Slag-encrusted crucible rim sherds from Structure 1 pond area. left: KeDe-1:72 (slag on interior only); right: KeDe-1:86

Crucible plates. A second category of slag-encrusted ceramic appears to belong to a platter type of crucible (KeDe-1:71, 83; fig. 5.41) with thickened rim, ca. 10 cm diameter, and 0.5 cm thickness. Unslagged specimens have grey paste with air bubbles and a scraped surface finish. One unslagged specimen (KeDe-1:26-27-28; fig. 5.42) bears a yellow-brown glaze around its rim but lacks glaze on dorsal and ventral surfaces. Another unusual sherd has a grey slip or paint on the inside of its everted rim.

Fig. 5.39. Crucible cross-sections showing fused paste of a slag-encrusted specimen, KeDe-1:18 (top), and unfused paste of an unused specimen, KeDe-1:21 (bottom).

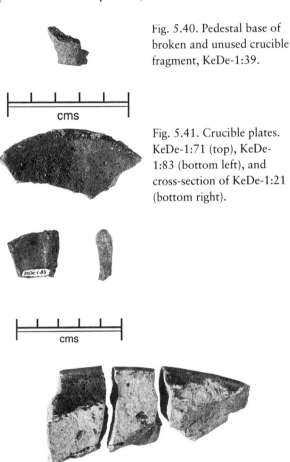

Fig. 5.40. Pedestal base of broken and unused crucible fragment, KeDe-1:39.

Fig. 5.41. Crucible plates. KeDe-1:71 (top), KeDe-1:83 (bottom left), and cross-section of KeDe-1:21 (bottom right).

Fig. 5.42. Crucible plate fragments, KeDe-1:26-27-28, with glazed edge.

Fig. 5.43. Ceramic rooftile fragments, KeDe-1:74 (left) and section of uncatalogued cross-section fragment (right) 1.5 cm thick.

CERAMIC TILES. Low-fired red-orange tile fragments (fig. 5.43) are among the most widely distributed Elizabethan artifact type found at the Frobisher sites, both in test pit collections and surface finds. Tile remains are also the most common European material encountered in Inuit camps on Kodlunarn, at Tikkoon, and in other sites. No whole tiles were recovered, so it is not possible to verify the presence of the double-perforated "English" rooftile (fig. 5.44) found by Kenyon at Fort Albany (ca. A.D. 1675) in Hudson Bay (Kenyon 1986), as opposed to the ridged Basque form. Kenyon described English tiles as follows:

These tiles are quite uniform, and measure 10.5" long, 6.25" wide, and 0.5" thick. The two suspension holes are punched from the top (i.e., the concave side), and this surface is invariably smoother than the bottom, or convex side. These specimens are quite different from the Spanish tiles that are scattered along the Straits of Belle Isle. (Letter to the author dated April 17, 1980)

Most tile fragments exhibit surfaces that are scraped and have impressions of sand grains; they have thicknesses of 1.4–1.5 cm, and are made with a red or orange paste tempered with silt- or sand-size particles often containing quartz and biotite minerals. The paste is frequently filled with lenticular air pockets aligned with the long axis of the tile. The edges of most tiles are squared and slightly lipped,

probably from being thrust against a flat surface when the wet clay was cut to flatten and smooth the edge. Sand seems to have been applied to tile surfaces when they were cut to keep them from sticking to other surfaces. Tile fragments often occurred in Kodlunarn Island sites as thin spalled plates, a fragmentation pattern that helps distinguish them from brick, which usually lacks this platey fracture.

Most of these tiles have the appearance of rooftiles, but some may have served other functions. One tile fragment from S1 (KeDe-1:77) has a slag- or glaze-coated edge. This specimen may be a fragment of a glazed tile of a type fairly frequently found in Frobisher Bay Inuit sites (Fitzhugh 1991) and present in Hall's collection from Kodlunarn Island (see fig. 1.6, item 14, which Klingelhofer (1976) identified as a 16th-century stove tile solely from the illustration). Specimens of this material have been found in early historic Inuit sites as far from Kodlunarn Island as Peterhead Inlet, near Iqaluit (Douglas Stenton, pers. comm. 1990) and at Inuit sites recently excavated at Kuyait and Kamaiyuk, both within 25 km of Kodlunarn Island (Fitzhugh 1991). Some of these tiles have abraded rounded edges indicating their use as polishers or as sources of abrasive paste used for polishing metal ornaments, as described by Inuit to Hall (1865b: 543; Rowley, this volume). Since no whole tiles have

Fig. 5.44. Early 17th-century English rooftile (courtesy of Walter Kenyon and Royal Ontario Museum).

been found on Kodlunarn that can be positively identified as rooftile, as opposed to stove tile whose glazed surface has spalled, questions of identification of rooftile in the Frobisher and Inuit sites remain to be answered. However, given the use of rooftile in other 16th-century settlements in the New World, such as at Red Bay, Labrador, and in England at the time, we may presume Frobisher's men brought rooftiles to cover their shore facilities.

BRICK. Brick was confined mostly to the S1 smithy collections, where it occurred in two forms: yellowish and reddish-brown or purple. The yellow form may be a fire-brick type. No specimens were found in pieces large enough to determine size or shape. Red bricks have a very sandy paste made of rounded sand (quartz and biotite or pyroxenite) grains; flint temper also occurs. The yellow brick has a more clayey paste and less sand admixture. Brick fragmentation is blocky and not lamellar, like rooftile.

SAMPLE MATERIALS

The following samples (appendix 4) were gathered from various Frobisher structures:

CHARCOAL AND WOOD. Charcoal was plentiful in most of the Frobisher structures tested, but wood was found only in S7 (longhouse) and S12 (ship's trench). Here it was preserved in abundance but was too decayed to be positively identified microscopically, although it appeared to be oak on macroscopic inspection. A complete analysis of wood and charcoal samples is presented elsewhere (Laeyendecker, this volume). These findings are important for substantiating the European origin of the site but do not present such clear-cut evidence in the case of the blooms themselves; the bloom samples analyzed to date contain coniferous and birch/alder charcoal which points more toward northern production possibly in Baffin rather than in England.

Previous research (Sayre et al. 1982) raised the possibility that the early bloom dates might have resulted from local smelting of iron with charcoal produced from arctic driftwood. In this regard, the discovery of a large bed of charcoal in S3, a small structure that might have served either as a charcoal kiln or as a storage area, is of interest. Identification of beech, willow, oak, birch, hazel, and maple in this

sample provides assurance that abundant supplies of European charcoal were available, as reported in the manifest lists of the expedition. Therefore, the necessity of local production of charcoal would seem to be highly unlikely. Further, the large volume of wood (probably oak) noted in test pits in the ship's trench (S12) also helps substantiate historical claims that the ship's trench was used as a ship repair facility or storage cache. The consistent pattern of charcoal from such species as oak, beech, ash, and hazel as a complex in most of the structures tested and the relative absence of local arctic species or coniferous arctic driftwood provide assurance that these structures are in fact of European origin and belong to a single occupation horizon. Many of these samples have been dated to the 16th century (table 5.3).

COAL. Soft coal was found in several Frobisher structures but was most common in S1 where it probably was used as the principal fuel for iron forging. Indeed, coal seems to have been used to rework bloom fragments in this structure (see below). Small amounts of coal were also found in S3 and S7. Future studies might help identify the source of this presumably English coal. Coal is also found, together with English flint, at several of the Frobisher mines in Countess of Warwick Sound, including Winter's Furnace on Newland Island, Denham's Mount in Victoria Bay, and at Anvil Cove 1 on Opingivik Island. Frobisher's reports indicate coal was used at various mines as fuel for assay furnaces (cf. Hogarth, this volume).

CINDER. As in the case of coal, cinder was relatively abundant in S1, further supporting interpretation of this structure as a smithing location. Cinder was also found in test pits in S2, S3, and S7.

SLAG. Slag also was abundant in collections from S1, and some of these "slags" later were identified as bloom fragments (Unglik, this volume). High sulfur content suggests that some of these bloom fragments were being reworked with coal rather than charcoal (Unglik, this volume)—a primitive procedure that produces worthless, brittle iron and seems unlikely to have been done by experienced iron-workers. Slag was also found in S11, a pit feature that has not yet been excavated and may have been used for smelting. The question of whether or not Frobisher's men smelted iron on Kodlunarn is one that has been

Fig. 5.45. Slag lumps with encrusted soil from test pit in Kodlunarn Island 1 smithy.

Fig. 5.46. Nodules of English flint found in coal deposit at Denham's Mount mine, which Kenyon named Judy Point (KeDd-1). To date all Frobisher coal deposits in Countess of Warwick Sound have contained small nodules of chert, which probably became inadvertently mixed with the coal in the holds of the ships. Coal was a commonly used as ship's ballast (photo: R. Auger/Laval University).

raised previously, but which now seems unlikely in view of more recent data and study (cf. Harbottle et al., Ehrenreich, this volume). Such activity would require large amounts of precious charcoal and would have produced large slag heaps, which have not been noted by Hall or later researchers. We did not search for slag during the 1981 survey, but in 1990 we searched Kodlunarn for smithing slag deposits and failed to find any.

MORTAR AND FLINT. Fenton's watchtower (S8), has been the primary location on the island producing mortar lumps, both in Hall's day and ours. A few samples were collected, but have not been studied. Some mortar contains crushed fragments of caramel- and tan-colored European flint, probably

brought as ship's ballast in Frobisher's vessels and later used as tempering material for the mortared masonry walls of this structure. Small chunks of European flint were also found in S1 and the adjacent pond bed. English flint is commonly associated with coal deposits at Frobisher's mine sites in the "Countess Sound" region. Hall learned that the Inuit collected the Frobisher flints to use as strike-a-lights (Hall 1864, 2:164).

DRIFTWOOD. A small collection of driftwood samples was gathered from storm tide lines in Countess of Warwick Sound as a check on the wood species being rafted into Frobisher Bay during recent times. Modern driftwood samples have not been collected from eastern Baffin Island previously and may be of interest in relation to the question of whether arctic driftwood plays a role in the early dating of iron blooms found at Kodlunarn Island. Most of the samples collected were of coniferous woods (Laeyendecker, this volume) and seemed by their form (uneroded logs, lumber, even a hockey stick fragment) to originate from modern occupations at Iqaluit. None suggested Siberian sources, and we did not note any driftwood samples on raised shorelines or upper marine terraces, but one sample recently analyzed has been identified as Yukon River driftwood cut in 1924 (Laeyendecker, this volume). Frobisher accounts indicate that driftwood was relatively abundant in the area.

IRON ORE. Because of the possibility that iron might have been smelted locally, in 1981, James Blackman looked for possible ore sources. A number of moderately iron-rich rocks were noted. Bogs were also tested for bog iron ore, with negative results. In 1990 Robert Ehrenreich noted local silicaceous iron-bearing rocks that might be suitable for smelting in "low tech" furnaces. If more evidence of local smelting of the Frobisher blooms becomes available, it would be useful to pursue the subject of iron sources further.

FROBISHER'S "BLACK ORE." Frobisher "gold" ore has been studied by Roy, Hogarth, and others. Small piles of these materials were noted on Kodlunarn Island near the mine/reservoir and the ship's trench. In 1990–91 we conducted detailed surveys of several of the Frobisher mines located on Newland Island (Frobisher's Winter's Furnace mine), at Judy Point (Denham's Mount mine), on Kodlunarn Island (Countess of Warwick mine), and at the Countess of Sussex mine north of Cape Sarah (Hall 1865b:363, 432; Kenyon 1975b:146, 1980/81:190). Analysis of these sites and materials is discussed elsewhere in this volume and in various papers by D. Hogarth.

KODLUNARN TENT CAMP COLLECTIONS

Few materials were collected from Inuit/Elizabethan tent sites on and near Kodlunarn Island during our survey. This was not due to any lack of material remains but to lack of time and our primary focus on the Frobisher sites. Most materials found at these sites were left in their original locations and have been noted in the site descriptions above. Exceptions were a rooftile fragment found in a Neoeskimo

structure at A8 on Kodlunarn Island (KeDe-1:4), probably collected by Inuit from the Frobisher sites at the other end of the island, and a brass cartridge (KeDe-1:5) from A12, undoubtedly of more recent origin, as is a lead bullet (KeDe-1:3) from A4 found with the metal detector 5 cm beneath the surface. Hall was given a similar round lead musket ball found by Inuit near the ship's trench (Hall 1865b:543). A chert microblade, KeDe-1:2, probably is witness to an earlier Dorset presence here. In 1990 we resurveyed the Kodlunarn Island tent camps and found a piece of early (i.e., 16th–17th-century European) ceramic in the A5 structure and in A7 the iron point noted above as well as a single bone or ivory pin, whose presence is a clue to the probable Inuit rather than Frobisher origin of this structure.

Site Conservation Issues

Surveys of Kodlunarn Island indicate that its archeological resources are threatened by two different agencies: marine erosion and vandalism. Evidence of the former is widespread in the lower Frobisher Bay region, due to the absence of extensive Pleistocene glaciation and limited postglacial rebound. While a few Paleoeskimo sites were found intact because they had been sited away from the shore, most of these sites are being destroyed rapidly by rising sea levels and erosion; even many Neoeskimo sites dating to the past 1000 years are now in the tidal zone and are being rapidly destroyed. This process is enhanced by high tidal amplitude, which exposes 25–30 vertical feet of the intertidal zone to marine erosion and frost action twice a day. Most of the shorelines in outer Frobisher Bay are presently undergoing active erosion and are fronted by sea cliffs. Many archeological sites dating to the past thousand years have eroded or are in the process of eroding into the sea at the crests of these sea cliffs. Kodlunarn Island is no exception, but the major losses to date seem to be recent Inuit camps rather than Frobisher sites because most of the latter are set back from the shore to a greater degree. Nevertheless, Kenyon and our team observed Frobisher remains eroding rapidly from the banks south of the smithy and S11 on both sides of Best's Bulwark, and we found remains in the ship's trench being steadily degraded. Reports of erosion have been submitted to Canadian authorities yearly following our fieldwork in 1981, 1990, and 1991.

The more selective process of destruction is the gradual damage to Frobisher sites and loss of material remains to collectors, be they professional, casual visitors, or unwitting vandals. The near-total destruction of the Frobisher house (S8) and its deposits is the most obvious casualty. Little remains intact here today except the structure's foundation. Similar attrition has been occurring at other localities, so that few Frobisher remains are noted on the surface today. Sadly, many visits by scientists have contributed to this cumulative loss by collecting or excavating without documenting collections or preparing scientific reports. The only solution to both of these problems is a concerted effort at evelation and assessment of current resources and excavation of those most threatened. Because the Frobisher sites are small, shallow, and relatively ephemeral, the best solution today probably is complete recovery, publication, and conservation of artifacts followed by stabilization and restoration of sites and structures within the framework of a national historic site. The Kodlunarn site area has tremendous historical and popular appeal and could be an important economic as well as scientific resource.

Dating Kodlunarn Island

As noted previously, our renewed interest in the Kodlunarn Island sites owes it origin to radiocarbon dates obtained from the analysis of the Smithsonian bloom by Brookhaven Laboratory. This dating was prompted by speculation that iron in early European sites in North America might not be of Frobisher origin, but possibly of Norse, or of others even less known. The results of this dating, reported in Sayre et al. (1982) and in Harbottle et al. (this volume), provide support for this idea with determinations from two samples of interstitial carbon contained in the iron (derived from charcoal used in the smelting process) dating to A.D. 1230–1400 and A.D. 1160–1280 (calib.). On the other hand, it seems possible that other factors are involved, such as local smelting with old arctic driftwood or smelting on Kodlunarn or in England using old heartwood fuel (Sayre et al. 1982:449). The latter seems unlikely, as noted by Laeyendecker (this volume), owing to the value of trunkwood as timber and the common practice of "coppicing," the harvesting of twigwood and small branches as a more efficient method of producing charcoal. The alternative explanation for producing early dates, local smelting with use of old arctic

driftwood, also seems unlikely, as it would require the reduction of approximately 2000 kg of wood (Ehrenreich, this volume) to produce enough charcoal for a single smelt. With the discovery of three more blooms at Kodlunarn Island in 1981, two of which have been dated and produced similar results of 200–300 years earlier than Frobisher (table 5.3), and a fourth (not yet dated) from Cyrus Field Bay in 1990, explaining early bloom dates on the basis of local smelting with arctic driftwood seemingly becomes even more difficult.[1] In any case, why would the six blooms found to date, produced at such cost, have been abandoned after so much effort? The average of the six dates run on carbon/charcoal from blooms 1 and 2 (table 5.3), excluding sample V2-1B as probably coal-contaminated, is calib. A.D. 1282, about 296 years before the 1578 Frobisher voyage.

Further complicating the picture is the fact that bloom 1 contained spruce-larch charcoal that, on the basis of species represented, might suggest a Frobisher driftwood origin (date calib. A.D. 1250–1440) more than an Elizabethan English origin; while bloom 2's birch-alder charcoal inclusion might well have been of local rather than of European origin (dates: calib. A.D. 1006–60, 1077–1125, 1136–50). In addition, the preservation of charcoal embedded in the surface of bloom 1 has to be considered in the light of its stability and curation (i.e., how the artifact was treated, physically, before burial). What is the chance of a fragile chunk of charcoal surviving on the surface of a bloom for several hundred years, as required by the Norse theory? The same question may be asked regarding possible transport from England or for use in rough work like anvils or carpenter's dollies. Might the preservation of such external charcoal not argue for a local origin and more gentle history for these artifacts?

It is against this confusing picture that we now consider ten radiocarbon dates from non-bloom materials from the 1981 survey. Four of these, SI-5521 from S1 on non-local oak and beech charcoal, SI-5522 from S2 on non-local beech charcoal, SI-5526 on non-local beech charcoal, and TO-2609 on non-local oak charcoal gave modern or too recent results, even though their European species and early

---

1. Contrary to previous observations on the lack of driftwood available in Countess of Warwick Sound in 1981, surveys in 1991 in Loks Land and outer reaches of Cyrus Field Bay revealed large deposits on the beaches facing the outer coast.

European typological association provides little alternative to a Frobisher or other early European association. The other six samples are more useful:

BETA-42660 from S1 (TP1) smithy (oak char.) calib. A.D. 1322–1340, 1392–1446

BETA-42659 from S2 assay shop (oak char.) calib. A.D. 1453–1657

SI-5523 from S3 charcoal store (oak, beech, birch) calib. A.D. 1407–1436

SI-5525 from S12 ship's trench, TP1 (oak?) calib. A.D. 1477–1665

SI-5527 from S12 ship's trench, TP1 (oak) calib. A.D. 1459–1529

SI-5528 from S12, ship's trench, TP2 (id.?) calib. A.D. 1435–1484

When these six determinations are averaged, the result is calibrated A.D. 1436–1452; its average at A.D. 1442 is 160 years later than the average of the six bloom-associated dates, but still more than 100 years before Frobisher's voyages. Individually (SI-5525) and averaged (SI-5525 + 5527), the two dates on oak wood and oak charcoal found with bloom 2 in TP1 of the ship's trench, and BETA 42659 on oak charcoal from the S2 assay shop, produced the only calibrated carbon-14 determinations that date to the Frobisher period.

An alternative approach to the bloom/non-bloom dating discrepancy averages only the youngest date from each of the three dated blooms on the assumption that these dates are the least likely to be contaminated with coal from the forging activities that may be suspected of having biased some of the early bloom dates. Recent work by Cresswell (1991a) suggests that the radiocarbon dates from bloom 2 demonstrate a pattern of increasing age toward the surface of the bloom, with the deepest samples (TO-712-3a, calib. A.D. 1400–1442) dating youngest, and surface samples (TO-712, calib. A.D. 640–717/742–760) dating oldest. This pattern is consistent with an explanation of dating errors resulting from contamination of surface samples by diffusion of carbon derived from forging the bloom in a coal furnace. In this case the youngest dates for blooms should be from the center of the bloom and should be a more reliable indication of bloom age than surface or average dates. Following this line of thinking we select only the bloom 1 date (628 ± 150 B.P.) from a spruce/larch charcoal sample that might be local or from arctic driftwood (therefore possibly early); the youngest date from bloom 2, an internal iron sample that is not likely to be contaminated,

500 ± 60 B.P.; and the youngest internal iron sample from the Smithsonian bloom, 679 ± 133 B.P. Averaged, these produce calib. A.D. 1409, only 33 years older than the average for non-bloom wood/charcoal dates from the Kodlunarn sites.

Selecting this method begins to resolve the dating discrepancies between the bloom and non-bloom dates, but does not provide understanding of why or how the blooms are being contaminated, whether by coal during reforging, by smelting with old arctic driftwood, or by smelting with charcoal from old English timber. Nevertheless, it begins to make more sense of the archeological context of the site itself. The blooms in the ship's trench all appear to be secure in their association with a single depositional event which, on the basis of historical analysis can hardly be other than that of the Frobisher expedition. The only other possibility is a pre-Frobisher history for this group of blooms. This is difficult to conceive of, especially given the large number of blooms found in Frobisher site context and the linkage of these specimens in the Frobisher records (Fenton's "osmundes") and Inuit oral history accounts of the Frobisher voyages. Apart from the radiocarbon dates, nothing else found to date at the "Frobisher" sites on Kodlunarn Island suggests anything other than a Frobisher occupation.

Climate and Little Ice Age

Data presently available from the Kodlunarn area sites does not permit assessment of the important question of the local and regional effect of the Little Ice Age (ca. A.D. 1500–1750) on European or Inuit occupations. However, data on air and water temperature from Frobisher area sites could be forthcoming from future geological and zooarcheological studies. Historical analysis of the Frobisher records, which are quite detailed as to recordings of ice conditions, provide data for comparison with modern baseline conditions and paleotemperature data. From information presently available from Kodlunarn Island, it would appear that water was more prevalent on the site during the Frobisher period than during our visits in early August of 1981, 1990, or 1991 when the frost was out of the ground and all of the ponds and drainages were dry, as was the S8 mine/reservoir. At least it appears that water was more prevalent on Kodlunarn in Frobisher's summers than in recent years. Observations by Best and Fenton on the frequency of skims of sea ice and routinely frozen ship rigging, as noted in the Frobisher narratives, have to take into consideration that the Julian calendar used in Elizabethan times was ten days in advance of today's Gregorian calendar, which was not adopted in Britain until 1752; but even so, there appears to have been much more summer frost and heavier sea ice conditions during the Frobisher voyages than in recent years.

Conclusions

As a preliminary study based primarily on analysis of 1981 field data, the results reported here can only provide an interim statement on the research conducted in outer Frobisher Bay and its bearing on problems relating to Martin Frobisher's presence here in 1576–78. It is clear however, that a great amount of research data relevant to these issues lies buried beneath the seemingly desolate, relatively barren surface of Kodlunarn Island. Not only has the 1981 season provided a large amount of new documentation on surficial cultural traces, but a rich store of information has been released from a very small amount of subsurface probing through use of remote sensing and limited application of direct test pitting.

The most important conclusion reached from this survey is that Hall's views and those of later visitors like Strong and Kenyon appear validated. There is little reason (other than radiocarbon dates) to question Hall's conclusion that the Kodlunarn Island sites are in fact the remains of Martin Frobisher's expeditions of 1577 and 1578. Although detailed analysis of the ceramic finds must await larger samples and comparison with British industrial wares, indications point toward a late 16th-century occupation that agrees closely with historical accounts in Frobisher's own records and Inuit oral history, especially in terms of ship-building and gold-mining activities conducted in the ship's trench, in the assay shop, and at various mines located by Hall, Kenyon, and Hogarth. A further degree of confirmation lies in the results of charcoal and wood analyses indicating the nearly exclusive presence of European species.

However, many questions relating to the Frobisher voyages remain unsolved and in fact have been rendered more mysterious by the results of more than ten years of research. Most importantly, the early dating of the iron blooms and wood/charcoal dates is not yet fully explained. This mystery is no longer that resulting from pioneering analysis of a single specimen, the Smithsonian bloom, and its Norse-period dating; we now have discovered four new blooms nearly identical to those Hall recovered and the two dated have produced Medieval dates. All dates obtained directly from the blooms and from three of four non-bloom dates precede the historical period of the Frobisher voyages. Nothing in the site layout, structures, or artifacts found suggests multiple European occupations. Still, until further research is done, it seems prudent to assume that a single depositional event occurred in the Frobisher period.

The question of the early dates is only one problem. Many others have been raised by the research initiated by these peculiar datings. Why, for instance, have we found evidence of coal-fired reworked iron blooms, made from different ore sources than bloom 2, in S1; and why are so many blooms, a precious commodity in an iron-starved arctic outpost, associated with the ship's trench and its probable ship-building activities? Are they in fact artifacts themselves, used by shipwrights as counterweights or "dollies" (Ehrenreich, this volume) for driving dowels and nails and clenching iron fastenings? The considerable amount of oak and other European hardwood buried in the ship's trench points toward both historical explanations: shipbuilding and material caching. Could these remains have been created by a band of Englishmen struggling, as Inuit accounts maintain, to rebuild a ship fit for a return to England, either in 1576 or 1578 (Fitzhugh, Chapter 14). Are these blooms the "osmundes" referred to by Fenton? And what are the possibilities of European visitors other than Frobisher to Countess of Warwick Sound? The locality is an admirable one for seafarers requiring respite from the rigors of travel along the rugged outer coast of Baffin Island, either earlier or later than Frobisher. Surely there were other visits to this region not recorded in the historical literature or in remembered Inuit accounts.

The archeological resources of outer Frobisher Bay are indeed considerable. Our surveys have pointed out the need for expanding studies of Paleoeskimo and Neoeskimo prehistory begun by Collins, Maxwell, and Stenton in the inner reaches of the bay, and Schledermann in Cumberland Sound to the north. Outer Frobisher Bay is particularly well suited for studies of European-Inuit encounters as this rich maritime hunting territory would have been the geographic locus for exploration and whaling contacts with Inuit in the early historical period. In addition, the question of European impact on the development of Neoeskimo culture since the 16th century needs investigation. Did Frobisher's arrival in Baffin contribute to the southward expansion of Neoeskimos into Labrador (Kaplan 1985) or establish new social, economic, and political alliances in the Eastern Arctic, perhaps contributing to social and demographic changes reflected in communal house development (Fitzhugh 1985a)? Did the influx of exotic European material goods have an impact on local subsistence and technological systems? Finally, how much interaction took place between Frobisher's men and the East Baffin Inuit, and was this a significant factor in their cultural development? or was it merely a minor technological and material stimulus? These questions are now being addressed through investigation of Inuit sites occupied at the time of the Frobisher voyages and are being related to Inuit occupations known from northern Baffin, Ellesmere, Greenland, and Labrador.

Most importantly, the 1981 and 1990 surveys have shown that the sites on Kodlunarn Island and probably also those occupied by Frobisher's men in other regions of Frobisher Bay hold important information that expands the written record of these exploration ventures. These sites are in themselves not described specifically in the historical literature and need to be investigated archeologically. They contain important materials that amplify the historical documents and provide an avenue to investigate little-known industrial processes and materials of the day.

They provide material remains of a pioneering European settlement and exploitation venture that resulted in the first European establishment in the Canadian Arctic, and the first English settlement in the New World. They may also suggest new interpretations not included in the historical literature. But most significantly, archeological study of the Frobisher sites provides a new body of documentation on an important event in the history of European expansion into the New World that was rapidly exploited by native peoples and may have had an impact on Inuit cultural development as a source of new materials and a foretaste of things to come.

Acknowledgments

A large number of individuals and institutions have helped to make this research possible. In addition to those mentioned in the text I wish to thank Dosia Laeyendecker especially for her long interest in and support of this research. I also wish to thank the Iqaluit Research Center for logistical support, Pauloosie Kilabuck for his many services in the field in 1981; project donors, crew members, and researchers noted herein; Prince of Wales Northern Heritage Centre; Parks Canada Conservation; Britt Williams, Marcia Bakry, and Julie Permutter for artwork; and Victor Krantz for photography. Jacqueline Olin, Martha Goodway, Garman Harbottle, Robert Ehrenreich, Richard Cresswell, Donald Hogarth, Susan Rowley and many others provided much-appreciated technical advice.

Fig. 6.1. This ancient Inuit camp at Kamaiyuk, only four kilometers from Kodlunarn Island, has been the site of a winter camp for Inuit and their ancestors for more than 2000 years. Today it probably looks as it did in 1577 when visited by Frobisher's lieutenant, George Best. With Inuit at summer camps elsewhere, Best was able to inspect the site carefully. His observations on housing techniques, artifacts, and customs in general, published in London later that fall, are the earliest "ethnographic" documentation of Canadian Inuit culture. Best's descriptions of physical objects are objective, but his notes on Inuit customs and social habits reveal the deep cultural gulf and bias that divided Englishmen from the Inuit Best called "this newe prey."

Upon the maine land ouer againſt the Counteſſes Iland we diſcouered, and behelde to our great maruell, the poore caues and houſes of thoſe countrie people, which ſerue them (as it ſhoulde ſeeme) for their winter dwellings, & are made two fadome vnder grounde, in compaſſe rounde, lyke to an Ouen, being ioyned faſt one by another, hauing holes like to a Foxe or Conny berrie, to kéepe and come togither. They vndertrench theſe places with gutters ſo, that the water falling from the hilles aboue them, may ſlide awaye without their anoiaunce: & are ſeated commonly in the foote of a hil, to ſhielde them better from the colde winds, hauing their dore and entrance euer open towardes the South. From the ground vpward they builde with whales bones, for lacke of timber, whiche bending one ouer another, are hanſomly compacted in the toppe togither, & are couered ouer with Seales ſkinnes, whiche in ſtead of tiles, ſenceth them from the rayne. In eache houſe they haue only one roome, hauing the one halfe of the floure rayſed with broad ſtones a fote higher than ỳ other, whereon ſtrawing Moſſe, they make their neſts to ſléepe in (Best in Steffansson and McCaskill 1938, 1:64–65).

6

Field Surveys in Outer Frobisher Bay

WILLIAM W. FITZHUGH

European-Inuit Contact Studies

Although archeology in the Arctic has been largely devoted to the study of Inuit (Eskimo) culture history, excavation of European sites is beginning to provide new sources of information on European activity in the North. But as elsewhere in North America, Native and European archeology have been conducted as two separate disciplines pursued largely in isolation of one another. Archeologists finding European material in Inuit sites have often treated these items as "external" to native culture rather than as evidence of cultural interaction, innovation, and adaptation. On the other hand, the archeology of European sites tends to be site-specific, Euro-centered, and unanthropological. In reality, Native and European history in the North is often closely intertwined. This fact is beginning to receive increased archeological attention (e.g., Barkham 1980; Gulløv and Kapel 1979; Hickey 1984; Jordan and Kaplan 1980; Kaplan 1983, 1985; Pastore 1987; Ross 1975, 1980; Savelle 1985; Sutherland 1985; Story 1982; Trigger 1982; Tuck 1981, 1982).

Like studies relating to the 1853 abandonment of the HMS *Investigator* and the impact of its scavenged remains on Copper Eskimo culture (Hickey 1984), the Frobisher voyages offer unusual opportunities for investigating European-Inuit contact and change. Among the advantages of the latter are tight chronological control and spatial delimitation, substantial historical records (Stefansson and McCaskill 1938; McDermott 1984), and existence of Inuit oral traditions relating to the event (Hall 1865b; Rowley, this volume). But unlike studies of the *Investigator*, where European impact was exclusively passive, the Frobisher voyages involved limited direct European-Inuit contact over three or more years (depending on the accuracy of Inuit reports of a wintering-over party). In addition, Inuit collected and made use of Elizabethan materials for years after Frobisher's departure in 1578. Hall even found Elizabethan tiles being used for polishing stones in 1861.

Studies of these rich historical and archeological resources can be enhanced by research involving social and institutional perspectives as well as more traditional approaches to culture change (Fitzhugh 1985b). Such a program should combine historical archeology of the Frobisher camps on Kodlunarn Island with a variety of studies—archeological, historical, ethnological, oral historical, and environmental—on East Baffin Inuit culture in both regional

Fig. 6.2. Inuit brought home to England by Martin Frobisher in 1577, from engraving in Dionyse Settle's *La Navigation . . .*, published in Geneva in 1578. The illustration fairly accurately shows Inuit material culture (kayak, throwing board, bird spear) exotic to Europeans, but errs in depicting Inuit tents in European style. Artists commonly followed European conventions of landscape, dress, hair, and facial features. Greater accuracy in the shape of Inuit artifacts resulted from European curiosity about these objects and the fact that many had been brought home to England and were available for inspection by artists.

and local settings. This aspect of the work requires knowledge not only of documented contacts but also of indirect effects of contact seen regionally and through time. Was the Frobisher period merely an isolated event in Baffin Inuit history resulting in a brief infusion of European material goods into the Native system (e.g., Jacobs and Stenton 1985; Stenton 1987) with little long-term effect? or did it result in significant change in social or political organization, ideology, settlement patterns, demography, or population distribution? Did the influx of European materials, especially of metals, reconfigure earlier patterns of Inuit trade and contact with Greenland and Central and Western Arctic Inuit? Did they influence Greenland–East Baffin–Labrador communal house development (Petersen 1974/75)? Solutions to these problems cannot be limited to the Frobisher voyages, for they must also consider the impact of John Davis's 1585–87 contacts with Cumberland Sound Inuit just to the north of Frobisher Bay. Both voyages have extensive written documentation that includes specific information on ships' stores, hardware, and trade goods, and many particulars of the expeditions' social contacts with the Inuit are described.

From an archeologist's point of view, studies of 16th-century European-Inuit interaction hold a special appeal because of the unique history of contact in this northern region. East Baffin Inuit met Europeans first during sporadic Norse voyages of the 11th and 12th centuries. Thereafter there was probably little if any European contact until the 16th-century voyages of Frobisher and Davis, which resulted in the first major transfer of exotic (from a native point of view) European material culture and technology into Inuit society. At this point Baffin culture history diverges from the pattern of all other regions in the New World where, when contact begins, interactions progressed steadily, with few if any breaks, through a developmental cycle of trade, European settlement, and thereafter more intensive phases of acculturation. North of Newfoundland this pattern is somewhat different than in arable lands farther south (Fitzhugh 1985b); but even in Labrador (e.g., Kaplan 1983, 1985) European engagement, once begun in the 16th century, was never broken off. In this regard, East Baffin Inuit contact history is unique, being more like that of West Greenland in the 14th to 17th centuries, for following the Davis voyages, Baffin Inuit slipped outside the European sphere until the onset of the whale fishery in the 1840s, 250 years after the departure of early English voyagers and miners. Thereafter, however, Baffin Inuit history fell back into the contact pattern that had begun three centuries earlier in southern Labrador and two centuries earlier in West Greenland: progression through cycles of exploration contacts, engagement with European whaling stations, post-oriented trapping and trading, and, in the 20th century, response to government and military activity. Archeological study of these aspects of East Baffin Inuit history and comparison with patterns of culture change and acculturation elsewhere in North America are among the long-range goals of the Frobisher project. However, for the present, our initial concern is with the period ca. A.D. 1500–1900, a time of Inuit history about which almost nothing is known archeologically and for which archeological remains are abundant, diagnostic, and highly informative.

The twin goals of historical archeology and early European-Inuit contact studies led to the development of an interdisciplinary regional plan that began in 1981 with a search for relevant archeological sites. Even though these first surveys were brief, several Inuit sites were found on Willows (Opingivik) Island, Cape Sarah, and Tikkoon, representing the major cultural phases defined for the Eastern Arctic. These include Paleoeskimo Pre-Dorset (4000–2500 B.P.) and Dorset (2500–1000 B.P.) cultures and the succeeding Neoeskimo groups identified as Thule (A.D. 1000–1500), Developed Thule (A.D. 1500–

1700), and historic East Baffin Inuit cultures (A.D. 1700 to present) (Collins 1950; McGhee 1984; Maxwell 1985; Stenton 1987). Inuit sites dating to the period A.D. 1500–1900 were especially abundant. Hall's (1865b), Kenyon's (1975b), and Donald Hogarth's (Hogarth and Gibbins 1984) surveys suggested that Frobisher's mine sites should also be investigated. In addition our plan called for search for other Europeans including Norse and post-Frobisher European exploring, trading, and whaling activities.

The purpose of the 1990 and 1991 surveys was to locate and document Frobisher sites that did not come to the attention of C. F. Hall, including mines, settlements, and skirmish sites; to investigate 16th-century Inuit sites for their potential in elucidating Frobisher-Inuit contact history; to develop a general outline of European and Inuit culture history; and to assess archeological site availability and conservation status for studying post-Frobisher and whaling-era contacts and Inuit culture change ca. A.D. 1500–1950. This chapter includes results of the original 1981 survey as well as highlights from the 1990 and 1991 surveys in Countess of Warwick Sound, the Kingait coast, and Cyrus Field Bay.

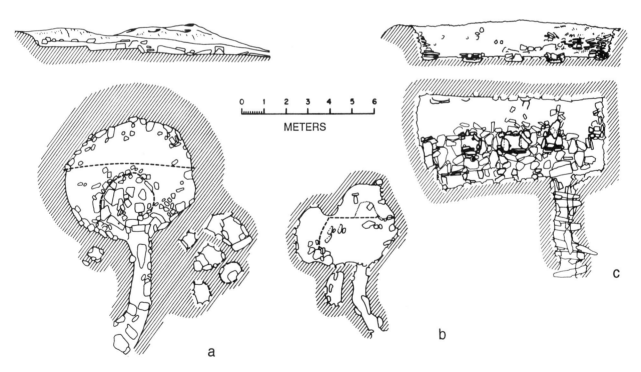

Fig. 6.3. Changes in Eastern Inuit dwelling styles in response to European contact ca. A.D. 1200–1900: *a*, small single-family prehistoric Thule house with one bench and hearth; *b*, bi-lobed, two-family house used in Greenland and Baffin Island ca. 15th–16th centuries; *c*, rectangular "communal" or longhouse with multiple rear sleeping platforms, used in Greenland and Labrador in 13th–20th centuries (from Gulløv 1985).

Fig. 6.4. RV *Pitsiulak* in Jackman Sound, August l991. Regional survey and field excavations in the rugged region of outer Frobisher Bay could not have been possible without the logistic support of this 51-foot research vessel, captained by Perry Colbourne and loaned to the Smithsonian by Stearns A. Morse of the University of Massachusetts, Amherst.

Field Activities, 1990–1991

The 1990 fieldwork plan involved use of the *Pitsiulak,* a 51-foot research vessel, as a mobile base of operations. The outer regions of Frobisher Bay where Frobisher's expeditions were centered cannot be studied by an interdisciplinary team without the logistic support, mobility, and safety provided by a large vessel. Dangers of ice, storms, and polar bears require a substantial investment in logistics, a means of rapid movement, and reliable communication between field parties and with Iqaluit. During 1988–89, the Smithsonian prepared for the Frobisher project by outfitting *Pitsiulak* with new engines, renovating her hull, installing safety, communications, and navigation gear, and assembling an experienced boat crew. The final element of the plan involved shifting the vessel from Newfoundland to Iqaluit for the duration of the project to avoid repeated and costly Newfoundland-Baffin transits.

The plan was activated by the vessel's movement in July from Port Saunders, Newfoundland, to Iqaluit, via Goose Bay, Nain, and Port Burwell. Today the coast from Nain, Labrador, to Iqaluit is probably the most isolated and rugged coastal passage in eastern North America, having no settlements and exhibiting notoriously difficult weather, pack ice, fog, and storm conditions. This passage was happily uneventful and gave us a chance to inspect the impressive landscapes and seascapes that early Inuit and European travelers confronted in this exposed region of the North Atlantic.

Our arrival in Iqaluit was made on schedule on 1 August. Two days later we departed down-bay, surveying Frobisher Bay islands en route. Because Countess of Warwick Sound (Kodlunarn Island, etc.) was still blocked with floating ice, we proceeded via Beare Sound and Lupton Channel to Cyrus Field Bay where we spent two days surveying its western shore. Here we located Dorset and recent Inuit sites at Itilikjuak, a caribou hunting place on the overland pass between Cyrus Field Bay and Countess of Warwick Sound. We returned to Gold Cove (north of Wiswell Inlet) to meet a charter flight from Iqaluit carrying Réginald Auger, Robert Ehrenreich, Garman Harbottle, Donald Hogarth, and a diesel fuel shipment on the 7th. August 7–12 were

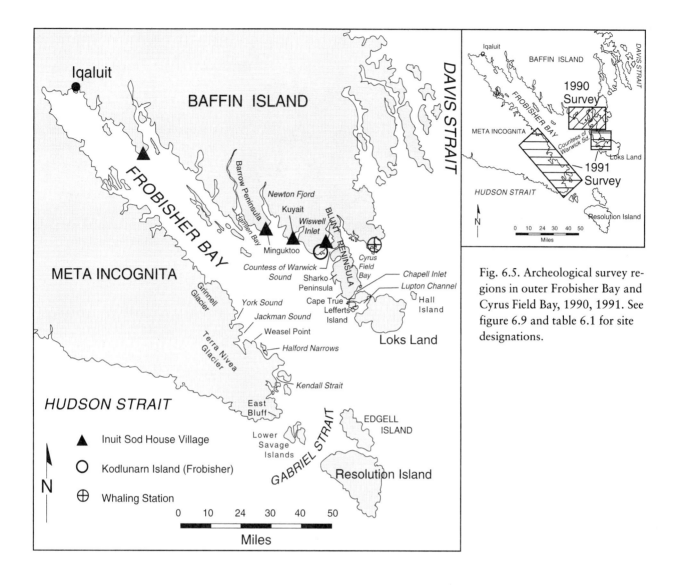

Fig. 6.5. Archeological survey regions in outer Frobisher Bay and Cyrus Field Bay, 1990, 1991. See figure 6.9 and table 6.1 for site designations.

spent surveying in Countess of Warwick Sound, giving special attention to the Frobisher mine sites. This group departed on the evening of the 12th, after which we returned to Cyrus Field Bay for two days to survey its northeastern shores and islands. Here Eric Loring discovered a missing Frobisher iron bloom similar to those found previously at Kodlunarn Island. We returned to Countess of Warwick Sound on the evening of the 17th to meet Charles Arnold, Robert McGhee, and James Tuck who had been airlifted to Kodlunarn Island. Surveys were conducted here and at Tikkoon Point on August 18–19, when Susan Rowley arrived and Auger, Arnold, McGhee, and Tuck departed. Surveys of Lincoln and Napoleon bays and excavations at Cape Sarah were then conducted, and on the evening of the 23d we returned to the outpost camp at Kuyait

before beginning the trip back to Iqaluit, with stops at Minguktoo and Imilik. We arrived in Iqaluit on the 25th. The last week of August was spent inventorying and photographing collections, packing equipment, and hauling the *Pitsiulak* ashore to her winter berth.

Considering the logistics shift from Newfoundland to Iqaluit and the limited number of days available for scientific work, the accomplishments in 1990 were substantial. These results could not have been done without the cooperation and assistance of many organizations and people in Newfoundland, Labrador, and Iqaluit, and of Inuit families in the Frobisher Bay outpost camps. Building community associations and explaining the goals of the Frobisher research program was an important part of our field effort.

Fig. 6.6. Despite fierce tidal currents, Beare Sound and Loks Land were target areas for our regional survey program because of their excellent hunting potential for polar bears, seals, walrus, and caribou. Driftwood, which is absent from other areas of Frobisher Bay, is brought here by arctic currents from Siberia and Alaska and probably attracted Inuit attention for thousands of years. It was abundant in this 20th century Inuit tentring inspected by Dosia Laeyendecker.

Fieldwork conducted in July and August of 1991 represented the first full season of work organized under the aegis of the Meta Incognita Steering Committee.[1] During this season excavations were conducted at two Inuit winter village sites, Kuyait and Kamaiyuk, located in 1990 near the Frobisher base-camp at Kodlunarn Island. Under field direction of Lynda Gullason (McGill University) and Anne Henshaw (Harvard University), two Inuit sod-walled winter houses and one fall qarmat tent house at Kuyait, and two sod-walled winter houses at Kamaiyuk, were excavated. In addition, regional surveys were conducted by a field team aboard the RV *Pitsiulak* in the surrounding outer Frobisher Bay and Cyrus Field Bay region. In addition to recovering information on contact-period Inuit dwellings containing Frobisher remains, these surveys found two new Frobisher mine locations and a large number of prehistoric and historic period Inuit settlements dating to the last 4000 years.

---

1. The Meta Incognita Project operates under the authority of a ministerial-level Canadian Government steering committee with representatives from Canadian Museum of Civilization (George MacDonald and Roger Marois), Government of the Northwest Territories through the Prince of Wales Northern Heritage Centre (Charles Arnold), Parks Canada (Christine Cameron and DiAnn Herst), and Town of Iqaluit (Tommy Owlijoot), under chairmanship of Thomas Symons (Trent University/Historic Sites and Monuments Board).

COUNTESS OF WARWICK SOUND

FROBISHER MINES

Investigations of the Frobisher camps on Kodlunarn Island were not allowed under our 1990 and 1991 permits, but we were able to locate, map, and gather preliminary data on other Frobisher sites in Countess of Warwick Sound and outer Frobisher Bay. Most of this work centered on documenting Frobisher mine sites, some of which had been located previously by Hall, Kenyon, and Hogarth. Three previously known mines in the vicinity of Countess of Warwick Sound were relocated and visited: Winter's Furnace (Newland Island), Denham's Mount (Judy Point), and Countess of Warwick (Kodlunarn Island). An important new mine, Countess of Sussex, was located for the first time on the mainland opposite Countess of Sussex Island. In addition, we found a large outcrop of black hornblende in the cove on the south side of Tikkoon Point (see fig. 6.18), which may have been mined as part of the Countess of Warwick works. As with the mines at the Kodlunarn ship's trench and mine/reservoir, coal dumps, stone structures, and mining trenches were discovered at Newland Island, and spoil piles were noted at the Countess of Sussex mine. Hogarth secured geological descriptions and ore samples at all five sites (Hogarth 1990, 1991) and is preparing reports on the geological settings, mining operations, and composition of ores obtained.

Our surveys verified the existence of coal dumps,

Fig. 6.7. Winter's Furnace mine on northeastern Newland Island. Mine trench to the right of pack, coal dump behind. View north.

Fig. 6.8. Donald Hogarth inspects "black ore" spoil pile at Countess of Sussex Mine. View north.

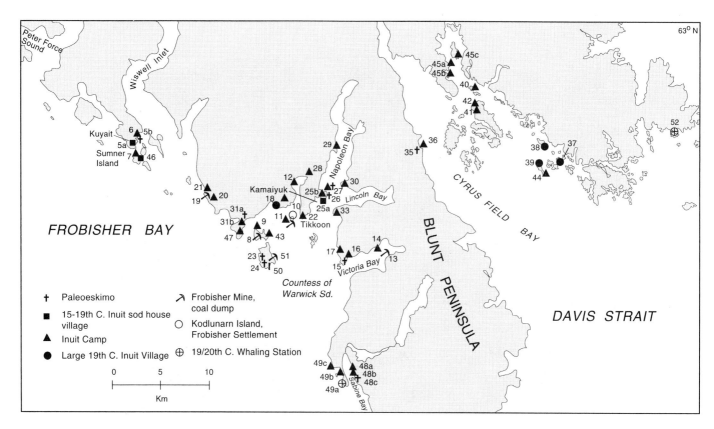

Peter Force Sound

Wiswell Inlet

63° N

Kuyait
6 5b
5a +
Sumner
Island
7 46

45c
45a
45b
40
42
41

52

38 37
39 44

29
28
12
Kamaiyuk
25b 27 30
+ 26
18 25a Lincoln Bay
10 22 33
11 Tikkoon
9
47 8 43

35 + 36

21
19 20
31a +
31b

17 16 14
15 13
Victoria Bay

CYRUS FIELD BAY

Napoleon Bay

BLUNT PENINSULA

DAVIS STRAIT

FROBISHER BAY

23 51
24 50

Countess of
Warwick Sd.

+ Paleoeskimo

■ 15-19th C. Inuit sod house
village

▲ Inuit Camp

● Large 19th C. Inuit Village

↗ Frobisher Mine,
coal dump

○ Kodlunarn Island,
Frobisher Settlement

⊕ 19/20th C. Whaling Station

49c 48a
49b 48b
49a 48c
Sabine Bay

0   5   10
|————————|————————|
Km

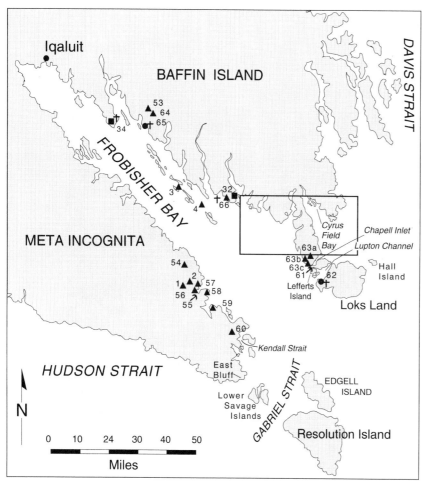

Iqaluit

BAFFIN ISLAND

DAVIS STRAIT

53
64
■ +
34 65

3

32
+ 66

4

FROBISHER BAY

META INCOGNITA

Cyrus
Field
Bay

Chapell Inlet
Lupton Channel

63a
63b
63c +
61 62
+

Hall
Island

54

1 2
56 57
55 58

Lefferts
Island

Loks Land

59

60

Kendall Strait

HUDSON STRAIT

East
Bluff

Lower
Savage
Islands

EDGELL
ISLAND

GABRIEL STRAIT

Resolution Island

N

0   10   24   30   40   50
|——|——|——|——|——|——|
Miles

Fig. 6.9. Archeological sites found in
1981, 1990, and 1991. Outline on
map to left shows location of map
above. See table 6.1 for site designations.

TABLE 6.1. Archeological sites recorded in 1981, 1990, and 1991

Site name	Map code	Culture*
KINGAIT COAST:		
York Sound 1	54	Bloody Point Inuit camp
Jackman Sound 1	1	Recent Inuit
Jackman Sound 2	2	Recent Inuit
Jackman Sound 3	55	Frobisher "silver" mine
Jackman Sound 4	56	Inuit tentring camps
Jackman Sound 5	57	Inuit tentring camps
Weasel Point 1	58	Inuit tentring camps
Halford Island Narrows	59	Inuit tentring camps; Cesna crash
Kendall Strait	60	Inuit pinnacles
LOWER FROBISHER BAY:		
Idlaulitoo Outpost Camp	53	Modern Inuit outpost
Tongue Cape 1	64	Dorset/Neoeskimo camp
Tongue Cape 2	65	Modern Inuit field camps
Ikkerasukudunuk 1	3	Neoeskimo/Recent Inuit
Minguktoo 1	32	Thule/Neoeskimo sodhouse village
Minguktoo 2	66	Dorset/Neoeskimo tentring camps
Imilik 1	34	Dorset/Neoeskimo sodhouse village
Gabriel Island	4	Neoeskimo camp
Kuyait 1	5a,b	Dorset/Thule/Neoeskimo village
Kuyait 2	6	Neoeskimo tentring camps
Sumner Island 1	7	Neoeskimo tentring camps
Sumner Island 2	46	Inuit sod house village
Newland Island 1	8	Frobisher mine and coal dump
Newland Island 2	9	Neoeskimo tentring camps
Newland Island 3	43	Neoeskimo tentring camp
Kodlunarn Island 1	10	Frobisher sites
Kodlunarn Island 2	11	Neoeskimo camps
Diana Marsh Outcrop	12	Neoeskimo grave site
Judy Point 1	13	Frobisher coal dump
Judy Point 2	14	Neoeskimo tent camps/structures
Victoria Bay 1	15	Dorset camp
Victoria Bay 2	16	Neoeskimo tent camps
Victoria Bay 3	17	Neoeskimo cave site
Hall Peninsula 1 (Paksakha)	18	Recent Inuit spring camp
Countess of Sussex 1	19	Frobisher Mine
Countess of Sussex 2	20	Dorset camp
Countess of Sussex 3	21	Neoeskimo camps
Tikkoon Point 1	22	Frobisher(?)/Neoeskimo structures
Willows Island 1	23	Dorset midden/Thule/Neoeskimo camps
Willows Island 2	24	Dorset midden
Willows Island 3	50	Dorset midden and winter village
Anvil Cove 1	51	Frobishercoal dump; Inuit camps
Napoleon Bay 1 (Kamaiyuk)	25a,b	Dorset midden/Thule/Neoeskimo vill.
Napoleon Bay 2	26	Dorset/Thule/Neoeskimo camps
Napoleon Bay 3	27	Dorset/Thule/Recent camps
Napoleon Bay 4	28	Recent Inuit camps
Napoleon Bay 5	29	Caribou blind
Lincoln Bay 1	30	Neoeskimo camps
Harris Point 1	33	Recent Inuit
Cape Sarah Neck 1	31a,b	Paleoeskimo (Transitional)
Cape Sarah 1	47	Thule/Inuit qarmat and tent site
Sabine Bay 1	48a,b,c	Dorset/Neoeskimo tent sites
Sharko Peninsula 1	49a,b,c	Thule/Inuit/European whaling station
Beare Sound 1	62	Dorset/Neoeskimo TR village
Lefferts Island 1	61	Frobisher mines and Inuit camps
CYRUS FIELD BAY:		
Itilikjuak 1	35	Dorset village/Neoeskimo tent camps
Itilikjuak 2	36	Caribou drive system
Chappell Inlet 1	63a	Old Inuit tentring
Chappell Inlet 2	63b	Neoeskimo caribou drive system
Chappell Inlet 3	63c	Neoeskimo tentring camps
Cyrus Field Bay 1 (Lookout I.)	37	Historic and Recent Inuit camps
Cyrus Field Bay 2	38	Paleoeskimo/Neoeskimo camps
Cyrus Field Bay 3	39	Thule/Neoeskimo/recent Inuit camps
George Henry Island 1	40	Recent Inuit
George Henry Island 2	41	Thule/Neoeskimo camps
George Henry Island 3	42	Thule/Neoeskimo camps
Island-95 1	43	Unknown stone structure
Island-95 2	44	Neoeskimo camps
Cyrus Field Bay Survey	45a,b,c	Recent Inuit (inner bay surveys)
Cape Haven 1	52	European whaling station

*Recent Inuit = 19/20th century; Neoeskimo = undatable but of Thule/Inuit tradition; Thule = prehistoric Neoeskimo, ca. A.D. 1000–1550; Early Historic Neoeskimo = A.D. 1550–1800; Dorset = 2500–1000 B.P.; Transitional Paleoeskimo = ca. 3000–2500 B.P.; Pre-Dorset = ca. 4000–2800 B.P.

Fig. 6.10. Inspecting the coal deposit at Denham's Mount Mine (Kenyon's "Judy" Point), Victoria Bay.

known and occasionally utilized by Inuit for many years, at Newland, Judy Point, and Kodlunarn. These dumps were left at mine sites where coal had been used both for general amenities (tea) and for "trying" (assaying) prospective ore samples before and during excavation. The coal was invariably associated with pebbles of English flint (see fig. 5.46) probably by mixing with flint ballast in the holds of the ships. Like tentrings on Kodlunarn Island, the stone structures found at these mines are not easily segregated into Inuit and Elizabethan types. All were fairly simple circular rings lacking internal features or diagnostic artifacts. Although none could be attributed specifically to the Frobisher miners, Fenton's reports indicate that his men worked and slept in tents at these sites. After Frobisher's departure the sites were utilized by Inuit both for hunting and for scavenging European materials. So we may expect a mixed assemblage whose identity will only be settled by excavation.

In 1991 three new mine/coal dumps were located, two of which—Lefferts Island and Jackman

Sound—are mentioned in the Frobisher reports, while the third, a coal dump at Anvil Cove on Opingivik Island, was not reported by Frobisher as a mine site. The Lefferts Island mine is located on the east side of the island which forms the west side of Beare Sound. This mine is one of several outcrops of black hornblende occurring along the Beare Sound coast of Lefferts Island and shows signs of having been quarried. A piece of chert, possibly European, was found here, but no coal or other remains. Today the sea washes over this site at high tide. One wonders if this outcrop is large enough to have produced the 330 tons of ore Frobisher took from his Beare Sound (Sussex Island) mine. Some of the other outcrops on the north side of Lefferts Island may have been mined, but evidence of working is not obvious today.

The Jackman Sound mine (KbDg-1) is interesting for several reasons, but primarily because it was probably the first "mine" Frobisher's men located when the expedition returned to Frobisher Bay in 1577 explicitly to locate gold and silver ore sources.

Fig. 6.11. Lefferts Island black ore quarry on Beare Sound. View east.

Fig. 6.12. Quartz outcrop in inner reaches of Jackman Sound, probably Frobisher's "Smithes Island silver mine."

Exploring the south shore of the bay, George Best reports "Upon a small island, within this sounde, called Smithes Island (because he first set up his forge there) was found a mine of silver, but was not won out of the rocks without great labor" (Best, in Stefansson and McCaskill 1938, 1:61). This description matches a quartz outcrop on a small island in the narrow southern extension of Jackman Sound. Although only a small outcrop, it is conspicuous and

bears evidence of quarrying. Its prominent location and the fact that silver may occur as veins in large quartz outcrops suggest this is the "Smithes Island" quarry. No other outcrop that might have been taken by Elizabethans as a potential silver mine was noted in Jackman Sound. It seems that this first "mine" identified on the Frobisher voyages was as unproductive as those to be found later and was abandoned after only moderate disturbance.

buried coal lens

Fig. 6.13. Anvil Cove 1 site, location of Inuit tent camps found above a remnant lens of Frobisher coal, eroding at the bank.

The Anvil Cove location at the southeast end of Opingivik Island produced only a small buried lens of Frobisher coal and was associated, as usual, with flint pebbles. Most of this coal deposit has eroded into the sea. Frobisher does not report a mine at this location, and we did not find "black ore" outcrops here.

Work in 1990 at the Frobisher sites confirmed the scientific and historical importance of full-scale excavation of these endangered sites, particularly at localities on Kodlunarn Island. Although surface indications of Frobisher activity other than evidence of sod and rock foundations are nil, owing to centuries of scavenging by Inuit and later relic-hunters, Frobisher deposits do exist in situ and show promise for excavation. None of these structures or localities appears to have serious complications requiring elaborate conservation measures or extraordinary excavation infrastructure. The Frobisher structures are small and discrete, with archeological deposits ranging from a few to 30 cm in depth. Only in the ship's trench, where wood remains exist, will special conservation measures be required.

INUIT SITES

Most of the remainder of this report concerns evidence of historic-period Inuit sites found in southeastern Frobisher Bay having a direct bearing on European-Inuit acculturation and contact history. Special attention was given to locating traditional Eskimo (Inuit) archeological sites occupied at the time of the Frobisher voyages. While the accounts of the Frobisher voyages record a variety of friendly and hostile encounters, archeological information on European-Inuit contacts is unavailable, and oral historical accounts (cf. C. F. Hall 1864, 1865) are scanty. For these reasons locating Inuit sites contemporary with the Frobisher voyages was an important goal of our research.

WILLOWS ISLAND 1 (KeDe-2). A large multicomponent site was found on a broad, sod-covered ledge on the western side of Willows Island (Opingivik; Hall's "Oopungnewing") where the shore is protected by an offshore barrier island. This grassy expanse of marshy ground, partially underlain by permafrost, is watered by a small pond from which two small streams drain to the sea. Walrus and seal bones are scattered about, having been gathered together from crevices and caches recently by Inuit searching for ivory and bone carving materials. Exposures are seen only along the stream beds and in the badly eroding front edge of the bank. In 1981 we found a polished slate Thule harpoon endblade eroding into the northernmost stream bed a few meters above its mouth; a level beneath the point contained a grey chert biface and quartz-crystal artifacts. Upon returning to this site in 1990 we located the only Pre-Dorset artifact recovered from the outer bay region to date—a spalled burin. The reason for the paucity of early Paleoeskimo sites in Southeast Baffin is clear; few early sites have escaped destruction by erosion on these rapidly submerging shorelines.

Willows Island 1 appears to have been occupied periodically during the past four thousand years by Paleoeskimo, Thule, and recent Inuit groups. The absence of sod houses suggests it was not used during the midwinter period by early Neoeskimo peoples, although later groups may have lived here in winter after sod houses gave way to snow houses in the 19th century (see fig. 5.2). Inuit use of the site results from its proximity to excellent late winter and early spring walrus and seal hunting at the *sina* (ice edge), which lies close offshore.

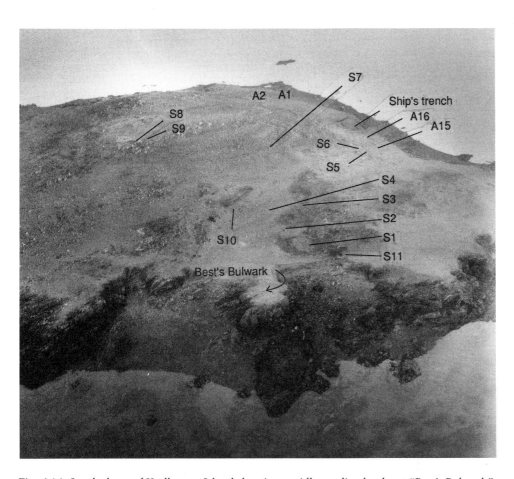

Fig. 6.14. South shore of Kodlunarn Island showing rapidly eroding banks at "Best's Bulwark" and smithy area sites.

Fig. 6.15. Late Dorset implements collected from eroding bank at Willows Island 1 (KeDe-2). Ground chert burin-like tool at bottom, second from right, below serrated-edge biface. Traces of an eroded Pre-Dorset component (spalled burin, not illustrated) were also noted. (Photo: R. Auger/Laval University.)

Our work in 1981 had indicated the presence of permafrost. In 1990 we returned but failed to locate productive organic-bearing Neoeskimo levels. However, the site's Dorset deposits were found to be extensive, with some bone preservation, and extend hundreds of meters along the front of the terrace, around the western headland into the northern cove and into "driftwood" cove (Willows Island 2) to the south. The combined sites probably constitute the largest Dorset settlement area in Countess of Warwick Sound.

WILLOWS ISLAND 2 (KeDe-8). The most productive Dorset deposit found in 1990 was recovered from the eroding northern shore of the small cove south of Willows Island 1. The location features a black earth midden 15–20 cm thick which appears to be the remains of a Dorset winter house. The sample recovered from the erosion face included chert, crystal, and soapstone artifacts (triangular points, side-notched points, microblades, scrapers, vessel fragments) typologically comparable to South and West Baffin Middle Dorset. In 1991 we returned

to test the deposits away from the eroding back. Expecting to find little of the site remaining, we discovered that 100 square meters of this very productive midden is intact, stratified below a Neoeskimo level.

Fig. 6.16. Willows Island 2 (KeDe-8) Late Dorset implements from eroding bank (photo: R. Auger/Laval University).

Fig. 6.17. Walrus mandibles nested tooth-side up in part of a 5-meter line at Willows Island 2; compare with the row of walrus heads in figure 5.2.

At the crest of the beach south of the Dorset site we found a string of walrus mandibles protruding from the sod (fig. 6.17; cf. fig. 5.2) near an alignment of whale vertebrae. The mandible alignment is east-west, perpendicular to the hillslope. It is composed of 25 mandibles, nested tightly, tooth side up, and extends for a distance of 5 m. These unusual bone deposits appear to represent a previously undescribed form of Thule or Dorset hunting ritual. No cultural materials were found in the area, but radiocarbon dates on the bone should provide clues to authorship.

WILLOWS ISLAND 3 (KeDe-12). In 1991 we found a large Dorset midden on the sloping grassy hillside at the extreme southern end of Willows Island. The site is unusual because it is one of the few Dorset sites in the outer bay region that is not being actively eroded. Test pits produced late Dorset implements, preserved faunal remains, and charred rock slabs in a 20–30-cm-thick deposit. A marshy gully north of the site contained thick deposits of wood, walrus hide, baleen, and other faunal remains. This site would be an excellent prospect for excavation.

ANVIL COVE 1 (KeDe-13). A series of Inuit sites was found in a small cove on the southeast side of Willows Island in an area we informally named "Anvil Cove." This is the site of an Inuit camp visited by Hall in 1862 while searching for the Frobisher anvil Inuit said had been taken here from Kodlunarn Island and which they reportedly threw off the cliff onto the tidal flat six years before Hall's visit (Hall collection inventory in Collinson 1867:373). According to Inuit in earlier days it was still to be seen at low tide. Hall's search was not successful (Hall 1865b:451, 498), nor was ours, without a metal detector or low tide. Perhaps the anvil has sunk into the mud. Hall considered it might also have been carried off with the ice in spring breakup.

In 1991 we continued our search here and identified numerous tentring sites along the shore. At L1, the northernmost, we found the historic Inuit tentring camp with caches and hearth features above a 1–2-cm-thick lens of coal (described above). We searched for the lost Frobisher anvil, again without success. At the south end of the terrace, under the protection of the hillside, we found masses of faunal remains embedded in the wet moss, including butchered walrus, seal, small whales, and caribou.

Fig. 6.18. Nestled walrus mandibles at Anvil Cove 1, part of a sinuous 25-meter-long alignment in which all mandibles have been buried tooth-side down.

Wood was occasionally preserved. The site setting, the dispersed and unburied nature of the bone deposit, and the absence of tentrings suggested the area had been used as an Inuit snowhouse village sometime during the last few centuries; quite likely it is the same village visited by Hall in spring 1862 (see fig. 5.2) as he indicates an igloo village here on a sketch map of the island in his field notes.

At the northeast end of the bone bed we found another partially buried alignment of walrus mandibles. Unlike the similar feature at Willows Island 2, which lies directly in line on the other side of the hill, this feature is much larger, extending 25 m in an easterly direction, and its ca. 95 mandibles are all nested *tooth side down*. All teeth had been removed from the jaws. A walrus jaws alignment was noted on Oopingivik/Willows Island by C. F. Hall in 1861, but his reference speaks of jaws placed two feet

apart extending over the top of the hill at the *north* end of the island. Our feature is at the south end of the island and does not extend over the hill. Hall's reference seems to be mistaken; we have surveyed the north end of Willows Island and have found no such feature there. Neither Hall nor his Inuit companions knew the function of the feature. Almost certainly it represents hunting ritual.

TIKKOON POINT (KeDe-4). Located due east of and only one kilometer from Kodlunarn Island, Tikkoon Point figures strongly in the cultural geography of Countess of Warwick Sound. The Frobisher reports note that natives sometimes climbed the Tikkoon hills to shout taunts across to miners on Kodlunarn. Hall makes frequent note of Tikkoon as an old Inuit camp, and it was here that he recovered the bloom "time-worn with ragged teeth," probably the one that he later presented to the Smithsonian (Hall 1965:430, 437).[2] MacMillan also visited the site, and Walter Kenyon used it for his camp. Our surveys also included visits to Tikkoon; like Hall and Kenyon, we noted evidence of many Inuit camps, but also evidence of early Europeans. One of its many interesting features is a large island of black rock outcropping in the landing cove. Although Frobisher is not known to have mined this site, its rock appears similar to that of known mines.

Tikkoon lies on a well-watered, sheltered point at the end of the peninsula separating Diana and Napoleon bays. The entire beachpass across to Napoleon Bay is scattered with the remains of dwellings, most of which date to the Neoeskimo (Thule and recent) period, but Dorset occupations occur as well. We noted 20 to 30 tentrings and other structures, most of which are located on the western beaches. This area was tested by Walter Kenyon, whose pits are visible, and in one we found tan chert flakes and a Dorset side-notched biface. Structures were also noted in the marshy area between the western beach plateau and the crest, on the crest itself, on the eastern slope facing Napoleon Bay, and along the rocky ground toward the point. Unlike tent camps on Kodlunarn, most sites at Tikkoon are sod-covered.

2. Despite Hall's assertion (1965:437) that his Tikkoon bloom was sent to the Smithsonian and the Kodlunarn bloom to Britain, he may be mistaken, for the Smithsonian bloom, which resembles his figure on page 437, is smooth, not "ragged toothed."

Fig. 6.19. Tikkoon Point west beaches, overlooking black ore outcrop on shore and Kodlunarn Island. In distance, left to right are Willows Island, Newland Island and Cape Sarah. View to northwest.

In 1981, in a windy exposure at the top of the beach, we located a feature Kenyon noted but had not tested: two small oval depressions (10 × 20 × 3 cm) set in a carbonaceous deposit that cemented the surrounding surface gravel into a hard, black mass (fig. 6.20). Several rock slabs were also associated with this feature. The depressions were clearly defined, not at all eroded, and the mass of material was fused by exposure to fire. Our metal detector indicated the presence of iron. Excitement was heightened because the depressions matched the size and shape of the Frobisher iron blooms. We wondered if Kenyon's feature might be the base of an early iron furnace.

Upon excavation the mass of encrusted slag and charcoal turned out to be solidified tar which had seeped into the ground and hardened above a 1.5-m-diameter cement slab. The tarry residue contained cinders, charcoal, iron bits, wire nails, remains of

Fig. 6.20. Tar-encrusted hearth base with two kettle-bottom depressions at crest of Tikkoon beachpass.

Fig. 6.21. Remnants of one of several unusual rectangular stone pavements (S4) at Tikkoon, partially buried under slopewash. These structures appear to be the prepared floors of snowhouses (R. Auger, pers. comm.).

two-strand burlap-like fabric, and calcined small-mammal bone. Rather than an Elizabethan smelter, the feature is a 19th-century whaling hearth used to tar nets and rigging whose pot bottoms had left circular depressions in the fused deposit. Team member Caroline Phillips had seen similar hearths at European whaling stations in Cumberland Sound.

Our 1981 survey also included testing the site's marshy areas for bog iron, but no iron-rich deposits were found. Elsewhere, peat and driftwood samples were collected. In 1990 we returned to map and test other structures, discovering the site to be much larger and more complex than noted in 1981. At this time we noted several unusual rectangular stone pavements that seemed unusual by Inuit standards. Samples of rooftile, brick, and a chunk of iron were found in some of the Tikkoon tentrings that appear to be of Inuit type; several in situ Dorset components were discovered also.

In 1991 Réginald Auger returned to test several of these structures and determine their Frobisher connections. Among the sites investigated were three stone foundations along the side of the northern hillslope (S4, S20, and S21) and a group of tentrings (S14, S17) with Frobisher ceramics on the surface. The hillside pavements (fig. 6.21) were found to contain sled runners and historic Inuit materials, suggesting that they are stone floors and sleeping platforms for snowhouse dwellings. Excavation of

the S14 tentring produced Elizabethan tiles, a fragment of brass, and faunal remains. Tests in the S7 structure produced a small wedge of iron (see Wayman and Ehrenreich, this volume). Thus, all the Tikkoon sites tested so far appear to be Inuit camps. If Frobisher settlements exist at Tikkoon, they will be difficult to find in the thick sod cover of the western beach.

CAPE SARAH NECK 1 (KeDe-3). Several sites were found at Cape Sarah on raised beaches at the neck of a small peninsula enclosing the northwestern corner of Countess of Warwick Sound. This neck is a popular spot, visited by Inuit travelers waiting for the wind to drop before continuing by boat to their summer camps at the entrance of Diana Bay. A similar motive inspired our 1981 visit, and during the time available we located several sites. The most extensive of these (Area 1) lies east of the stream and consists of Neoeskimo tentrings containing seal and walrus bones and partially buried Paleoeskimo structures associated with grey chert flakes. A fallen rock slab pinnacle similar to those known from Ungava Bay and northern Labrador (where they seem to be of late Thule origin) lies toppled at the eastern end of the beach. Area 2, west of the stream gully, consists of several boulder clusters that seemed to be remains of Paleoeskimo dwellings. These sites lacked bone but contained chert flakes and had Paleoeski-

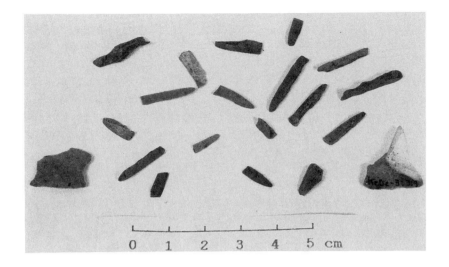

Fig. 6.22. Cape Sarah Neck 1 (KeDe-3), Transitional Dorset, ca. 2500 B.P., ground and spalled burins and spalls (photo: R. Auger/Laval University).

mo axial floor plans. Near the crest of the beach-pass, Area 3 contained tentrings, slab pavements, and other signs of activity. No diagnostic artifacts were found, and no excavations were made. Absence of more substantial dwellings suggested that Paleoeskimo and Neoeskimo groups camped occasionally at Cape Sarah Neck but had primary settlements elsewhere.

At the end of the 1990 season we returned to this site to excavate the A2 structure that seemed likely to provide us with an undisturbed early Paleoeskimo collection and house plan. Having seen nothing but eroding Dorset middens all summer, our hopes were high, and we were encouraged by the rapid recovery of a burin spall with ground edges indicating a "Transitional" or "Groswater" Paleoeskimo component ca. 2500 B.P. Transitional (or Groswater, as they are called in Labrador) sites are fascinating because their lithic assemblages usually consist of various types of beautifully made tools. But soon our enthusiasm began to flag as burin spall after burin spall was unearthed and no other tools were found (fig. 6.22). No Labrador cherts were noted, and finally we even decided that the structure might not be associated with the spalls. The site is probably the most specialized Transitional Paleoeskimo site ever excavated, testimony to a hunter's single-minded dedication to the carving of ivory or bone implements.

HALL PENINSULA 1 (KeDe-7). Surveys along the north shore of Countess of Warwick Sound in 1981 located several Neoeskimo sites, one of which (known as Kussegeerarkjuan) is a historic period winter village that was in use at the time of Hall's and Boas's research. The site is located several hundred meters east of the prominent sea cliff scar referred to by Kenyon (erroneously) as "Fenton's Fortune." Kussegeerarkjuan was the site from which an iron bloom was transported by Inuit to the Lookout Island site in Cyrus Field Bay (see below). Our work here in 1990 produced a preliminary site map and artifact samples from some of the site's 26 structures (fig. 6.23). The dwellings consist of a distinctive type of low rock- and sod-walled tentring having an excavated floor surrounded by a three-sided sleeping platform. This house form is transitional between the deep Neoeskimo winter pit houses and summer tentrings. Although the lack of heavy rock walls removes this house type from the more heavily constructed qarmat-type structures, its form suggests this type of dwelling functioned as a single-family fall or late spring house. Among the more common artifacts recovered were round and tubular glass trade beads, rifle and shotgun shells, a variety of iron, tin, and copper ornaments and implements, transfer print and other 19th-century ceramics, pipestems, European flint, and objects of worked bone, ivory, and wood. The many unusual forms can be clearly linked with social, economic, and technological changes in late 19th-century Southeast Baffin Inuit culture as it responded to the European whaling and exploration era. Hall's documentation is especially important for this period.

Fig. 6.23. This large early winter site, Hall Peninsula 1, was visited by Hall in 1862 (Kussegeerarkjuan). Its low-walled sod and stone houses, known as qarmats, were used by Inuit in the 19th and early 20th centuries as replacements for earlier styles of large multifamily winter houses. This site was also known to Franz Boas.

Fig. 6.24. Kuyait site area (KfDf-2), view to south.

KUYAIT 1 (KfDf-2). The 1990 surveys proved extremely fruitful in expanding the 1981 work to other Inuit sites and resulted in discovery of several winter villages located near Frobisher's camps on Kodlunarn Island. The largest of these, Kuyait, at the southwestern entrance of Wiswell Inlet opposite Sumner Island, consists of at least eleven semisubterranean sod structures ranging from small single-room dwellings to large multiroom "clover-leaf" type dwellings, a number of tentrings, and at least one fall dwelling or qarmat. Test pits in these structures and elsewhere on the site revealed late Pre-Dorset, Dorset, Thule, and historic Inuit occupations. Most of the visible sod houses date from ca. A.D. 1200 to the present and contain both tradition-al Inuit and European materials, including Frobisher tile fragments and later materials like clay pipes, glass, ceramics, metal, and beads. Wood and bone are present but generally not well preserved. Kuyait will be a key site detailing outer bay Neoeskimo cultural development with crossties to the Frobisher expeditions.

Three houses were excavated here in 1991 by Lynda Gullason, Anne Henshaw, and the author. House 3, a "single-room" rectangular structure with a long entrance passage, originated as a prehistoric Thule structure and was later utilized in the early 20th century. Between the two occupations, the structure and most of its deposits and original architecture were destroyed by a frost boil which erupted

Fig. 6.25. Earlier types of winter dwellings were deeply excavated into the earth, were bilobate in form, and had two sleeping platforms. Kuyait House 8, here under excavation, represents this traditional early Baffin Inuit form whose use began as early as the 13th century. Entrance passage at lower left; cold trap at inner end of passage; floor paving in center; hearth piles immediately to left and right of passage entry; sleeping benches at upper left and right.

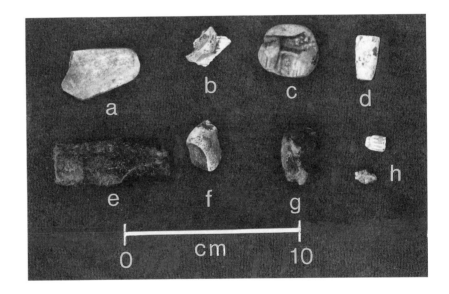

Fig. 6.26. European materials found in Kuyait House 8: *a,* white ceramic, *b,* slag-encrusted ceramic crucible fragment, *c,* green-glazed stove tile with molded surface and abraded edges, *d,* large tubular bead, *e,* piece of iron strap, *f,* English flint nodule, *g,* chunk of coal, and *h,* red and white barrel-shaped bead and bead fragment.

in the center of the house. A small assemblage of slate points and knives was recovered from the badly disturbed Thule levels.

More productive excavations were conducted at House 8, a large bilobed sod house with excellently preserved entrance passage, floor pavements, hearths, and two sleeping platforms. This location had previously been the site of earlier Dorset and Thule structures, and many of their artifacts were found in wall and subfloor deposits. The latest occupation, that of the bilobed structure, contains a small number of traditional artifacts like harpoons, dog trace buckles, soapstone vessel fragments, and a few glass bead, ceramic, and iron finds that appear

to date to the 18th or early 19th century. The collections also include Frobisher artifacts such as flint nodules, glazed stove tile, rooftile, and some early period glass trade beads. Preliminary analysis suggests the house dates to the early contact period before the appearance of whalers brought a large influx of European materials into Frobisher Bay Inuit society. The Frobisher finds appear to be the result of scavenging Elizabethan artifacts needed for various purposes, such as fire-making and polishing kits from the Kodlunarn Island sites.

A third structure excavated, House 12, was a qarmat, a subrectangular low sod- and rock-walled tent probably used during the fall or early winter. This

Fig. 6.27. Kamaiyuk site (Napoleon Bay 1, KfDe-5), view south. Tikkoon Point and Kodlunarn Island are a short distance around the point to the right. Figure 6.1 shows the area at low tide. The site, now eroding badly, appears to have been under threat of inundation for many years. When George Best visited it in 1577 he noted that Inuit had dug ditches to keep water from collecting in their houses. Through Best's report (see p. 98), Kamaiyuk became the first Native archeological site to appear in English literature.

structure contained several hundred late 19th-century European artifacts of all descriptions, from metal knives and ulu blades to toy soldiers, and traditional Inuit material culture, overlying deposits containing Dorset and Pre-Dorset implements. These materials date the qarmat to the whaling period and document the substantial impact of sustained local contact with European whalers that began in the middle of the 19th century. Excellent faunal collections were also recovered. This structure is architecturally similar to structures at Kussegeerarkjuan (Hall Peninsula 1, KeDe-7), contains similar cultural materials, and probably dates to the same period.

SUMNER ISLAND 2 (KfDf-5). On the island opposite Kuyait 1 we found a group of four small sod winter houses some of which were occupied, according to Ooleetoa Pishuktie, during the 20th century by his family. House 1 was partially eroded into the sea; House 2 is a small bilobed structure with entrance lintel uprights; House 3 had a single platform paved with gravel; and House 4 was bilobed and grassed over. These structures and nearby tentrings contained seal and walrus bones and have been used during the winter and spring hunting season. The sod houses appear to mark a return to the use of this house type for winter habitation in the 20th century, after several decades in the late 19th century (documented by Hall and Boas) when Inuit abandoned permanent winter dwellings for snow houses and qarmats, probably in response to the presence of European whalers and winter trading opportunities.

KAMAIYUK (KfDe-5). A third important sod-house site was located in 1990 at Kamaiyuk near the southwest entrance of Napoleon Bay, only a few kilometers from Kodlunarn Island. Three of Kamaiyuk's four sod-walled houses are two-room structures; the fourth is a large rectangular structure somewhat resembling "communal" houses in Labrador and Greenland (Kaplan 1985; Petersen 1974/75). Two other small single-room structures are also represented. Exposures in the middens and fronts of these houses revealed faunal remains, Inuit artifacts, and early European materials including Frobisher tile and ceramics, English flint, glass, and slag, and other materials. Like Kuyait, the Kamaiyuk winter houses are underlain by a thick Dorset midden, and its houses and middens are being severely eroded by the sea. The large amount of Elizabethan material links these structures to the Frobisher voyages and suggests Kamaiyuk was occupied during and after the Elizabethan expeditions.

In 1991 Lynda Gullason and Anne Henshaw excavated House 2 and most of the "longhouse" (House 1), and the middens and other structures were tested. House 2 proved to be a bilobed, two-family dwelling with a central stone roof support similar to House 8 at Kuyait. As at Kuyait, its walled and subfloor deposits held substantial amounts of Dorset and Thule artifacts, as well as Frobisher rooftile, glazed stove tile, glass, a pewter (?) ulu blade, bits of iron, and a few European wood artifacts most likely originating from contact with the Frobisher party or scavenging its camps. Post-

Fig. 6.28. Kamaiyuk House 2 in process of excavation. Entrance passage extends out to lower right.

Fig. 6.29. Artifacts collected from eroding Kamaiyuk houses. Clockwise from upper left: encrusted iron or slag; flint nodule; roof tile and brick fragments; drilled (bronze?) fragment (photo: R. Auger/Laval University).

Frobisher historic artifacts were found as well, but in very small numbers. House 1 revealed a similar picture of occupation before the European whaling period. The latest occupation floors of both houses appear to postdate the Frobisher contact era by at least a century, indicating that this site, which was described by George Best in 1577 (Stefansson and McCaskill 1938, 1:64), had progressed through several stages of reoccupation by the time of its final abandonment. Even though these structures do not appear to document an active period of Elizabethan contact, they contain Frobisher-period materials in a variety of stages of use, reuse, modification, and adaptation to both new and traditional Inuit needs. Upon excavation, the form of House 1 appeared less like a Labrador or Greenland communal structure and more like a modified form of a bilobed two-family dwelling, with sleeping benches placed in a single alignment rather than at the typical 120-degree angle. Further work will be required to clarify the dating and form of this multifamily house. Houses 3 and 4 appear to date earlier than Houses 1 and 2 by virtue of being of smaller size, being built with larger rocks, and having more Frobisher artifacts in evidence. Future excavations will be directed at these structures in an attempt to isolate earlier stages of European/Frobisher contact at Kamaiyuk.

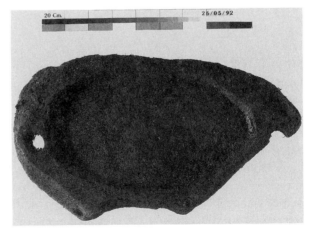

Fig. 6.30. Whalebone plaque with inset rim and perforations for mounting, found at base of House 2, Kamaiyuk (courtesy Canadian Museum of Civilization).

Fig. 6.31. Minguktoo site at Brewster Point, Barrow Peninsula. Foundations of fifteen sod houses dating from Thule period to the present are situated around this cove. As in most cases in outer Frobisher Bay, these sites are being destroyed by marine submergence and erosion.

Fig. 6.32. The well-preserved house depressions at Imilik (Ward Inlet) date to Dorset and Thule times. Their stability is linked to their location near the geological "hinge"; to the northwest, land surfaces and sites are still emerging from glacial "rebound" while to the south and east they are being submerged and destroyed.

MINGUKTOO AND IMILIK. Other sod-house villages identified in Frobisher Bay include the large site of Minguktoo (KfDg-1) at Brewster Point (Barrow Peninsula) which contains fifteen or more houses dating from Thule times to the present, and Imilik, a smaller village with eight Neoeskimo sod house foundations dug into a large Dorset winter site near the mouth of Ward Inlet. These sites were mapped and photographed but were not tested. A return visit to Minguktoo in 1991 resulted in discovery of several components containing Transitional Dorset, Early Dorset, and Late Dorset artifacts at eroding shoreside locations.

IDLAULITOO OUTPOST CAMP. This modern settlement site at the mouth of Waddell Bay contains a large building whose sod wall and roof provided interesting parallels for interpreting early sod house construction techniques. The walls consisted of a tapered foundation of sods one meter high; the roof, of floor carpet—a good replacement for scarce and smelly walrus hide—was secured down on top of the wall with large flat-sided boulders. The collapse of such a structure results in the walls and perched rocks falling inward onto the floor, filling the house with a thick level of wall sods and angular boulders.

COUNTESS OF WARWICK SOUND: SUMMARY

The 1981/1990 data suggest that the outer regions of Frobisher Bay have had a long and prolific human settlement spanning the past 4000 years. Although early Paleoeskimo (Pre-Dorset) sites are very rare, probably owing to their long exposure to coastal submergence and erosion, late Paleoeskimo Dorset sites are numerous and rich in material remains. A somewhat surprising result of our work was the relative absence—in areas we surveyed—of early Thule culture sites. On the other hand, Thule signs are nearly universally present in the larger village sites, but the houses and middens of this period have been disturbed by reoccupation of these sites by successive generations. Factors of geography, faunal availability, coastal submergence, and lack of sod for building winter houses except in locations enriched by previous occupation have contributed to rendering Thule settlement less visible than historic period occupations. This said, however, Neoeskimo sites dating to the post-1500 period of European-Inuit contact do appear to be more numerous, and of these, sites containing Frobisher material were noted frequently in Countess of Warwick Sound. These sites offer a unique opportunity to study Frobisher's impact on East Baffin Inuit culture; they also permit study of indirect effects of European contact on broader aspects of Eastern Arctic Inuit political, economic, and demographic systems. This work will be faciliated, as noted previously, by the fact that following Frobisher's and Davis's visits in the late 16th century, East Baffin Inuit slipped back outside the sphere of European influence for 250 years, until the arrival of whalers in the 1830s.

Finally, we noted considerable variety in Inuit house styles dating to the period ca. A.D. 1400–1900. These houses are found both with and without historic materials, and their architectural features vary from single-room "Thule" structures to multiple-room "clover-leaf" forms. Of special interest is the Kamaiyuk site, whose structures appear to represent a chronological sequence of multiroom houses, all of which contain Frobisher materials and which seem likely to date ca. 1550–1800. The latest and largest of the Kamaiyuk structures may represent a transitional type between the local bilobed architectural tradition and the rectangular Greenland/Labrador-style communal house. This structure form is unique so far among historic Inuit dwellings noted in Frobisher Bay. Evidently, Labrador influence in Frobisher Bay is as lacking in Neoeskimo sites as Ramah chert and other Labrador lithic types are in Dorset sites here.

KINGAIT COAST SURVEYS

During late August 1991, a brief survey was made along the southern coast of Frobisher Bay from York Sound to East Cape, the southeastern tip of Baffin Island. This region had looked very promising for archeological surveys in our transit inbound for Iqaluit in 1990, and it had never been surveyed. Of special interest was that this area figured prominently in accounts of Frobisher's 1577 voyage.

Fig. 6.33. Modern Inuit dwelling in Waddell Bay with sod walls, carpeted roof, and hold-down rocks.

Fig. 6.34. York River entering York Sound and gravel bar on which Inuit were probably camped at time of the arrival of Frobisher's ships in 1577. York Sound 1 site is located halfway out on the other side of the bay. View north.

YORK SOUND 1 (KcDh-3). One of the most dramatic incidents during the Frobisher voyages occurred on the Kingait (south) side of Frobisher Bay early in the summer of 1577, when Frobisher's men attacked an Inuit camp, killing several people and taking a woman and her baby hostage (Stefansson and McCaskill 1938, 1:67). The location of this event can be identified as being on the north shore of York Sound. Earlier, the Elizabethans had visited a York Sound fishing camp from which the Inuit had fled upon their approach. Here the men discovered clothing they thought belonged to the lost 1576 sailors. This site must have been on the gravel beach at the mouth of the York River, which today is a storm bar regularly overswept by the sea. Searching here in August 1991 we found no traces of sites, old or recent. According to the accounts, the Inuit fled to a second site—the one later attacked—on a point farther out on the north shore.

Surveying this coast we found there to be only one possible site location suitable for such a camp: York Sound 1 (fig. 6.35). Here, against a dramatic backdrop of mountains and glaciers, we identified four separate settlement loci, of which L1, L2, and L3 are of early historic age. These sites consist of tentring clusters, caches, stone enclosures, and remains of possible kayak supports. The dwelling sites are covered with moss and no artifacts were visible. A short distance to the east is a rocky promontory answering the description of "Bloody Point," the location at which the fleeing Inuit were overtaken and attacked.

Fig. 6.35. View south over York Sound 1 site, probably the Inuit camp attacked by Frobisher's men in 1577, from which they fled by boat and were overtaken at "Bloody Point."

"WEASEL POINT" 1 (KbDg-2). A low peninsula with a shallow but protected harbor complex five kilometers south of the entrance of Jackman Sound has been used extensively for summer hunting camps. Eight loci were identified, some of which contained as many as eight to ten tentrings. The camps all appear to date to a distinct early historic period during which U-shaped hearths were used. Shreds of canvas were noted, and in one location a cache was discovered containing a dowel-pinned section of ship's timber (oak) and large iron spikes (fig. 6.36).

HALFORD ISLAND NARROWS (KbDg-3). Several small camp sites containing tentrings and caches were found on the mainland (west) side of Halford Island Narrows. An isolated find of a Paleoeskimo biface fragment was also made, the only Paleoeskimo sign we found during our survey from York Sound to East Bluff. Equally unusual was the discovery of the hulk of a Cessna 185 airplane lying upside down in the middle of a bog. The crash probably occurred about ten to fifteen years ago. Parts of the plane have been scavenged. No human remains or loose articles were present.

KENDALL STRAIT. We spent one afternoon surveying the channels and islands on the north side of Kendall Strait and south among the small islands west of Gross Island. Surprisingly few settlement traces were found in this area. We had expected Inuit activity to pick up as one approached the southeastern tip of Baffin Island, known for its strong currents and tidal mixing. However, other than a few isolated tentrings and stone pinnacles, there were few Inuit sites. Another surprise, considering the rocky nature of East Baffin (often thought to be Norse "Helluland," or flatstone land), was the extensive deposits of sand in the form of huge kame terraces along the hillsides, sand-filled valleys, and bridging sand bars between islands. While our surveys here were not thorough enough to be definitive, they create the impression of very light Neoeskimo occupation. Paleoeskimo sites were not noted, probably due to erosion loss. The apparent lack of Inuit use of this area is probably related to poor hunting potential. Today, the outer reaches of eastern Meta Incognita shore are rarely visited by Inuit, although early summer beluga and walrus hunts were conducted here in the past. We saw few signs of caribou and little evidence of seal, walrus, or whale. Time

Fig. 6.36. "Weasel Point" cache of ship's timber, dowel, and iron spikes.

did not allow us to extend our survey to the Lower Savage Islands and the Resolution/Edgell Island region.

CYRUS FIELD BAY

During August of 1990, while surveying various regions of outer Frobisher Bay, we spent a few days in Cyrus Field Bay, a small bay east of Blunt Peninsula frequented by Inuit who lived in Countess of Warwick Sound. Inuit often travel between the two bays by way of a short, low pass at the head of Lincoln Bay. This pass is also an excellent place to hunt caribou. The close contact between the two locations was noted by Hall, who also recorded a story that Inuit had once taken an iron bloom from Kodlunarn Island to Cyrus Field Bay (Rowley, this volume). It seemed useful to explore Frobisher and later European contacts beyond the confines of Countess of Warwick Sound in this direction.

We made two visits to Cyrus Field Bay in 1990. The first was in early August when we surveyed the west side of the Lincoln Bay Pass, finding some excellent Dorset sites, caribou hunting blinds, and historic Inuit camps. Later in the month we returned to survey the east side of the bay where we found several large Thule and historic tent camp sites. In 1991 we attempted to reach the old whaling station Cape Haven at the eastern end of Cyrus Field Bay in early August, but could not do so because of unusually heavy ice conditions. This project was realized, though briefly, with helicopter transport in early September. The following summarizes highlights of these surveys (see table 6.1 for complete site listing).

Fig. 6.37. Eric Loring, Ned Searles, and Pauloosie Pishuktie at Late Dorset Itilikjuak site (KfDd-2), House 1, view east.

ITILIKJUAK. Several sites were located during our brief reconnaissance at Itilikjuak ("place to get through") on the west side of Cyrus Field Bay at the Lincoln Bay overland pass. In addition to discovering a system of caribou hunting blinds and caches at the mouth of the pass (A2 area) near a prominent raised delta or ice-marginal feature, we found, mapped, and tested a series of historic Inuit camps (A3 area) and a group of Dorset houses (A1 area). The former sites contained a rich inventory of early 20th-century "Euro-Inuit" material culture, excellent faunal preservation, and house structure detail. Excavation of these and other historic period Inuit structures at this crossroads location should prove highly rewarding. Likewise, tests at the Dorset site

recovered in situ Late Dorset artifacts (tan/brown chert microblades, triangular points, broadly notched bifaces, scrapers, burin-like tools and quartz-crystal cores and microblades) in five sod-covered subrectangular houses. Faunal remains are present although their condition is poor.

CYRUS FIELD BAY 1 (KfDc-1). The most important find of the summer came from a large Neoeskimo spring camp on the large island (probably Hall's "Look-out Island" at his "Rescue Harbor") three kilometers southwest of Mount Budington. Here we literally stumbled upon a 17.5-lb iron bloom similar to those recovered from Kodlunarn Island (see fig. 5.35).

Cyrus Field Bay 1 has several spatially (and probably chronologically) distinct groups of tentrings, caches, cairns, and graves spread over several hundred square meters of rough bouldery ground. No Paleoeskimo traces were noted, and most of the tentrings and artifacts noted on the bouldery surface seem to date from the historic period. We noted historic period Inuit remains made from both traditional Inuit as well as European materials. Many of these artifacts were scattered about in a way that suggested they had been associated with winter snow house camps rather than with summer/fall tentrings.

The Lookout Island bloom was found a meter from the shore in a group of tentrings whose seaward portions had already been carried away by rising sea levels and sea-ice scour. In one of these rings, barely a meter beyond the seaweed cast up by the last high tide, Eric Loring stumbled on a brownish

Fig. 6.38. Late Dorset finds from Itilikjuak: notched end-blade, microblade, triangular point, ground burin-like, and base of notched biface (photo: R. Auger/Laval University).

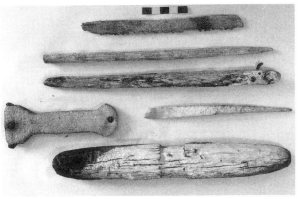

Fig. 6.40. Surface finds from Cyrus Field Bay 1 (Lookout Island) site (KfDc-1): notched stick (noise-maker?), pins of wood and ivory, knife handle with iron blade and rivets, large toggle; scale in cm (photo: Anne Henshaw).

object that was slightly browner and rustier looking than other rocks in the beach. Inuit accounts of a bloom having been transported from Kodlunarn Island to Cyrus Field Bay several hundred years ago would hardly convince a researcher that such an object could be found. But unless one presumes that blooms are scattered across southeastern Baffin Island like tektites after a meteor impact, the Lookout Island bloom can be none other than that noted in Inuit tales as having been carried here by the Inuit Annawa and Manabing from Kussegeerarkjuan near Diana Bay in 1859 (Rowley, this volume). Hall himself found this bloom two years later, in 1861, and

stated in his book that he "obtained" it. If he did, it was never heard of again, for on his return Hall seems to have had only two blooms (Washburn, this volume). Hall's failure to collect the bloom may result from the fact that he had just arrived in Baffin and had not yet learned of the Inuit stories of Kodlunarn Island or blooms or made the Frobisher connection. Our find was a fortunate one indeed, especially as this lost Frobisher relic was about to be swept into the sea.

Fig. 6.41. Lookout Island finds: lamp wick trimmer, glass bottle modified into a scraping tool, clay pipestem, glass fragments, ivory float nozzle; scale in cm (photo: Anne Henshaw).

Fig. 6.42. Lookout Island iron bloom in situ in bed of rust flakes.

The bloom rested on end with its edge embedded in the rocky ground in a bed of rust, with a 2-cm-long iron spall lying alongside. The spall appeared to have been physically detached from the bloom purposefully, perhaps with the aid of fire, as the rust bed included chunks of charcoal. No artifacts were

found nearby, but those found in other areas of the site date to the 19th to 20th century (figs. 6.40, 6.41). The bloom and samples were collected and sent to Yellowknife together with other early iron finds from the 1990 season.

CYRUS FIELD BAY 2 (KfDc-2). Another large tent camp site was found at the southern end of the big island directly west of Mount Budington. Our activity here produced a field sketch map of the 20–30 or more tentrings and other features and observations on occupation sequences. This site appears to have been an important seal and caribou hunting camp. As in the case of the George Henry Island sites, few walrus bones were present. A wide variety of European and traditional Inuit artifacts were noted, most of which date to the 20th century. Excellent preservation of structures and large numbers of artifacts makes this an excellent site for ethnoarcheological study, especially as some of the Inuit who lived here are still alive.

ISLAND 95 1 (KfDc-3). Located only a few hundred meters west of Lookout Island is an island of similar size and shape, the most seaward of the Budington group, on whose summit is a geodetic marker registering its elevation as 95 m, hence our appellation, "Island 95." This island was surveyed first in 1990 and was found to have three site locales: a

Fig. 6.43. Island-95 lookout hill structure inspected by Skipper Perry Colbourne.

large grassy area with scores of tentrings at its north end, a summit "lookout" house at its crest, and a small site at its southern end having several tentrings, hunting blinds and caches. We revisited this island briefly in 1991 and found the north camp to contain historic trade materials similar to those from Cyrus Field Bay 1, 2, and 3. The sites appear to be spring and summer camps. Most seem undisturbed.

The hilltop structure was unusual and probably not of Inuit origin. It is built with several courses of rocks resting on ridges of bedrock around a natural declivity in the summit of the hill. These walls enclose the west, north, and east sides; no wall is present on the south. Several wood planks, including 2 × 4s, possibly of later date than the rock walls, were found inside the enclosure. The geodetic marker is in the center of the structure. No other artifacts or signs of use were found. Possibly this structure resulted from activities of the surveyors who placed the marker in the recent past, but the lichen-covered rocks suggest an earlier time. The site is most suitable as a lookout for game—seals, polar bears, walrus, or caribou—all of which are abundant in this region. Perhaps the structure dates to Hall's time and was used by the crew of the *George Henry* as a lookout. But if so its location, or Hall's use of "Lookout Island" for the neighboring island to the east, is in error.

GEORGE HENRY ISLAND 1 (KfDd-4). Another large tent camp site was found on the northwestern point of George Henry Island. From the style of its

Fig. 6.44. Ned Searles and Eric Loring mapping George Henry Island 1 (KfDd-4) Thule/Recent Inuit site, Structure 20. View to west.

heavily rocked tentrings, massive caches, grave cairns and other architecture, this site appears to date to the late Thule/early contact period, probably ca. A.D. 1500–1850. Few artifacts were noted on the surface, but from a cache eroding at the shore we recovered a bone point, an awl, a bronze gun trigger guard, and a sheet of lead. Early faceted-head iron nails and other objects were also found. The burial cairns and caches we saw had already been opened and their contents were missing.

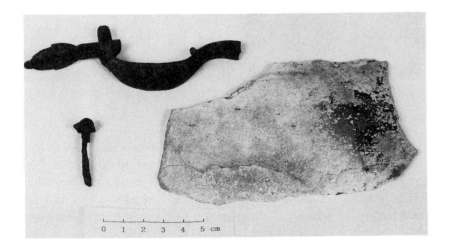

Fig. 6.45. Lead sheet, nail, and trigger guard, the latter found eroding into the sea from a small cache in Structure 1, KfDd-4, George Henry Island 1 (photo: R. Auger/Laval University).

Fig. 6.46. Aerial view of Cape Haven whaling station, view east.

Fig. 6.47. Corner of main structure at Cape Haven showing large paving stones and sea-washed wood remains and driftwood. The Cape Haven whaling station was used as a whaling and walrus hunting station for several decades at the end of the 19th and early 20th centuries. Inuit were hired to help hunt and staff the rendering operation on land. Remains of some of the heavy machinery used still exists at the site.

CAPE HAVEN WHALING STATION (KfDb-1). The whaling and trading station known to Inuit as *Singaijaq* on the south side of William Peninsula near Cape Haven, Cyrus Field Bay, was visited briefly during a helicopter survey. This site was visited several years ago by Douglas Stenton with Iqaluit elders, who retrieved a whaling harpoon gun here.

Our visit provides further documentation on this important site, which was occupied by various Scottish and English whaling concerns during the late 19th and early 20th centuries. The site covers several hundred square meters of bedrock barely above sea level between a small pond and the sea. Its most obvious features are three huge iron tanks, two large

Fig. 6.48. Anne Henshaw and Lynda Gullason inspecting Inuit tentrings at the Cape Haven station. The remains of Inuit camps at this site probably date to recent times as well as to the period when the station was active. Later visits were occasioned by Inuit desire to obtain useful raw materials from the huge stores of European materials abandoned here after the station closed, as Inuit had done previously for hundreds of years at Kodlunarn Island. Huge iron rendering kettles and sea mammal oil storage tanks decorate the site.

iron kettles, machinery parts, pipes, barrel hoop iron of various sizes, and heavy chain. A large building foundation with several construction phases and adjacent slab pavements occupy the center of the site, flanked by smaller slab and boulder features. A boulder platform has been built up as a high-tide dock. European objects of all descriptions and sizes—industrial and domestic—are strewn over the barren bedrock surface, at the bottom of ponds, and in shallow turf deposits in the central occupation area. Most are of European materials and types, but some, like an Inuit-style iron walrus harpoon found on the wave-washed face of the ledge, indicate Inuit influence if not Inuit origin. The site is covered with wood—both local lumber and driftwood—whose deposition pattern suggests that storm seas occasionally wash over the entire site. Great volumes of bone materials, mostly of seal and walrus but also including whale and caribou, are found everywhere. The site is extremely productive archeologically. Our activities were confined to mapping, testing, and sampling small finds. In addition to the European remains, Inuit-style tentrings are found, some of which appear to be outbuildings to the main foundation and may have been occupied by Inuit station employees; other tentrings that occur in the middle of the station "plaza" seem to be post-European Inuit occupations. These rings also contain rich deposits of bone and European artifacts, including trade beads.

As a small, well-preserved whaling station, Cape Haven offers excellent potential for archeological research, both into the operation of a commercial establishment and as a locus for European-Inuit contact and cultural exchange. Its value as a research site is greatly enhanced by its small size. Unlike whaling stations like Kekkerton, Cape Haven could (and should) be excavated completely. The rapid pace of erosion of its exposed and thinly buried deposits calls for urgent archeological attention.

Fig. 6.49. Iron nauluk, based on traditional Inuit design, with a chunk of weathered and sawn ivory found eroding from the bank into the sea at the Cape Haven site.

Project Summary: Culture History

During a few days in 1981 and one month each in 1990 and 1991, we located and documented about 75 archeological sites (see site list and maps) in southeastern Frobisher Bay and Cyrus Field Bay. Unfortunately we had no time en route from Labrador to Iqaluit to survey Resolution Island, Gabriel Strait. These sites contained 95 distinct archeological components, including 2 Historic European, 7 Frobisher sites/mines, 51 recent Inuit, 15 Thule, 18 Dorset, and 2 Pre-Dorset, covering the full 4000-year range of human occupation of the Eastern Arctic. (See table 6.2.)

Because the 1981 survey had indicated the presence of prehistoric and historic Inuit sites in Countess of Warwick Sound, our primary objective in 1990 and 1991 was to amplify this survey and extend it into other areas of the sound and adjacent regions. Specific tasks included determining prospects for developing a culture history outline for the outer bay region, locating and sampling selected sites, developing preliminary site conservation profiles, and assessing geological and environmental data sources. In terms of Frobisher studies we planned to explore for Frobisher sites and mines and to search for 16th–19th-century Inuit sites that could be targeted for contact studies beginning with the Frobisher period and proceeding through the European whaling era to the modern day.

Our survey data allow us to present a number of preliminary conclusions concerning Inuit culture history, results of historical archeology of Kodlunarn Island having been presented in the previous chapter. The first and most obvious result of the regional survey is that the outer reaches of Frobisher Bay have very few sites of Pre-Dorset, Transitional, and Early Dorset cultures. Except for a few sites placed well above the active shorelines, like Cape Sarah Neck, all have been lost to the combined forces of submergence and erosion. The decreasing frequency of sites from modern to Pre-Dorset times suggests that site destruction and shoreline submergence has been progressive and active for at least the past 4000 years; we may not expect to find many early sites left in the outer coast region. However, in contrast to the absence of early Paleoeskimo sites, there is a relative abundance of late Paleoeskimo sites of Middle-Late Dorset times consisting of large sodhouse villages with thick middens (often lacking bone) and spring/fall tent camp settlements. Almost all these Dorset sites are undergoing extensive shorefront erosion, and many are in terminal stages of loss, as illustrated at Kuyait, Kamaiyuk, and Willows Island 2. Others (e.g., Itilikjuak) are entirely preserved and contain evidence—though often without much bone preservation—of an entire short-term occupation Dorset village. Most of these Dorset sites date to the latter part of the Middle Dorset period or to early Late Dorset times (ca. A.D. 500–1200).

One of the surprising results of the survey is the relative scarcity of early Neoeskimo sites ca. A.D. 1000–1300. While we know Early (A.D. 1000–1300) and Developed Thule (A.D. 1300–1600) people occupied the inner reaches of Frobisher Bay at Crystal II (Collins 1950) and Peale Point (Stenton 1987), sites of these periods are rare in Countess of Warwick Sound. Traces of these settlements have been found as early components at Kuyait and Kamaiyuk, but the limited number of sites with abundant baleen—a period indicator for early Thule occupations—and absence of summer sites with "Thule type" (i.e., heavy rock) stone contruction points toward limited early Thule presence here. It seems that the primary locus of early Thule whaling was in other areas such as the Iqaluit region that are more frequented by whales, and perhaps in Loks Land and other seaward locations.

We have already noted the presence of many Late Thule and Historic Inuit winter villages dating to the period A.D. 1400–1900 which contain abundant evidence of Elizabethan materials, presumably of Frobisher and Davis origin, and later materials dating to the 19th-century whaling era. But in general, it seems that the Countess of Warwick Sound and adjacent regions of Frobisher Bay were not highly productive whaling regions, which no doubt accounts for the absence of both Thule and European whaling sites, the latter having been conducted primarily out of Cyrus Field Bay. Finally, we noted the impact of large 19th–20th-century Inuit occupations in nearly every available location in our survey region. Many of these sites were visited by Hall, who noted a large Inuit population in the 1860s. At this time these groups were becoming accommodated to European whaling activities, and this more than any other factor probably accounts for the presence of this large outer bay population aggregate.

As noted previously, traditional Inuit economy in the outer regions of Frobisher Bay today is based primarily on caribou, seal, and walrus, and we found this to be the case for Inuit sites of the past

Fig. 6.50. Kamaiyuk Houses 3 and 4 showing whalebone and collapsing walls. The fronts of all six Kamaiyuk houses are being destroyed by wave and ice erosion.

200 to 300 years. Earlier sites dating to the Late Thule/Early Inuit period, however, contain baleen and whalebone. Finally, the absence of parallels in artifact types and house forms and the absence of exchange of lithic raw materials suggest that early Inuit groups of southeast Baffin throughout their 4000-year history had little contact with Inuit groups south of Hudson Strait in Labrador and Ungava. Dorset sites in particular were found to have western rather than southern connections and contained no Ramah chert or Labrador Dorset tool styles. Likewise, Labrador Dorset and Thule sites contain few materials of East Baffin origin.

Site Conservation and Geological Observations

While Frobisher Bay has been the subject of previous archeological studies, to date all of these efforts have been located in the inner bay regions surrounding Iqaluit. In these areas archeological sites have been preserved by a regime of geological uplift resulting from the continuing effects of postglacial land adjustment following glacial melting and ice retreat from the coast. In contrast to the "uplift positive" inner bay region, outer Frobisher Bay, like other coastal regions of northern Labrador and eastern Baffin, reached its maximum relative uplift several thousands of years ago. Since then, rising relative sea levels have taken a heavy toll on archeological sites.

As noted above, virtually all archeological sites found in 1981, 1990, and 1991 have suffered attrition to one degree or another from coastal submergence and erosion. Erosion is not limited only to the earliest Inuit/Eskimo sites, but is severely impacting Frobisher and historic period sites as well. Erosion appears to have removed all but the barest traces of Baffin's earliest peoples—the 4000-year-old Pre-Dorset culture, and artifact-rich middens of 2000-year-old Dorset culture are toppling into the sea at an alarming rate. Thule sites have lost most of their middens, and many house entrances and front walls have been destroyed. Even 19th- and 20th-century Inuit sites are slipping into the sea, while the Hall bloom from Lookout Island was found virtually in the "landwash," about to be carried off by waves or spring ice. Clearly, cultural resources of the outer Frobisher Bay region are an endangered resource whose loss will make it impossible to recover information on Inuit and European culture history from this formerly densely populated area of southeast Baffin.

An unusual and disturbing discovery is that site erosion appears to have increased substantially during recent years. Arctic archeological sites are particularly sensitive indicators of changes in rates of submergence and coastal erosion, because they tend to be situated directly at the coast and their ages can be determined with precision. Research in northern Labrador and southeast Baffin Island shows that even the most recent archeological sites are being

Fig. 6.51. Recent Inuit tentring near "Best's Bulwark" half-eroded into the sea.

rapidly eroded. The probable causes of this phenomenon are higher tidal amplitudes and increased frequency of fall storms whose high waves and swells attack archeological sites most violently when they are not protected by shore ice. These observations suggest the danger of increased rates of loss of archeological resources on submergent northern coasts in the future. They also suggest that studies should be directed at the sensitive archeological site/sea level interface to see if data from these sites can provide a new means of investigating climatic and sea-state changes reflecting broader patterns of global change.

In conclusion, our preliminary surveys show that the outer coastal region of Frobisher Bay has a rich but distinctly endangered set of archeological resources. There is ample evidence of a full range of human occupation for the past 4000 years from early Paleoeskimo times to the modern day. Most Pre-Dorset sites have been lost to submergence and erosion, but Dorset and Neoeskimo sites are abundant and can be expected to reveal much about the prehistory and early history of this unknown region. Inuit sites dating to the Frobisher era are also common and even before excavation reveal traces of Elizabethan material culture. It seems certain, therefore, that at least the Inuit part of the twin goals of the Frobisher project—historical archeology of the Frobisher voyages and impact of early English expeditions on Inuit culture history in Baffin Island—can be achieved with a high degree of success.

Acknowledgments

Funding for 1990 and 1991, the first two years of a planned multiyear project, came from the Smithsonian's Scholarly Studies Program and the Arctic Studies Center. The Iqaluit Research Center (Bob Longworth/Science Council of the Northwest Territories and his associates) provided assistance in the form of planning and logistics support, radio scheds, and living accommodation. Initial project coordination in Iqaluit was also assisted by Bruce Rigby, then of Arctic College (Iqaluit Campus), and Iqaluit residents Bruce Hulen, Pauloosie Pishuktie, Pauloosie Kilabuk, Harry Kilabuk, Al Rigby, Mary Ellen Thomas, and others. Assistance from the Iqaluit Town Council (Kathryn Garven), Elders Council, Iqaluit Coast Guard, Department of Transportation, and Sealift personnel was much appreciated. Special thanks are due to Bill McKenzie and Bryan Pearson for help with local transportation and equipment storage, and to the Inuit families at Minguktoo, Tungait, Gold Cove, and Kuyait who provided information and support for our work in their territory. Special thanks are due to Karen Moran and Kim Wells for administrative assistance, and to Britt Williams, Julie Permutter, Marcia Bakry, Réginald Auger, Lynda Gullason, and the Canadian Museum of Civilization for scientific illustrations and photographs. We gratefully acknowledge Stearns A Morse for the loan of the research vessel *Pitsiulak* to the Smithsonian Institution.

Fig. 6.52. 1990 field team. Back row, left to right: Lynda Gullason, Jim Walters, Sophie Morse, Ned Searles, Eric Loring, Darrell Kaufman, Réginald Auger; front row: Scott Biggin, Pauloosie Pishuktie, Anne Henshaw (out of focus: Perry Colbourne and Bill Fitzhugh). Also present for part of the season were Charles Arnold, Robert Ehrenreich, Garman Harbottle, Donald Hogarth, Robert McGhee, Susan Rowley, and James A. Tuck.

Fig. 6.53. 1991 field team. Back row, left to right: Lynda Gullason, William Fitzhugh, Ooleetoa Pishuktie, Kim Gardener, Patrick Saltonstall, Dosia Laeyendecker, Daniel Odess, Michael Bradford; front, left to right: Pauloosie Pishuktie, Sophie Morse, Ned Searles, Anne Henshaw, Jeanette Smith. Missing: Skipper Perry Colbourne, Juta Ipeelie.

We also thank our 1990 boat team: *Pitsiulak* skipper Perry Colbourne, mate Sophie Morse, and guide Pauloosie Pishuktie; field directors Anne Henshaw (Harvard) and Lynda Gullason (McGill), and assistants Scott Biggin, Eric Loring, and Ned Searles; geologists Darrell Kaufman and Jim Walters of the Institute of Arctic and Alpine Research, University of Colorado; archeologist Robert Ehrenreich (National Security Council/Washington); geologist and Frobisher historian, Donald Hogarth (Ottawa University); chemist and dating specialist Garman Harbottle (Brookhaven National Laboratory); historical sites archeologist Réginald Auger (Laval University); and anthropologist Susan Rowley (University of Alberta) and her amautiq-swaddled son Jason Kiuvik Fareidon Dowlatabati. The 1991 field team included Juta Ipeelie as a *Pitsiulak* assistant, and excavations crews of Auger, Gullason, and Henshaw, noted above, assisted by Michael Bradford, Kim Gardner, Dosia Laeyendecker, Daniel Odess, Ooleetoa Pishuktie, Patrick Saltonstall, Edmund Searles, and Jeannette Smith; and field consultants Davin Ala, Donald Hogarth, Darrell Kaufman, and Bill Manley.

Fig. 7.1. A fanciful depiction of a Frobisher mine in the third expedition, by Aa (1706:ff. 63), recording European misconceptions of the 18th century, including the use of the double-tined pick, underground mines, and the general topography of the area. Published with permission of the British Library.

7

Mining and Metallurgy of the Frobisher Ores

Gold was the principal incentive for the second and third voyages of Martin Frobisher. On first landing in the "New Land" (July 20, 1576; Little Hall's Island, entrance to Frobisher Bay), Robert Garrard collected from the cobblestone pavement "a blacke stonne as great as a halfe pennye loafe" (Lok ca. 1581:2R–2V). Subsequently, this specimen was presented to Michael Lok, director of the enterprise, who had it analyzed by several assayers (M. Lok in Stefansson and McCaskill 1938, 2:79–90). Samples, some of which returned 4 oz Au/cwt (2400 ppm), kindled the interest of the speculative royalty and public, and were responsible for the second voyage, mainly fielded for prospecting (Ellis 1816), and the third voyage, sent out to mine and return at least 800 tons of "ore" to England ("Instructions" in Stefansson and McCaskill 1938, 2:155–161).

The first voyage was of normal size for an early arctic expedition (2 ships, 1 pinnace, 36 men). The second voyage was large (3 ships, 145 men). The third voyage was the largest arctic voyage of all time (15 ships, more than 400 men). Names, assigned ships, and occupations are listed by the author in appendix 1 of this volume. The Cathay Company directed, through appointed commissioners, the financial affairs of the voyagers (Shammas 1975).

Frobisher's landfalls in the Canadian arctic islands (including the exact location of the Countess of Warwick Mine and three coal deposits) were established by Captain C. F. Hall in 1861 (Hall 1864). The most complete compendium of all works concerning the three expeditions is by Stefansson and McCaskill (1938). Geology is described by Blackadar (1967) and Hogarth et al. (1985), the "ores" by Roy (1937) and Hogarth (1985), and the contained precious metals by Hogarth and Loop (1986).

Useful data were found in an anonymous criticism of Frobisher, partly written in Michael Lok's hand (Lok ca. 1581). Further information has been drawn from three unpublished manuscripts (Lok 1578a; Lok et al. 1576–78, 1578–81) containing accounts of the Cathay Company that were used as testimony before the Exchequer. Recently, these accounts have been transcribed by McDermott (1984).

This paper will be concerned with mining and metallurgy in Baffin Island and vicinity; it will not touch upon the "small sayes" in London or the metallurgical plant established at Dartford, except in an indirect manner.

DONALD D. HOGARTH

Personnel

Mining, during the second expedition, was conducted on a modest scale. There were eight miners, seven from the Forest of Dean and one from Cornwall. On occasion, these numbers were enhanced by mariners. In addition, there were three assayers ("goldfiners") with Jonas Shutz, an experienced German metallurgist, in charge. With him were Gregory Bona, another German metallurgist, and Robert Denham, a London goldsmith (Lok et al. 1576–78).

During the third voyage, mining and metallurgy were pursued on a much larger scale. After conflicts with Frobisher, Shutz refused to participate and was replaced as chief assayer by Robert Denham, who had assisted Shutz in London throughout the winter and was granted a patent of £50 a year to practice

metallurgy (Lok ca. 1581:12). He was accompanied by William Humphrey Jr., John Lambell, Robert Peacock, and Gregory Bona. Bona may have been prospector as well as assayer because, distinct from the others, he is listed as *goldfinder* in the second and third voyages (Lok et al. 1576–78:143; Lok 1578a:19) but *goldfiner* in the second voyage (Lok et al. 1576–78:111). At times Edmond Stafford, Edward Fenton, and Frobisher, himself, helped in the assaying. However, Fenton's journal (Kenyon 1980/81) suggests that Denham alone was competent to part gold from silver. For miners, Frobisher recruited 147 men, mainly from Cornwall, but many were inexperienced in this profession. Denham appears to have been their supervisor and Edward Sellman acted as their paymaster (Lok 1578a; Lok et al. 1578–81).

TABLE 7.1. Tonnages of ore shipped in the third voyage (1578)

Ships	Localities and estimated weights (tons)							Official weight (tons)
	Countess of Sussex Mine	Beare Sound	Denham's Mount	Queen's Foreland	Countess of Warwick Mine	Winter's Furnace	Fenton's Fortune	
COMPANY'S SHIPS								
Ayde	20	110	–	–	–	–	–	132
Gabriel	–	20	–	–	–	–	–	9
Michael	–	20	–	–	–	–	–	13
Judith	80	–	–	–	–	–	–	60
COMMISSIONED SHIPS								
Thomas Allen	100	60	–	–	–	–	–	166.2
Anne Francis	–	–	–	130	–	–	–	116.0
Hopewell	–	–	140	–	–	–	–	136.1
Moon of Fowey [Foy]	–	–	–	100	–	–	–	98.2
Francis of Fowey [Foy]	80	–	–	–	50	–	–	126.9
Thomas of Ipswich[a]	–	–	–	–	–	–	–	–
Beare Leicester	–	–	100	–	–	–	–	84.0
NONCOMISSIONED SHIPS								
Salomon of Weymouth	60	60	–	–	10	–	–	100.4
Armonell of Exeter	85	–	–	–	5	5	5	94.2
Emanuel of Bridgwater[b]	30	60	20	–	–	–	–	–
Bark Dennis[c]	–	–	–	–	–	–	–	–
TOTALS	455	330	260	230	65	5	5	1136

SOURCES: Estimated tonnages from E. Sellman (Stefansson and McCaskill 1938, 2: 69–70); Official weights from Lok et al. 1576–78:211; Lok et al. 1578–81:67–85, 92.
a. Deserted, August 8.
b. Discharged ore in Ireland, ca. November 1.
c. Sunk near Resolution Island, July 2.

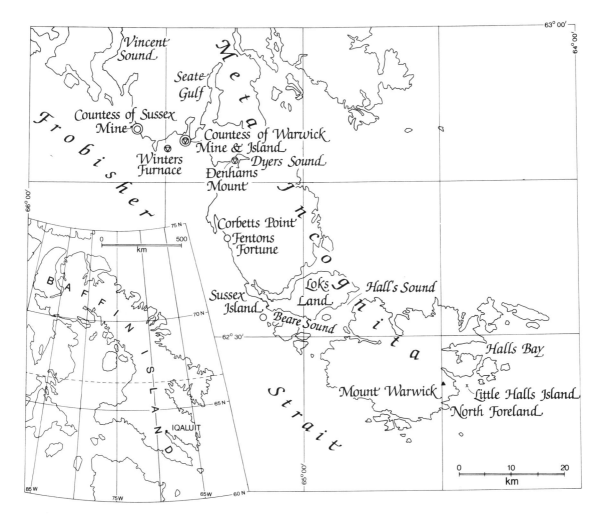

Fig. 7.2. Location map showing established and probable mines (double circles), approximate position of other mines (open circles) and coal deposits (triangles). Names are those of the 16th century (old script) as interpreted by the author from manuscript data. Published sources include Hall (1864), Stefansson and McCaskill (1938), and Kenyon (1980/81).

Mining

THE MINES

"Ore" in the second expedition was supplied by a single mine (the Countess of Warwick Mine) and in the third expedition, by seven mines (table 7.1). Of these, the locations of the Countess of Warwick and Countess of Sussex mines only can be regarded as firmly established, although it is highly likely that the location of the Winter's Furnace Mine, given below, is also correct. *Fenton's Fortune* of Kenyon (1975b:145) is a doubtful mine and cannot represent the *Fenton's Fortune* in Fenton's journal (Kenyon 1980/81), which is on the opposite side of Countess of Warwick Sound.

Figure 7.2 shows the location of the mines and coal deposits on the north side of Frobisher Bay ("Frobisher Strait"). The latter have been pinpointed from information in Hall (1864) and observations in 1990. The mines have been located from published and unpublished data, as well as personal observation.

COUNTESS OF WARWICK MINE,
COUNTESS OF WARWICK ISLAND
(PRESENT-DAY KODLUNARN ISLAND)
Location: 8-hectare island; 62°49'N, 65°26'W
1/250,000 NTS map sheet: 25I–15L (Loks Land)

The "ore" returned to England from the second voyage weighed 158.4 tons (Lok et al. 1576–78, 1578–81). It was essentially derived from the Count-

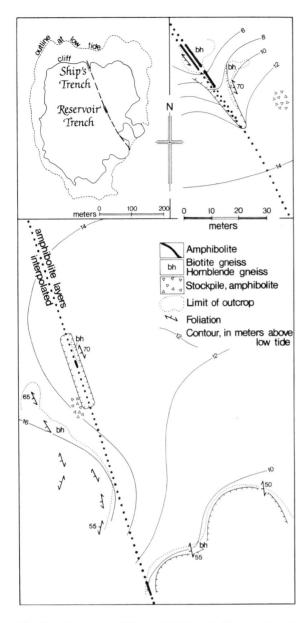

Fig. 7.3. Countess of Warwick Mine, Kodlunarn Island. Top left, outline of island, showing location of amphibolite payzone; top right, ship's trench; bottom, reservoir trench. Survey by Walter Gibbins and Donald Hogarth, 1983.

"payzone" is in the southeast where a solid layer attains a thickness of 0.5 m. Details of the "mine" are shown in figure 7.3.

The most northerly trench appears to have been the original excavation. A spy planted on the second expedition by the newly appointed Spanish ambassador to England (Don Bernardino de Mendoza) reported that, at departure from the island in 1577, this trench was three fathoms deep, the approximate depth today. No mention was made of the other trench (Hume 1894:567–9). From this we may conclude the north trench was essentially finished in the second voyage and subsequent mining was confined to the southerly and more interior trench.

The original excavation, the northerly or "ship's trench" of Hall (1864, 2:150), is about 20 m long. It widens to 13 m and deepens to 6 m in the north end. The later trench, the "reservoir trench" of Hall, is 26 m long, 4 m wide, and up to 1.6 m deep. Hall showed that the ship's trench could have been used as a dry dock as well as a mine, but there is no evidence that the reservoir trench was ever used for water collection.

Remains of two stockpiles of "ore" are evident at the northeast end of the ship's trench and the southwest end of the reservoir trench. The stockpile at the ship's trench may have been a central storage depot for ore from various nearby localities, whereas that of the reservoir trench, being further inland, was probably derived from the adjacent trench alone. This conclusion is consistent with chemical and mineralogical similarities of a specimen collected in situ with two specimens collected from the old stockpile.

Precious metal values from the two trenches (derived in situ and from stockpiles) were low. For example, the three specimens of "ore" from the reservoir trench contained 130 ± 40 ppb Ag and 11 ± 3 ppb Au (Hogarth and Loop 1986). These values are similar to those of average ultrabasic rock (80 ppb Ag, 11.4 ppb Au) and slightly higher than those of the Earth's crust (Boyle 1979:16, 38). The original 16th-century assays were approximately 10^5 times higher in silver and 10^4 times higher in gold than the new values. In discussing the reason for these discrepancies Hogarth and Loop concluded that they "are probably due mainly to mistakes in analytical procedure by the Elizabethan assayers." Very likely appreciable silver was inadvertently added as argentiferous lead during the fusion stage.

ess of Warwick Mine, although a small portion may have been taken from Beare Sound. The same mine produced another 65 tons in the third voyage (table 7.1).

"Ore" was taken from two aligned trenches, put down on a steeply dipping layer of hornblende-rich rock (amphibolite), which transects the island for 350 m in a NNW direction. The widest part of this

COUNTESS OF SUSSEX MINE, FROBISHER BAY

Location: small peninsula; 62°50'N, 65°36'W

1/250,000 NTS map sheet: 25I–15L (Loks Land)

The Countess of Sussex Mine was the largest Frobisher mine, accounting for some 450 tons or 30% of the ore returned to the British Isles in 1578 (E. Sellman in Stefansson and McCaskill 1938, 2:69–70). Since that date, the location has remained a mystery. However, manuscript data suggested the mine was situated on mainland Baffin, about 10 km WNW of Kodlunarn Island, Frobisher's center of operations.

In 1985, this part of the coast was carefully searched by helicopter and a "notch" in the rock, the only possible location of former workings, was examined on the ground. The "notch" can be followed for 450 m, and the surrounding landscape closely resembles that portrayed in the old reports. The "notch" overlies closely spaced layers of dark amphibole-rich rock, the widest about 6 m across and containing solid black layers up to 3 m thick. A precipitous hole at the south end looks particularly suspicious as a man-made excavation.

While a quick search did not reveal any stockpiles of "ore," evidence for this being the Countess of Sussex Mine was provided in the rather distinctive bed rock (hornblendite) composed of about 60% hornblende, 20% diopside, 10% forsterite, 5% hypersthene and 5% calcite and opaque minerals. It is similar to a specimen collected from a former Frobisher storage bin in Dartford, England, and others collected at Fort Dún-an-Óir, Ireland, where one of Frobisher's vessels was wrecked on return from the third voyage (Hogarth 1989). However, the ore bears little resemblance to the ore at Kodlunarn Island. The adjacent layers of amphibole gneiss (60% hornblende, 30% plagioclase, 10% diopside) may represent the "mixed ore," said to be closely associated.

In 1990, during the Smithsonian's expedition to Baffin Island, further evidence of mining was found on another peninsula 300 m south. "Black ore" had been dug from a shallow trench, intermittently put down along a length of 77 m. Two closely spaced pay zones, interlayered with hornblende gneiss, attained maximum thicknesses of 1.2 m. The ore, hornblende interspersed with microscopic grains of diopside, closely matched a rock type collected from Frobisher's storage site at Dartford.

Analyses showed very little precious metals. Gold was less than 1 ppb in both the "black ore" and surrounding hornblende gneiss. This is less than the crustal abundance of 3.5 ppb quoted by Boyle (1979:16). Silver was less than 1000 ppb compared to the crustal abundance of 75 ppb (ibid.:16).

Contrary to public opinion the "ores" were *not* fool's gold (pyrite). The confusion probably originated with the word marcasite (variously spelled *marquesite* and *markesyte*) used by assayers to describe rock collected in the first voyage (M. Lok in Stefansson and McCaskill 1938, 2:83–84). Elsewhere the rock is described (many times, contemporary descriptions) as *black ore*. The present author found surprisingly little sulfide mineralization in both the ore stockpiled at Dartford, England, and in the Baffin Island area. This absence, incidently, may account for the unusually low content of precious metals in a rock of this general composition (ultrabasic rock).

WINTER'S FURNACE MINE

Location: Newland Island; 62°48'N, 65°30'W

1/250,000 NTS map sheet: 25I–15L (Loks Land)

Newland Island, Winter's Furnace in Frobisher's day, "an Ilande verie apte to ancour bye," is a place of historic significance. It was here, on July 22, 1578, that Master Robert Wolfall "preached a godly sermon" and conducted the first Protestant service in North America (Kenyon 1980), and it was also here, on August 16, 1578, that four of Frobisher's company, who probably had succumbed to scurvy, were ceremoniously laid to rest. "Black ore" had been discovered by Edward Fenton, in mid-July 1578. However, in less than a week that mine was abandoned. The men loaded 5 tons into the *Armonell* (E. Sellman in Stefansson and McCaskill 1938, 2:70).

Loose coal, no doubt used to fuel an assay furnace, was discovered on the north side of the island by Hall in 1861 and relocated during the 1990 Smithsonian expedition. The largest deposit covered an area 35 × 20 m, a smaller deposit lay immediately northwest. To the southeast was an 18-m notch in the overburden, possibly marking the location of Fenton's Mine. On the seaward side were blocks and fragments of a hornblende-rich black rock, probably the remains of an old spoil heap. Similar rock, composed of hornblende, hypersthene, and plagioclase, has been observed in Frobisher's ore at Dartford.

Loose coal, on a peninsula in Victoria Bay (Dyer's Passage of Frobisher) was also reported by Hall, and presumably marks the location of another furnace. The deposit was pinpointed during the 1990 Smithsonian expedition but search for the Denham's Mount Mine, which must have been nearby (fig. 7.2 gives the approximate location), was unsuccessful.

A representative collection of typical specimens from each mine, with precise locations, was assembled by Robert Denham during the third voyage but, unfortunately, never reached England (Kenyon 1980/81; Lok ca. 1581).

MINING METHODS

By all reports, mining methods were primitive. Open pits were excavated by sheer man power and abandoned when the rock refused to yield. The Countess of Warwick Mine, the first producer, "fayled being so hard stone to breke" (E. Sellman in Stefansson and McCaskill 1938, 2:70) and the Fenton's Fortune Mine was abandoned because the ore was "founde to lie so uncerteinlie and crabbedlie to gett" (Kenyon 1980/81:190). For leverage, loosening and comminution the miners relied on weighty *iron crowbars* (some to 30 lb), *sledges* (some to 20 lb), *pickaxes* (some to 8 lb) and *wedges* (some to 8 lb). An inventory of mining equipment is given in the Exchequer papers and is presented in table 7.2. A separate inventory for the cargo of the *Ayde* in the third voyage (Commissioners in Stefansson and McCaskill 1938, 2:165–66) also includes one drill, one gauge and four chisels. Another equipment list for the third voyage appears in the inventory of the *Judith* (Fenton 1578:8R), which duplicates certain items in the list of table 7.2. Notable additions and differences are: 20 while [wheel] barrows, 20 hand barrows, 300 helves for pick axes, as well as 120 trenchers and 12 sledges of 24 lb each [instead of 20 lb]. Similar tools are described in Agricola (1950:148–53) and are pictured in figure 7.4.

Of special interest are the large wedges. Postlethwaite (1976:70 f.n.) described period wedges in England with chains attached, and such wedges may have been used in Baffin Island. A method used widely in the 16th century for hard-rock mining was *plug-and-feather* or *stope-and-feather* (Raistrick and Jennings 1983:67; Agricola, 1950:118), where wedges ("stopes" or "plugs") were driven into a

TABLE 7.2. Miners' tools appearing in the bills of lading

A. Second Voyage
 Bills of John Fyshe[r], smith, and others
  140 tools (448 lb net) including:
   11 iron crow bars
   6 sledges
   96 shovels and spades
   an unspecified number of wedges, mattocks, hammers and pickers
   120 baskets to carry ore
   452 lb Spanish iron and 56 lb steel to fashion miners' tools
   4 leather bags [for drinking water]

B. Third Voyage.
 1. Bill of Geoffrey Turvile and Richard Bowland
   120 shovels
   36 spades
   100 mattocks
   800 baskets

 2. Bill of Richard Lane, smith
   10 iron crow bars of 30 lb each
   10 iron sledges of 20 lb each
   10 iron sledges of 10 lb each
   35 iron wedges of 8 lb each
   34 iron wedges of 5 lb each
   30 pick axes of 8 lb each
   32 small plate wedges
   8 iron hoopes

 3. Bill of Robert Crokey, smith
   81 pick axes of 7.1 lb each
   64 iron wedges of 5.0 lb each
   30 small picks of 3.6 lb each
   4 iron wedges ⎤
   24 iron plates │
   1 'scrap' [scraper?] ├ 568 lb total
   36 great hammers │
   3 small hammers ⎦
   12 iron crow bars of 30 lb each
   24 iron wedges of 7 lb each

 4. Bill of Edward Sellman for purchase at Plymouth
   77 pickaxes
   110 iron wedges
   10 sledges
   30 shovels and other [unspecified] miner's tools

 5. Bill of William Wilson
   36 1-gallon, leather bags ['jacks'] for drinking water

SOURCES: Second voyage, Lok et al. 1576–78:104, 120; third voyage, Lok 1578a:9R–12R.

crevice or hole drilled along the grain and plates ("feathers") forced into the rock between them. All of these implements are included in the company's inventory (table 7.2). Kenyon (1975b:143) illustrates chisel marks at a crevice on the side of a trench in one of the old pits, perhaps an abandoned plug-and-feather operation. A *mattock* (a small pick) had its iron head fashioned into a hammer at one end and pick or axe at the other. *Pikes* were used to pry and loosen soft rock. A *picker* was a long, narrow chisel that was held in one hand and a

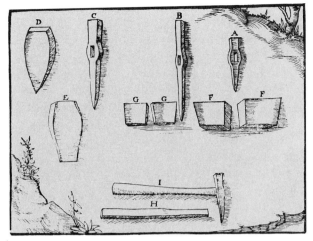

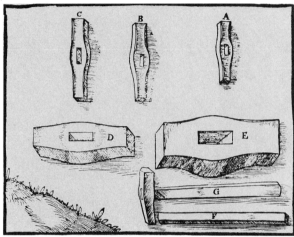

Fig. 7.4. 16th-century mining tools. From Agricola (1561), in a private collection. Upper frame: *A, B, C, D,* pick heads of various sizes (*B* and *C* are ca. 45 cm long); *H,* pick handle; *I,* assembled head and handle; *E, F,* wedges; *G,* iron plate. Lower frame: *A, B, C,* hammer heads of various sizes; *F,* hammer handle; *G,* assembled head and handle; *D, E,* sledge heads. *E* (ca. 30 cm long) was used in combination with pick *D* (upper frame) to break especially hard rock (like that at Baffin Island!).

hammer blow dealt to it with the other. It was used to remove loose rock from a face. At this time, *picks* were tined at one end only and, when combined with the hammer, were particularly useful in loosening soft or fractured rock (see fig. 7.5).

The tools needed frequent sharpening and case hardening, and this imposed a heavy demand on the blacksmiths. Thus we find two blacksmiths grouped with the mining men (in addition to a gunsmith) in the second voyage (Lok et al. 1576–78:112, 143) and four blacksmiths in the third voyage (Lok

1578a:16; Lok et al. 1578–81:160). In preparation for the third voyage, orders were sent to Robert Hopkins for tools for the blacksmiths forge, Giles Fleming for two anvils weighing 2 cwt each, William Villars for 50 chalders of sea coals, Richard Tomkins for another 30 chalders of sea coals, and to John Roberts for seven pairs of bellows (Lok 1578a:10R–11R). Part of the coal and perhaps some of the bellows were used in the assay operations.

As far as is definitely known, neither gunpowder nor quicklime were used to fracture rock. In England, explosives were introduced in mines about 1650 (Shaw 1975:20; Raistrick and Jennings 1983:133). The old method used to break rock in mines of Germany, that of firing a face and then dousing the scorching rock with cold water, was probably used sparingly, if at all, because of fuel shortage.

Metallurgy

The technology of fire assaying was well advanced by the time of the voyages. Available publications included Georgius Agricola (1950), Lazarus Ercker (1951) and Vannoccio Biringuccio (1942). Jonas Shutz, chief metallurgist in the second voyage, was from an active mining region in present-day East Germany and must have been acquainted with this technology.

At Baffin Island, the metallurgical process probably involved (1) crucible fusion with the aid of a flux and metallic lead, whereby the precious metals were dissolved in lead, which sank to the bottom of the molten charge and were separated, when cool, as a lead button, with a sharp blow of the hammer, (2) cupellation of the lead button, permitting the lead to diffuse into the cupel wall, the silver and gold remaining as bullion bead, (3) parting of gold and silver, by acid (HNO_3) dissolution of silver, and (4) precipitation of silver as insoluble $AgCl_2$ by addition of seawater. In other words, fire assaying at the end of the 16th century was essentially the same process as that of today. The technology is discussed by Agricola (1950:218–65) and Ercker (1951:19–181).

The following bills of lading, "for Implements and other necessaries for the mynes of [the] New Land," pertain to the third voyage (Lok 1578a:10R–12R):

(1) To Oliver Skinner, for iron bars and plates of various sorts, which he delivered to John Fisher, smith, to construct 3 iron furnaces for small assays.

Fig. 7.5. Etching in the anonymous Mining Laws and Statutes of Bohemia (Anon. 1616), copied from an unidentified 16th-century woodcut, showing curved, single-tined picks, weighty sledges, and the combined pick and sledge operation of breaking rock in a European mine. From a private collection.

(2) To John Gunne for iron plates, which he delivered to John Fisher, smith, to make [the same?] 3 iron furnaces.

(3) To John Fisher, smith, for iron work for construction of the furnaces and procuring necessary additional material for the furnaces.

(4) To Jacob Johnson for 223 earthenware pots [crucibles?] for 8 stoves.

(5) To Jeronias [?], miner, for 2 iron stoves.

(6) To Robert Denham, goldsmith, for additives [details not specified] to make assays of the mines in the New Land.

These data indicate that materials were provided for at least three furnaces (possibly eight). The equipment of the *Judith* (Fenton 1578:7R, 8V) included 1000 lb lead (partly for crucible charge) and two balances with weights.

Lazarus Ercker illustrates an assay furnace of 1574 (fig. 7.6) which probably resembled those used in the Frobisher expeditions. It was described (Ercker 1951:22) as having a square cross-section, made of strong sheet iron, reinforced inside with iron bars, and lined with refractory clay. It could be unscrewed and dismantled into five parts.

Countess of Warwick Island must have been a major assaying center during the third voyage. Edward Fenton (Kenyon 1980/81) mentions assaying during 17 days in August 1578. The assays were from "ores" from various sites on the north and south side of the "Straits" and all of these assays were made on Countess of Warwick Island. Additional evidence is provided by the discovery of scorched brick, broken crucibles, and partly fused rock (including amphibolite and sillimanite gneiss) on the northern part of the island.

Assay furnaces were also set up on Newland Island (Winter's Furnace), Victoria Bay and possibly Sussex Island (Beare Sound). The very name Winter's Furnace suggests an assay site. It is probably identical with the locality of coal described by Charles Hall (Hall 1864, 2:77–78). As for the Sussex Island Mine, Sellman specifically mentions assays made by Denham at Beare Sound, August 14–15, complete with HNO_3 parting (Sellman 1578). "Ores" from Beare Sound and Winter's Furnace are not mentioned as those assayed at the Countess of Warwick Island in Fenton's journal (Kenyon 1980/81).

Fig. 7.6. 16th-century assay laboratory in Ercker's *Beschreibung Allerfürnemsten . . .,* reproduced from an English translation (Ercker 1951:138), with permission of the University of Chicago Press. *A* is an iron furnace, *B* an iron sheet for collecting assays, *C* an eye-protecting slit to observe the furnace in operation, *D* an acid (HNO$_3$) parting flask, *E* shows density determination of gold and silver. Assay equipment employed in the third expedition may have been similar to items *A* and *D*.

Acknowledgments

Field research was supported by Canadian Department of Indian Affairs and Northern Development (DIAND) contracts during the summers of 1983 and 1985 and by the Smithsonian Institution in 1990. Walter Gibbins (DIAND) took care of field logistics and accompanied the author to the sites in 1983 and 1985. Precious metal analyses were made by John Loop (University of Ottawa). Permission to publish was granted by the following: British Library (fig. 7.1 and ref. to Lok 1581, Sellman 1578), Huntington Library (ref. to Lok 1578a), The Marquess of Salisbury, Hatfield House, Hertfordshire (ref. to Lok 1578b), Public Record Office (table 7.2 and ref. to Lok et al. 1576–78, 1578–81), University of Chicago Press (fig. 7.6), and a private collector, who prefers to remain anonymous (figs. 7.4, 7.5). The author is indebted to H. Wiseman, Trent University, for providing a transcript of Fenton (1578), made for Walter Kenyon. The thesis of James McDermott (1984) proved very helpful in interpreting the account books of Michael Lok (Lok 1578a; Lok et al. 1576–78, 1578–81). The manuscript was typed by Julie Hayes and figures 7.2 and 7.3 were drafted by Edward Hearn.

It is regrettable that assay values or details of the methodology are not available for the second and third voyages. The Book of Register, appearing at least four times in Fenton's journal (Kenyon 1980/81), recorded all assays, but mysteriously disappeared on the homeward voyage of 1578 (Lok 1581). However, Denham reported (Lok 1578b) that the overall lading of the third voyage could be expected to average "almost an onse of gold in C [1 cwt] of ewer." This is equivalent to 20 ounces to the ton or 600 ppm, exceedingly rich ore by any standard, and further evidence of assay error made by those associated with the Company of Cathay.

8

Sixteenth-Century Ceramics from Kodlunarn Island

The following summary amplifies discussion of the 1981 ceramic finds discussed by Fitzhugh (this volume) and is confined to a small sample of ceramics recovered during a brief 1990 survey of Kodlunarn, which was limited to three days. Most of our time at Kodlunarn was spent surveying in order to understand the settlement organization. Limited test-pitting was carried out for half a day in the ship's trench, the assay office, and the area of the smithy. We also surface-collected artifacts from the eroding bank in front of the smithy, around the house foundation on the highest point of Kodlunarn, in the ship's trench, and about the western shore of Kodlunarn Island. This contribution links some of the identified ceramics to the pyrotechnological work carried out at Kodlunarn during the 16th century.

Fifty-eight ceramic fragments (table 8.1) were recovered from Kodlunarn Island and three fragments were collected from two contemporaneous Inuit sites nearby. The function of 47 fragments can be determined, but it remains conjectural for 11 others due to their smallness. The three ceramic fragments recovered from two Inuit sites are readily identifiable.

TABLE 8.1. Ceramics inventory from Kodlunarn Island and two Inuit sites

Category	No. frag.	Description	Provenience	Fig.
A	1	Utilitarian decorated vessel salmon-color, green glaze	A	8.2a
B	2	Coarse earthenware culinary vessel no glaze	B,C	8.1
	2	Utilitarian/industrial coarse earthenware, no glaze	B	
C	1	Crucible	D	8.2b
	5	Crucible with glassy surface	E,D,A	8.2c
D	4	Cupel	E,D	8.2d,f
	2	Cupel with glassy surface	E,D	8.2e
E	14	Refractory ceramic	F,D	8.3a-c
	7	Red brick	E,D	
F	11	Red tile	E,G,F	8.3d-f
	9	Unidentified brick or tile fragment	E	
G	1	Beige fabric with lead glaze and specks of iron	Lincoln Bay-1	8.6a
	2	Red fabric coarse earthenware	Napoleon Bay-1	8.6b

PROVENIENCE: A = general surface collection; B = eroding bank front of smithy; C = surface of A5 tentring; D = 1990 test pit in assay office; E = cleaning of the 1981 test pit in assay office; F = ship's trench; G = surface of A9 structure.

REGINALD AUGER

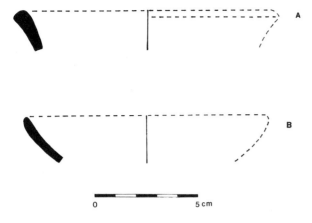

Fig. 8.1. Coarse earthenware culinary vessels, rim sherds: A, storage jar (KeDe-1:131); B, possible saucer sherd (KeDe-1:108).

Dating of these ceramics is established by their association with the Frobisher voyages, that is, the time capsule 1576–1578. The identifiable specimens are attributed to seven functional categories as described below.

A. Utilitarian Decorated Vessel

This waretype is represented by a single body fragment whose interior surface is missing (see fig. 8.2a, KeDe-1:110). It is a coarse earthenware with a salmon-colored fabric. Micaceous temper is identified in the fabric. Its outer surface shows a motif applied when the clay was still plastic and possibly represents a flower. It is finished with a dark green lead glaze on the outside.

B. Coarse Earthenware Culinary Vessel

This waretype is a coarse earthenware whose brownish orange colour fabric shows a considerable amount of mica inclusions and coarse temper. Two fragments are included; their hardness suggests that they were fired at a very high temperature.

The fragment found in the eroding bank in front of the smithy (fig. 8.1a, KeDe-1:131) has an outwardly projecting lip which thickens at the edge, and the rim flares out slightly. It is suggested that this sherd belongs to a storage jar whose rim was designed to receive a cap. The second rim sherd (fig. 8.1b, KeDe-1:108) was recovered on the surface of a

tentring on the west side of the island. Its lip thickens very slightly toward its edge and flares out. This sherd, though small, may come from a saucer. Parallel lines on the inner and outer surfaces of both sherds suggest that these utilitarian culinary vessels were made on a potter's wheel.

Two other fragments with a similar fabric are also reported in table 8.1, but their hinge-shape attributes defy any interpretation. Their hardness shows that they were fired at a very high temperature, and they are classified as culinary/industrial for they could be either a type of ceramic required in the pyrotechnology carried out at Kodlunarn Island or culinary wares. If they are from culinary wares, they have no counterparts in the 17th-century English vessel typology presented by Pope (1986). Further research on pyrotechnology might allow us to determine their function.

C. Crucible

The ores mixed in with fluxes are placed in crucibles to assay their gold and silver content. Crucibles used to assay copper are usually thicker than those used for gold and silver. Crucibles are made with either clay or ashes; those of clay vary in size and shape. Some are even made in the shape of a moderately thick scorifier (Agricola 1950:229; fig. 8.3).

Six such fragments are identified in the Kodlunarn collection (fig. 8.2b,c, KeDe-1:107,114). They are all

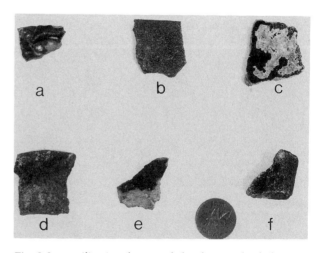

Fig. 8.2. a, utilitarian decorated sherd, green lead glaze on plastic decoration (KeDe-1:110); b, c, crucible sherds (KeDe-1:107,144); d–f, cupel sherds (KeDe-1:116-118). Note vitreous finish on c and e.

made of a grey clay and show signs of having been submitted to intensive heat. Five fragments show that a coarse grit was added to the clay. The thickness of their walls is 3 mm on average. The inner surface of five out of six fragments has a vitreous finish, while the sixth specimen is a rim fragment and has no vitreous deposition.

Blackburn's (pers. comm. April 1991) preliminary results from the microprobe and thin sectioning of the vitreous finish and the crucibles show that they have an identical composition. A mixture of quartz and clay is present on both the crucibles and their vitreous finish. The similarities in composition suggest that, although different in appearance, the vitreous finish could represent the melting at the surface of the crucibles rather than the solidification in the crucibles of the minerals in fusion. Additional support for this hypothesis is also found in the chemical composition of the vitreous finish and the black ore (amphibolite) the English were smelting. Whereas amphibolites contain iron and magnesium, those two elements are absent from the vitreous finish of these crucibles.

D. Cupel

Another object used in assaying ores is the cupel (see fig. 8.3). The cupel is a small refractory recipient, not unlike in function to a crucible, and used to refine gold or silver. It differs from the crucible in that a cupel is made from pulverized bones mixed with ashes from the previous smelts (Aitchison 1960:387).

Fig. 8.4. *a–c,* refractory ceramics (KeDe-1:120-122), note soot deposition on *c; d–f,* red tile fragments (KeDe-1:100).

Pending further analysis of the fabric, it is suggested that we have six possible cupel fragments (fig. 8.2d–f, KeDe-1:116–118). They are thick-walled fragments (5–7 mm in thickness) whose fabric is rather porous. Their density is also less than the crucible fragments discussed above. Among the six sherds studied, two have the same vitreous finish on their inside walls as observed on the crucibles. Three other fragments are portions of a base and wall. The sixth specimen is a rim sherd which shows signs of having been submitted to intensive heat.

E. Refractory Ceramic

Refractory clay or heat-resisting clay, which is relatively pure and iron-free (Rhodes 1976), is used in the manufacture of refractory parts for ovens and in the production of crucibles. Altogether 14 such pieces of refractory clay have been recovered (fig. 8.4a–c, KeDe-1:120–122). Except for three small fragments from the ship's trench, they all come from a stratigraphic context in a test pit sunk into the assay office. They are buff-colored sherds and their surface shows a rough finish. They are made of a very fine-grained clay, and the glassy sound they make when two fragments are knocked together suggests that they have been submitted to a high temperature. Moreover, convergent lines on their surfaces suggest that the object to which they belonged was not made on a potter's wheel, as was

A—SCORIFIER. B—TRIANGULAR CRUCIBLE. C—CUPEL.

Fig. 8.3. Scorifier, crucible and cupel, from Agricola (1950).

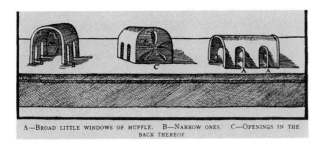

A—BROAD LITTLE WINDOWS OF MUFFLE. B—NARROW ONES. C—OPENINGS IN THE BACK THEREOF.

Fig. 8.5. Muffle, from Agricola (1950).

customary for the production of culinary vessels in 16th-century Europe. Another clue is the asymmetry of an edge fragment (5 cm long), which is thicker at one end than at the other. This feature certainly is not characteristic of mass-produced culinary vessels. Thus, the roughness of its finish and the asymmetry of the edge fragment point out that we have an irregularly shaped object rather than a vessel. Consequently, taking into consideration that it was recovered from the assay office, it is suggested that the object may have been a muffle.

Muffles (fig. 8.5) are clay objects which act as covering for the scorifiers that contain the ores being assayed; they prevent the coal dust and ashes from interfering with the assaying of the ore. They correspond roughly in size to the mouth of the furnace. "The muffle is as thick as a fairly thick earthen jar; its upper part is entire; the back has two little windows, and each side has two or three or even four, through which the heat passes into the scorifiers and melts the ore" (Agricola 1950:228). In addition, that same edge fragment also shows traces of soot on its inner and outer surfaces which could come from the combustion of coal in the furnace.

Clays used for making muffles must be very refractory (heat resistant), yet plastic enough to be modeled and, once cooked, dense, hard, and resistant to repeated thermal changes. They are reputed to become buff-colored when heated (Rhodes 1976:29).

RED BRICK. According to Agricola (1950) various types of assay furnaces were used during the 16th century. Furnaces were either made of brick, metal or clay. "Those of brick can be prepared more quickly, while those of iron are more lasting, and those of clay are more suitable" (ibid.:226). Moreover, the brick furnace must remain stationary while

the iron and the clay furnaces can be carried from one place to another. In shape, furnaces may be round or rectangular.

The documents indicate that the English used portable clay furnaces at the various mines identified in the research area, and coal deposits have been located at two mine sites. It is also possible that a semipermanent brick furnace was used at the base camp on Kodlunarn Island. In describing the mode of building an assay furnace, Agricola reported that "the one of bricks is built on a chimney-hearth which is three and half feet high; the iron one is placed in the same position, and also the one of clay" (Agricola 1950:224).

Seven brick fragments have been unearthed in the assay office, all of which are reddish orange brown. Some of them have a coarse temper, and one fragment displays traces of combustion. It is likely that these brick fragments originated from the construction of a chimney-hearth associated with a clay furnace.

F. Red Tile

Assaying at Kodlunarn was carried out in order to see if the ores to be mined could be advantageously smelted. "By tests of this kind miners can determine with certainty whether ores contain any metal in them or not" (Agricola 1950:219). Assaying differs from smelting only by the small amount of material used in the assay furnace.

Thus, earthenware tiles are part of the hardware used in assay furnaces. They are used in clay furnaces for the same purpose as a bed-plate is used in the iron assay furnace. The bed-plate has holes in it and is placed over the furnace chamber to act as a tray to receive crucibles. The holes allow the ash to fall from the burning charcoal, and the draught blowing through it stimulates the fire. Two tiles are used so that when the upper one is damaged by the heat of the fire (a frequent event) it can be easily replaced with the other one.

Eleven reddish orange tile fragments have been recovered in association with architectural features identified at Kodlunarn (fig. 8.4d–f, KeDe-1:100). Owing to their wide distribution over the site, they may not all be from bed-plates for a clay oven, but a case can be made for that interpretation.

Alternatively, their abundance suggests that the red tiles identified on Kodlunarn Island could have been roofing tiles to cover some of the shelters built on the island. Tile roofing was a common roofing technique in 16th-century Europe. Further testing of the various features should verify the hypotheses suggested.

G. Ceramics from Inuit Sites

Two of the Inuit sites tested during the 1990 survey yielded 16th-century European-made artifacts. The ceramics sherds were found in association with an unusual summer tentring and a winter house at the Lincoln Bay-1 and Napoleon Bay-1 sites, respectively. The Lincoln Bay-1 tentring is unusual in that its front part is completely paved with slabs and a hearth is built in the center of that feature. The single ceramic sherd is from that hearth. The ceramics from Napoleon Bay-1 are in association with an Inuit winter house built over a Dorset midden which is now eroding into the bay.

The Lincoln Bay-1 sherd (fig. 8.6a, KfDd-1:1) is a beige fabric finished with a clear lead glaze clouded with flecks of manganese or iron on its inside surface. Moreover, the parallel lines visible on the inside surface show that it was made on a potter's wheel and was probably a bowl. Burned fat on a broken edge suggests that the bowl was used for a while even though it was fragmentary. Both Napoleon Bay-1 sherds (fig. 8.6b, KfDe-5:1–2) are reddish brown coarse earthenwares and seemingly from the same object. The fabric has some coarse temper included, and neither of them shows any traces of having been glazed. Their fragmentary state prevents us from determining to what type of object they belong, but we know it was made on a potter's wheel. In addition to the ceramics, Napoleon Bay-1 has also yielded tile fragments, flint detritus, and an unidentified bronze piece with drilled holes. Three houses at the Napoleon Bay-1 site have yielded European-made materials. Needless to say, those two sites have a valuable archeological potential for documenting Inuit/European contact.

To summarize, although archeological research on 16th-century English occupation in North America is in its infancy, the styles of ceramics recovered from Frobisher's basecamp and Inuit sites fit well, in

Fig. 8.6. *a*, bowl sherd, beige fabric, clear lead glaze (KfDd-1:1); *b*, reddish brown coarse earthenware sherd (KfDe-5:1-2).

terms of their fabrics and glaze, with late 16th-century European styles (G. Gusset, pers. comm. December 1990).

By their abundance of European-made items and their contemporaneity with the Frobisher voyages, both Inuit sites demonstrate their archeological potential for documenting the European/Inuit acculturation contact studies. As for the industrial sites on Kodlunarn Island, the description of the ceramics recovered in 1990 has refined our understanding of the function of the features recorded by the 1981 Smithsonian Expedition (Fitzhugh this volume). Further archeological research at Kodlunarn will focus on the pyrotechnology for rendering the minerals, mining technology, blacksmithing, and the logistics related to maintaining an English camp in the 16th-century Arctic. It will provide us with the material evidence, such as the architecture and the artifacts, which will improve our understanding of explorations and contacts.

Acknowledgments

This paper was written while the author was supported by the Social Science and Humanities Research Council of Canada through a Post-Doctoral Fellowship and by the Faculté des Lettres, Université Laval. Support for field research was provided in part by the Arctic Institute of North America and the Smithsonian Institution.

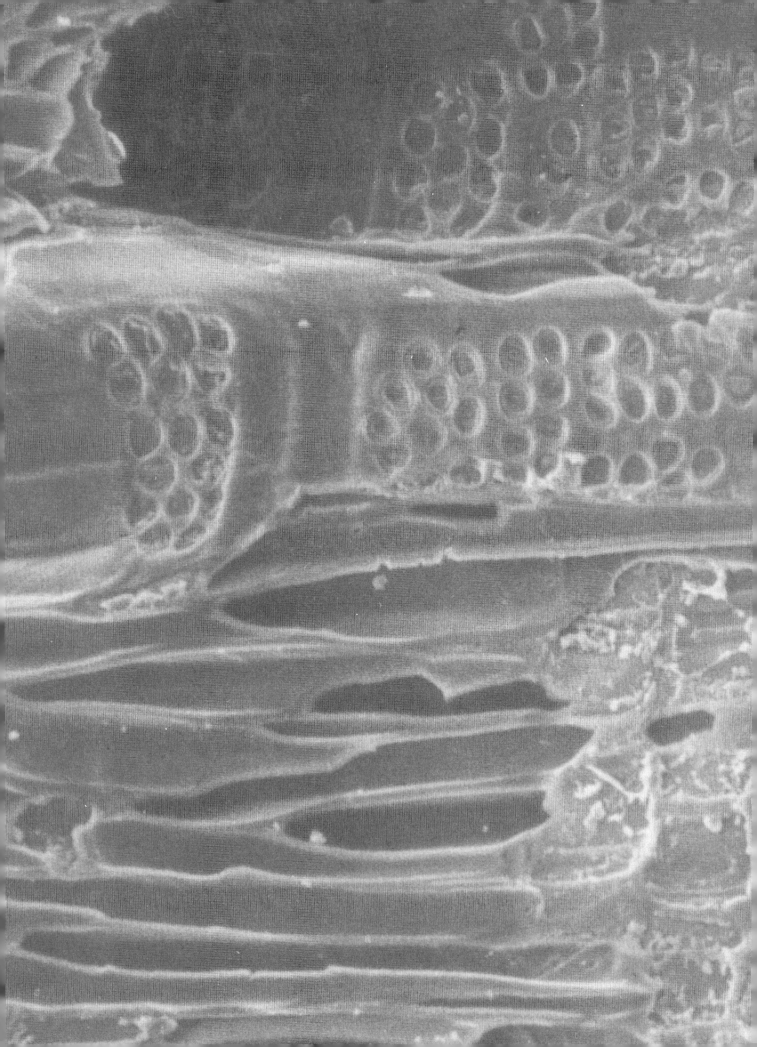

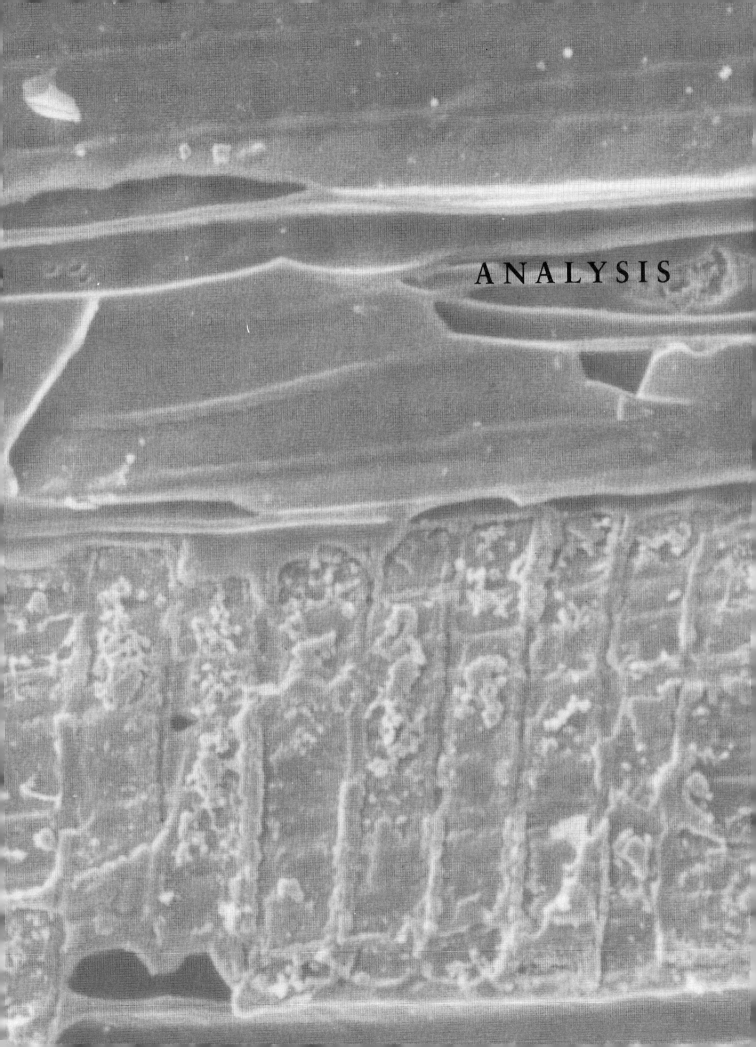

ANALYSIS

Fig. 9.1. Early dates and the presence of conifer charcoal embedded in some of the Frobisher iron blooms have raised questions about the possibility of local smelting of iron ore, or forging of iron blooms, from charcoal made from local driftwood. Driftwood is commonly found on the outer Baffin coast today, as it was during Frobisher's day. While modern driftwood contains much modern flotsam, old logs are also encountered. Some of these may have originated in Siberia or Alaska. Dendrochronological analysis suggests one driftwood sample came from a conifer that ceased growing in Alaska in 1924. This photo shows an occurrence of driftwood on the Chapell Inlet beach (photo by D. Laeyendecker).

PREVIOUS PAGES: Willow (*Salix* sp.), radial section, × 350, charcoal fragment from S1, sample 1981-49

9

Wood and Charcoal Remains from Kodlunarn Island

In 1861, Charles Francis Hall discovered an early European mining site on Kodlunarn Island in Frobisher Bay, NWT, Canada, which he attributed to Martin Frobisher's expeditions (1576–78). He reported on the site and made a collection, which he divided between the Smithsonian Institution of Washington and the Royal Geographical Society of London. Both collections were subsequently lost, but one of the Smithsonian relics, an iron bloom, was recently rediscovered. This bloom has subsequently been known as the "Smithsonian bloom." However, the early radiocarbon dates received from this bloom (Sayre et al. 1982) placed it in a time period before the Frobisher expeditions. This result led to the Smithsonian Kodlunarn Island project.

In 1981, an interdisciplinary Smithsonian team conducted fieldwork at the Frobisher site on Kodlunarn Island. Several structures were surveyed and mapped, including foundations of buildings and remains of a ship-repairing site, the "ship's trench." Test pits were excavated in and around these structures. Samples were collected of coal, slag, tile, ceramics, crucible fragments, chert, brick, mortar, iron, wood, and charcoal. Three iron blooms were also recovered. Samples from wood chips and charcoal fragments were analyzed at the Smithsonian Institution. The results of the analysis of these wood and charcoal remains are discussed in this paper.

Wood and Charcoal in the Frobisher Accounts

The Frobisher accounts have numerous observations relating to wood and driftwood, including the following quotes.

About driftwood:

> We traversed these seas by the space of 26 days without sight of any land and met with much driftwood and whole bodies of trees (Best, in Stefansson and McCaskill 1938, 1:54).

About building a small fort during the second voyage:

> We began to make a small Fort for our defence in the Countess island and entrenched a corner of a cliff which on three parts like a wall of good height was encompassed and well fenced with the sea and we finished the rest with cakes of earth to good purpose and this was called Best Bulwark after the lieutenant's name who first devised the same (ibid. 1:72).

DOSIA LAEYENDECKER

Fig. 9.2. Charcoal production in Elizabethan England, sequential illustrations. Wood was stacked to form a cone, which was coated with a claylike mixture of earth and charcoal dust (above, left foreground). The coating kept the inside temperatures to a minimum, so that the wood was converted to charcoal and not ash.

About burning wood:

> We plunked down our tents and everymen hasted homeward and making bonfires upon the top of the highest mountain of the island . . . we gave a volley of shot for a farewell (ibid. 1:76).

About building a house for the purpose of leaving a hundred men behind, during the third voyage:

> Whereupon there was a strong Fort or house of timber artificially framed and cunningly devised by a notable learned man here at home, in ships to be carried there (ibid. 1:81).

> Within the ship that was drowned there was part of our house which was to be erected for them that should stay all the winter in Meta Incognita (ibid. 1:89).

They began to consider the erecting up of the house or Fort . . . but first they perused the bills of lading . . . and found that there was arrived only the east side and the south side of the house and yet that not perfect and entire . . . also there was found want to drink and fuel to serve one hundred men . . . so they agreed upon giving up the idea of wintering there (ibid. 1:105).

The masons finished a house . . . of lime and stone upon the Countess of Warwick island . . . and to allure those brutish and uncivil people to courtesie against other time of our coming, we left therein diverse of our countrie's toys, as bells and knives . . . also pictures of men and women in lead, men on horseback, looking glasses, whistles and pipes. Also in the house was made an oven and bread left baked

Fig. 9.2 (*continued*). After being coated, the cone was lit (above, left foreground), and the wood slowly reduced in size to charcoal (counterclockwise) (courtesy of University of California, Santa Barbara, Library Special Collections; from Perlin 1989).

therein. We buried the timber of our Fort (ibid. 1:116).

Why they lost their beverages other than water:

The great cause of this leakage and wasting was for that the great timber and sea coal which lay so weightly upon the barrels broke, brused and rotted the hoopes (ibid. 1:117).

About the local Inuit and their wood sources:

They have nothing in use among them to make fire with, save a kind of heath and moss which growth there and they kindle their fire with continual rubbing and fretting one stick against the other, as we do with flints (ibid. 1:126).

They have no wood growing in their country thereabouts and yet we find they have some timber among them which we think does grow far off to the south of this place, about Canada, or some other part of Newfoundland, for there the trees standing on the cliffs of the seaside, by the weight of the ice and snow in winter overcharging them with weight, when the summer thaw comes above and also the sea stretching under them below which wins delay of the land, and they are undermined and fall down from those cliffs into the sea and with the tides and currents are driven to and fro upon the coasts further off and are taken up there by these country people to serve them to planks and strengthen their boats and to make bows and arrows and such other things for their use. . . . And of this kind of driftwood we find all the sea over in great store, which being cut or sawed, by reason of long drifting in the sea is eaten by worms and full of holes of which sort theirs is found to be (ibid. 1:127).

About availability of wood:

> However at Orkney the people are destitute of wood. Their fire is turf and cow shardes. There is no wood at all (Dionyse Settle, in Stefansson and McCaskill 1938, 2:12, 23).

Wood (including timber) and charcoal are mentioned on the supply lists of the ships of the Frobisher expeditions (Stefansson and McCaskill 1938, 2:98), including at least 14 tons of wood and at least 10 tons of charcoal. In manufacturing charcoal (fig. 9.2), it is recognized that two cords of hardwood produce one ton of charcoal. In production, wood loses 75% in weight and 50% in volume. Charcoal has a greater heating power per cubic foot than wood. The lack of sulfur and phosphates makes charcoal valuable for metallurgic uses, especially the smelting of iron ore (Schenck 1904). Wood is only 57% as efficient as coal for fuel (Graves 1919).

It is supposed that Frobisher's expedition brought along wood for general repairs and possibly for fuel. For house construction timber was used. Traditionally, timber and wood mean different things. Timber comes from the trunks of timber trees and is suitable for beams, planks, gateposts, and such. Wood comes in poles, brushwood, and similar small stuff suitable for light construction, firewood, and charcoal burning (Rackham 1980:3). As timber was mentioned elsewhere in the accounts, the wood mentioned on the supply list together with sea coal and charcoal was probably shipped in the form of smaller sticks. Sea coal must have been used for fuel. Charcoal probably served specialized uses, in smithies and in assay furnaces. Several smiths were on board ship with bellows and iron (Stefansson and McCaskill 1938, 2:116, 117) and an assayer was employed on the second and third voyages (ibid. 2).

Summarizing, we learn that Frobisher and his men set up camp on the Countess of Warwick Island (now Kodlunarn Island) by erecting an earth-walled fortification, setting up tents (an account notes two sums of money paid to Morris, the tent maker; Stefansson and McCaskill 1938, 2:118), and building a stone house. They buried timber and supplies for future use. They noticed the sparseness of local fuel wood and made observations about the availability of driftwood, which they erroneously supposed drifted up from Labrador and Newfoundland.

Analysis of Wood and Charcoal

ARCHEOLOGICAL PROVENIENCE

In 1981 the Smithsonian team mapped and surveyed several structures on Kodlunarn Island, including foundations of buildings and a ship's trench (see fig. 5.4). Test pits were dug in and around most of these structures. Important to this study were the wood and charcoal samples (appendix 4) collected from these test pits and also from the iron blooms that were recovered. The wood and charcoal samples were dried, cleaned, and identified at the Smithsonian Institution before a selection was made for radiocarbon dating. Calibration of radiocarbon dates was based on the Radiocarbon Calibration Program, 1987, developed by the University of Washington Quaternary Isotope Laboratory following Stuiver and Pearson (1986).

All the wood samples came from the ship's trench. The wood was very deteriorated and the cell structure mostly beyond recognition. The charcoal samples were associated with four workshop structures and also with the iron blooms found in and near the ship's trench. Compared to the wood, the charcoal was in good condition. Tiny rootlets present were easily removed and did not infest the charcoal fragments themselves. Some fragments were good-sized chunks of a centimeter or larger. The straight growth rings indicate that these fragments were derived from trunk wood. Other fragments were round twig forms with curved growth rings, derived from branches. These had a diameter of 2 cm or larger, the largest fragment being 4 cm in diameter.

METHOD

Identifications of wood and charcoal samples follow the same basic principles. Characteristic features in the anatomical cell structure (figs. 9.3, 9.4) of the unknown species must be microscopically studied and compared to the features of known species in woodslides, micrographs, and descriptions (Greguss 1955, 1959; Jane 1956; Panshin and de Zeeuw 1970; Phillips 1948; Schweingruber 1976, 1978, 1990). A combination of several characteristic features is used for proper identification. In the case of subfossil wood where the wood structure is usually deteriorated, or charcoal where the features are slightly shrunken and the wood structure is difficult

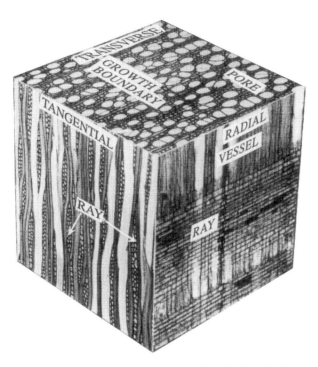

Fig. 9.3. Microscopic features of hardwood (dicotyledonous wood) (after Panshin and de Zeeuw 1970).

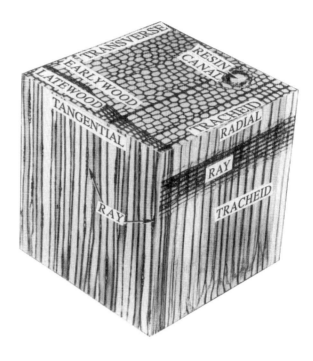

Fig. 9.4. Microscopic features of coniferous wood (after Panshin and de Zeeuw 1970).

to see, it may be impossible to find this combination of features and the sample remains unidentified.

For identification, the wood was cut by hand with a razorblade along transverse, tangential, and radial planes (fig. 9.5). Sections were placed on a slide in distilled water or ethanol and studied with a standard research microscope under transmitted light. The magnification used varied between 40 and 500 times. Charcoal fragments were broken by hand along the transverse, tangential, and radial sections. These surfaces were studied with a reflected light microscope (Zeiss with epiplan objectives) under the same magnifications. To view the transverse section at lower magnifications, a dissecting microscope is sometimes more effective. Wood and wood-slide reference collections were used from the Smithsonian Department of Botany. Photomicrographs were taken in the SEM laboratory of the Smithsonian's Museum of Natural History.

RESULTS

The wood samples excavated at Frobisher's site on Kodlunarn Island were usually too deteriorated to be identified. However, the charcoal fragments could be identified to genus in most instances, as their cell structure was generally well preserved. As certain

species are native to certain geographic areas, identification of the species helps to indicate the point of origin of the charcoal fragment. However, the nature of charcoal is such that minute details in the cells cannot be observed easily and therefore analysis of charcoal does not normally permit identification to the species level.

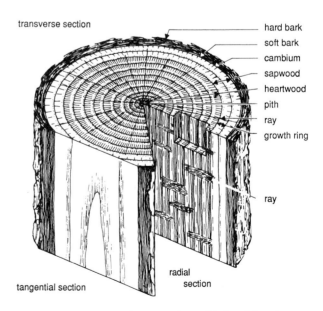

Fig. 9.5. Macroscopic features of wood (after Schweingruber 1990).

STRUCTURE 1, a rectangular structure built of sod walls and rocks, is possibly the remains of a smithy. Fragments of tile, brick, charcoal and slag were found scattered around and also in the disturbed southwest corner in a pile of dirt, probably left from Walter Kenyon's excavation (Kenyon 1975b). Four charcoal samples were collected, one on the surface and three in a test pit 5 cm below the surface:

1981-41, surface collection, structure 1
few charcoal fragments, identified as oak

1981-48, test pit 1, structure 1
small charcoal sample, identified as oak, ash, willow

1981-49, test pit 1, structure 1
charcoal sample, 10 g, identified as:

oak	2.8 g
willow	2.1 g
ash	0.7 g
beech	0.5 g
coniferous sp.	0.5 g (spruce/larch type)
birch	0.4 g
unidentified	3.0 g (hardwood)

A radiocarbon date was run on 2.8 g of oak charcoal. It dated to 510 ± 80 ^{14}C years B.P. (Beta-42660). The calibrated dates are A.D. 1322–1340 and 1392–1446.

1981-61, test pit 1, structure 1
charcoal sample, 12.0 g, identified as:

oak	5.5 g
birch	2.1 g
willow	0.9 g
beech	0.5 g
coniferous sp.	0.2 g (spruce/larch type)
unidentified	2.8 g (hardwood)

A radiocarbon date was run on a combination of oak (5.5 g) and beech (0.5 g). It dated –20 ± 65 ^{14}C years B.P. (SI-5521).

STRUCTURE 2 is a rectangle of stone foundations and may have been the assayer's workshop. Many crucible fragments were found here, but no coal and very little slag. A large charcoal sample was collected in a test pit in the interior of this structure. Other small charcoal samples were collected in a test pit north of this structure.

1981-17, test pit north of structure 2
shiny fragments, some 4 cm diameter
identifications: beech, oak

1981-18, test pit north of structure 2
small charcoal sample, identification: oak

1981-22, interior test pit, structure 2
charcoal, 15.6 g, fragments 2–4 cm diameter:

beech	5.6 g
oak	2.7 g
birch	1.2 g
maple	0.3 g
willow	0.5 g
hazel	0.1 g
unidentified sp.	5.2 g (hardwood)

A radiocarbon date was run on 5.6 g of beech charcoal. The result was 65 ± 60 ^{14}C years B.P. (SI-5522). Another sample of 2.7 g of oak charcoal dated to 320 ± 90 ^{14}C years B.P. (Beta-42659), calibrated to A.D. 1453–1657.

STRUCTURE 3 is another rectangular rock foundation. Samples of charcoal, coal, and slag were collected in a test pit in the center of its interior.

1981-19, test pit 1, structure 3
charcoal, 7.8 g, identified as:

beech	3.6 g
willow	0.8 g
oak	0.6 g
birch	0.4 g
hazel	0.4 g
maple	0.2 g
unidentified sp.	1.8 g (hardwood)

A radiocarbon date was run on a combination of beech, birch and oak, totaling 4.6 g of charcoal. The result was 500 ± 35 ^{14}C years B.P. (SI-5523), calibrated to A.D. 1407–1436.

STRUCTURE 7 is a linear structure, about 22 m long. Small charcoal samples were collected from two test pits.

1981-24, test pit 1, structure 7
small fragments of oak, beech, birch

A radiocarbon date was run on 0.2 g oak charcoal. The result was 210 ± 60 ^{14}C years B.P., calibrated to A.D. 1645–1683, 1739–1805, or 1934–1955.

1981-25, test pit 1, two tiny fragments of oak

1981-30, test pit 3, small sample of oak

1981-31, small sample of oak and beech

STRUCTURE 12, the ship's trench, is a feature that was probably used as a mine and as a tidal dry dock for ship repair. "On the shore of the north side of the island I found also an excavation, which I called a ship's trench" (Hall 1865b:427). Two test pits were excavated at locations indicated by metal detector signals. These test pits produced two iron blooms. One of the blooms was found imbedded in layers of wood, charcoal, and decayed "amorphous" carbon. The other bloom was associated with layers of wood. Both test pits were about 60 cm deep.

Charcoal was collected in test pit 1. The charcoal fragments were rather large, about 2 cm long. The growth rings were straight, indicating that the fragment was derived from trunk wood and not from small branches. Wood fragments, which were very "mushy" and so deteriorated that the wood structure had almost disappeared, were collected in test pit 1 and test pit 2. Bloom 2 was found in test pit 1, Bloom 3 was found in test pit 2.

Test pit 1 (structure 12). Bloom 2 from test pit 1 was analyzed for carbon-14 at the IsoTrace Laboratory of the University of Toronto by Richard Cresswell. Small samples of charcoal were found inside the bloom. The charcoal was in the form of powder, but one tiny fragment of about 1 mm could be identified as a hardwood species probably alder or birch. This charcoal was dated to 970 ± 60 ^{14}C years B.P., which was calibrated to A.D. 1006–1060, 1077–1125, or 1136–1150. A sample of iron from the surface of the bloom was dated at 1340 ± 70, calibrated to A.D. 640–717 or 742–760. Two more samples from different sites within the bloom were also analyzed, yielding two more dates, 550 ± 60 B.P., calibrated to A.D. 1307–1355, and 500 ± 60 B.P., calibrated to A.D. 1400–1442 (Harbottle et al., this volume).

1981-68, test pit 1, structure 12
charcoal, 13.5 g
   oak   10.0 g
   beech   3.5 g

   Both fractions of this sample were radiocarbon dated: 1981-68 A, 3.5 g of beech charcoal, came out to 103.7% modern (SI-5526); 1981-68 B, 10 g of oak charcoal, yielded a date of 355 ± 45 (SI-5527), which calibrated to A.D. 1459–1529.

1981-69, test pit 1, structure 12
charcoal, 4.4 g
   oak   3.7 g
   beech   0.6 g
   unidentified sp. 0.1 g (hardwood)

1981-70, test pit 1, structure 12
charcoal, 18.5 g
   oak   17.3 g
   beech   1.0 g
   hazel?   0.1 g

1981-71, test pit 1, structure 12, from just below bloom 2.
wood, 24.5 g, oak(?)

   A radiocarbon date was run on this sample. The result was 290 ± 85 ^{14}C years B.P. (SI-5525), calibrated to A.D. 1477–1665.

1981-72, test pit 1, structure 12
wood, 17.9 g, oak(?)

Test pit 2 (structure 12).

1981-73, test pit 2, structure 12
wood 51.1 g, unidentifiable

1981-74, test pit 2, structure 12
wood, unidentifiable

1981-75, test pit 2, structure 12, from 10 cm below bloom 3
wood, oak (?)

1981-76, test pit 2, structure 12, from east floor
wood 51.7 g, unidentifiable

   A radiocarbon date was run on this sample. The result was 415 ± 50 ^{14}C years B.P. (SI-5528), calibrated A.D. 1435–1484.

1981-77, test pit 2, structure 12, from just below bloom 3
bark (?)

Bloom 1 was discovered at a depth of 10 cm in the sandy soil a few meters south of the ship's trench. A charcoal sample was removed from the external surface of the bloom. This sample (total weight 115 mg) consisted of tiny charcoal fragments (2 mm), charcoal powder, sand and a few tiny rootlets; 55 mg of charcoal fragments were separated and sent to the Brookhaven National Laboratory for dating.

1981-83, from bloom 1
charcoal, 55 mg, identified as coniferous sp.(spruce/larch type)
   Radiocarbon date, 628 ± 150 ^{14}C years B.P. (Brookhaven), calibrated to A.D. 1250–1440.

Discussion

The charcoal in the samples from Kodlunarn Island derived from a variety of trees. Oak (*Quercus* sp.) and beech (*Fagus* sp.), separate or in combination, form the larger part of the samples. Birch (*Betula* sp.) and willow (*Salix* sp.) occur in smaller amounts, while ash (*Fraxinus* sp.), hazel (*Corylus* sp.), maple (*Acer* sp.) and coniferous sp.(*Larix* sp./*Picea* sp. type) appear only occasionally (table 9.1).

The question is, where did this charcoal come from? In view of the early dates of some of the charcoal samples, there are three possible sources:

1. The charcoal was imported by the Frobisher expedition as mentioned in the accounts (Stefansson and McCaskill 1938, 2:98).

2. The charcoal was burned on the site and derived from local dwarf bushes or from driftwood.

3. The charcoal was imported by people who visited the island on an earlier date than the Frobisher expedition.

Let us discuss hypothesis 3 first. Norse people from Greenland or Scandinavia may have and probably did venture to Baffin Island between the years A.D. 1000 and 1350 (Stefansson and McCaskill 1938, 1:21, 23; Jones 1968:269). The Norse settlement in L'Anse aux Meadows, Newfoundland, has a median date of A.D. 1000 (Ingstad 1977). The calibrated radiocarbon date on charcoal associated with bloom 1, A.D. 1250–1440, places the bloom in the Norse period, although late. The calibrated dates from the carbon extracted from the Smithsonian bloom, A.D. 1240–1400 and A.D. 1160–1280, also

place that bloom in the period of the late Norse occupation of Greenland (Sayre et al. 1982; Harbottle et al., this volume).

It is possible that Norsemen from Greenland visited Kodlunarn Island. Norse copper was found in the form of a late Dorset amulet in Hudson Bay (Harp 1974), and an Inuit carving of a Norseman has been found in a Thule site in south Baffin Island (Sabo and Sabo 1978). Norsemen from Greenland may have burned local dwarf bushes and coniferous driftwood. However, they are unlikely to have left charcoal from temperate-zone trees. Hearth charcoal from the late Norse Site V51 Sandnes in Greenland (McGovern 1984) consisted of only willow and coniferous species. Wood chips from that Viking site were all from coniferous trees, and twigs were identified mostly as willow and occasionally as birch and alder. In 30 kilos of wood and charcoal samples only one fragment of oak (charcoal) was found (Laeyendecker n.d.).

Bloom 2, from test pit 1 in the ship's trench, is associated with oak charcoal, which yielded a calibrated date of A.D. 1459–1529 (SI-5527). Oak wood from just below this bloom dated to A.D. 1477–1665 (SI-5525). Both these dates are post-Norse. Bloom 3 from test pit 2 in the ship's trench was associated with wood that dated to A.D. 1435–1484 (SI-5528), also post-Norse, but before Frobisher's visit. It is possible that people other than Greenlanders or Frobisher's men visited the island. Not all exploring expeditions were so well documented. Also, because of possible profitable prospects some ventures may have been secret.

Hypothesis 2 is that wood and charcoal was derived from the local vegetation or driftwood. The local vegetation on Kodlunarn Island at the time of Frobisher's visit consisted of a kind of heath and moss, according to the account of George Best (Stefansson and McCaskill 1938, 1:126). Dwarf bushes of willow, birch, and possibly alder may have grown in sheltered places. The available firewood was very scarce, however, and only small amounts of tiny fragments of charcoal would have remained in the site.

A great deal of driftwood occurred in the ocean and along most beaches of the Arctic, as mentioned in the excerpts from the Frobisher voyages noted above. This wood has its main origin in the boreal and subboreal forest regions of Scandinavia, northern USSR, Alaska and Canada. The rivers that drain into the Arctic Ocean from these areas carry large

TABLE 9.1. Occurrences of identified charcoal in different structures. Numbers indicate weight in grams in the separate samples.

	S1	S2	S3	S7	Ship's Trench
Oak	(2.8);(5.5)	(2.7)	(0.6)	(0.2)	(10.0);3.7;17.3
Beech	0.5;(0.5)	(5.6)	(3.6)	+	(3.5);0.6;1.0
Birch	0.4;2.1	1.2	(0.4)	+	
Willow	2.1;0.9	0.5	0.8		
Ash	0.7				
Maple		0.3	0.2		
Hazel		0.1	0.4		+
Conif	0.5;0.2				

+ = present.

( ) = fraction of sample used for radiocarbon dating.

quantities of driftwood. Oceanic currents catch the wood and are responsible for its transportation and eventual deposition along the arctic shores. Eurola (1971) summarized the research carried out on identification of driftwood of the Arctic Ocean and the locations where this driftwood was found. During the turn of the century, interest in driftwood research was high. Ingvarson (1910) published probably the most extensive paper on identification of driftwood from Ellesmere Island obtained during the *Fram* expedition.

Recent research (e.g., Blake 1961, 1972, 1975) has focused on dating identified subfossil driftwood on ancient beaches in the Canadian Arctic Archipelago. Changes in driftwood penetration would be dependent on the direction of the currents and the sea ice conditions (enough ice for the transportation of the wood as well as enough open water for the delivery of the wood on the beaches). This may indirectly indicate changes in postglacial climate. However, these data can be quite complex and may seem contradictory (Dyke and Morris 1990). Haggblom (1982) studied identified driftwood on Svalbard, finding that wood floating in water has a limited buoyancy (coniferous woods about 10 months, hardwoods about 6–10 months). In order for driftwood to reach distant beaches it must be frozen into pack ice. During climatic conditions with greater percentage of open water, only wood with good buoyancy survives as driftwood; other woods sink. In such warm periods, driftwood was notably absent from the beaches of Svalbard. Caution must be exercised, however, as native people have regularly collected driftwood from arctic beaches for fuel and tool-making. Especially in areas where driftwood is scarce, for instance east of the Mackenzie River in northern and arctic Canada, coastal people have collected every scrap of wood near communities and sometimes had to use skin and bone as wood substitutes. In the western Canadian Arctic and Alaska no shortage of driftwood has ever been felt (Giddings, 1941).

Eurola (1971) mapped all the driftwood identifications and occurrences to date and presented them in a table of 680 recorded specimens (fig. 9.6). He distinguishes American and Siberian driftwood regions according to the origin of the wood. To establish origin, wood must be identified to species, because different species of the same genus occur in different geographic regions. However different species of spruce and larch are impossible to identi-

fy. It is sometimes even difficult to distinquish between spruce and larch, although some methods have been developed to solve this problem (Bartholin 1979). Driftwood from American and Siberian rivers enters the Arctic Ocean during the three or four months of the year when the rivers are ice free. The movement of the ice pack over the Arctic Ocean follows two main currents, the Pacific Gyral in the area between the pole and arctic Canada and the Transpolar Current from the New Siberian Islands to Fram Strait between Svalbard and Greenland (Sokolov 1966; Weeks 1978). The Transpolar Current continues as the East Greenland Current, which rounds the southern point of Greenland and turns northward. The western shores of Baffin Island belong mainly to the American driftwood region. In Frobisher Bay, driftwood from North American rivers is deposited via arctic Canada and also from closer sources, like Hudson Bay. Some driftwood of Siberian and European origin could find its way via the East Greenland Current to eastern Baffin Island; but it is unlikely for driftwood to come up from the south, from Labrador and Newfoundland, as George Best had thought (Stefanson and McCaskill 1938, 1:127), because the Labrador Current would carry it to the south and not to the north (fig. 9.6).

Dendrochronological methods (Baillie 1982, Schweingruber 1989) have been applied to the study of the origin and age of driftwood. Climatic indications, temperature, and precipitation are factors usually reflected in the tree rings. Consistent variations in ring thickness, when they occur in a large number of trees in a sizable area, constitute the basis for the study of dendrochronology. Coniferous trees at the arctic tree line are particularly favorable for this study. Careful selection of samples is essential, because not all trees near the tree line record temperature accurately. To establish a master chronology for a certain region one has to sample a transect, a collection of trees at regularly spaced intervals. The measurement data are presented in the form of curves. Cross-dating is the process of identification of a sequence of tree ring widths in an unknown sample and comparing this pattern with an established chronology. Giddings (1941, 1952, 1954) has cross-dated archeological driftwood in Alaska. Bartholin and Hjort (1987) established the origin and age of driftwood from Svalbard by cross-dating tree ring patterns with master chronologies from the European part of northern USSR. Eggertsson (1991)

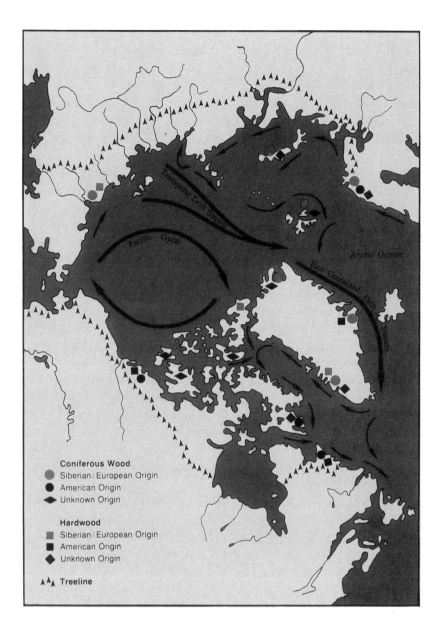

Fig. 9.6. Major directions of ice drift and surface currents in the Arctic Ocean and Northeast Canada, showing treeline of the subarctic region and driftwood occurrences and origins (compiled from Eurola 1971 and Haggblom 1982).

Coniferous Wood
● Siberian / European Origin
● American Origin
◆ Unknown Origin

Hardwood
■ Siberian / European Origin
■ American Origin
◆ Unknown Origin

▲▲▲ Treeline

was able to use some of his pine samples from Iceland for cross-dating with a master chronology from northwest Siberia. He concluded in his preliminary report that driftwood on the coast of Iceland originates from rivers draining into the Barents Sea in the west and from rivers in eastern Siberia, the Lena and the Yenisey. Eggertsson cross-dated two spruce samples from northeastern Greenland with a mean curve from the Yukon River region in Alaska and one spruce sample with a curve from the Mackenzie Delta in Canada. He also correllated a driftwood sample collected from Frobisher Bay in the 1991 field season to master chronologies from the Yukon River valley in Alaska. The outermost tree ring of the sample was dated to 1924 (Eggertsson, pers.

comm. April 1992). Dendrochronology and wood anatomy together applied to driftwood samples, as well as the study of the sea currents in the Arctic Ocean, have great potential to detect the origin and age of arctic driftwood, which is of special interest to the archeologist.

It appears that most driftwood is derived from coniferous woods. Haggblom (1982) mentioned that among driftwood samples from Svalbard, coniferous trees were predominant and wood from birch (*Betula* sp.), willow (*Salix* sp.) and alder (*Alnus* sp.) occurred only rarely. Of a total of 208 driftwood samples from the northwest and northeast coast of Iceland, Eggertsson (1991) identified 73% as pine (*Pinus* sp.), 16% as spruce (*Picea* sp.), 9% as larch

(*Larix* sp.) and 2% as hardwood trees (these driftwood finds are not included on fig. 9.6). Eggertsson also studied 30 driftwood samples from northeastern Greenland. Of these, he identified 60% as spruce (*Picea* sp.), 20% as larch (*Larix* sp.), 13% as spruce-larch type, and 7% as hardwood species. Kindle (1921) reported vast quantities of driftwood between Herschel Island and the Mackenzie Delta, which he identified as largely spruce (*Picea* sp.) and poplar (*Populus* sp.). This wood originated from the Mackenzie River. In 1978, 39 driftwood samples were collected from the northern coast of Labrador by Smithsonian and Bryn Mawr College archeological crews. These samples were identified as spruce (*Picea* sp., 9 specimens), larch (*Larix* sp., 7), willow (*Salix* sp., 14), alder (*Alnus* sp., 2) and birch (*Betula* sp., 1). From Frobisher Bay, the Smithsonian team collected 8 driftwood samples in 1981, which were identified as pine (*Pinus* sp., 1 specimen), spruce (*Picea* sp., 5) and willow (*Salix* sp., 2) (Laeyendecker n.d.).

During the field seasons of 1990 and 1991, driftwood was collected in the mouth of Frobisher Bay not far from Kodlunarn Island. These samples have not yet been analyzed but will be identified at the Smithsonian Institution. It was observed that driftwood was scarce in most areas. However, two beaches that were surveyed in 1991, along Chapell Inlet and Lefferts Island, had an abundance of scattered driftwood (fig. 9.1). Because in the mouth of Frobisher Bay the land is sinking and the beaches are eroding away, driftwood remains of recent centuries are found in a single horizon at the highest storm tide line, and not at different levels according to age, the way they can be found on raised beaches of emergent coastal areas. Thus it will also be important to date some of these samples.

So far, no occurrences of oak, beech, ash, hazel, or maple were found among northern driftwood samples nor have such references been noted in the literature. Only the coniferous charcoal in samples from Kodlunarn Island could have been derived from driftwood.

This leaves us to discuss hypothesis 1. Were the wood and charcoal deposits found at the sites of Kodlunarn Island imported by the Frobisher expedition? This seems plausible for wood and charcoal fragments from oak, beech, ash, hazel, and maple. However, coniferous charcoal is possibly from driftwood origin and birch and willow may have been local brush vegetation. The only coniferous tree that

was indigenous to England was the pine from the Scottish Highlands, which was not exploited commercially (Rackham 1980). Coniferous wood was imported to England from the Baltic and from Norway for timber, but probably not for charcoal.

According to Oliver Rackham's works (1980, 1986), charcoal was a common industrial and urban fuel in Elizabethan England. It was made by burning wood in an insufficient supply of air in pits, in earth-covered stacks, and later in kilns. However, there is little in the way of precise records of charcoal manufacturing processes. In some woodleases it was specified that charcoal pits should be filled, in others charcoal burning was specifically forbidden. Charcoal was made from what remained after the underwood was cut at about the height of a foot. These lower parts of the underwood (coti) were then cut close to the ground and made into charcoal. Quantity and value depended on the variable quality of the coti.

Woods were treated in different ways and had different economic uses. Oak was generally cut young. Straight knot-free boards of oak were usually imported. Oaks were extensively exploited, so there must have been lots of coti for charcoal making. Beech coppice was extensive in the 16th century. In some wood pastures, beech was pollarded (cut high above the ground). In England, beech was never as popular as timber, but was a high-priced fuel wood. Beech had been used for ironworks since the Roman occupation. Ash, maple, and hazel were among the more common underwood species in 16th-century surveys of woods in England. Although they all had specialized uses, ash for all kinds of tools and handles, hazel for barrel hoops and thatching, maple for musical instruments and furniture, these woods were commonly found in charcoal pits. Birch use is not well documented. Its use for fuel does not seem to have been great. Willow was at one time used for making charcoal (Brimble 1946). The charcoal of oak, beech, ash, hazel, and maple, and possibly birch and willow, could have been readily available near Frobisher's points of departure at Radcliffe, Blackwall, and Harwich.

Conclusions

Two samples from the Smithsonian bloom were dated at Brookhaven National Laboratory to calibrated ages of A.D. 1240–1400 and 1160–1280 (Sayre et al. 1982). Three blooms were found by the Smithsonian

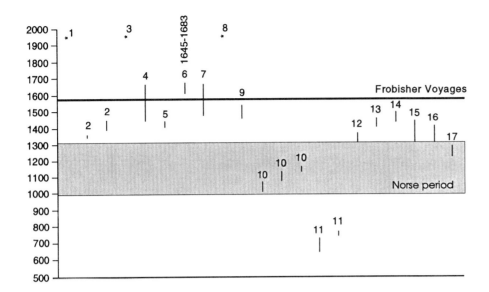

Fig. 9.7. Radiocarbon dates (calibrated 1 σ range) from Kodlunarn Island (KeDe-1). * = modern date. Graphed numbers refer to entries in table 9.2.

field team in 1981; bloom 1 was dated from samples of adhering coniferous charcoal by Brookhaven to a calibrated age of A.D. 1250–1440 (Harbottle et al., this volume). Bloom 2 produced four dates, one on charcoal included in the iron and three on iron from different locations in the bloom. The results of these dates are diverse, but the youngest dates, from the innermost part of the bloom, give a calibrated age of A.D. 1307–1355, 1383–1427 and 1400–1442 (nos. 12, 13 in fig. 9.7). If one compares the youngest date of the Smithsonian bloom with the date from bloom 1 and the youngest dates from bloom 2, then a relationship between these three blooms is obvious (fig. 9.7). These dates are about two hundred years before the Frobisher time period. If these iron blooms were of Frobisher origin, they would have been smelted with charcoal made from local driftwood, which could explain the early date, because driftwood found at present shorelines in the Arctic can be several hundred years old (Blake 1975, Haggblom 1982). However, it is difficult to imagine that enough driftwood could have been collected to fabricate charcoal for the smelting process. The discrepancy between the ages of the sample from the surface of bloom 2 (A.D. 640–717 and 742–760) and the samples from its inner parts (A.D. 1307–1355, 1383–1427, and 1400–1442) may indicate refiring of the bloom with coal, which also hints at a shortage of charcoal.

Wood and charcoal samples associated with blooms 2 and 3, excavated from the ship's trench in 1981, yielded three calibrated dates—A.D. 1477–1665 (wood, SI-5525), 1459–1529 (charcoal, SI-5527) and 1435–1484 (wood, SI-5528)—that fall within or close to the time period of Frobisher's voyages. Oak and beech were the woods found in these samples. As no coniferous charcoal or wood was identified, driftwood cannot be a factor in these dates.

Summarizing, we can say that blooms 1, 2 and 3 were found in association with wood and charcoal of English derivation. These wood and charcoal samples dated within or close to the Frobisher time period. However, the blooms themselves dated earlier. Two of these earlier bloom dates were run on charcoal samples extracted from the blooms and identified as coniferous species (bloom 1) and alder or birch species (bloom 2). This charcoal could possibly have been derived from driftwood (coniferous species) or local vegetation (alder or birch species) and thus probably not imported by the Frobisher expedition. The earlier dates of the blooms and the identifications of the charcoal they were dated on together indicate that these blooms were not smelted by Frobisher's men on Kodlunarn Island, at least not by using the English charcoal that must have been available (10 tons of charcoal mentioned in the supply lists), as samples of this charcoal were found in several of the Frobisher site structures. The origin of the blooms remains unknown, but they must have been used and left by the Frobisher expedition, because the wood and the charcoal that was excavated in association with these blooms certainly came from England with the Frobisher expedition.

TABLE 9.2. Radiocarbon dates from wood and charcoal samples from Kodlunarn Island (KeDe-1). Numbers 1-17 correspond with numbers on Fig. 9.7

	Provenience	Sample No.	Material	^{14}C Years B.P.	Calibrated Age A.D.
1	Structure 1 Test Pit 1	(1981–61) SI-5521	Charcoal 5.5 g oak 0.5 g beech	-20 ± 65	
2	Structure 1 Test Pit 1	(1981–49) Beta-42660	Charcoal 2.8 g oak	510 ± 80	1322–1340 1392–1446
3	Structure 2 Interior Test Pit	(1981–22) SI-5522	Charcoal 5.6 g beech	65 ± 60	
4	Structure 2 Interior Test Pit	(1981–22) Beta-42659	Charcoal 2.7 g oak	320 ± 90	1453–1657
5	Structure 3 Test Pit 1	(1981–19A/B) SI-5523	Charcoal 4.6 g oak beech, birch	500 ± 35	1407–1436
6	Structure 7 Test Pit 1	(1981–24) TO-2609	Charcoal 0.2 g oak	210 ± 60	1645–1683 1739–1805 1934–1955
7	Structure 12 Ship's Trench Test Pit 1	(1981–71) SI-5525	Wood 24.5 g oak(?)	290 ± 85	1477–1665
8	Structure 12 Ship's Trench Test Pit 1	(1981–68A) SI-5526	Charcoal 3.5 g beech	103.7 % modern	
9	Structure 12 Ship's Trench Test Pit 1	(1981–68B) SI-5527	Charcoal 10.0 g oak	355 ± 45	1459–1529
10	Structure 12 Ship's Trench Test Pit 1 Bloom 2	IsoTrace V2-2/7 TO-347	Charcoal birch/alder inclusion in iron	970 ± 60	1006–1060 1077–1125 1136–1157
11	Bloom 2	IsoTrace V2-1B TO-712	Iron	1340 ± 70	640–717 742–760*
12	Bloom 2	IsoTrace V2-1A TO-712.2	Iron	550 ± 60	1307–1355*
13	Bloom 2	IsoTrace H1-2A TO-712.3a	Iron	500 ± 60	1400–1442*
14	Structure 12 Ship's Trench Test Pit 2 (Bloom 3)	(1981–76) SI-5528	Wood 51.1 g id.?	415 ± 50	1435–1484
15	Test Pit south of Ship's Trench Bloom 1	(1981–83) Brookhaven	Charcoal 55 mg spruce/larch	628 ± 150	1250–1440*
16	Smithsonian Bloom	Brookhaven	Iron	679 ± 133	1240–1400*
17	Smithsonian Bloom	Brookhaven	Iron	792 ± 107	1160–1280*

*Harbottle et al., this volume

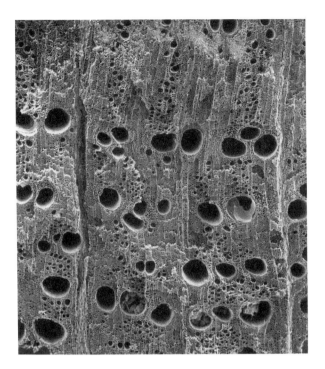

Fig. 9.8. Oak (*Quercus* sp.), transverse section, × 40, charcoal fragment from S2, sample 1981-22. Ring-porous wood with large pores in early wood and small pores in late wood in more or less radially oriented groups; two broad rays and many narrow rays can be seen.

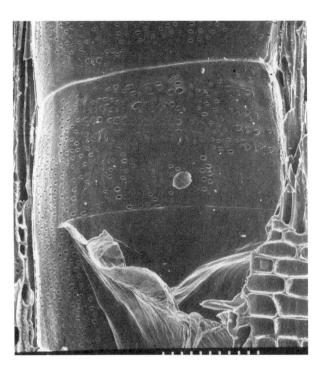

Fig. 9.9. Oak (*Quercus* sp.), radial section, × 300, charcoal fragment from S12, sample 1981-70. Close-up of vessel with simple perforation plate and minute intervessel pits.

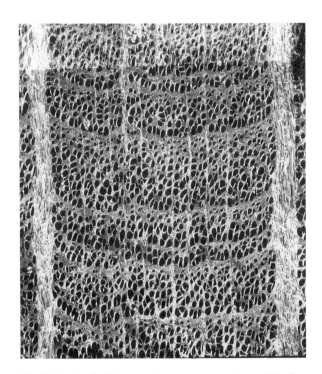

Fig. 9.10. Beech (*Fagus* sp.), transverse section, × 50, charcoal fragment from S12, sample 1981-70. Diffuse-porous wood with many small pores; growth ring is distinct, broad and narrow rays are visible.

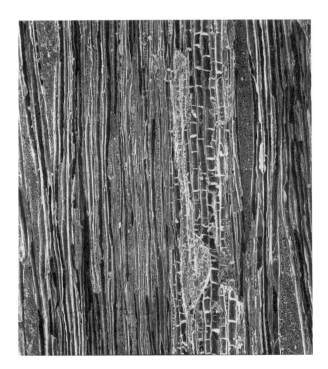

Fig. 9.11. Beech (*Fagus* sp.), tangential section, × 60, charcoal fragment from S12, sample 1981-70. Broad and narrow rays seen in cross section.

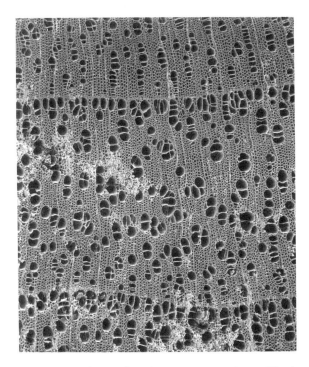

Fig. 9.12. Birch (*Betula* sp.), transverse section, × 80, charcoal fragment from S2, sample 1981-22. Semi-ring-porous wood with distinct growth rings.

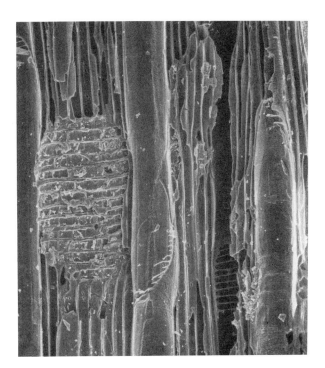

Fig. 9.13. Birch (*Betula* sp.), radial section, × 300, charcoal fragment from S2, sample 1981-22. Vessels show scalariform perforation plates and minute intervessel pits. Ray is homocellular, consisting of all procumbent cells.

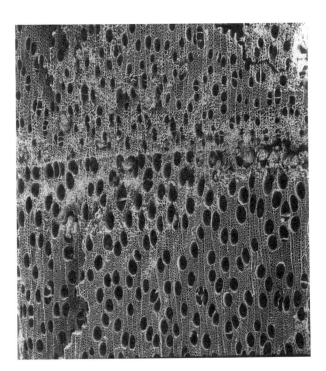

Fig. 9.14. Willow (*Salix* sp.), transverse section, × 50, charcoal fragment from S1, sample 1981-49. Diffuse-porous wood with many small vessels.

Fig. 9.15. Willow (*Salix* sp.), radial section, × 350, charcoal fragment from S1, sample 1981-49. Vessels show simple perforation plates and large intervessel pits. Ray is heterocellular, consisting of procumbent and upright cells.

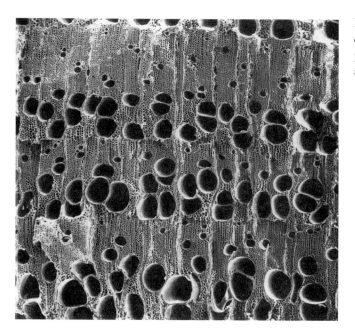

Fig. 9.16. Ash (*Fraxinus* sp.), transverse section, × 50, charcoal fragment from S1, sample 1981-49. Ring-porous wood with distinct growth rings, smaller pores arranged in radial files.

Fig. 9.17. Ash (*Fraxinus* sp.), tangential section, × 250, charcoal fragment from S1, sample 1981-49. Rays are two or three cells wide, vertical strand is a group of parenchyma cells.

Fig. 9.18. Ash (*Fraxinus* sp.), radial section, × 350, charcoal fragment from S1, sample 1981-49. Large vessels have simple perforation plates and small intervessel pits. Ray is homocellular, all procumbent cells.

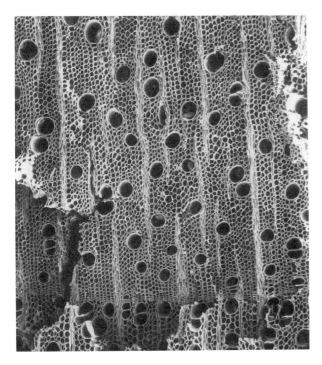

Fig. 9.19. Maple (*Acer* sp.), transverse section, × 100, charcoal fragment from S2, sample 1981-22. Diffuse-porous wood with small pores sparsely and evenly distributed.

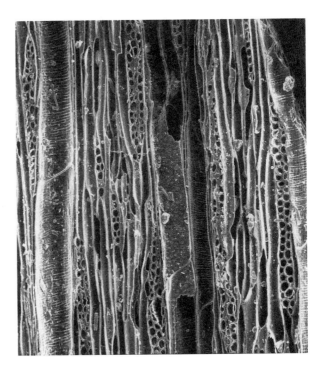

Fig. 9.20. Maple (*Acer* sp.), tangential section, × 200, charcoal fragment from S2, sample 1981-22. Vessels show simple perforation plates and spiral thickening in walls. Rays are two to three cells wide.

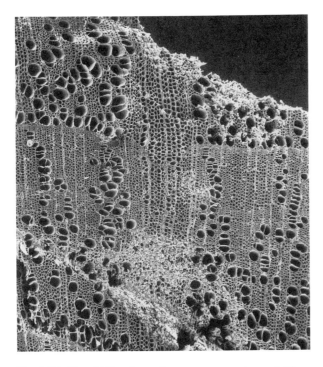

Fig. 9.21. Hazel (*Corylus* sp.), transverse section, × 100, charcoal fragment from S2, sample 1981-22. Diffuse to semi-ring-porous wood, pores radially filed. Very wide ray is an aggregate ray, a composite ray including vessels and fibers. Narrow uniseriate rays also present.

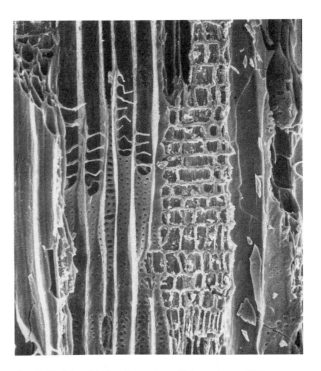

Fig. 9.22. Hazel (*Corylus* sp.), radial section, × 500, charcoal fragment from S2, sample 1981-22. Scalariform perforation plates seen in vessels; ray is heterocellular (procumbent and upright cells).

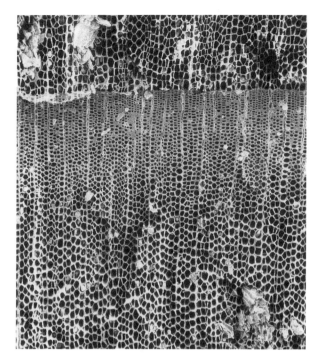

Fig. 9.23. Coniferous sp. (*Picea-Larix* type), transverse section, × 50, charcoal fragment from S1, sample 1981-49. No vessels, gradual early to late wood transition. This is probably spruce.

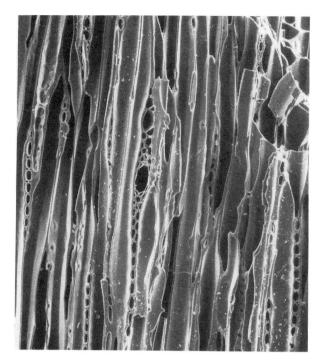

Fig. 9.24. Coniferous sp. (*Picea-Larix* type), tangential section, × 200, charcoal fragment from S1, sample 1981-49. Transverse resin canals incorporated in ray.

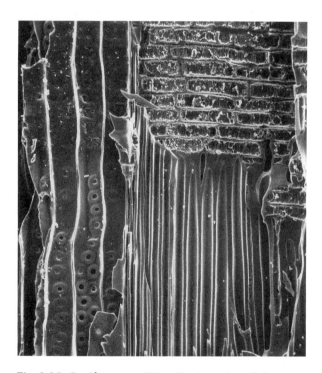

Fig. 9.25. Coniferous sp. (*Picea-Larix* type), radial section, ×·250, charcoal fragment from S1, sample 1981-49. Bordered pits show on radial walls of tracheids, small piceoid pits in crossfields of ray.

10

Carbon-14 Dating of Iron Blooms from Kodlunarn Island

It sometimes happens that discovery of a single extraordinary, inexplicable artifact will touch off a whole train of archeological, literary-historical, or laboratory research, and such has been the impact of the Smithsonian Frobisher bloom. Its finding (Hall 1865a), loss through being mislaid (Stefansson and McCaskill 1938), rediscovery and laboratory investigation (Sayre et al. 1982) are part of the background that gave rise to the Smithsonian interdisciplinary survey of Kodlunarn Island in 1981, and to the present volume. That expedition unearthed three additional blooms, and in this chapter we refer to research on the "Frobisher blooms," identified as bloom number 1, 2, or 3. The original bloom preserved at the Smithsonian Institution as catalog number 49459 is referred to as the "Smithsonian bloom."

It has always been clear that with the Smithsonian bloom, as with any archeological artifact whose date may not necessarily be the same as that of the materials with which it was found in context, to establish an independent date for the smelting of the iron could prove decisive in evaluating competing theories for the object's origin and archeological deposition. For example, if a reliable date for the Smithsonian bloom were found to be nearly synchronous, within a small error, with the Frobisher voyages (1576–78) one could argue that the iron was smelted in Elizabethan England and transported to the site by Frobisher's men. Indeed, in the detailed list of supplies assembled for the third Frobisher voyage (1578) there is an entry that must be discussed in this connection. The journal of Edward Fenton, who was captain of the *Judith* on the 1578 expedition, is preserved in manuscript in Magdalene College, Cambridge (Fenton 1578). In the list of supplies[1] appears the entry "Yron lampes xii" that is, 12 iron lamps. Kenyon (pers. comm.) read this as "Iron loupes," or "lumpes," and in the Oxford Unabridged English Dictionary one finds the following meanings for these words in the 1600s: "*Loop*, A mass of iron in a pasty condition . . . a bloom," "*Lump*, A bloom or loop of malleable iron."

Through the kindness of Donald Hogarth, one of us (GH) has been able to examine a photocopy of the Fenton manuscript page 9, and there seems little question that the handwritten word is "lampes" and

GARMAN HARBOTTLE,
RICHARD G. CRESSWELL, AND
RAYMOND W. STOENNER

1. The late W. A. Kenyon made available to one of us (GH) the list of supplies, which was not included in the part of Fenton's journal published by Kenyon (1980/81).

not "loops" or "lumpes." Hogarth concurs in this opinion (pers. comm.) and it would seem that we must discard this item as being a record of an English origin for the blooms.

To add to this there are two additional important references in the Fenton journal (op. cit.), the first for Monday July 21, 1578: "Then we wente to the Countesse Ilande to view the same wherein our judgments all things remayned at [as] we left them in so much as we founde divers osmondes which we lefte uncovered lying in their places untooched of [by] the people and we reatorned to our Shipp." The second reference, on July 27, describes a visit of "The Master" (Charles Jackman, master of the "Judith") to an island called "Winters fornace" (i.e., furnace): "upon a pointe of that Ilande they [i.e., Jackman and Master Wolfall, the Anglican clergyman who accompanied the voyage] founde ... certein osmondes of iron caried thither by the people of the Countrey."

The word "osmonde" presents something of a problem. In Scandinavian archeometallurgy it is often used to describe a refined, superior iron, usually supplied (in the Baltic countries) in pieces the size of a matchbox, about 300 g. As such, it was the starting material for making tools, fishhooks, and such, and could not be mistaken for a bloom of the type found by Hall, and by the 1981 expedition, at Frobisher Bay. On the other hand, the Oxford English Dictionary also lists an attributed meaning for osmond: "osmond furnace—a small primitive sort of furnace for reducing bog-iron ore, formerly used in Sweden, Finland etc.," and in a reference of 1864 (Percy 1864:619): "I shall distinguish it by the name of an Osmund furnace, from the Swedish word osmund, which was applied to the bloom produced in this kind of furnace." These uses are compatible with Fenton's possible identification of the Frobisher blooms as "osmondes" (see also Schubert 1957:111, 120, note 1, 297 et seq. which clearly documents "osmond" as a term for iron blooms). Neither Hall nor the 1981 expedition found any 300-g osmondes of "superior iron," or anything that resembled it.

Thanks to the research of N. van der Merwe (1969), it is possible to carry out carbon-14 dating on iron itself, subject to certain limitations of interpretation as will be seen. When iron ore is smelted with charcoal, the reduction of the oxidized iron to metal is not accomplished by a high-temperature reaction of the ore with solid carbon, but rather with gaseous carbon monoxide coming from the partial combustion of the carbon.

In the bloomery furnace, at about 1150°C:

$$O_2 + 2C \text{ (charcoal or coke)} \rightarrow 2CO, \qquad (1)$$

followed by the overall reduction

$$2\,Fe_2O_3 + CO \rightarrow Fe_3O_4 + FeO + CO_2, \qquad (2a)$$
$$Fe_3O_4 + CO \rightarrow 3\,FeO + CO_2, \qquad (2b)$$
$$FeO + CO \rightarrow Fe + CO_2. \qquad (2c)$$

Some oxide combines with impurities to give a liquid slag which separates from the reduced iron. The latter in turn forms a pasty slag-rich lump or bloom. While hot and in a reactive state this bloom iron can also interact with CO or CO_2 to form iron carbide (van der Merwe 1969):

$$5\,Fe + CO_2 \rightarrow Fe_3C \text{ (cementite)} + 2\,FeO. \qquad (3)$$

Thus the iron retains, in the form of solid carbides, carbon having essentially the same isotopic composition as the carbon which was burned to carbon monoxide in eq. (1). If the carbon input was charcoal from contemporary vegetation, then the iron carbides might be expected to have a carbon-14 level reflecting that fact. Unfortunately for carbon dating, bloomery iron generally has no more than 0.1–0.2% carbon in the form of cementite by weight.

There are several possible and rather obvious sources of error. If, for example, the charcoal were replaced by coke, which is made from coal (having no carbon-14), the carbon monoxide in eq. (1) would be too "old" and this error would persist into the carbide phase, and in the dating. Likewise, if calcite (a natural calcium carbonate mineral usually containing "dead" carbon) were present in the ore charged into the bloomery furnace, then at high temperature:

$$CaCO_3 \rightarrow CaO + CO_2 \qquad (4)$$

followed by

$$CO_2 + C \rightarrow 2\,CO \qquad (5)$$

and a net reduction of carbon-14 content in the carbon monoxide would occur when the carbon monoxide from eq. (5) mixed with that from eq. (1). Despite these problems, van der Merwe was able to obtain reliable dates from several samples of iron of known age, including Roman bloomery iron (van der Merwe 1969).

By 1964 the mislaid Smithsonian bloom was rediscovered by Wilcomb Washburn (this volume;

Sayre et al. 1982) and in the light of the Viking discoveries of the Ingstads in Newfoundland (Ingstad 1977) it became a matter of paramount importance to attempt to date the bloom. Clearly, the technique of van der Merwe would be used, but unfortunately, bloomery iron has such a low carbon content (as noted above) that even if the whole bloom were sacrificed, only ca. 5 g of carbon would be obtained, and that was insufficient for conventional radiocarbon dating.

What was obviously needed was a miniaturization of the carbon-14 dating procedure, so that determinations could be made on bloom iron samples of moderate size. In the mid 1970s the accelerator mass spectrometer (AMS) technique for micro carbon-14 determination had not yet been invented, and a miniaturization of existing proportional-counter technology seemed to be the best bet. At Brookhaven Laboratory these miniature counters had been highly developed for counting a few atoms of argon-37 generated in large masses of chlorine-37 by solar neutrinos (Kummer et al. 1972, Davis 1978); this same technology was now exploited to miniaturize carbon-14 proportional counting down to a level of 10 mg of carbon (Sayre et al. 1981, 1982; Harbottle et al. 1979). This counter project was funded by the Smithsonian Institution, precisely with the goal of dating the original Smithsonian bloom.

At about this same period, great progress was being made by the General Ionex–Toronto–Rochester group at the University of Rochester in adapting the Tandem Van-de-Graaf accelerator to serve as a mass spectrometer, permitting the direct counting of carbon-14 present in very dilute (about 1 in 10^{14}) mixtures in archeological or other carbon specimens (Purser et al. 1977; Bennett et al. 1977, 1978; Maugh 1978). This procedure exploits the fact that carbon readily forms negative ions which can be accelerated to a positive potential terminal; nitrogen does not. The enormous discrimination of carbon-14 from nitrogen-14 provided by this quirk of nature is what permits AMS to be used in carbon dating.

As originally developed, AMS was capable of dating carbon samples of the order of a few milligrams; today the sensitivity has improved and submilligram specimens can be handled.

For this report, both the proportional counter and AMS techniques were employed; the former earlier, at Brookhaven (Sayre et al. 1982), the latter more

recently, at the IsoTrace Laboratory at the University of Toronto (Cresswell 1991b).

Carbon Dating the Blooms

Four iron blooms recovered from or traceable to the Frobisher site are listed in table 10.1. Blooms 1, 2 and 3 were found during the 1981 expedition (this volume); the fourth is that discovered by Hall (Hall 1865a) and rediscovered at the Smithsonian Institution in 1964. A fifth bloom, not yet cataloged or dated, was found in 1990 (table 10.1). Unfortunately, we cannot be sure as to the exact place of discovery of the Smithsonian bloom (Catalog 49459) in Countess of Warwick Sound. Hall himself is not very clear which of the three blooms he found (at Tikkoon Point, Kodlunarn Island, and Lookout Island) went to the Smithsonian Institution (Hall 1865a:437).[2] He does say that the Kodlunarn bloom was "sent to the British Government early in the year 1863, through the Royal Geographic Society of London." On the other hand, the 1864 and 1865 editions of Hall illustrate a bloom accompanying the account of the Kodlunarn discovery that appears to be identical with the Smithsonian specimen (see fig. 2.5d). Also, the account of this discovery says it was "a piece of iron, semi-spherical in shape, weighing twenty pounds," a rather good description of the Smithsonian object, while the Tikkoon bloom is described as "Iron—time-eaten, with ragged teeth! . . . weighing fifteen to twenty pounds," which does not fit so well. In any case two of the three blooms are today lost.

The dating procedure used with the Smithsonian bloom is fully described in Sayre et al. (1982). A very similar procedure was used to date the bit of charcoal which was found stuck into a small pit in bloom 1: the charcoal was combusted to carbon dioxide in a vacuum line, collected, purified, and forced into a miniature counter for measurement. This research was carried out at Brookhaven National Laboratory.

The dating of different components of bloom 2 was carried out at the IsoTrace Laboratory at the University of Toronto, utilizing the Accelerator Mass Spectrometer (Beukens et al. 1986, Kieser et al. 1986). An included sample of charcoal was cleaned

---

2. It seems likely that the Lookout Island bloom was found by Hall but was not collected by him (Fitzhugh, this volume, Chapter 5).

TABLE 10.1. Radiocarbon dates of the iron blooms from Kodlunarn Island

Bloom number	Accession or catalog number	Provenience	Material dated	Method	Age, ^{14}C years, B.P.	Calibrated radiocarbon date A.D.[a]
Smithsonian	49459	C.F. Hall, Kodlunarn I. or Tikkoon Pt.	Iron	Proportional Counter	679 ± 133	1240–1400
"	"	"	"	"	792 ± 107	1160–1280
1	Ke De–1:91	Kodlunarn I., S of ship's trench	Charcoal[b] external on bloom	"	628 ± 150	1250–1440
2	Ke De–1:87	Kodlunarn I. test pit 1, ship's trench	Charcoal[b] inclusion in iron V2-2/7	AMS	970 ± 60	1006–1150
"	"	"	Iron V2-IB	AMS	1340 ± 70	640–760
"	"	"	Iron V2-IA	AMS	550 ± 60[d]	1307–1355
"	"	"	Iron HI-2A	AMS	500 ± 60	1400–1442
3	Ke De–1:90	Kodlunarn I. test pit 2, ship's trench				
4	e	Cyrus Field Bay				

a. Tables of Stuiver and Pearson (1986) (1 σ confidence)
b. From spruce or larch
c. From birch or alder
d. Average of this and the following date (HI-2A) give a calibrated date of A.D. 1290–1456 for 95% confidence.
e. Present location, Prince of Wales Centre, Yellowknife, NWT, Canada. Found on 1990 expedition.

with a dilute acid-alkali-acid treatment, then combusted to carbon dioxide. Whereas the Brookhaven proportional counters were simply filled at this point, to supply a solid source of carbon for the Iso-Trace AMS the carbon dioxide was converted to acetylene, then cracked to amorphous graphite on aluminum. The graphite targets were then bombarded with caesium ions in the ion source of the mass spectrometer, producing negative carbon ions which could be analyzed using accelerator mass spectrometry, with the ratios of carbon-12, -13 and -14 measured relative to a standard.

NON-IRON SAMPLES

It is important that the non-iron dating samples (table 10.1) be described precisely. When dug from the ground the surface of bloom 1 was pitted, and embedded in this pock-marked surface was a small piece of charcoal weighing 55 mg. One might assume as a working hypothesis that the charcoal became embedded during the smelting process; thus the carbon date of the charcoal might be related to the (approximate) date of smelting. The charcoal has been identified as of coniferous (spruce/larch type) wood (Laeyendecker, this volume). The radiocarbon age obtained at Brookhaven was 628 ± 150

years. Unfortunately, at this radiocarbon age, the calibration curve has a serious "wiggle" resulting in a threefold redundancy in calibrated calendar dates (Stuiver and Pearson 1986) (fig. 10.1; table 10.1). This has the effect of considerably broadening the span of calendar dates corresponding to this one radiocarbon age, given its standard deviation.

The second non-iron sample is a 47.2-mg fragment of charcoal that was extracted from the interior of bloom 2 when it was sectioned by Parks Canada for metallurgical examination. Parks Canada designated the metallurgical section V2; the charcoal inclusion was designated V2-2/7 (Unglik 1987). This charcoal has been identified by one of us (RGC) as of birch-type wood. As mentioned above, the charcoal was purified, resulting in a residue of 16.5 mg. Of this, 11.4 mg was combusted to carbon dioxide, processed, and analyzed by AMS. The radiocarbon age was 970 ± 60 years; as above, the calibrated calendar date is listed in table 10.1.

The third non-iron sample was a 30.3-mg cinder lump, designated 53-16 by Parks Canada, analyzed at IsoTrace in the same manner as the charcoal. This lump was not closely associated with bloom 2; it came from the smithy site, S1, and gave a radiocarbon age of 25,640 ± 220 years B.P., suggesting that the cinder consisted of at least 95% coal, coke, or other nonradiogenic carbon.

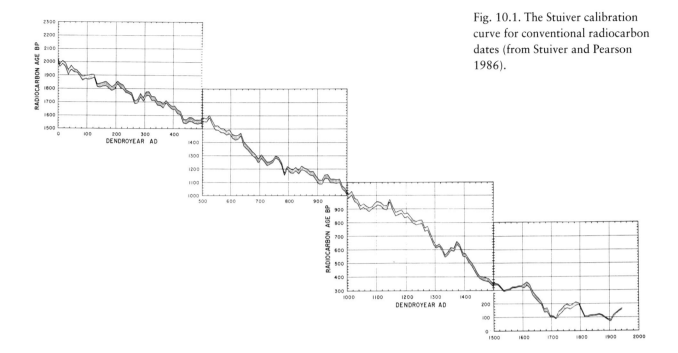

Fig. 10.1. The Stuiver calibration curve for conventional radiocarbon dates (from Stuiver and Pearson 1986).

IRON SAMPLES

The Smithsonian bloom (Catalog 49459) was dated by the van der Merwe (1969) procedure as follows (Sayre et al. 1982:446).

Approximately 1 kg was milled into powder. Two separate, identical iron samples were taken. The first sample, weighing 40 g, was pretreated with three 100-ml portions of 0.1 N HCl, followed by distilled water washing, and drying in vacuo. The second, also 40 g, was similarly treated except that three washes with 0.1 N NaOH preceded the acid treatment. Because the apparatus could only accomodate 10 g of iron at a time, three 10-g portions of iron from each sample were individually treated, and the resulting carbon dioxide combined. The iron was burned in a stream of oxygen; the overall reaction is

$$4 \, Fe + 3O_2 \rightarrow 2 \, Fe_2O_3, \qquad (6)$$

accompanied by the oxidation of the small quantity of iron carbide (cementite) present:

$$4 \, Fe_3C + 13 \, O_2 \rightarrow 6 \, Fe_2O_3 + 4 \, CO_2. \qquad (7)$$

The carbon dioxide was separated from the excess oxygen by trapping at liquid nitrogen temperature, then further purified by passage over copper wool at 700°C and, after adding more oxygen, by passage of the mixture over silver wool at 750°C. After still further purification on activated charcoal at 0°C, and several cycles of pumping to remove all traces of residual gases, the carbon dioxide was forced into a miniature counter at four atmospheres pressure, and the carbon-14 count rate determined.

The radiocarbon dates, and corresponding calibrated calendar dates obtained, are listed in table 10.1.

Bloom 2 was dated at the IsoTrace Laboratory as follows. Three samples shown to contain sufficiently high carbon for radiocarbon analysis (Unglik 1987) were cut from sections cut by Parks Canada. Sample V2-1A (3.21 g) was cut from section V2-1 (Parks Canada designation), approximately 30 mm from the outer surface and 30 mm from the base of the bloom. V2-1B (1.34 g) is an outer surface sample from the same section. H1-2A (3.40 g) was cut from section H1-2, approximately 50 mm from the outer surface and 10 mm from the base. Each sample was placed in a zirconia crucible, loaded into a quartz combustion chamber, and located within the coil of a 3-kW induction furnace. To increase the load for V2-1B, 6.48 g of carbon-free iron flux was added to this sample. Each sample was then preheated to 500°C to remove surficial contamination, then gradually brought to its melting point in a stream of pure oxygen. The derived carbon dioxide was then trapped and prepared for AMS analysis as described above.

Carbon dioxide yields were 7.3, 9.7, and 3.7 cc for samples H1-2A, V2-1a, and V2-1B, respectively. Assuming an 85% efficiency (Cresswell 1987), this gives carbon contents (by weight) of 0.14, 0.19, and 0.17%. These compare to an average of 0.06% for the Smithsonian bloom, but are consistent with the variable carbon contents reported for bloom 2 by Unglik (1987).

The radiocarbon and calibrated dates are given in table 10.1. For the Smithsonian bloom, duplicate radiocarbon determinations were made and these are listed separately. For the AMS dates on bloom 2, each aliquot of carbon dioxide was converted into a pair of targets, analyzed on two separate runs, and the results averaged.

In all samples reported here, including the charcoal, the isotopic abundance of carbon-13 was measured and used to correct the radiocarbon age in the usual manner (Michael and Ralph 1971, Sayre et al. 1982, Beukens et al. 1986). All radiocarbon ages were calculated using the conventional Libby mean life of 8033 years, corresponding to a radiocarbon half-life of 5568 years. Calibrations were effected using the Stuiver dendrochronological calibration curve (Stuiver and Pearson 1986).

The range of iron dates obtained by AMS dating of bloom 2 (table 10.1) requires comment. The greater age of the near-surface sample (V2-IB) could be taken to indicate possible diffusion and reaction of carbon monoxide of radiocarbon age greater than that of the bloom interior iron, taking place inward from the surface during some post-bloomery reworking. For example, if the bloom were reheated in a coal fire the surface carbon would be apparently "older." However, one knows that such a treatment would be metallurgically useless as the high sulfur content of coal leads to brittle, unusable iron. Also, the measured sulfur content of bloom 2 (Unglik, 1987) is normal for charcoal-smelted iron: if coal had been used for smelting or reheating, the sulfur would be as much as ten times higher. It was also noted by the analysts that sample V2-IB was taken in a part of the bloom where the iron contained much slag; this may have influenced the radiocarbon age.

It is clear from this range of dates that more carbon-14 dating measurements ought to be made, on several of these blooms, as a function of depth.

Interpretation of the Bloom Dates

If the bloom, and embedded/inclusion charcoal, dates are not systematically in error, we must explain or rationalize the observation (table 10.1) that they all fall significantly earlier than the Frobisher voyages (1576–78). Because of the great value of oak timber in Elizabeth's England, charcoal for any purpose was traditionally manufactured by use of smaller branches or cuttings from trees: wood that had no great value and would otherwise have been wasted (Tylecote 1962; Schubert 1957; Laeyendecker, this volume; Rackham 1980, 1986). We would argue, then, that if blooms of Elizabethan manufacture were present, whether smelted with charcoal in England or with English charcoal brought over by Frobisher, the iron carbide radiocarbon age ought to calibrate to not more than ca. 50 years before the 1570s, or ca. A.D. 1520 as a lower limit. Charcoal (1981-19) (a mixture of beech, birch and oak) from structure 3 (Laeyendecker, this volume) dated about a century earlier (A.D. 1410–1435, radiocarbon date 500 ± 35 B.P.), while oak charcoal from test pit 1 (1981-68B) dated to A.D. 1450–1535, 355 ± 45 B.P., the latter about what one would expect for charcoal brought from England. The former is similar to dates of the most interior of the iron samples; in this connection, it would be very desirable to date some more "Frobisher" charcoal, perhaps from the purported smithy area, that looks as though it might have been brought along as fuel.

Several authors (Laeyendecker, this volume; Sayre et al. 1982; Rostoker and Dvorak 1986) have commented on the idea that the pre-Frobisher dates observed for the iron blooms might have resulted from a local smelting operation using charcoal derived from driftwood, which can have an age of several hundred years. Laeyendecker (this volume) cites references on the age of driftwood, and notes that oak, beech, ash, hazel, or maple is generally not observed in northern driftwood. She concludes that only the coniferous charcoal on Kodlunarn Island at the Frobisher site could have been derived from driftwood. In general, she rejects the idea of local smelting using driftwood-charcoal.

A similar objection is registered by Rostoker and Dvorak (1986) who carried out earlier metallographic studies on the Smithsonian bloom. They have calculated that, to smelt the roughly 100 pounds of "Frobisher" blooms either recovered or recovered and then lost, some 8000 pounds of driftwood would have to have been collected and converted to charcoal by Frobisher's men. There are other strong arguments that can be made against this idea. Frobisher came three times, but in the first voyage, what with difficulties with the ice and the

Inuit, he barely set foot on land and made no camp, let alone gather iron ore, convert driftwood to charcoal, or smelt the iron to blooms. There was no motive, no reason, no time, and certainly no written record of smelting on the first voyage, and we may surely eliminate that possibility (see Stefansson and McCaskill 1938). On both the second and third voyages, substantial quantities of charcoal were taken along in the ships, for use in the smithies and for fire-assay of the "gold ore": second voyage, "charcoale 1 ton" (ibid. 2:98); third voyage, many tons of charcoal (Hogarth, pers. comm.)[3]. This being the case it is hard to understand why the expedition would squander their precious few days in Frobisher Bay gathering driftwood to burn to charcoal to smelt iron. It is worth noting that a typical charcoal "burning" involves many cords of wood and more than three weeks time (Zeier 1987). Also, suitable iron ore, probably bog ore, would have to have been located and reprocessed. Finally, there is no written record of any of these activities (Stefansson and McCaskill 1938, Fenton 1578) despite rather complete coverage of the events of the second and third voyages.

Indeed, the impression one gets in reading the eye witness accounts of these latter two voyages is of a constant struggle to save the boats from the shifting, deadly icebergs and floes, followed by desperate haste, once they were ashore, to mine the precious gold ore, test it, and somehow load tons of it into the ships before the ice came back again. It is difficult to see how driftwood collection, charcoal production, iron-ore mining and smelting can possibly have played any role under those circumstances. No archeological evidence has been found of charcoal pits, exploited iron ore deposits, or smelting slags.

If we accept Fenton's phrases about the "osmondes" as indicating that bloom iron was already present on Kodlunarn Island at the time of the second voyage, then we are rather strongly compelled to the conclusion that the iron blooms were already in the area before the Elizabethans arrived—a conclusion that is consistent with the iron carbide and embedded/inclusion carbon dating (table 10.1). Considering the metallographic quality and composition of the Smithsonian bloom, Rostoker and Dvorak (1986) reached the same conclusion as did Unglik (1987): the bloom was not likely brought from England.

Before we conclude that the data are consistent with a Viking origin of the blooms, there is one further possibility that needs to be mentioned. In the decades before Frobisher, there was a large fleet of fishing and whaling vessels operating out of Bordeaux, La Rochelle, other French ports, and the Côte Basque, making annual voyages to the St. Lawrence, Labrador, and Newfoundland waters (Turgeon 1986). For example, in 1565, a total of 80 ships were involved, while in Frobisher's era, ten years later, this number may have increased to as many as 350–380 ships (from all European ports; ibid:529). It does not seem impossible that some of these ships could have gone farther north, pursuing whales and even trading with the Inuit (Tuck 1985). Indeed, Stefansson and McCaskill several times note that the natives that Frobisher encountered already seemed to be familiar with people who came in ships (1938, 1:49 note 1, commenting on the Best narrative of the voyage) and Best himself noted that "they [the Inuit] use to traffic and exchange their commodities with some other people, of whom they have such things, as their miserable country, and ignorance of art to make, denyeth them to have, as bars of iron, heads of iron for their darts" (Stefansson and McCaskill 1938, 1:126). These authors assert that "the greater probability, because of the sum of the evidence, is, then, that ships were on the West Greenland and East Baffin coasts either habitually or sporadically before Frobisher" (ibid. 1:126 note 1).

If, however, these pre-Frobisher northern voyagers brought smelted iron blooms with them during roughly the first half of the 16th century, there would still be no obvious reason why those blooms should have iron carbide dates two to three centuries earlier.

The hypothesis that iron was brought to Frobisher Bay by the Vikings was not even considered by Stefansson and McCaskill (1938: appendix 9). However, in the years since 1938 much has happened to reshape our views and render this hypothesis more plausible. An increased knowledge of the Viking settlements in Greenland, coupled with the Ingstads' discovery of an unmistakeable Viking site at L'Anse aux Meadows in Newfoundland, plus some informed speculation on Viking navigation practice (Ingstad 1969, Ingstad 1977) has been persuasive.

---

3. Hogarth's research among contemporary archives relating to the third voyage has uncovered references to payments to suppliers of charcoal for that voyage. The total weight of charcoal was at least 12 tons.

Fig. 10.2. Iron smith at work expelling slag from a bloom using hammer and tongs while co-worker operates the bellows. This scene would have been a common one at ca. A.D. 1100 when this portal detail in the stave church at Hylestad, Aust-Agder, Norway, was carved. The source of the iron would have been bog ore. Similar technology was used by Norse in Iceland, Greenland, and at the Newfoundland L'Anse-aux-Meadows site. The bloom shown in this illustration is about half the size of the ones recovered from Kodlunarn Island (photo courtesy Universitetets Oldsaksamling).

At L'Anse aux Meadows, an iron-smelting furnace, smelted iron, iron slag, bog-iron ore, and a charcoal pit were excavated (Ingstad 1969:198; Ingstad 1977). At a Thule site in southern Baffin Island, an Inuit ivory carving may be taken to represent a Viking (Sabo and Sabo 1978). Tuck (1985) tells of finding Inuit artifacts at Red Bay, Labrador, amid the remains of a 16th-century Basque whaling station, and Schledermann (1980) discovered Norse finds at Ellesmere Island.

There is no longer any question of a Viking presence in these waters after about A.D. 900–1000 (Morison 1971:chapter 3). Frobisher Bay lay rather directly on the important sea route from Greenland to Markland, Helluland, and Vinland (Ingstad 1969). The Vikings smelted bog iron to blooms in their Vinland settlement (Ingstad 1977) and were thoroughly skilled in the practice. Taking all available evidence into account, it now appears probable that the blooms found at Frobisher Bay were indeed a product of Viking industry during the great period of their voyages to Northern America (see fig. 10.2).

Acknowledgments

The Brookhaven portion of this research was supported by contract DE-AC02-76CH00016 with the Department of Energy and supported by its Office of Basic Energy Science. The IsoTrace portion of this work was supported by the National Science and Engineering Research Council of Canada through grants to J. C. Rucklidge and A. E. Litherland and an infrastructure grant to the IsoTrace Laboratory. The authors thank the above, also R. P. Beukens for help and stimulating discussions, and D. Hogarth for many valuable additions and corrections.

11

Metallurgical Study of an Iron Bloom and Associated Finds from Kodlunarn Island

A metallurgical study was carried out on an iron bloom and associated finds, including lumps of slag, iron fragments, and pieces of fuel, at the request of the Smithsonian Institution in Washington, with the agreement of the Prince of Wales Northern Heritage Centre in Yellowknife, Northwest Territories. The artifacts were recovered from the 16th-century site of the Frobisher expeditions on Kodlunarn Island in Countess of Warwick Sound, adjacent to Baffin Island in the Canadian Arctic. This material together with two other iron blooms was found in 1981 in the course of an archeological survey conducted in Frobisher Bay by a Smithsonian team headed by Jacqueline Olin and William Fitzhugh.

The major Frobisher features were identified as a "ship's trench" (a long narrow excavation that had the appearance of a dry dock), a blacksmith's shop, "assay office," water reservoir or mining trench, "sentry house," a possible long shed or barracks, two large caches, pits and other structures. The blooms came from isolated buried spots. Bloom 1 was found in a sandy soil near the opened cache pits. Blooms 2 and 3 were from the ship's trench in association with pieces of 16th-century ceramics, European oak wood, charcoal, and rust. The slags came from entirely different sites, in the smithy and assay structures, several hundred meters from the ship's trench.

Iron Bloom

DESCRIPTION OF BLOOM

The designation, size and weight of the three blooms recovered from Kodlunarn Island are given in table 11.1.

All three blooms were in the shape of a cake of roughly the same height (figs. 11.1, 11.2, 11.4a,b,c). Bloom 1 was rounded, while blooms 2 and 3 were tapered on three sides, resembling somewhat a truncated cone with one flat side. As shown in table 11.1, blooms 1 and 3 were of similar diameter and

TABLE 11.1. Designation of iron blooms from Kodlunarn Island

Provenance no.	Code no.	Size (cm)	Weight (kg)
KeDe-1.87.981	2	Ø17/12×9	5.4
KeDe-1.91.981.4	1	Ø22×10	12.6
KeDe-1.90.981.4	3	Ø21.5/16.5×9	10.9

HENRY UNGLIK

181

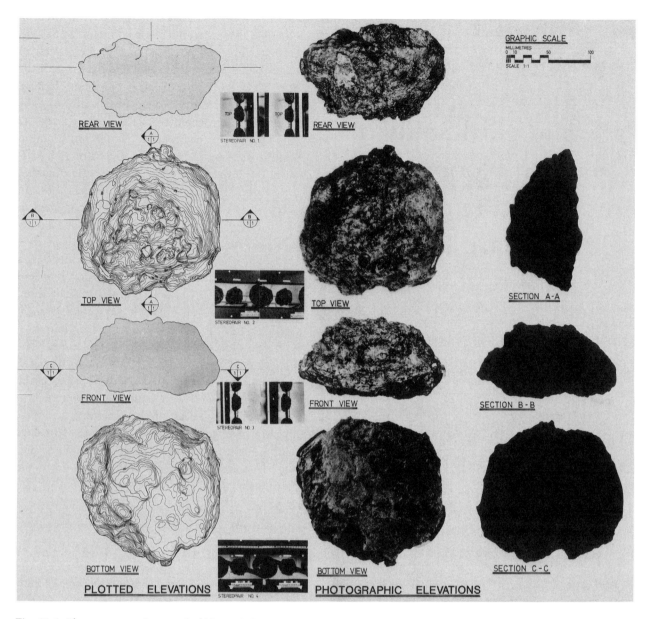

GRAPHIC SCALE
MILLIMETRES
0 10   50   100
SCALE 1:1

REAR VIEW

STEREOPAIR NO. 1

REAR VIEW

A
1|1

B
1|1

TOP VIEW

B
1|1

STEREOPAIR NO. 2

TOP VIEW

SECTION A-A

A
1|1

C
1|1

FRONT VIEW

C
1|1

STEREOPAIR NO. 3

FRONT VIEW

SECTION B-B

BOTTOM VIEW

PLOTTED ELEVATIONS

STEREOPAIR NO. 4

BOTTOM VIEW

PHOTOGRAPHIC ELEVATIONS

SECTION C-C

Fig. 11.1. Photogrammetric record of bloom 2, KeDe-1.87.981 (courtesy of Parks Canada).

weight. The weight of bloom 2, having a smaller diameter at one end, was about half that of the other blooms.

Visual observations showed the blooms to be heavily corroded; uneven magnetic pull varied within a single bloom from nonmagnetic to strongly magnetic. The dark-brown surfaces were rather porous and cracked in several places. Bloom 1 was cracked at the top, close to the edge. Bloom 2, with

a rough, irregular slag-like upper part and pieces of wood and charcoal adhering to the surface, was also cracked at the top. Bloom 3 was in the poorest state of preservation with large portions transformed to powdered rust, flaking off at the side.

Several large slices were taken from bloom 2 in the horizontal and vertical directions (fig. 11.3).The two horizontal slices (H1 and H2) were cut at the blooms widest end, throughout its entire width. This

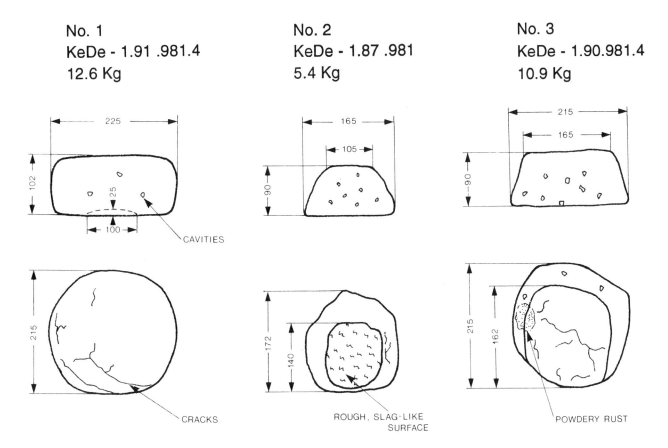

No. 1
KeDe - 1.91 .981.4
12.6 Kg

225
102
25
100
CAVITIES
215
CRACKS

No. 2
KeDe - 1.87 .981
5.4 Kg

165
105
90
172
140
ROUGH, SLAG-LIKE
SURFACE

No. 3
KeDe - 1.90.981.4
10.9 Kg

215
165
90
215
162
POWDERY RUST

Fig. 11.2. Sketches of iron blooms. Scale 1:6.

part of the bloom, with the larger diameter and about 40 mm high, henceforth will be called part H. The three vertical slices (V1, V2 and V3), beginning at and running parallel to the side surfaces, were cut through the bloom's height. This part, from the side with the smaller diameter, about 60 mm wide and 50 mm high, will be called part V.

Sectioning revealed that the bloom consists of a mixture of iron, slag, and void space (fig. 11.4d,e,f). The proportion of non-metal in the bloom was estimated from the surface area of the sections to be about 40%. Part V of the bloom contains about twice as much slag as part H. Macroscopic examination was used to investigate the structure of large areas. The macro-etching revealed considerable variations in carbon content and even distribution of sulfur. It appears that most of part H of the bloom (at its widest end) is lightly carburized, with some zones being heavily carburized. The remaining portion of the bloom (part V) shows very little or no carburization.

PART H

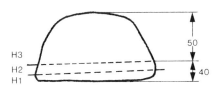

H3
H2
H1
50
40

PART V

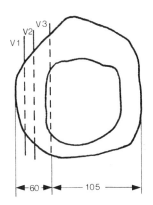

V1 V2 V3
60
105

Fig. 11.3. Location of macrosections in bloom 2.

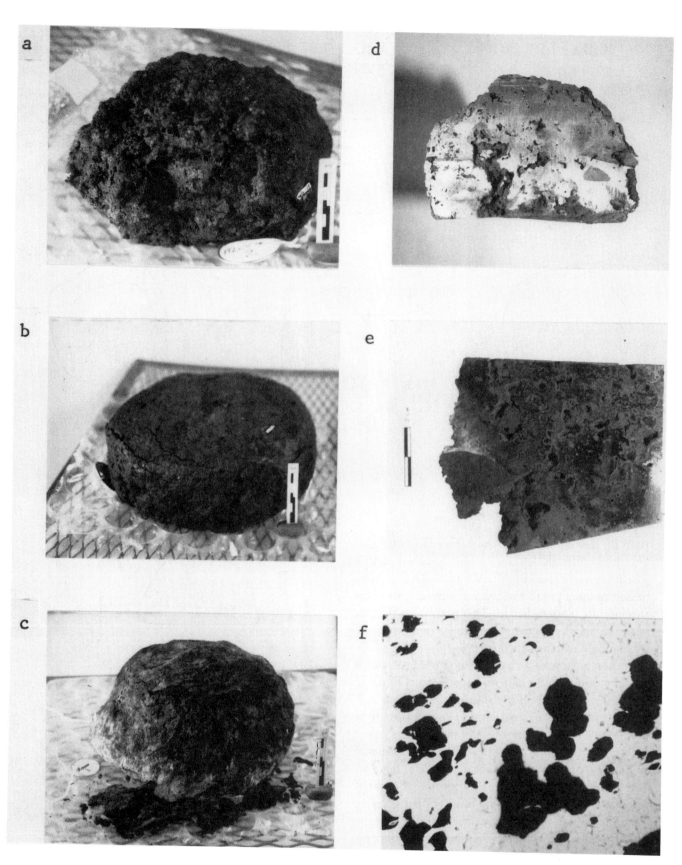

Fig. 11.4. Iron blooms before and after sectioning: *a,* bloom 2, × 0.3; *b,* bloom 1, × 0.3; *c,* bloom 3, × 0.3; *d,* bloom 2 after sectioning; *e,* macrosection H1-1; *f,* microsection H1-4/4, × 50.

METAL IN BLOOM: STRUCTURE AND COMPOSITION

In general, there is a clear separation between the large areas of metal and slag randomly intermixed in the bloom. Some parts of the bloom are almost completely free from slag but other parts contain a great deal of slag. In some samples many small and rather compact slag inclusions of duplex structure are visibly dispersed throughout the metal matrix (see fig. 11.8b). The lack of iron consolidation is evident in the samples containing large cavities in the metal matrix (fig. 11.4f).

Part H (horizontal sections) and part V (vertical sections) of the bloom clearly differ in structure, carbon content, grain size, and hardness of the material (table 11.2, figs. 11.5 and 11.6). The white areas in figures 11.5 and 11.6 (designated as iron) indicate the metallic parts of the bloom (ferritic iron) which were macro-etched, but were not subjected to microscopic examination. Part H (fig. 11.5) has a heterogeneous structure characterized by large variations in carbon content. A structure of ferrite with variable amounts of pearlite and a low to medium carbon content (0.2–0.5% C) is predominant here (fig. 11.7a,b,c). In addition, present in part H are highly carburized zones (ca. 0.7–0.8% C) with coarse colonies of pearlite and grain boundary ferrite (fig. 11.7d); very low carbon areas (< 0.05% C) with ferrite grains only are present in part V (fig. 11.8b).

Ferrite is a soft, low carbon phase with less than 0.05% C (nearly pure iron), while pearlite is much harder than ferrite and contains about 0.8% C. The average microhardness of ferrite and pearlite in the

TABLE 11.2. Microstructure of iron bloom 2

Code no.	Phase[a]	% C[b]	Grain size ASTM	Hardness HB	Structure[c]
H1-1/1	F+P	0.2–0.4	–	–	Widmanstätten str.
H1-1/3	F+P	0.2–0.3	3	–	Equiaxed grains
H1-1/4	F	<0.05	≥1	106	Equiaxed grains 0.1–1.2 mm, slag incl., phs. segreg.
H1-2/1	F+P	0.3–0.5	–	112	Widmanstätten str., variation in C
	P	≈0.8	–		
H1-3	F+P	0.2–0.3	–	–	Widmanstätten str., slag incl.
H1-4/2	F+P	0.2–0.5	–	120	Widmanstätten str., variation in C
H1-4/4	P+F	0.3–0.6	≥1	135	Widmanstätten str., wave str.,
	P	0.7–0.8			variation in C, equiaxed grains
H2-2/2	F+P	0.2–0.3	3	–	Equiaxed grains
H2-2/3	F	<0.05	1/2	124	Equiaxed grains, slag incl., phs. segreg.
H2-4/2	F+P	0.2–0.5	–	–	Widmanstätten str., wave str., slag incl.
H2-4/4	F+P	0.3–0.4	–	125	Widmanstätten str.
V1-1	F	<0.05	1/3		Equiaxed grains, wave str., slag incl.
V1-2	F+P	0.1–0.2	–	103	Equiaxed grains
V2-2/2	F	<0.05	≥1/2		Equiaxed grains, phs. segreg.,
	(F+P)	(0.1–0.2)			Widmanstätten str.
V2-3	F	<0.05	1	–	Equiaxed grains, slag incl., phs. segreg.
V3-1/2	F	<0.05	≥1/2	116	Equiaxed grains, phs. segreg.
	(F+P)	(0.2–0.3)			
V3-2/1	F	<0.05	1/2	101	Equiaxed grains
V3-3/1	F	<0.05	≥1/2	–	Equiaxed grains, nitrides, slag incl., phs. segreg.
V3-3/3	F	<0.05	≥2	–	Equiaxed grains
V3-3/6	F	<0.05	3/4	104	Equiaxed grains
	F+P	0.2–0.3			

[a]F = ferrite, P = pearlite
[b]Carbon content estimated metallographically
[c]phs = phosphorus, C = carbon

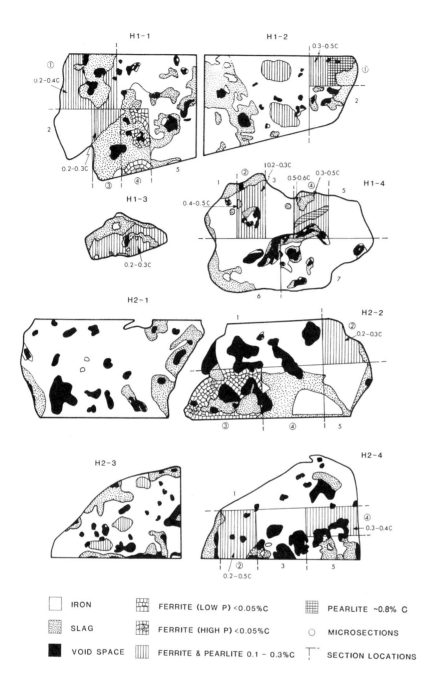

Fig. 11.5. Structural phases in iron bloom 2: Part H (at widest end).

H1-1   H1-2
0.3-0.5C
① 0.2-0.4C
①
2
2
0.2-0.3C
③   ④   5
H1-3
②   3 0.2-0.3C 0.3-0.5C
0.5-0.6C ④ 5 H1-4
0.4-0.5C ②
0.2-0.3C
6   7
H2-1

H2-2
② 0.2-0.3C
③   ④   5
H2-3   H2-4
④ 0.3-0.4C
② 3 5
0.2-0.5C

☐ IRON	⊞ FERRITE (LOW P) <0.05%C	☷ PEARLITE ~0.8% C
▦ SLAG	▦ FERRITE (HIGH P) <0.05%C	○ MICROSECTIONS
■ VOID SPACE	⦀ FERRITE & PEARLITE 0.1 - 0.3%C	⊤ SECTION LOCATIONS

bloom is 163 HV$_{50}$ and 264 HV$_{50}$, respectively (table 11.3). Since ferrite developed a Widmanstätten pattern, the general structure of the metal is not markedly granular. This type of structure, named after Alois von Widmanstätten, was first encountered in meteorites. It is found in more or less pronounced state in steel castings which have been cooled from a very high temperature without being worked.

Part H of the bloom actually consists of two types of equally prevalent structures. One is that of a pearlite matrix with Widmanstätten pattern of par-

allel ferrite plates and needles at prior austenite grain boundaries and within grains. The holding of iron and steel at a very high temperature for any considerable length of time necessarily develops a very coarse grain structure, and the metal is then said to be overheated. Slow cooling also will tend to coarsen the structure. At the same time the more carbon and the higher the rate of cooling, the smaller the amount of proeutectoid ferrite to be found. The other type of structure is that of coarse equiaxed ferrite grains with pockets of pearlite.

Fig. 11.6. Structural phases in iron
bloom 2: Part V (at smallest end).

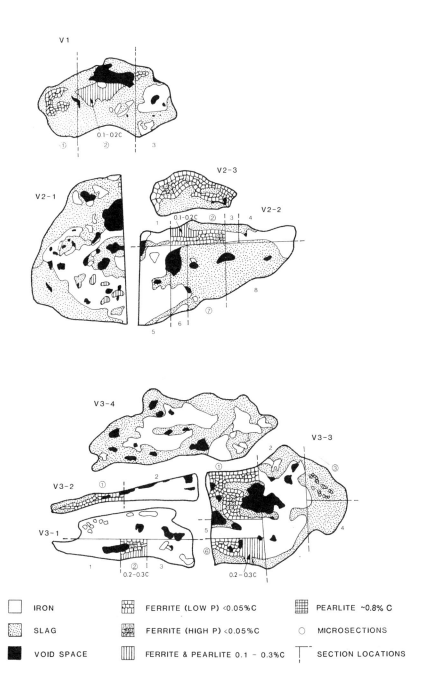

The Widmanstätten distribution of ferrite suggests that this portion of metal was cooled from a
high temperature at a fairly fast rate. Average hardness of the material in part H of the bloom is 120
HB. This overheated (say at 1100–1200°C), coarse-
grained structure with Widmanstätten pattern of ferrite is evidence that the metal is without any mechanical treatment such as hammering. Overheated
and coarse-grained iron has usually lower strength
and may have lower ductility.

The low carbon structure of part V of the bloom

(fig. 11.6) consists essentially of extremely coarse,
equiaxed ferrite grains ASTM No. 1/2 or larger (fig.
11.8a,b). Only small portions of metal contain ferrite with pockets of pearlite.

The carbon present as pearlite is concentrated locally to the extent of 0.1–0.3%. The average hardness of part V of the bloom, 106 HB, indicates a soft
but tough and ductile material. The huge ferrite
grains suggest a very low cooling rate from a high
temperature; the bloom was probably cooled in a
furnace.

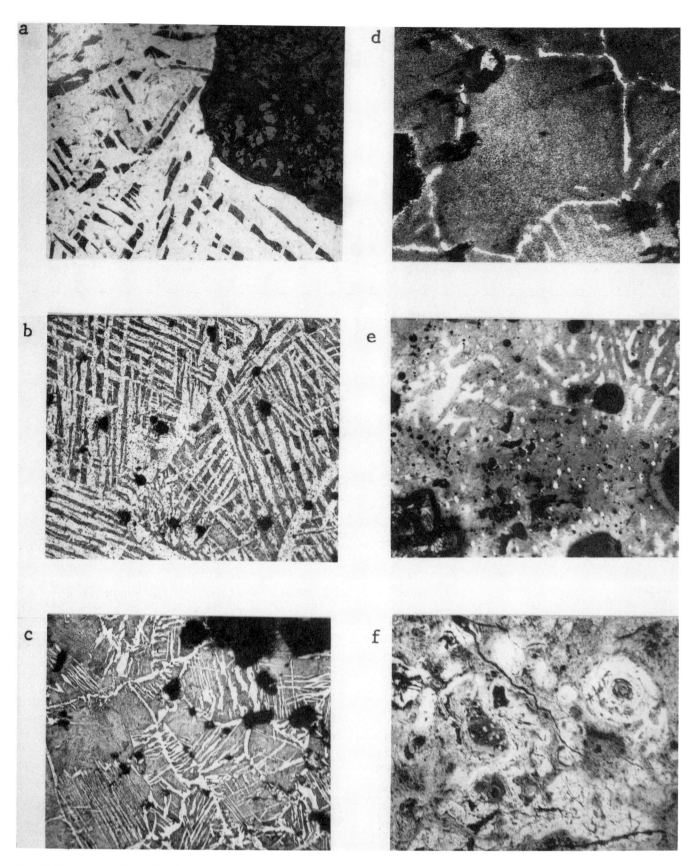

Fig. 11.7. Structure of metal in bloom (Part H): *a*, 0.2–0.4% C, × 100; *b*, 0.4–0.5% C, × 100; *c*, 0.5–0.6% C, × 50; *d*, 0.7% C, × 100; *e*, Oberhoffer reagent, × 50; *f*, mineralized iron, × 50.

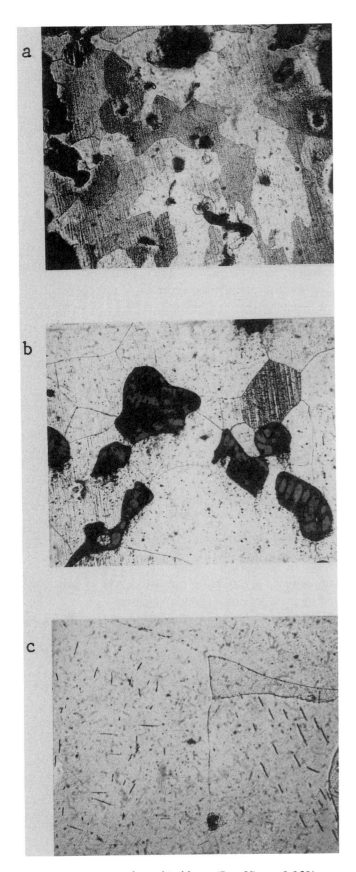

Fig. 11.8. Structure of metal in bloom (Part V): *a*, <0.05% C, × 50; *b*, < 0.05% C, × 100; *c*, nitride needles, × 300.

TABLE 11.3. Microhardness of phases in iron bloom 2, HV_{50}

Code no.	Ferrite		Pearlite
	P-poor (dark area)	P-rich (light area)	
H1-1/1	181	–	257
H1-1/3	136	–	279
H1-1/4	169	214	–
H1-2/1	168	–	245
H1-3	168	–	280
H2-4/2	181	–	257
V2-3	136	–	–
V3-1/2	167	183	–
V3-3/1	157	212	–
AVERAGE	163	203	264
RANGE	136–181	183–212	245–280

Though some phosphorus segregation was observed in the bloom, selective etching with the Oberhoffer reagent revealed that most of the low carbon ferrite matrix is also low in phosphorus. Serrated zones of ferrite due to phosphorus segregation are shown in figure 11.7e. The P-poor dark etched areas clearly contrast with the P-rich areas of ferrite which on etching remain light. Since the presence of phosphorus increases hardness (Piaskowski 1970:207; Tylecote 1986:145), it was not surprising that the P-rich ferrite yielded higher hardness (avg. 203 HV_{50}) than the P-poor ferrite (avg. 163 HV_{50}). Hot working of the bloom would result in banded structure in the portions with phosphorus segregation, leading to cold-shortness, that is, brittleness at ordinary temperatures. Due to the heterogenous distribution of phosphorus in the ore and the lower diffusion rate of this element in iron at 1300°C compared with that of carbon, large variations in phosphorus content occur frequently in the structure of iron (Stead 1918:396f; Todd and Charles 1978:74). Phosphorus is a ferrite-stabilizing element, causing diffusion of carbon away from such phosphorus-rich regions that transfer first to ferrite on cooling. It is not uncommon to find isolated areas of high phosphorus content, even in low phosphorus iron.

Interestingly enough, the presence of iron nitrides was detected in the bloom. Figure 11.8c shows the ferrite grains with nitride precipitates in the form of rather long needles. In some areas of the bloom the metal corroded away leaving behind a matrix consisting of ferrous oxides (fig. 11.7f). The structure of

TABLE 11.4. Comparison of part H and part V of bloom 2

	Part H (at widest end)	Part V (at smallest end)
Proportion of slag	≈20%	≈40%
Proportion of nonmetal	≈30%	≈50%
Hardness	120 HB	106 HB
Carburization	considerable	little or none
Structure	F+P, (P,F) Widmanstätten, equiaxed grains	F, (F+P), equiaxed grains
Grain size	coarse	extremely coarse
Amount of carbon	variable, 0.35%C, (0–0.8%C)	little carbon, ≤0.1%C (0–0.3%C)
Rate of cooling	moderate	very slow

the mineralized iron zones may be described as "wave" structure due to the configuration and different shades of various oxide layers usually surrounding large corrosion cavities. Most likely, the light-gray areas represent magnetite, the light oxide areas are hematite, while the dark-gray regions are hydrated ferric oxides, or compacted ordinary rust. The comparison of part H with part V is made in table 11.4, recapitulating the characteristic features of bloom 2.

Part H of the bloom compared with part V contains less slag, the metal is characterized by uneven primary carburization, it is harder, and cooled from high temperature at a faster rate. Part V of the bloom, with considerably more slag, virtually no carbon, and extremely coarse grains, is softer and was cooled very slowly from high temperature. The hardness testing of the metal in the bloom yielded values ranging from 101 to 135 HB, the average value of the metallic material being 115 HB. Such hardness suggests a relatively tough material with equivalent tensile strength approximating 400 MPa. The considerable variation in hardness is due to the pronounced heterogeneity in structure. It should be added that the strength and toughness of an iron bar made from the bloom would be primarily governed by the size and distribution of slag stringers present in that bar (Gordon 1983:613, 1988:127).

The bloom's heterogeneity, as shown by the presence of low carbon content areas surrounded by others of very much higher carbon content, indicates that the material had never been fully molten. This great variability in the structure and carbon content was one of the most notable characteristics of bloomery iron. Extreme heterogeneity, as that in part H of the bloom, was typical of the material produced by the Roman bloomery process. Widmanstätten structure with large variations in carbon content was observed, for example, in the Forewood bloom from Sussex examined by Smythe (1936/37:198), and in the bloom found at Lower Slaughter, Gloucester (O'Neil and Brown 1966:31).

Chemical analysis of metal in the bloom was carried out after completion of microscopic examination on samples of known structure selected from areas with high, medium, and low carbon contents, as well as from P-poor and P-rich areas (for details of chemical procedure see appendix of this chapter). The results of chemical analysis (table 11.5) indicate that the iron samples contain a variable amount of carbon, very low in part V of the bloom and quite high in part H of the bloom reaching as much as 0.63% C. The predominantly P-poor iron portions of the bloom contain 0.1%P, while the few P-rich areas have a higher content of 0.25%P. As would be expected, the sulfur content of metal in the bloom is very low.

The exceptionally high silicon and manganese concentrations in iron can only come from the silica and manganese oxide contents of slag adhering to the metal in the bloom, which found its way to the analysis. This was corroborated by the electron-beam analysis performed by Richard Cresswell, University of Toronto, on sample H1-2. It showed the sample to be a very pure iron with traces of cobalt and no presence of silicon or manganese.

Generally, in bloomery iron, carbon is usually on the order of 0.1% or below, although in some cases it may rise as high as 0.3% or higher. Silicon and manganese contents are on the order of 0.05%, normally negligible in alloyed association with the metal, higher amounts existing almost entirely in the slag inclusions. Also the sulfur content of bloomery iron is low (less than 0.1%), a value below 0.04% being quite common. Phosphorus ranges from 0.03% to 0.5% with a tendency to be in the lower range limit. There are on record examples of blooms investigated over the past half-century or so. Of these examples several are reported in table 11.6 showing the composition of various Roman blooms in England and Medieval blooms in Ireland.

TABLE 11.5. Analysis of selected iron samples in bloom 2, wt. %

	H1-1/1	H1-2/1	H2-2/3	V3-1/2	V3-2/1	Average
C	0.09	0.63	0.05	0.07	0.07	0.26/0.07*
Si	1.34	0.95	4.19	1.46	0.86	1.8
Mn	0.38	0.37	1.59	1.01	0.31	0.7
P	0.12	0.11	0.30	0.23	0.08	0.1/0.25**
S	0.02	0.05	0.04	<0.02	<0.02	0.03
Cu	0.011	0.013	0.011	0.014	0.016	0.01
Ni	0.003	0.002	0.002	0.003	0.004	0.003
Co	0.005	0.009	0.002	0.005	0.008	0.006
As	<0.001	<0.001	0.004	0.006	0.004	0.003

*Carbon values in part H and part V of bloom, respectively.
**Phosphorus values in P-poor and P-rich areas of bloom, respectively.

SLAG IN BLOOM: STRUCTURE, COMPOSITION, AND CONSTITUTION

Testing (see appendix) showed the slag in the bloom to have a high specific gravity varying from 4.8 to 5.3. The specific gravity of a number of old bloomery slags from different European countries analyzed by Neumann (1954:38) varies between 2.7 and 4.4, averaging around 4.0. Serning (1973:17) determined the specific gravity of slag from Dalarna, a prehistoric iron center in Sweden, to be 2.4–3.4. Osann (1959:1208) gave a higher figure (approx. 3.7) for the majority of slags from a Germanic settlement of Salzgitter-Lobmachtersen dated to A.D. 200. The specific gravity of the slag in the bloom (5.0 avg.) is closest to the upper value given by Nielsen (1930:205) for primitive iron slag, ranging from 3 to 5.

Microscopic examination showed the structure of slag in the bloom to consist of a large amount of primary phase of wüstite (FeO) in a fayalite-glass matrix, the fayalite being an iron silicate ($2FeO \cdot SiO_2$) and the glass presumably approximating the composition of anorthite ($CaO \cdot Al_3O_2 \cdot 2SiO_2$). Wüstite appears white under reflected light and forms rounded dendrites. The predominant phase of fayalite usually occurs in the matrix as light-gray randomly oriented columns (fig. 11.9). The hardness of various phases differs by a significant though not a very large amount (table 11.7). Wüstite dendrites are considerably softer than fayalite or glass. Fayalite is only slightly softer than glass, and it has a tendency to crack, mainly from the corner. For comparison, table 11.7 also lists the microhardness values of bloomery slags from Roman Britain, the Norse site of L'Anse aux Meadows, Newfoundland, and Carthage, North Africa.

TABLE 11.6. Average composition of English and Irish blooms, wt.%

	Corbridge, Northumberland (Roman)	Forewood, Sussex (Roman)	Cranbrook, Kent (Roman)	Lower Slaughter, Gloucester (Roman)	Co. Fermanagh, Ulster (Medieval)	Downpatrick, Ulster (13th Century)
C	0.097	≤0.3	1.27	≤0.8	≤0.47	0.08
Si	0.046	–	0.2	tr.	0.01	0.16
Mn	0.040	–	–	tr.	0.01	0.02
P	0.044	–	0.02	0.085	0.072	0.061
S	0.025	–	0.027	0.007	0.017	0.038
Weight (kg)	18	1.24	0.71	11.0	5.2	≈0.7

SOURCES: For Corbridge: Bell 1912:127; for Forewood: Smythe 1936/37:197f; for Cranbrook: Brown 1964:502; for Lower Slaughter: O'Neil and Brown 1966:33; for Co. Fermanagh: Evans 1948:62; for Downpatrick: Schubert 1957:340, 140

TABLE 11.7. Microhardness of slag phases in bloom 2, HV$_{50}$

Code no.	Wüstite	Fayalite	Glass
H1-1/4	409	638	683
H1-4/4	401	613	666
H2-2/3	473	623	713
H2-2/4	435	628	733
V1-1	460	655	766
V2-2/7	480	766	841
V3-2/1	463	707	773
V3-3/1	473	759	825
AVERAGE	449	674	750
Britain (Roman)[a]	510	716	713
Carthage (Roman)[b]	574	665	760
L'Anse aux Meadows (Norse)[c]	584	867	753

[a]Wingrove (1970:264)
[b]Unglik (1986:110)
[c]Unglik and Stewart (1979:117)

The types of basic microconstituents identified by microscopic examination and microhardness measurements were confirmed by x-ray diffraction, which showed the presence of wüstite and fayalite in all the analyzed slags. The x-ray diffraction samples were taken directly from the polished slag sections after microscopic identification of the phases was completed.

In addition to the main phases, the presence of small granules of metallic iron was quite frequently observed in the slag structure (fig. 11.9b). These blobs of irregular shape were not melted completely during smelting. Also a piece of charcoal was detected in the bloom.

Fig. 11.9. Structure of slag in bloom: *a*, × 100; *b*, × 100; *c*, × 500.

The composition of individual samples and the average composition of slag in bloom 2 is given in table 11.8. The slag has a very high iron content. The lime content is uniformly low, not exceeding 1.5%. The slag is also low in other oxides like silica, alumina, and magnesia. Manganese oxide is less than 3.5%, alkali less than 1%, and titanium dioxide less than 0.1%. Phosphorus pentoxide is within 0.5–0.6%, and the sulfur content does not exceed 0.015%.

The trace element level of the bloom slag is generally low, the amounts of As, Cu, Ni, Mo, U, and B being less than 10 ppm, that of Co, Sn, Sb, and Zn less than 20 ppm, and that of Cr, V, and Bi ranging from 20 to 70 ppm. Only the level of Pb reached about 300 ppm.

A number of chemical analyses of typical bloomery slag from various countries was compiled (and averaged) in table 11.9 in accordance with information found in the literature. Direct comparison

TABLE 11.8. Analysis of slag in bloom 2, wt.%

	Individual samples				Average
	H12	V2-2/7	V2-2/8	V3-3/4	
Fe tot.	55.46	56.58	57.91	58.47	57.0
FeO*	71.35	72.79	74.50	75.22	73.5
SiO$_2$	11.59	12.30	9.17	7.99	10.3
CaO	1.00	1.38	0.91	0.83	1.0
Al$_2$O$_3$	1.97	2.33	1.71	1.47	1.9
MgO	0.27	0.38	0.29	0.26	0.3
MnO	2.50	3.26	2.30	2.18	2.6
P$_2$O$_5$	0.60	0.62	0.50	0.50	0.6
S	0.008	0.014	–	<0.01	0.01
TiO$_2$	0.06	0.07	0.06	0.05	0.06
Na$_2$O	0.09	0.13	0.03	0.06	0.08
K$_2$O	0.39	0.56	0.37	0.32	0.4
LOI	<0.05	<0.05	<0.05	<0.05	<0.05
TOTAL	90.07	94.04	90.02	89.10	
TRACE ELEMENTS (ppm)					
As		<5		<5	<5
Cu		<1		<1	<1
Ni		<1		<1	<1
Co		<1		14	7
Cr		38		39	39
Mo		4		8	6
V		64		56	60
Sn		19		18	19
Sb		15		<5	10
Pb		303		270	287
Ag		<0.5		<0.5	<0.5
Zn		11		8	10
Bi		27		19	23
U		<10		<10	<10
B		<5		–	<5

*All iron reported as FeO

TABLE 11.9. Average composition of ancient bloomery slags from various countries, wt. %

	Britain Early Iron Age[a]	Britain Roman[b]	Britain Early Medieval[c]	Britain Medieval[d]	Britain 13–17th century[e]	L'Anse aux Meadows, Canada Norse, 10–11th century[f]	Dalarna, Sweden Norse, 8–10th century[g]	Carthage, North Africa Roman, 5–7th century[h]	Germany Prehistoric[i]	Bohemia and Moravia until 12th century[j]	Poland Prehistoric—Medieval[k]	Russia 10–14th century[l]
FeO*	69.3	66.8	59.3	50.4	50.2	69.5	65.1	69.0	63.2	60.3	61.7	67.6
SiO_2	19.3	20.7	23.5	26.9	25.6	17.4	21.0	22.9	22.3	24.8	20.9	16.4
CaO	1.8	2.3	3.1	4.9	4.9	1.7	2.1	1.1	3.1	2.1	2.9	4.1
Al_2O_3	2.8	4.9	5.1	9.5	9.5	3.6	4.3	1.4	2.7	4.3	5.0	3.5
MgO	0.5	1.0	0.6	2.6	3.1	1.0	0.4	0.3	0.7	–	0.4	–
MnO	0.4	0.4	1.9	1.5	1.7	0.8	4.3	0.9	2.0	1.0	3.1	1.3
P_2O_5	0.8	0.3	1.1	0.7	1.0	0.6	0.3	–	3.3	0.6	3.7	2.4
S	0.02	0.06	0.09	0.03	0.05	0.06	–	–	–	–	–	–
TiO_2	0.3	0.4	0.3	0.3	0.3	0.3	–	0.3	–	–	–	–

a. Tylecote 1986:146 (omitted no. 5) (12 slags)
b. Morton and Wingrove 1969a:1559 (omitted nos. 7, 8, 11, 12, 13) (15 slags)
c. Tylecote 1986:186 (omitted nos. 1, 2, 10, 11, 20, 21, 23, 24, 25, 26) (17 slags)
d. Morton and Wingrove 1972:481f (23 slags)
e. Water powered; Tylecote 1986:209 (omitted no. 9) (8 slags)
f. Unglik and Stewart 1979 (24 slags)
g. Serning 1973:18, 37, 38, 68, 87, 103 (21 slags)
h. Unglik 1986:105 (omitted nos. 1036, 1142b, 1529a) (18 slags)
i. Oelsen and Schürmann 1954:509 (omitted nos. 3, 5, 6, 7, 10, 11, 31, 32, 60, 62, 69, 74, 83, 85, 97, 101) (85 slags)
j. Pleiner 1958:283 (omitted nos. 1, 2, 6, 9, 16, 20, 24, 31, 32) (25 slags)
k. Piaskowski 1961:266; 1964:147; 1972:449; 1973:263, 1981:435 (omitted nos. 8, 10; –; 1-3, 3-1, 3-2; 2;–) (33 slags)
l. Kolchin 1953:41 (omitted no. 6) (12 slags)
*All iron reported as FeO

indicates that there is more FeO and less of the remaining oxides, except MnO, in the bloom slag than in the typical smelting slag. It can be seen in table 11.9 that in Britain, there is a change in slag composition with time. The FeO content decreases while the contents of SiO_2, Al_2O_3 and other oxides increases considerably. Apparently, the development of bloomery furnaces made it possible to use poorer and less pure iron ores and increase the efficiency of the bloomery process. It might also be noted that the content of P_2O_5 is lower in the Roman period than in the early Iron Age and it increases again by early Medieval times.

In numerous analyses of ancient slag, researchers showed that bloomery slag is basically an iron silicate with a low content of oxides of other metals, with the main structural phases being wüstite and fayalite in a glass matrix. Bloomery slags from many ancient sites were shown to have a melting point ranging from 1100 to 1200°C. Good examples of those are La Tene slags from Siegerland (Gilles 1936:257), prehistoric slags from Tarp near Flensburg, Germany (Oelsen and Schürmann 1954:511), Roman slags from British Isles (Morton and Wingrove 1969a:1556) and Carthage, North Africa (Unglik 1986:105), and Viking slags from Dalarna, Sweden (Serning 1973:18, 37, 48, 68, 87) and L'Anse aux Meadows, Newfoundland (Unglik and Stewart 1979).

Bloomery slags are always very rich in iron. Such slags are liquid at the temperatures that can be attained using a direct method of iron manufacture. The reduction in a bloomery furnace was a smelting operation in which part of the iron contained in the charge acted as flux to the siliceous gangue material of the ore, thus causing high iron loss to the slag. Morton and Wingrove (1969b:55) consider that in the early bloomery process the iron content of the slag was on the order of 40–50%. Neumann (1954:34) maintains that even in more recent slags the iron content rarely drops below 32–35%; in older slags, however, it climbs up to 50–58%.

The Morton and Wingrove (1969a:1557) procedure was adopted in determination of the bloom slag constitution. According to them, the properties of bloomery slags are determined by the characteristics and properties of the mineral phases they contain and not merely by the properties of the oxides themselves.

Morton and Wingrove (1969a:1564) have concluded that bloomery slag consists of three phases: wüstite, fayalite, and anorthite. They considered that lime and alumina take up all the silica required to form anorthite ($CaO \cdot Al_2O_3 \cdot 2SiO_2$) and that residual silica then combines with iron to form fayalite ($2FeO \cdot SiO_2$). Using these assumptions, the original tap analysis was calculated from the chemical analysis of the slag by accepting that all the iron was present initially as ferrous iron. The tap analysis was in turn used in the calculation of the relative proportions of the three principal phases, and of three mineral constituents (FeO, SiO_2 and anorthite) necessary for estimation of the slag melting point. It should be pointed out that Morton and Wingrove allude at times to anorthite as a crystalline mineral phase, where it is more accurate to call it glass with the composition of anorthite. Thus, calculated amounts of microconstituents of the bloom slag are given in table 11.10. On average, the bloom slag contains $62.5 \pm 7.1\%$ wüstite, $31.8 \pm 6.2\%$ fayalite and $5.7 \pm 1.1\%$ glass with the composition of anorthite.

The melting temperature was estimated from the chemical analysis of the slag by plotting the calculated major constituents on a FeO-SiO_2-anorthite ternary phase diagram (Levin et al. 1956:171) and assuming that the whole slag has been molten. The

TABLE 11.10. Constitution of slag in bloom 2, wt.%

	Code no.				Average
	H12	V2-2/7	V2-2/8	V3-3/4	
ANALYSIS					
FeO	71.35	72.79	74.50	75.22	73.5
SiO_2	11.59	12.30	9.17	7.99	10.3
CaO	1.00	1.38	0.91	0.83	1.0
Al_2O_3	1.97	2.33	1.71	1.47	1.9
MgO	0.27	0.38	0.29	0.26	0.3
MnO	2.50	3.26	2.30	2.18	2.6
P_2O_5	0.60	0.62	0.50	0.50	0.6
S	0.008	0.014	–	<0.01	0.01
TiO_2	0.06	0.07	0.06	0.05	0.06
Alkali	0.48	0.69	0.40	0.38	0.5
TAP ANALYSIS					
FeO	79.35	77.44	82.81	84.47	81.0
SiO_2	12.89	13.09	10.19	8.97	11.3
CaO	1.11	1.47	1.01	0.93	1.1
Al_2O_3	2.19	2.48	1.90	1.65	2.1
MgO	0.30	0.40	0.32	0.29	0.3
MnO	2.78	3.47	2.56	2.45	2.8
P_2O_5	0.67	0.66	0.56	0.56	0.6
S	0.01	0.02	–	0.01	0.01
TiO_2	0.06	0.07	0.07	0.06	0.07
Alkali	0.53	0.73	0.44	0.43	0.5
MINERALOGICAL CONSTITUENTS					
FeO	83.2	82.1	86.4	88.0	84.7
SiO_2	11.0	10.8	8.4	7.3	9.4
Anorthite	5.8	7.2	5.2	4.7	5.7
MICROCONSTITUENTS					
Wüstite	56.9	56.3	66.4	70.5	62.5
Fayalite	37.4	36.5	28.4	24.8	31.8
Anorthite	5.8	7.2	5.2	4.7	5.7

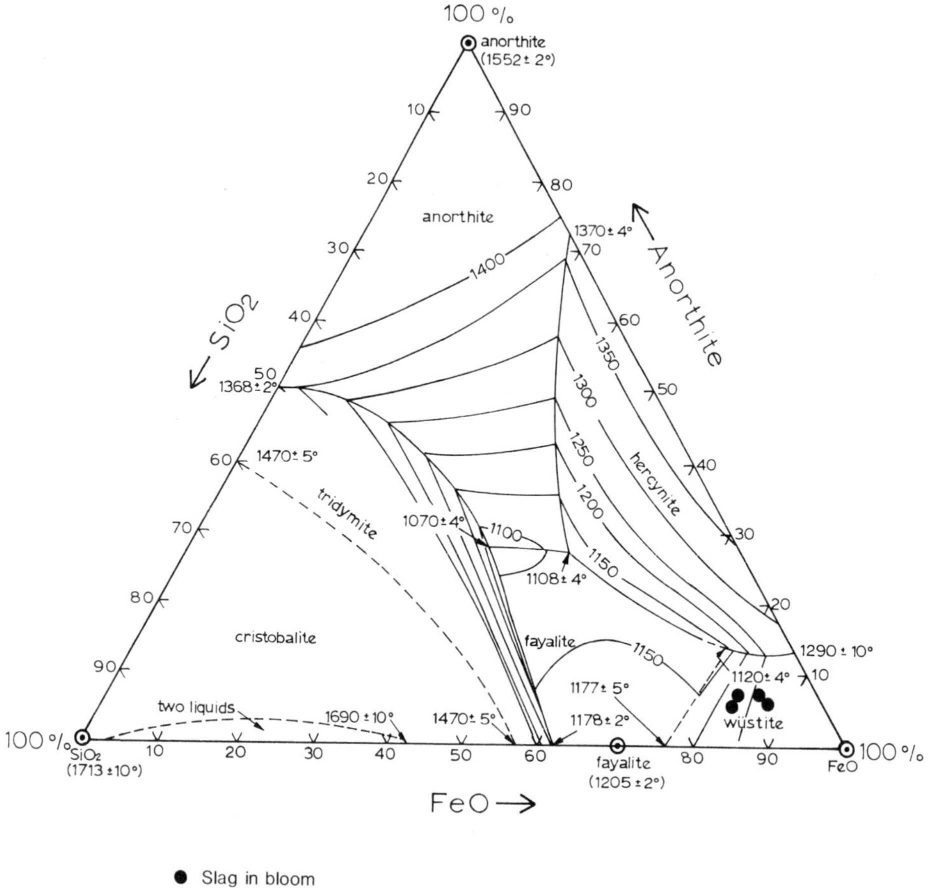

Fig. 11.10. Constitution and melting point of slag in bloom 2.

● Slag in bloom

ternary diagram in figure 11.10 demonstrates that the mineralogical constitution of the bloom slag is concentrated in a wide range of low melting compositions, at temperatures of 1150–1200°C, around the wüstite-fayalite region. Formation of such low-melting slags is essential if the production of bloomery iron is to succeed.

Associated Finds

CHARACTERIZATION OF ASSOCIATED MATERIAL

Apart from the blooms, a large number of various samples was collected several hundred meters from the site where bloom 2 was found. These included cinder, slag, some iron, lumps of fuel, stone, etc. (table 11.11).

Description of the finds, based on the results of preliminary examination, is given in table 11.12, which reports the approximate size, weight, specific gravity, and iron content of the individual samples. Out of five pieces of iron two are metallic iron (bloom fragments 53-39 and 58-1) and three are

completely mineralized. The lumps of fuel are small and very light (total of 90 grams), resembling coke rather than charcoal. Most of the samples in table 11.12 (c. 0.6 kg) represent waste material formed in the course of iron working. Visual observations showed these samples to be small lumps, on average $3 \times 2.5 \times 1.5$ cm in size and 13 g in weight. The largest lumps were $8 \times 5.5 \times 3$ cm in size, 51 g in weight, and another one 73 g in weight. The lumps basically include two by-products of iron working of

TABLE 11.11. Location and material of associated finds

Prov. no.	Material	Location
45	Layered pieces	Outside blacksmith's shop
46	Layered pieces	(Pond, Structure 1)
53	Cinder, slag, iron	Blacksmith's shop
54	Lumps of fuel	(Test pit No. 1, Structure 1)
58	Iron, slag	
89	Lumps of fuel	Pit (Structure 11)
97	Cinder	Outside blacksmith's shop

TABLE 11.12.   Description of lumps of slag and associated material

Code no.[a]		Approx. size (cm)	Weight (gram)	SG	Approx. % Fe[b]	Material[c]
45		2.5 × 2 × 2	14	–	–	Silicious fragment
46		3 × 2 × 1.5	19	–	–	Silicious fragment
53-1		5 × 4 × 4	73	3	53	Slag
53-2	(cl, ss)	4.5 × 4 × 1.5	18	3	14	Cinder
53-3		4.5 × 2.5 × 2	14	1.8	26	Cinder/Slag
53-4	(ss)	3 × 2.5 × 2	14	2.7	42	Slag/Cinder
53-5		4.5 × 3 × 3	16	2	5	Cinder
53-6		4 × 3 × 1	9	2.3	44	Cinder/Slag
53-7		3.5 × 2.5 × 1.5	11	2.4	35	Cinder
53-8	(ss)	4 × 3 × 1.5	13	2	37	Cinder/Stone
53-9		3 × 1.5 × 2	12	3.8	56	Slag
53-10	(cl)	3 × 3 × 2	9	2.3	5	Cinder
53-11		3 × 2 × 1.5	11	3.8	60	Slag
53-12		3 × 2 × 2	8	1.9	–	Stone
53-13	(ss)	8 × 5.5 × 3	59	1.9	33	Slag/Cinder
53-14	(cl, ss)	4.5 × 3.5 × 2	20	1.8	5	Cinder
53-15	(cl, ss)	3.5 × 3.5 × 3	23	2	20	Cinder
53-16	(cl, ss)	4.5 × 4.5 × 3	32	1.8	18	Cinder
53-17		4 × 4 × 2.5	21	2.2	33	Slag/Cinder
53-18		4.5 × 3 × 2	26	2	5	Cinder
53-19		3 × 3 × 1.5	10	2.1	–	Stone
53-20		2.5 × 2.5 × 2	16	2.2	21	Cinder
53-21	(ss)	2 × 1.5 × 1	3	2.5	22	Cinder
53-22		1.5 × 2 × 1.5	4	2.0	15	Cinder
53-23		2 × 1.5 × 1.5	2	2.1	16	Cinder
53-24		3 × 1.5 × 1	5	2.6	13	Cinder
53-25	(m)	2.5 × 2 × 1	3	2.5	28	Slag/Cinder
53-26	(m)	2.5 × 2 × 1	4	4	46	Slag
53-27	(m)	2.5 × 2 × 1.5	4	2.1	10	Cinder
53-28	(m, ss)	2 × 1.5 × 1.5	4	2.3	32	Cinder/Slag
53-29		3.5 × 2.5 × 1.5	5	1.8	43	Slag/Cinder
53-30		2.5 × 2 × 1.5	4	2.2	15	Cinder
53-31		2.5 × 2 × 2	6	2	19	Cinder
53-32		3 × 2 × 1	5	1.8	21	Cinder (w. Fe blobs)
53-33	(cl)	2.5 × 1.5 × 1.5	4	1.8	33	Cinder
53-34		2 × 1.5 × 1.5	8	3.3	56	Slag
53-35		2.5 × 2 × 1.5	6	2.5	44	Slag (w. Fe blobs)
53-36		2 × 1.5 × 1	3	2.2	8	Cinder/Slag
53-37		2.5 × 1.5 × 1.5	4	1.9	19	Cinder
53-38	(ss)	1.5 × 1.5 × 2	3	2.1	29	Cinder
53-39	(m)	2 × 2 × 1.5	15	–	–	Bloom fragm.
53-40	(m)	3 × 2 × 1	5	–	–	Mineralized iron
53-41	(m)	1.5 × 1.5 × 1.5	4	–	–	Mineralized iron
53-42	(m)	1.5 × 1.5 × 1	2	–	–	Mineralized iron
53-43		3 × 2.5 × 1.5	12	3.9	59	Slag
53-44	(cl)	3 × 2.5 × 1.5	6	2	19	Cinder
53-45		3 × 2.5 × 2	5	–	–	Lump of coke
53-46		3.5 × 2.5 × 1.5	10	–	18	Silicious fragment
53-47		3.5 × 2.5 × 1	9	–	30	Silicious fragment
53-48		3 × 2.5 × 1.5	9	1.9	27	Cinder (w. Fe blobs)
54		2.5 × 2.5 × 2	51	–	–	Lumps of coke
58-1	(m)	4 × 3.5 × 1.5	25	–	–	Bloom fragm.
58-2		3 × 2 × 1.5	12	3.5	59	Slag
89			35	–	–	Coke, bituminous coal
97-1		4 × 3 × 2.5	22	–	–	Stone
97-2	(cl)	5 × 3 × 2	25	2.2	30	Cinder/Slag (w. Fe blobs)
97-3		4 × 3 × 2	9	1.9	33	Cinder
97-4	(ss)	2 × 2 × 2	8	1.8	23	Cinder/Slag (w. Fe blobs)
97-5		1.5 × 1.5 × 1	16	2	13	Cinder
97-6		2 × 1.5 × 1	2	1.9	33	Cinder
97-7		1.5 × 1.5 × 1	2	1.7	5	Cinder
97-8		5.5 × 2 × 2	22	–	–	Stone

a. cl = coal; ss = silicious stone; m = magnetic

b. Approximate iron content determined semi-quantitatively by EDX surface analysis

c. As identified by microscopic examination

a distinctly different character. About two-fifth of the lumps are slags or contaminated slags, while the remaining lumps are cinders.

To clarify the terminology, in this paper smelting slag is a term applied to the iron-silicate complex formed in the molten condition in the furnace hearth during iron smelting. Cinder, as defined by Morton and Wingrove (1969a:1556, 1969b:57), is a drossy solid mass infusible at the working temperature of the hearth and embedded in a partially fused material often intermixed with slag. It collects on top of molten slag and never reaches a molten or free-flowing condition. Contaminated slag is a mixture of slag and cinder. Finery (and chafery) slag is related to the indirect process of wrought-iron production by refining pig iron, while smithing slag is a waste material of a blacksmithing operation during forging of iron to a desired shape.

The slag lumps have a compact, regular shape, steely color with a tinge of green, a rather smooth surface, and a solid glassy texture (fig. 11.11a). The exposed surface of some of the lumps exhibits a rippled appearance (fig. 11.11b), a sign of viscous flow from the furnace. The cinder lumps are somewhat lighter and have a black or steely-gray color. With few exceptions, the slag and cinder lumps were found to be nonmagnetic. The slag lumps have a high iron content ranging from about 45 to 60% and a relatively high specific gravity. The cinder lumps, as might be expected, have a lower iron content and lower specific gravity than the slags. About two-thirds of the cinders contain less than 15% iron. The contaminated slag lumps have intermediate values of iron and specific gravity.

The lumps of fuel were identified as coke and bituminous coal. In several lumps, mainly of cinder, pieces of coal were embedded in the matrix (fig. 11.11c). These coal fragments are remnants of the fuel originally used in the iron working. The white and yellowish fragments of stone, entrapped in a large number of cinder or contaminated slag lumps, consist predominantly of amorphous or crystalline silica with a small amount of iron. The coloration found on some of these pieces was most likely caused by high temperature and reaction with iron-containing slag. Another piece, consisting mainly of crystalline silica, is probably a loosely consolidated form of sandstone or schist, altered by heat and partly impregnated with cinder. This evidence suggests that the stone samples are likely remains of a siliceous furnace lining.

LUMPS OF SLAG AND CINDER: STRUCTURE, COMPOSITION, AND CONSTITUTION

As in the slag from the bloom, the structure of the slag lumps consists basically of three phases: fayalite, forming columnar crystals; wüstite, which is very often dendritic; and the glass phase, presumably of anorthite (tables 11.13, 11.14).

The predominant phase is that of large fayalite columns in a glass matrix. In several lumps small columns of secondary fayalite accompany the primary fayalite columns. The amount of primary dendrites of wüstite varies from sample to sample, but most of the slag lumps contain a large or considerable amount of this phase (fig. 11.11d). The lumps of slag contaminated with some infusible material display structural features common for both slag and cinder. The structure of contaminated slag 53-25 shows fayalite columns penetrating a fused matrix, typical of a slagged furnace lining material. In several lumps the iron oxide phase is not dendritic, but in the form of plates, probably of magnetite rather than wüstite.

TABLE 11.13. Microstructure of lumps of slag

Code no.	Fayalite columns	Wüstite dendrites	Glass	X-ray diffraction
53-1	3c	0	2	F
53-4*	3m	0	2	–
53-9	4c	2m	1	–
53-11	4c	3m	1	–
53-13*	3c	1f	2	–
53-17*	3m	1m	3	–
53-26	4m	2f	1	–
53-34	4c	3f	1	–
53-35	3f	0	3	–
53-43	3m	4f	1	F,W
58-2	3m	2f	1	F,W

Quantity: 0 = none, 1 = small amount, 2 = considerable amount, 3 = large amount, 4 = very large amount. Size: f = fine, m = medium, c = coarse. XRD compound: W = wüstite, F = fayalite.
*Contaminated slag

TABLE 11.14. Microhardness of phases in slag lumps, HV_{50}

Code no.	Wüstite	Fayalite	Glass	Iron blob
53-1	–	719	788	–
53-9	500	726	625	–
53-11	445	834	687	–
53-34	513	799	709	–
53-35	422	701	748	131
53-43	454	761	658	–
AVERAGE	467	757	703	
Slag in bloom (avg.)	449	674	750	

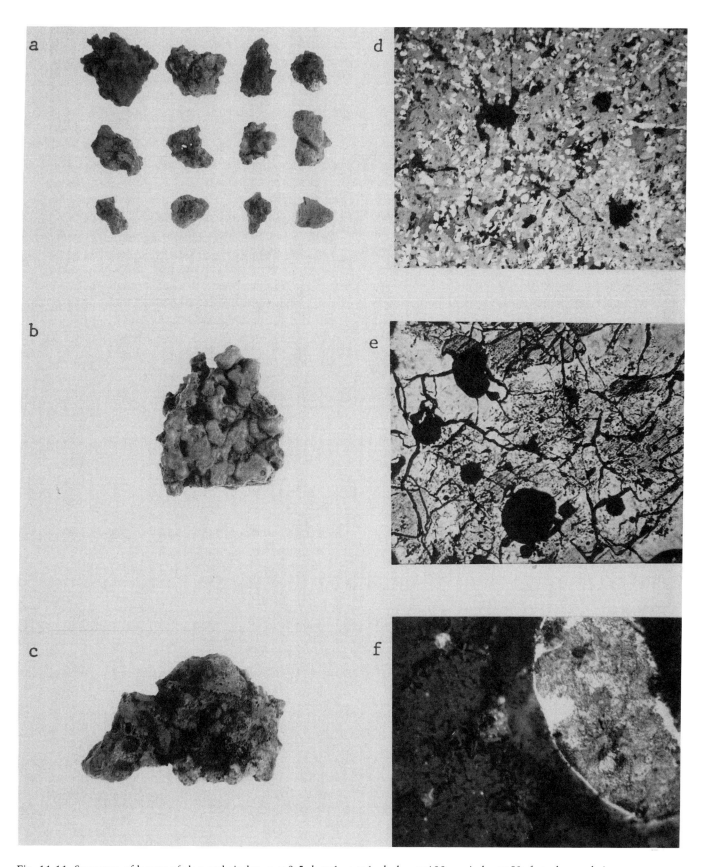

Fig. 11.11. Structure of lumps of slag and cinder: *a*, × 0.5; *b*, × 1; *c*, × 1; *d*, slag, × 100; *e*, cinder, × 50; *f*, steel granule in cinder, × 800.

TABLE 11.15. Microhardness of phases in cinder lumps, HV$_{50}$

Code no.	Matrix	Iron blob
53-37	762	–
53-32	752	190
53-47	673	–
53-48	759	278
97-2	713	202
97-4	726	271
AVERAGE	731	235

The cinder lumps have a different structure from that of the slag lumps. Microscopic examination did not reveal essentially any definitely recognizable mineralogical phases as it did in slag lumps. Typical microstructure under ordinary illumination consists of an almost featureless matrix with numerous pores and often many particles of sand (fig. 11.11e). Polarized light disclosed a large number of colorless and yellowish particles of silica embedded in a fused, amorphous matrix. Microhardness of the fused matrix corresponds closely to the microhardness of the fayalite phase in slag (table 11.15).

The structure of cinder resembles a mass infusible at the working temperature of the furnace embedded in a partially fused material, often intermixed with slag. Interestingly enough, some of the cinder and slag lumps contain irregular metallic iron blobs. The metallic iron granule in slag 53-35 is soft. Its low microhardness (131 HV$_{50}$) is indicative of the low carbon ferrite phase (<0.05% C). The structure of the much harder iron blob in cinder 53-48 (278 HV$_{50}$) is that of the high carbon pearlite phase (0.8% C, fig. 11.11f). The high microhardness of the iron blobs present in cinder lumps (avg. 235 HV$_{50}$) suggests that the granules are closer in structure and in the amount of carbon to steel than to iron.

TABLE 11.16.   Average composition of lumps of slag and cinder, wt. %

	Slag lumps (5 samples)	Contaminated slag (7 samples)	Cinder lumps (7 samples)	Slag in bloom (4 samples)
Fe tot.	46.4	19.9	12.1	57.1
FeO	59.7	25.5	15.5	73.5
SiO$_2$	21.7	47.7	54.0	10.3
CaO	0.9	2.1	3.2	1.0
Al$_2$O$_3$	6.7	12.9	14.9	1.9
MgO	0.7	0.9	0.9	0.3
MnO	0.08	0.06	0.06	2.6
P$_2$O$_5$	0.2	0.35	0.3	0.6
S	1.5	0.5	0.17	0.01
TiO$_2$	0.3	0.5	0.6	0.06
Na$_2$O	0.5	1.2	1.3	0.08
K$_2$O	0.6	1.0	0.4	0.4
TRACE ELEMENTS, ppm				
As	<5	≤8	≤5	<5
Cu	120	92	73	<1
Ni	62	98	77	<1
Co	24	38	34	7
Cr	98	173	130	39
Mo	15	6	3	6
V	109	265	208	60
Sn	15	10	<10	19
Sb	15	8	8	10
Pb	203	83	39	287
Ag	3	6	5	<0.5
Zn	13	13	12	10
Bi	16	≤6	≤2	23
U	<10	<10	<10	<10
B	<5	<5	10	<5

The material of the lumps is uniformly low in CaO, MgO, MnO, and alkali, and shows great variation in FeO, SiO₂, Al₂O₃, P₂O₅, S and TiO₂ (table 11.16). The trace element level though generally low is also somewhat variable, the noticeable elements being Cu, Ni, Co, Cr, V and Pb.

Table 11.16 demonstrates that the slag contains a large amount of FeO, substantial amounts of SiO₂, Al₂O₃ and TiO₂, and a very large amount of sulfur. Cinder lumps are lower than the slag lumps in FeO and S but they are significantly higher in such oxides as SiO₂, CaO, Al₂O₃ and TiO₂. Contaminated slag, comparing with cinder, has more FeO and S, less SiO₂, CaO and Al₂O₃ and basically the same amounts of MgO, MnO, P₂O₅, TiO₂ and alkali. It is then evident that the furnace lining, or some other material infusable at the working temperature of the hearth, contributes to the slag considerable amounts of Si, Al, Ca and Ti, while Fe and S clearly come from the slag. The furnace lining intermixture also resulted in partial enrichment of slag in such trace elements as Cr and V, and dilution in Pb, Cu, Mo and Sb.

The composition of the slag lumps, with high iron content, low silica, lime, alumina and other oxides, and no presence of copper, lead or tin is typical for slag resulting from a direct method of iron manufacture. As much as 40 to 50% iron is often present in the slags from ancient smelting furnaces (Aitchison 1960:200). The cinders resemble pumice or basalt lava and have often a very low iron content ranging from 6 to 19%. They could only be clearly identified as product of smelting on the basis of their metallic iron inclusions. The same type of cinder was found for example at Sigerland, a La Tène prehistoric site in Germany (Gilles 1936:258). It should be noted that the approximate iron content at the surface of the lumps (from the EDX analysis) is considerably higher than that obtained using DC plasma spectroscopy. This can be accounted for by the heterogeneous character of the lumps which often consist of fused fragments of slag and cinder, pieces of cinder coated or impregnated with slag, and pieces of coal and siliceous stone permeated with cinder or slag.

Similarly to the bloom slag, the constitution and melting points of lump slag and cinder were calculated from their chemical analyses using the Morton and Wingrove approach (table 11.17). In this method, the minimum operating temperature range in a furnace was estimated from the lump slag composition by matching these compositions against

TABLE 11.17. Constitution of lumps of slag, wt.%

	53-1	53-9	53-11	53-43	58-2
ANALYSIS					
FeO	49.94	60.74	64.61	64.24	58.76
SiO₂	26.80	21.90	19.50	18.30	22.10
CaO	1.43	0.78	0.59	0.67	0.91
Al₂O₃	7.84	6.67	6.30	5.99	6.87
MgO	0.77	0.50	0.40	0.71	0.85
MnO	0.10	0.06	0.05	0.09	0.11
P₂O₅	0.38	0.56	0.12	0.01	0.04
S	1.36	1.46	0.75	2.29	1.83
TiO₂	0.38	0.32	0.29	0.26	0.30
Alkali	1.65	0.94	0.93	0.81	1.30
TAP ANALYSIS					
FeO	55.09	64.67	67.13	68.80	63.14
SiO₂	29.56	23.32	20.26	19.60	23.75
CaO	1.58	0.83	0.61	0.72	0.98
Al₂O₃	8.65	7.10	6.55	6.41	7.38
HgO	0.85	0.53	0.42	0.76	0.91
MnO	0.11	0.06	0.05	0.10	0.12
P₂O₅	0.42	0.60	0.12	0.01	0.04
S	1.50	1.55	0.78	2.45	1.97
TiO₂	0.42	0.34	0.30	0.28	0.32
Alkali	1.82	1.00	0.97	0.87	1.40
MINERALOGICAL CONSTITUENTS					
FeO	61.8	71.6	75.3	76.0	70.4
SiO₂	29.4	23.9	21.3	20.0	24.2
Anorthite	8.8	4.5	3.4	4.0	5.4
MICROCONSTITUENTS					
Wüstite	–	14.6	24.5	28.3	12.7
Fayalite	87.7	80.9	72.1	67.7	81.9
Anorthite	8.8	4.6	3.4	4.0	5.4
Free SiO₂	3.5	–	–	–	–

previously determined isotherms on a ternary phase diagram. Both the slag lumps and the cinder/contaminated slag lumps contain fayalite and a glass phase, but the slag lumps have an excess of wüstite, whereas cinder lumps have an excess of free silica (table 11.18). Comparing with lumps of slag, the lumps of cinder/contaminated slag contain much less fayalite and more anorthite. The lack of free SiO₂ in the microstructure is due to nonequilibrium conditions resulting from rapid cooling outside the furnace which shifts the system toward the FeO side of the phase diagram and the formation of free SiO₂ is suppressed (Morton and Wingrove 1972:480).

The estimated melting temperature indicates that the lumps of slag fall within the normal working range of the bloomery iron production process, being usually 1100–1300°C (fig. 11.12). The lumps of contaminated slag, and even more explicitly those of

TABLE 11.18. Average content of microconstituents in lumps of slag and cinder, wt.%

	Slag			Cinder/Contaminated slag		
	$\overline{x}$	s	Range	$\overline{x}$	s	Range
Wüstite	16.0	11	0–28	–	–	–
Fayalite	78.1	8.0	67–88	32.0	14.5	6–55
Anorthite	5.2	2.1	3–9	15.7	14.0	3–49
Free SiO2	–	–	–	48.2	14.2	30–72

$\overline{x}$ = mean; s = standard deviation

experienced in the bloomery, confirming that this material is a product caused by poor furnace technique or an abnormally high operating temperature.

The slags from Kodlunarn Island are compared in figure 11.13 with a large number of bloomery slags studied by Oelsen and Schürmann (1954:510). The relationship between these slags is expressed graphically by means of a ternary diagram in terms of (FeO + MnO), SiO_2, and (Al_2O_3 + CaO + MgO + P_2O_5). The composition range of about 130 slags is marked by a broken line area, while the slag in the bloom and the lumps of slag and cinder are concentrated in distinct fields encircled by a solid line.

BLOOM FRAGMENTS: STRUCTURE AND COMPOSITION

It was quite unexpected to find bloom fragments among the slag/cinder lumps and associated material. The completely mineralized ferrous pieces show a wave structure with only few small metallic remains

cinder, are far removed from the fayalite region and are dispersed in the area of the cristobalite or tridymite monotectic shelf. The melting points of cinder/contaminated slag lumps are very high and fall outside the range of normal working temperatures

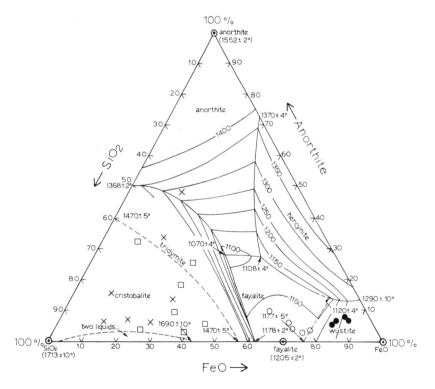

Fig. 11.12. Constitution and melting points of lumps of slag, contaminated slag, and cinder.

- ● Slag in bloom
- ○ Lumps of slag
- □ Lumps of contaminated slag
- ✕ Lumps of cinder

Fig. 11.13. Constitution of slag from Kodlunarn Island in terms of (FeO + MnO), SiO$_2$, and (CaO + Al$_2$O$_3$ + MgO + P$_2$O$_5$).

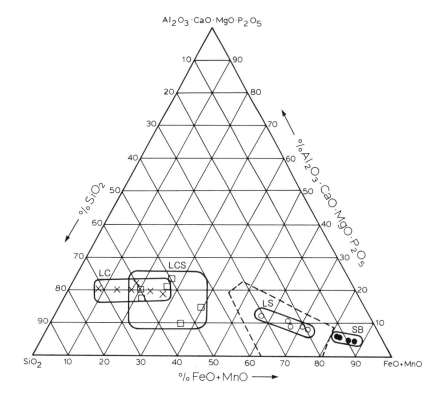

SB Slag in bloom
LS Lumps of slag
LCS Lumps of contaminated slag
LC Lumps of cinder
- - - Composition range of about 130 bloomery slags
studied by Oelsen and Schurmann (1954 : 510)

in the iron oxide matrix. The corroded metallic lumps 53-39 and 58-1 are small in size, not larger than 4 × 3.5 × 1.5 cm, and weigh 15 g and 25 g, respectively. They show a high carbon structure characteristic for a bloom material (tables 11.19 and 11.20).

Sectioning of the iron pieces, containing many large cavities, revealed a lack of metal consolidation (fig. 11.14a). The bloom fragments have a Widmanstätten structure with a widely varying carbon content (0.2 to 0.7%) and no slag inclusions. Ferrite occurs here along boundaries of very coarse prior austenite grains and as plates within grains (fig. 11.14b). These structural zones are intermixed with zones containing various proportions of ferrite and pockets of pearlite (fig. 11.14c,d). Pearlite has a structure of parallel alternate plates of ferrite and cementite. The coarse pearlite lamellae are easily resolvable at higher magnification. The large interlamellar spacing indicates a slow rate of cooling. The

After etching with Oberhoffer reagent, the bloom fragments also exhibited pronounced phosphorus segregation (fig. 11.14e). The microhardness of dark etched, P-poor ferrite grains is 154 HV$_{50}$, while that of light etched, P-rich ferrite grains is 224 HV$_{50}$, almost as high as that of pearlite (230 HV$_{50}$).

Analysis of the bloom fragments (table 11.21) revealed that the metal contains very little manganese, a relatively high amount of carbon, which is consistent with the fragments' structure, a considerable amount of phosphorus, and a very high sulfur content. It is unlikely that any of the silicon showed in the analysis is in the metal. Silicon and part of the sulfur are due to the residual slag admixed with metal in the bloom fragments.

Since the two bloom fragments have almost identical structure, they may have come from the same bloom. They share with part H of bloom 2 a similar structure and hardness, considerable carburization, variable amount of carbon, and large grain size. The

TABLE 11.19.   Microstructure of bloom fragments

Code no.	Phase[a]	% C[b]	Brinell hardness	Structure
53-40 53-41 53-42	Mineralized iron			Wave structure, metallic remains
53-39	P + F	0.6–0.7	125	Widmanstätten str., variation in carbon,
	F + P	0.4–0.5		phosphorus segreg.
	F + P	0.2–0.3	116–135	
58-1	P + F	0.6–0.7	123	Widmanstätten str., variation in carbon,
	F + P	0.4–0.5		phosphorus segreg.
	F + P	0.2–0.3	108–144	

a. P = pearlite; F = ferrite
b. Carbon content estimated metallographically

TABLE 11.20.   Microhardness of phases in bloom fragments, HV$_{50}$

| Code no. | Ferrite | | Pearlite |
	P-poor (dark area)	P-rich (light area)	
53-39	150	219	234
58-1	157	228	226
AVERAGE	154	224	230

TABLE 11.21.   Analysis of bloom fragments, wt. %

| | Bloom fragments | | | Bloom 2
(average) |
	53-39	58-1	Average	
C	0.35	0.22	0.3	0.26/0.07
Si	1.88	0.28	1.1	1.8
Mn	0.01	0.02	0.02	0.7
P	0.15	0.15	0.15	0.1/0.25
S	0.37	0.18	0.3	0.03
Cu	0.030	0.023	0.03	0.01
Ni	0.025	0.018	0.02	0.003
Co	0.007	0.006	0.007	0.006
As	0.005	0.001	0.003	0.003

two bloom fragments are similar in structure to the piece of iron produced by a postmedieval bloomery furnace at Muncaster, Cumberland (Brown 1970: 29). They may have been broken off when the bloom was taken out of the furnace, or at the first attempt of forging this brittle material.

Method of Manufacture

In the old direct-reduction process, a mixture of pure and rich iron ore and charcoal was heated in a bloomery furnace at relatively low temperatures of about 1100–1300°C (Pleiner 1969:484, Wynne and Tylecote 1958:346). The separation of iron oxide from the gangue and its reduction to metallic iron occurred simultaneously. A fluid slag was formed by the fluxing of silica with some of the iron oxide. The iron oxide was reduced by CO formed by partial combustion of charcoal with the blast air forced into the furnace through a tuyere. The iron ore in this process must not be too close to the tuyere or the gas will not contain sufficient CO to reduce the iron (Tylecote 1986:130).

The iron was first reduced from the ore in the form of small carbon-free foils rapidly carburized by the reduction gases even at the relatively low temperatures (Pleiner 1968:316f.). The tiny granules gradually coalesced under surface tension forces into a sponge (Killick and Gordon 1988:122) and descended in a mushy, semiliquid state. In the lower part of the furnace, the metallic sponge was sintered and fused into larger and more compact lumps, which during passage through the oxidation zone in the vicinity of tuyere were again decarburized and solidified. The liquid silicate slag formed in the furnace protected the iron from carburization (Forbes 1972:201, Schubert 1957:26).

Certain portions of the charge would absorb more carbon than others in the upper part of the furnace, and if this part did not get too near to the

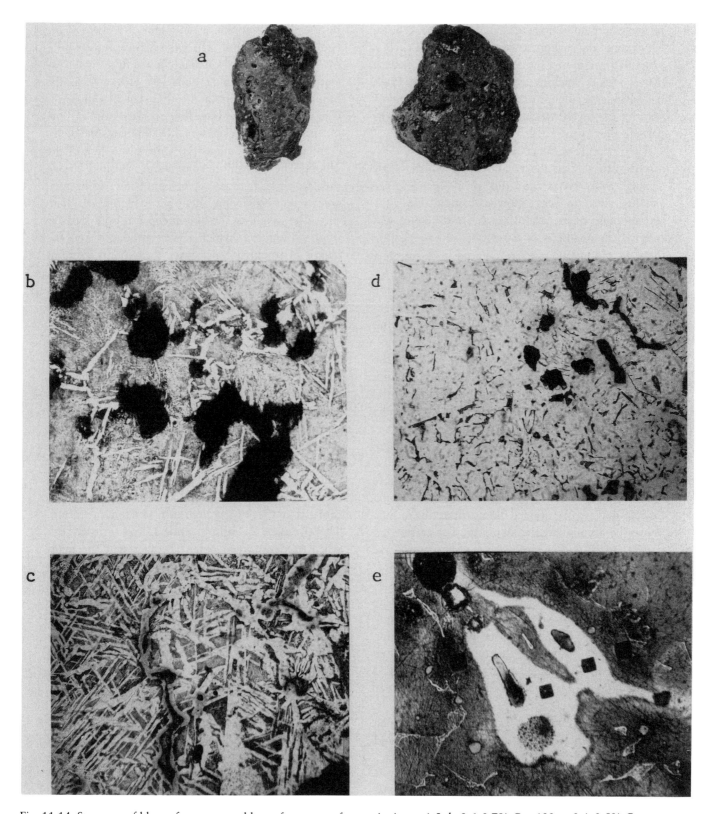

Fig. 11.14. Structure of bloom fragments: *a*, bloom fragments after sectioning, × 1.5; *b*, 0.6–0.7% C, × 100; *c*, 0.4–0.5% C, × 100; *d*, 0.2–0.3% C, × 100; *e*, Oberhoffer reagent, × 300.

tuyere where conditions are conducive to the burning away of the carbon, it would form a high-carbon area in the bloom (Tylecote 1986:173). In fact, it was shown in smelting experiments (Straube 1964: 937, Pleiner 1969:486) that the regions directly in front of the tuyere would have less carbon than the parts farther away.

The resulting product was a pasty mass of iron mixed with slag of the fayalite type, which partly drained away from the crude iron sponge. The smelting furnace was allowed to cool and the spongy mass of metallic iron, the raw bloom, was removed. A small bloom was produced by reheating the raw bloom in a separate furnace (a smithing hearth), or in the same one that had been used for smelting, and by initially forging it at a temperature above 1300°C in order to compact the iron and expel slag (Avery et al. 1988:264). After consolidation, the metal, usually in the form of a forged, semi-finished product, was ready for further shaping. The efficiency of the direct process was very low because the iron was used to flux the gangue material of the ore. Its poor yield was 20 to 55% of the iron in the ore; the remainder was lost in the slag.

It follows from the mechanism of the bloomery process that part V of the bloom (at the smallest end), having a ferritic structure and considerably more slag than part H, was facing the bottom of the furnace and was positioned close to the tuyere, just above the accumulated molten slag. The carburized part H (at the widest end), with less slag, must have been relatively close to the heap of charcoal, at some distance from the oxidizing zone near the mouth of the tuyere and the decarburizing influence of the molten slag. The inverted position would facilitate removal of the bloom from the furnace, assuming that much of the top of the furnace was broken away to gain access after each smelt. It would also account for the fact that part H was cooled faster than part V.

The large amount of wüstite in the bloom slag signifies low efficiency of the bloomery process and suggests that a primitive technique was used in manufacture of the bloom. The larger the amount of iron oxides appearing in the slag, the lower the efficiency of the process (McDonnell 1987:52; Scott 1990:157). As pointed out by Morton and Wingrove (1969c:66), some iron enters slag in the form of wüstite, and the quantity of this microconstituent may be partially controlled by the worker in order to obtain a good yield of iron, the aim being to produce a slag containing a minimum of wüstite at the end of the operation. The examination results indicate that the bloom was likely made in a man-powered bloomery running with low efficiency at the minimum temperature at 1100°C. The bloom slag is characterized by a low lime content and a low lime/silica ratio. This practically eliminates the deliberate addition of lime as flux during smelting of the bloom. The low sulfur contents in iron and in slag indicate that charcoal, a very pure low sulfur fuel, was used as a reducing agent in the bloom manufacture. The weight of the bloom depends upon the size of the furnace in which it was produced and the length of smelting time. Since the blooms in point are relatively small and light in weight, the dimensions of the furnace(s) were likely not much larger than those of the bowl-hearth furnaces still prevalent in the Roman period.

Let's consider now how the bloom fragments and the lumps of slag and cinder were manufactured. The composition of the lumps of slag indicates that no flux has been added to the ore. Given the high sulfur content, it is almost certain that the bloom fragments and the lumps of slag had been worked with S-containing fuel, probably the coked pieces of coal found at the site. The high-S bloom fragments and lumps of slag and cinder are probably a product of an unsuccessful attempt at smelting with coal, rather than that of a regular iron smelting operation. The presence of sulfur renders iron brittle both when hot and when cold. The fact that the manganese content is low makes it even worse, ensuring that all sulfur occurs as iron sulfide inclusions, which by inducing hot shortness in iron are so detrimental to its properties. The coarse-grained Widmanstätten structure of the bloomery fragments might be corrected by annealing, the cold shortness of brittleness due to phosphorus segregation does not preclude hot working, but the sulfur makes iron unforgeable at red heat and ultimately useless.

The fact that the bloom slag, comparing with the lump slag, contains much more wüstite and less fayalite suggests that the efficiency of the iron making process which resulted in the bloom slag was considerably lower than that which resulted in the lump slag. It appears that in the case of lump slag, other factors than the iron loss to slag, as expressed by the amount of wüstite present in the microstructure, contributed significantly to the relatively low efficiency of iron extraction. The refractory attack of the furnace lining by the slag is one of the factors;

the use of rather poor iron ores with a high alumina content is another. This, and possibly the lack of proper maintenance of the hearth after breaking the furnace walls to recover the bloom, would account for the extraordinary number of lumps of cinder and contaminated slag, almost five times as large as that of lumps of slag.

It was noticed earlier that the lumps of cinder frequently contained fragments of siliceous stone and coal. Apparently, the furnace, which operated at low temperatures of 1150–1200°C, was lined with siliceous stone. The many pieces of siliceous stone probably found their way into the cinder matrix when pieces of refractory fell off the walls of the bloomery furnace and were fused together by the molten slag mixed with reduced iron granules. We are also dealing with lumps of cinder from the furnace which thoroughly sintered rather than completely melted, and had not yet separated from the enclosed coal. Some of the refractory remains were actually shown to be a form of sandstone altered by heat. Sandstone would be quite handy for lining pits because it is relatively soft and often striated, thus permitting easy cutting or splitting into blocks or shapes for use in the raw state (Lankford et al. 1985:38). Although sandstones are normally well-jointed and easy to work, they are sometimes quite porous and consequently weathering action may have a very deleterious effect upon them.

Knowing the background of the Frobisher site one would be remiss not to consider the possibility that the lumps of slag and cinder were made in an assaying operation rather than by smelting iron ores. Assaying was in the 16th century an advanced field of applied science (Smith and Forbes 1957:59ff., Smith 1967:149). It refers to the examination of ore, especially of precious metal ore, to analyze the nature and proportion of its ingredients, to determine its purity, to find the yield of metal that could be expected from it and the possibility of profitably working it. The assaying operations were intended to reproduce quantitatively, but on a miniature scale, the operations of smelting. The purpose of assaying was to separate the metal when a roasted ore had been melted with flux and a reducing agent.

The fluxes for the assay of precious metal ores contained such ingredients as silica glass, salt, and borax, with a collector which was almost always lead. The most commonly used flux was the black flux, made by igniting a mixture of crude tartar and saltpeter (potassium nitrate, KNO_3) with a piece of charcoal. The materials heated leaving a blackish mass, consisting of a mixture of potassium nitrite, potassium carbonate, and carbon. Trial in a smith's forge was the most important assay of iron ores. The iron ore would be first magnetically separated then melted with saltpeter in a crucible in a blacksmith's forge. Analyses have shown that the lumps of slag and cinder contain very little potassium and only traces of boron and lead, the latter element being even in lesser quantity than in the bloom slag. This demonstrates that the lumps of slag and cinder are more than likely associated with iron working, and are not a product of assaying.

Origin

The structure and composition of metal and slag in the bloom can provide information on the origin and the iron making method used in its manufacture. In a bloomery process, where the smelting temperature was low and the iron was solid rather than liquid, the main source of impurities is the ore. It contains varying proportions of Si, Al, Ca, Mg, Mn, P and S, besides oxides of iron. At the temperatures operating in the bloomery process, most of the associated gangue minerals in the ore are not reduced into the iron but remain in the slag. The main exceptions to this are phosphorus and sulfur (Tylecote 1986:144, 169, 175; Schürmann 1958:1303f.). Often, the slag composition can be more useful than that of iron in finding the provenance of the iron objects and giving some indication about the nature of the smelting technique. The composition of bloomery slag depends on the composition of the ore and fuel and any reactions that take place between the slag and the furnace lining. In addition to the already mentioned elements, the presence of specific impurity such as V, Cr, Ti, and Mo can be used to identify ore source with unique local characteristics. Two elements in particular—manganese and phosphorus—represent important criteria for determining the origin of the ore on the basis of the chemical composition (Sperl 1979:82). Manganese, though often present in the ore, is not reduced during the normal smelting process and finds its way almost exclusively into the slag (Tylecote 1986:169).

Phosphorus can be reduced and taken up by the iron, although a portion of it finds its way into the slag. Arrhenius (1959, 1967) considers that iron with phosphorus content lower than 0.25% most likely is produced from low-phosphorus metalliferous ores. According to Tylecote (1986:175), the phosphorus content of the metal is about 0.5 to 0.25% of that of the slag. Piaskowski (1989:51) gives a wider range (0.26–0.8%) and estimates that only 5 to 15% of the phosphorus content of the ore goes to iron; in other words more than 80% goes to slag. Sulfur is a detrimental element in iron. Iron ores are generally very low in sulfur, and it is usually introduced by fuels such as peat and coal. Charcoal irons rarely show more than 0.05% S (Tylecote 1986:144). Though charcoal was the fuel ordinarily used for direct smelting of iron ore, much larger amounts of sulfur have been found in primitive irons believed to be smelted with coal. In fact there is abundant evidence that coal has been used for smithing and has perhaps been tried for smelting (ibid.:168). It was not until the late 17th century that coke was first successfully used in place of charcoal, and the full transition to coke followed in the 18th century (Coghlan 1977:22).

Now let's consider the implications of the composition of slag and metal in the examined bloom. The low silica, alumina, lime, and magnesia and the high iron oxide content, exceeding 70%, suggest that the slag in the bloom has been made from very pure and rich iron ores according to modern standards. Since in the bloomery process manganese hardly ever appears in the iron, the high manganese contents reported for the metal in the bloom are due to an incomplete separation of the slag before analysis. According to Gilles (1957:182), at 10% SiO_2 in the ore, the manganese content can be assumed to be about one third of that in slag, and at 25% SiO_2, about half of that in slag. Thus, the original ore used for smelting bloom 2 probably contained about 0.6% Mn, while the ore which resulted in the lump slags was much lower in this element, probably less than 0.05% Mn. The lower phosphorus content of iron and slag in the bloom suggests that low-phosphorus ores most likely were used in smelting the bloom. It figures from Piaskowski's and Tylecote's partition ratios that these ores would probably contain 0.3 to 0.5% P. The slag in the bloom is unlike most bloomery slags, because of the extremely low titanium content, less than 0.04%. This low titanium content may provide a means for tracing the ore source. The uniformly low lime content in slag, in no case exceeding 1.5%, could have easily come from the ore.

The bloom fragments and the lumps of slag show some similarity to the bloom, as well as important differences. For example, the bloom fragments and the lumps of slag were made from low phosphorus metalliferous ores. In contrast to the bloom slag the uniformly low manganese content is very noticeable in the lump slag and the bloom fragments, giving an indication that both are a product of smelting practically manganese-free iron ores. The alumina content in the lump slag is high compared to that usually found in primitive smelting slags, but not as high as in the Medieval slags. Piaskowski (1970:192) classified the slags from the territories of Poland on the basis of Al_2O_3, MnO, and P_2O_5 contents. According to that classification, the lump slag is a high Al_2O_3 (>6%), low MnO (<3.5%) and low P_2O_5 (<0.75%) slag. This excess alumina probably came from the ores used.

It was shown that the bloom slag and the slag in the form of lumps are compositionally different. The lump slag, comparing with the bloom slag, contains on average less FeO and more SiO_2, Al_2O_3, MgO and alkali. More significantly, the lump slag is substantially lower in MnO and P_2O_5, and much higher in S and TiO_2. The difference in manganese and titanium contents between the slag/cinder lumps and the slag in the bloom is worthy of note as illustrating the effect of different ore sources. Not less important is the fact that the trace element level of Cu, Ni, Co, Cr and V is visibly higher in the lump slag than in the bloom slag. When comparing the composition of slag with that of metal, it is interesting to note that both the slag and metal in the bloom are relatively high in manganese and low in sulfur. In contrast, both the lumps of slag and the bloom fragments are relatively low in manganese and high in sulfur. Furthermore, the levels of Cu, Ni, Co and As are significantly lower in slag than in metal, indicating that these trace elements are being easily reduced during smelting.

All of this leads to an inescapable conclusion that bloom 2 and the bloom fragments with associated lump slag do not share a common origin. Both are associated with iron working, but come from two different sources. The bloom 2 and the bloom fragments with associated lump slag differ in the type of ore used, the type of fuel, and the efficiency of the iron-making process. The presence of lumps of slag and cinder indicates that some sort of iron working was taking place at the Frobisher site resulting in these lumps and the bloom fragments.

Where bloom 2 was made is less clear. Some clues are provided by the size of the bloom and the composition of metal and slag. Schubert (1957:345), Tylecote (1986:211) and others reported on the progression of bloom size in the British Isles. There was a steady growth in the size of the bloom produced from the pre-Roman period up to the middle 14th century. In prehistoric Britain, the maximum weight of the bloom produced in the early bowl-hearth type furnace is given as 1 to 3 kg (Coghlan 1977:38, Schubert 1957:33). In the Roman period, large bowl furnaces and shaft furnaces were used, and bloom size increased from 5 to 10 kg (Coghlan 1977:38, Schubert 1957:54). In the migration period, most of the blooms found have proved to be somewhat smaller than the Roman maximum (Tylecote 1992: 75). The production of one bloom per day weighing about 15 kg may be taken as typical for an English bloom of medium size in the first half of the 14th century (Schubert 1957:139, Tylecote 1992:75). Though according to Aitchison (1960:200) and Forbes (1972:202), early furnaces were capable of producing in antiquity a bloom of about 20 kg.

Around 1400, when the application of water power was introduced more generally, the production was much higher, the bloom increasing in size to over 100 kg (Schubert 1957:140, Tylecote 1992: 76). In 1408–9, blooms weighing about 90 kg were obtained from smelting at Byrkeknott (Schubert 1957:140), and a bloomery in Eardale, Co. Durham, produced blooms weighing 100 kg (Tylecote et al. 1971:342f.). In about 1540, the normal weight of a bloom was about 130 kg, as for example in 1546 at the ancient Cistercian Abbey of Rievaulx in the North Riding of Yorkshire (Schubert 1957: 148). We can see that blooms comparable in size to bloom 2 were made in Britain in the Roman period, while those similar in weight to blooms 1 and 3 were produced between the 9th and the mid-14th centuries, long before Elizabethan times.

In Elizabethan times, the bloom reached about 130 kg in size, mainly due to the use of water power. As far as the composition is concerned, only the phosphorus content shows substantial variation with time in British iron and slag (Tylecote 1965: 165ff., 1986:199, 1992:66). The use of high-P ores was fairly general in the Iron Age (1st century B.C.), while low-P ores were in common use in the Roman period (1st–4th century A.D.). There was again a general tendency to use high-P ores in the Dark Age to early Medieval period (6th–13th century A.D.), culminating in the Saxo-Norman period (9th–11th century A.D.), and followed by a search for ores con-

taining low phosphorus in the later Medieval period (14th–15th century A.D.). Bloomery iron and slag with low phosphorus contents similar to the metal and slag in bloom 2 were typical for the Roman period and the late Medieval period.

The iron bloom recovered by Hall in the mid-19th century and deposited at the Smithsonian Institution was submitted for microscale carbon-14 dating performed at Brookhaven National Laboratory. It has been radiocarbon dated with their small counters at A.D. 1214 ± 175—three centuries earlier than the Frobisher voyages and within the period of Norse travels along the Baffin coast (Sayre et al 1982:447f.). This bloom, 18 cm in diameter and 9.1 kg in weight, was recently examined by the Conservation Analytical Laboratory of the Smithsonian (Anon. 1983:50). It was concluded that the bloom was probably not made or brought over by Frobisher, but rather made or introduced during the Norse occupation of Greenland in the 12th–13th centuries. Rostoker and Dvorak (1986:279, 287f.) made a similar claim, on the basis of a metallographic study of this bloom. They reasoned that the bloom would have been more likely produced on the northeast coast of North America rather than brought from Europe. As far as the new blooms are concerned, a piece of coniferous charcoal from the surface of bloom 1 was dated at Brookhaven to A.D. 1322 ± 150 (Laeyendecker 1987). This is probably about 150 years before the disappearance of the Norse community in Greenland. The Smithsonian's conventional radiocarbon dates on oak and beech type wood and charcoal associated with blooms 2 and 3 fall within the 16th and 17th centuries, a time period of Frobisher's voyages.

Recently, Cresswell (pers. comm. 1987), using accelerator mass spectroscopy at Isotrace Laboratory, University of Toronto, has carbon dated a sample of charcoal from inside bloom 2 at A.D. 1025 ± 50. The carbon dating of charcoal from bloom 2 (A.D. 1025), charcoal from bloom 1 (A.D. 1322), and iron from the Smithsonian bloom (A.D. 1214) gives dates consistent with the period of Norse occupation of Greenland and exploration of the North American coast. Norse accounts of voyages to the American mainland are reported in Viking sagas (Brøndsted 1965, Magnusson and Palsson 1965). Stefansson and McCaskill (1938, 1:xxi) mention the possibility of Norse travels from Greenland or Scandinavia to Baffin Island between A.D. 1000 and 1350. The Dorset Eskimos who also had lived in Greenland

and had been in direct contact with the Norse colonists, procured the terrestrial iron provided by the Norse and utilized it between the 10th and 15th centuries in the eastern and central Canadian Arctic (McCartney and Mack 1973:328f, 336). Norse iron was available from the area of Melville Bay by at least the 12th century A.D. Norse iron from the Silumit site on the western coast of Hudson Bay is the most southerly known and the earliest radiocarbon dated in the central area (A.D. 1140 and 1260). The most prolific Norse finds in the Canadian Arctic came from Thule villages in the region of eastern Ellesmere Island (Schledermann 1980). When Frobisher reached the area of Baffin Island, he found the Eskimos already in possession of some iron. Rickard (1934:538f.) thought that these bits of iron were obtained from driftwood which possibly came from northern Europe.

In fact, excavations at L'Anse aux Meadows, Newfoundland, have shown strong evidence that the site, dated to about A.D. 1000, was a Norse settlement from the Viking period (Ingstad 1977, Wallace 1977). Metallurgical examination of iron, slag, and ore revealed that smelting and smithing of iron were carried out at this site (Unglik and Stewart 1979). The use of a primitive, low efficiency process and the small size of bloom 2 tend to suggest that this crude piece of iron was unlikely to have been produced in 16th-century England and brought over by Frobisher to Kodlunarn Island. It should be pointed out, however, that if the bloom was made by Frobisher's men at the Baffin Island site under primitive field conditions, or by his contemporaries in a local, let's say, country bloomery, then indeed it could be smaller in size than the blooms typical for the Elizabethan period. The early carbon date might also result from charcoal smelting using old wood or driftwood.

Is it significant that blooms 1 and 3 as well as the Smithsonian bloom are of similar weight, while bloom 2 is smaller by about a half? The smaller size could possibly be explained by smelting bloom 2 for an appreciably shorter time than the other blooms. [Another explanation is loss of weight due to post-depositional rusting; see pages 83,84.–WWF] How likely is it that the several additional blooms found were made or introduced to the site by Frobisher? Who attempted to smelt iron using coal, thus producing the two bloom fragments and the lump of slag and cinder? These questions are not easily answered. We know that several blacksmiths with bellows and iron, as well as an assayer, were present on the ships' board during the second and third voyages (Stefansson and McCaskill 1938, 2:116f.). The list of supplies for the second voyage mentions also one ton of charcoal and 30 tons of coal (Stefansson and McCaskill 1938, 2:98). It would not make much sense for the Frobisher crew to smelt iron, if iron or iron blooms easily available for further processing were in their possession. The iron smiths aboard the Frobisher ships must have been aware that it was necessary to use charcoal rather than coal in iron smelting. With supportive carbon dating evidence obtained for blooms 1 and 2 and the Smithsonian bloom, it appears that these relics were left at the site not by Frobisher, but by some earlier visitors.

Conclusions

Bloom 2 is a normal product of smelting iron ore by the direct process where charcoal was used as fuel and no flux was added. It is a raw, unworked bloom made as a single piece in one smelt. It has not been melted and it does not show any signs of forging. No heat treatment had been given beyond such as would naturally accompany furnace cooling. The large amount of wüstite in the bloom slag signifies low efficiency of the bloomery process and suggests that a primitive technique was used in making the bloom. Smelting was carried out utilizing a low-phosphorus, low-manganese, and titanium-free ore. It was a pure and very rich iron ore, low in other oxides and trace elements. The iron extraction was likely conducted in a hand or foot powered bloomery at the minimum furnace temperature of 1100°C. The size of the furnace probably was not much larger than those of the bowl-hearth furnaces still prevalent in the Roman period.

Bloom 2 and the bloom fragments linked with the lump slag are not of common origin. Both are associated with iron working, but differ in the type of ore used, the type of fuel, and the efficiency of the iron-making process. Both the lumps of slag and the bloom fragments are relatively low in manganese and high in sulfur, in contrast to the slag and metal in the bloom being relatively high in manganese and low in sulfur. The lumps of slag are also relatively low in phosphorus and high in titanium, while the slag in the bloom is high in phosphorus and very low in titanium.

The metallurgical implications of the lumps of

slag and cinder must indicate that some sort of iron working was taking place at the Frobisher site. The bloom fragments and the lumps of slag and cinder most likely resulted from a smelting operation in which the same type of ore and fuel were used. This was a low-phosphorus and practically manganese-free iron ore, not as rich and pure as the ore used for making the bloom. Coal, not charcoal, was used as fuel. No attempt has been made to deliberately add lime as flux. The furnace was likely lined with siliceous stone and operated at temperatures of 1150–1200°C. The bloom fragments and the lumps of slag and cinder are a product of an unsuccessful attempt at smelting with coal, rather than that of a regular iron smelting operation. The presence of sulfur renders iron brittle both when hot and cold. Such iron is unforgeable at red heat and is useless in further processing. If in fact the Frobisher crew attempted to smelt any iron at the site, the small bloom fragments and the lumps of slag, both made with coal, would be most likely the products of their toil.

The blooms were carbon dated to a time span of several hundred years earlier than the period of the Frobisher voyages. Bloom 2 must have been made any time after A.D. 975, bloom 1 after A.D. 1172, and the Smithsonian bloom after A.D. 1039. A strict interpretation indicates that these carbon dates do not exclude either the pre-15th-century or the 16th-century origin of the blooms. However, if the carbon in wood used for charcoal was roughly contemporary with the making of the blooms, the probability that the iron is of 16th-century origin is very small indeed.

The important factors relevant to the origin of the blooms discussed here include the size of the bloom, the primitive, low-efficiency method of manufacture of bloom 2, the state of technology of iron making in Elizabethan England, the early carbon dates, and the amount of driftwood that would be needed to produce five blooms of iron. Most of these individual factors are on their own more likely indicative of a pre-15th-century provenance than one of the 16th century. These factors taken together make a stronger case for the earlier origin of the blooms.

In the context of the late European provenance, the small size of the bloom and the early carbon dates could be accounted for by smelting under primitive field conditions with charcoal made from old wood or driftwood. This explanation, though feasible, is speculative in nature and not based on evidence. The small size of the bloom and the early dates, within the period of Norse travels and the occupation of Greenland, coupled with the use of a primitive, low-efficiency process suggest rather that the bloom is of much earlier date, possibly of Norse origin. It appears that bloom 2 and the other blooms recorded to be from the Frobisher site were left there not by Frobisher, but by some earlier visitors, perhaps the Norse voyagers or their Greenlandic descendants, or those people who were in contact with them.

Acknowledgments

Many people in Canadian Parks Service, Environment Canada, have helped me with this project. In particular, I am indebted to John Stewart for reading the original manuscript and making useful suggestions for improvement, Frank Garrod for sulfur analysis and Joy Moyle for x-ray diffraction analysis of slag samples, Chris Sergeant for identification of fuel samples, Carole Piper for drafting figures, and George Vandervlugt for photographing the blooms. Thanks are due to Dave Norman of Canmet, Energy Mines and Resources, for supervising cutting of the bloom. My appreciation is extended to the Prince of Wales Northern Heritage Centre in Yellowknife, Northwest Territories, for giving permission to metallurgically examine the bloom. I also thank Robert Gordon of Yale University for reading the manuscript and preparing helpful comments.

Appendix: Methods of Examination

The main investigation procedures included macroscopic and microscopic examination, microhardness measurements, hardness testing, chemical analysis, x-ray fluorescence spectroscopy, x-ray diffraction, and specific gravity testing.

MACROSCOPIC EXAMINATION. The large sections were cut from the bloom using a water-cooled abrasive cut-off machine with a 2.4-mm-thick aluminum oxide cut-off wheel. Because of the intended carbon dating of the bloom, precautions were taken in sample preparation to avoid contamination of the iron and slag with sources of outside carbon. These included the use of a water coolant for cutting, emery papers for grinding (grit 2, 1,0, and 3/0), alumina powders (5-micron, 1-micron, and 0.05-micron size) and silk cloth for polishing, and water-based solutions for etching. To reveal the structure of large areas, various etching procedures were applied to the polished surface. The distribution of carbon was determined by etching in nital (5% HNO_3 water solution). The distribution of sulfur was revealed using a sulfur print (a silver-bromide photographic paper soaked in 2% H_2SO_4).

MICROSCOPIC EXAMINATION. The specimens for microscopic examination were cut from the macrosections using a low-speed saw with a diamond blade. After sectioning and cold-mounting in epoxide resin, the specimens were ground on silicone carbide abrasive papers Nos. 240, 320, 400, and 600. Rough polishing on a napless nylon cloth with 6-micron size diamond paste was followed by a medium-nap velvet cloth with 1-micron paste. Final polishing was done on a high-napped rayon cloth with a slurry of 0.05-micron gamma alumina. Then the metal specimens were etched in 4% nital to reveal the structure and in Oberhoffer reagent to show phosphorus segregation. The structure of polished and etched specimens was studied by reflected-light microscopy (Leitz "Orthoplan") at magnifications of 50 to 1000 diameters. The grain size was determined in accordance with the American Society for Testing and Materials Standard E 112.

MICROHARDNESS MEASUREMENTS. The relative hardness of the phases was measured using a Vickers type microhardness tester (Leitz "Miniload") with a diamond pyramid indenter under 50-g load. Each result was an average of five indentations according to the ASTM Standard E 384.

HARDNESS TESTING. Hardness measurements were taken on polished and mounted sections using the Rockwell Superficial method of hardness testing, according to the ASTM Standard E 18. Rockwell Superficial 30-T measurements, obtained with a ball of 1/16-in. diameter under 30-kg load, had been converted to standard Brinell (10-mm diameter ball under 3000-kg load) as approximate equivalent hardness (ASTM Standard E 140).

CHEMICAL ANALYSIS. Chemical analysis of the iron and slag samples was in most part carried out under contract by Bondar-Clegg & Company, Ltd., Ottawa. Before submitting for analysis, the metal samples were separated from slag to the extent it was physically feasible to do. The weight of the five metal samples forwarded for analysis varied from 13 to 17 grams (H1-1/1: 12.7 g, H1-2/1: 17.2 g, H2-2/3: 13.8 g, V3-1/2: 13.6 g, V3-2/1: 15.6 g), though only about 1 gram of homogenized drillings was actually used for each of the basic elements. The location of analyzed metal and slag samples taken from the bloom is given in figures 11.5 and 11.6 (slag sample H12 is a mixture of slag H1-1/3, H1-1/4, and H2-2/3).

Manganese, copper, cobalt, and nickel were determined using atomic absorption spectrophotometry, phosphorus and arsenic by colorimetry, silicon by gravimetry, carbon by combustion, and sulfur by x-ray fluorescence spectroscopy. All elements in bloom and lump slag, except for sulfur, were analyzed using directly coupled plasma atomic emission spectroscopy. The analysis of sulfur in bloom slag and in three lump slag samples was performed by Frank Garrod, Historic Resource Conservation, using a Leco sulfur analyzer. Several slag and cinder samples were also analyzed for boron by Barringer Magenta Limited, Toronto, using inductive coupled argon plasma emission spectroscopy. The fuel and stone material was examined by Chris Sergeant, Historic Resource Conservation, by means of optical microscopy, infrared spectrophotometry, and SEM-based x-ray microanalysis.

X-RAY FLUORESCENCE ANALYSIS. The EDX spectra were obtained with a Kevex computerized x-ray energy spectrometer (Model 7000) and a solid state lithium-drifted silicon detector, using a 3.7-gigabecquerels (GBq) Americium 241 radioactive source. The detection was limited to elements of atomic number above 20. Molybdenum for low-energy elements and cerium for high-energy elements were chosen as target materials. All spectra were accumulated over the energy range of 0–40 KeV and 10,000 predetermined counts were acquired for each spectrum.

X-RAY DIFFRACTION. X-ray diffraction of the slag microconstituents was done by Joy Moyle, Historic Resource Conservation. The x-ray diffraction unit (Enraf Nonius Delft, Diffractics 582) with a Gandolfi-type camera and monochromatic Co Kα radiation was employed to this end.

DETERMINATION OF SPECIFIC GRAVITY. The specific gravity of slag material was determined by measuring its weight in air and in water, and calculating the ratio of the weight in air to the loss of weight in water. The three slag samples from the bloom (V2-2/7: 15 g, V2-2/8: 8 g, and V3-3/4: 12 g) were about $2 \times 1.5 \times 1$ cm in size and contained about 57% iron. The size and the iron content of the lumps of slag is given in table 11.12.

12

Metallurgical Study of Small Iron Finds

The Smithsonian survey of the Countess of Warwick Sound in August 1990 yielded two important archeometallurgical results. First, the absence of slag heaps and smelting furnaces at Kodlunarn Island indicates that large-scale smelting did not occur. This, when correlated with the facts that several of the iron blooms have been recovered from Frobisher site contexts and that the reappraised carbon-14 date for the center of bloom 2 resolves the anomalously early dates (Harbottle et al., this volume),[1] supports the interpretation of Elizabethan origin for these artifacts (Ehrenreich, this volume).

Second, four additional iron objects, thought to be contact artifacts between the Frobisher expeditions and the indigenous population, were recovered from Inuit tentrings. The iron artifacts consisted of an arrowhead, a bloom, a wedge, and a flake. The arrowhead (catalogue 990.49.2) was a surface find discovered within the remains of an Inuit tentring on the western side of Kodlunarn Island (Chapter 5; fig. 5.36). The bloom and flake were recovered from an Inuit tentring on Lookout Island in Cyrus Field Bay, 15 miles north of Kodlunarn Island (Chapter 5; fig. 5.35). The bloom appears to have been hammered in a futile attempt to work it and the flake (catalogue number 990.49.1b) was apparently detached from the bloom during this process. The wedge (catalogue number 990.49.1a) occurred as a surface find in a tentring (S7) on Tikkoon together with pieces of Frobisher tile, chert flakes, a cut iron nail, and a percussion cap (Chapter 6). The rest of this structure has not been excavated.

Three of the iron objects were borrowed from the

MICHAEL L. WAYMAN AND
ROBERT M. EHRENREICH

---

1. Harbottle et al. show that the carbon-14 dates for the bloom gradate from exterior to interior, suggesting that the artifact was initially smelted with charcoal and later reworked with coal. Charcoal must have been used to smelt the bloom because the sulfur content of the artifact is too low (Unglik, this volume) and the reappraised Elizabethan carbon-14 date for the interior of the bloom is too recent for the artifact to have been smelted using coal as a fuel. However, coal could have been used during the heating and hammering of the artifact during its final shaping after smelting (Ehrenreich, this volume). The coal would not have affected the sulfur content of the iron, but would have skewed the carbon-14 dates. The carbon from the coal would have slowly diffused from the exterior of the artifact, causing the outer portions to have been contaminated the most and the resulting dates to be the oldest. Little or no "dead" carbon from the coal would have reached the interior of the bloom, however, and the interior dates should be more accurate. Thus, the Elizabethan date obtained from the center of the bloom is the most reliable for the artifact and would suggest that the artifact was produced during this period.

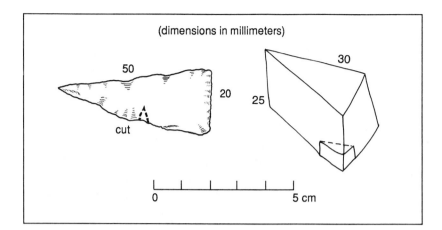

(dimensions in millimeters)

50

20

30

25

cut

0   5 cm

Fig. 12.1. Locations where samples were cut from original objects.

Prince of Wales Northern Heritage Museum in Yellowknife for further examination: the arrowhead, wedge, and small flake. Visual examination of the flake revealed that it consisted only of corrosion product, and hence it was not examined. The arrowhead and wedge were metallurgically analyzed to assist in the determination of (1) the possible dates of the artifacts (e.g., Elizabethan, Norse, other), (2) the potential origins of the artifacts (e.g., Britain, Scandinavian countries, Greenland, northeastern North America), and (3) the possible fabricators of the artifacts (e.g., iron smelters, blacksmiths, local Inuit).

Metallurgical Examination

The arrowhead and wedge were first visually examined using a stereobinocular microscope and a scanning electron microscope–energy dispersive analyzer (SEM-EDA) system. Both objects appeared to be ferrous material and both appeared likely to contain some metal as opposed to being entirely corrosion product. No elements other than iron and small amounts of normal soil contaminants were observed on the objects' surfaces (the SEM-EDA system used was not capable of detecting light elements such as oxygen).

To investigate these objects in greater detail, sections were cut from them, with the sampling geometries shown in figure 12.1. Sectioning of the arrowhead was successfully accomplished using a jeweller's saw. This was ineffective in the case of the wedge, however, and hence a low-speed diamond saw was used to cut a sample. The final detachment of this sample was accomplished by snapping a remaining uncut ligament, the material behaving in an

extremely brittle manner which is not expected from wrought or bloomery iron.

Both samples were found to be largely metallic and hence were prepared for metallographic examination using standard procedures. The samples were embedded in epoxy resin in 1.25-inch diameter mounts, with the transverse section of the arrowhead and the large longitudinal section of the wedge parallel to the mount surface for examination. The mounted samples were ground on 600-grit silicon carbide paper with water lubricant, then polished with 6-micron diamond compound on nylon cloth, and finally with 0.05-micron alumina slurry in water on short-napped microcloth. The polished samples were then examined unetched with the optical microscope and the SEM-EDA system. Microhardness measurements (Vickers) were made on the unetched samples using a diamond indenter with a 100-g load. The samples were then etched for 5 seconds by immersion in 2% Nital, and reexamined with the optical microscope and the SEM-EDA system.

ARROWHEAD

PRELIMINARY RESULTS. The arrowhead is not a planar sheet, but is slightly concave with a gentle curvature about its long axis. This curvature has no obvious relationship with the arrowhead's functionality, and could indicate that the artifact was fabricated from some previous object. However, the arrowhead could have been postdepositionally bent as well.

In the unetched condition, microscopy revealed a metallic matrix containing nonmetallic inclusions, that is, a microstructure typical of wrought iron.

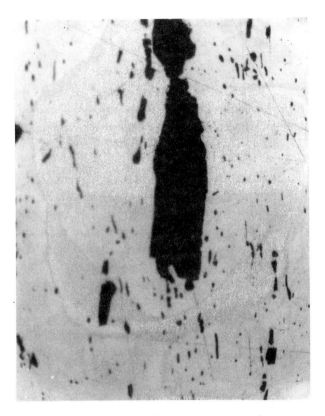

Fig. 12.2. Microstructure of transverse section of arrowhead, showing nonmetallic inclusions in metallic matrix. Optical micrograph, unetched, × 560.

Fig. 12.3. Microstructure of transverse section of arrowhead, showing nonmetallic inclusions in equiaxed ferrite matrix. Optical micrograph, nital etched, × 250.

Some of the inclusions appear to be oxides, which probably penetrated from the surface. However, most consist of a dark matrix phase containing a light globular dendritic phase (fig. 12.2), characteristic of slag inclusions invariably present in wrought iron. In the present case, the slag inclusions are not fractured, but are elongated, implying that the mechanical working of the iron was done at high temperatures where the slag deforms plastically rather than fracturing in a brittle manner as occurs at lower working temperatures.

No elements other than iron were detected by SEM-EDA in the metal phase; the limit of detectability of the SEM-EDA system is of the order of 0.5%. SEM-EDA showed that the dark matrix of the inclusions consists primarily of iron and silicon (i.e., an iron silicate) while the light globular dendritic phase is an iron oxide, almost certainly wüstite (FeO). Phosphorus, manganese, and a trace amount of calcium were detected in the inclusions, mainly in the dark matrix phase. It is believed that this matrix

phase is glassy; slag inclusions in wrought iron normally consist of a glassy iron silicate matrix (sometimes containing calcium, aluminum, etc.), with dendritic wüstite and in some cases fayalite crystals incorporated in it. In the present case, no crystalline fayalite was observed, and any calcium and aluminum in the matrix phase were below the detection limit of the analytical system.

Examination of the sample after etching gave results consistent with the observations reported above. The metallic component had the typical appearance of ferrite grains with no sign of iron carbides present, indicating a very low carbon content in the iron. The ferrite grains were equiaxed with a wide range of grain size, the mean being approximately 20 microns (fig. 12.3). No indications of elongated grain structure (i.e., cold work) were observed, even at the edge of the blade, which might be expected to have been chamfered or sharpened by cold hammering. The microhardness of the iron matrix was found to be HV195, which is relatively high

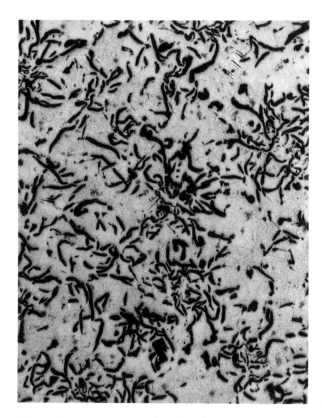

Fig. 12.4. Microstructure of wedge, showing distribution of graphite flakes in metallic matrix. Optical micrograph, unetched, × 56.

for wrought iron and suggests the presence of phosphorus in the metallic iron below the SEM-EDA detection limit.

With this possibility in mind, the arrowhead was analyzed for phosphorus using wavelength dispersive spectroscopy in an electron probe microanalyzer. Multiple analyses were carried out on both coarse-grained and fine-grained regions. The microprobe results confirmed that the arrowhead is made of phosphoric iron, with an average phosphorus content of approximately 0.17%, which is well above the 0.080% threshold used to distinguish phosphoric iron from low-phosphorus metal. No significant difference was observed between the coarse- and fine-grained regions.

PRELIMINARY CONCLUSIONS. The arrowhead is made of wrought iron typical of that produced over three millennia in many parts of the world. It is not possible to speculate as to the date at which the iron was smelted, or as to whether this is bloomery iron, fined pig iron, or puddled iron (the latter would definitely be post-1780s). The arrowhead is in the hot-worked condition, with little or no cold working having been done in the final shaping, at least in the section examined. The observed microhardness is also consistent with a wrought iron containing no carbon, no cold work, and an elevated phosphorus content.

The curvature of the arrowhead suggests that it may have been produced from a previous object. However, the fact that the microstructure shows it to be in the hot-worked condition is not in accord with the suggestion that the arrowhead might have been made by the local Inuit, who did not employ hot-working technology. It remains possible, however, that corrosion has removed the surface evidence of the local cold work, which would have been created if the Inuit had simply cut this arrowhead from a previous iron object without changing its thickness.

In summary, the examination of this object gives results that, while consistent with an Elizabethan origin, are unable to provide definitive evidence for or against this. Similarly there is no conclusive evidence for or against the arrowhead having been fabricated by the Inuit.

WEDGE

PRELIMINARY RESULTS. In the unetched condition, the microstructure of this object is typical of a gray cast iron with ASTM type B graphite rosettes (fig. 12.4). In the areas between the graphite rosettes, some microstructural evidence for solidification structure was observed in the form of rounded blobs within a reflective matrix. These rounded areas were identifiable as dendrite arms that in the SEM were visibly lighter than their surrounding matrix. The SEM-EDA showed that these dendritic regions contain only iron with minor amounts of silicon, while the darker matrix regions are also mainly iron, with less silicon than the dendrites but appreciable amounts of phosphorus. This high phosphorus level explains the reflective appearance when observed unetched in the optical microscope.

Also present in the microstructure are numerous blocky gray inclusions, which SEM-EDA showed to be manganese sulfides, possibly containing some iron with minor amounts of titanium, silicon, and

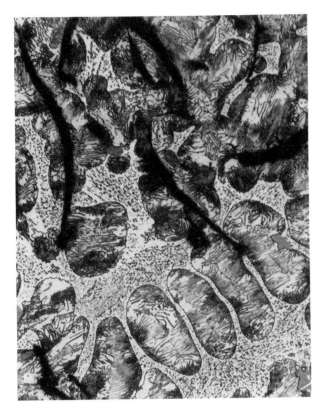

Fig. 12.5. Microstructure of wedge, showing graphite flakes embedded in a background structure that consists of pearlite dendrites in a matrix of eutectic steadite. Optical micrograph, nital etched, × 350.

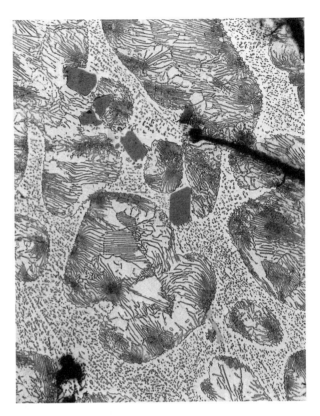

Fig. 12.6. Microstructure of wedge, showing details of the pearlite dendrites and the eutectic steadite. The blocky gray features are manganese sulfide inclusions. Optical micrograph, nital etched, × 560.

probably phosphorus. Some chlorine is present in the graphite flakes and voids, but this is likely the result of contamination.

Microhardness readings taken on the unetched sample show wide variability; some of this may be due to the proximity of hardness indentations to graphite flakes, but some is clearly caused by the heterogeneous nature of the matrix. The average microhardness was found to be HV410 with a standard deviation of 127.

After etching, the microstructure was confirmed as consisting of a background structure in which graphite flakes and sulfide inclusions are embedded. However, the etching was able to provide much more information about the background structure, which could be seen to be made up of pearlite dendrites in a matrix of steadite, the iron-iron phosphide eutectic constituent (figs. 12.5, 12.6). Microhardness readings taken in the pearlite gave HV319

whereas in the steadite, while it was not possible to make precise hardness measurements, values obtained were in excess of HV900.

PRELIMINARY CONCLUSIONS. The fragment is a high-phosphorus gray cast iron, with a carbon content of 3–4%. There is nothing in the microstructure of this material that could be used unambiguously to associate it with, or dissociate it from, the Elizabethan period. The object contains significant numbers of manganese sulfide inclusions, indicating moderate levels of both sulfur and manganese in the iron. Cast iron in Elizabethan times would have been smelted in a charcoal-fueled blast furnace and hence would be generally expected to have a low sulfur content. Coke smelting, which often creates high-sulfur iron, was not used before the early 18th century. Similarly, intentional manganese additions would not have been made prior to the mid-19th century. However, published analyses of some early cast irons do exhibit manganese and sulfur levels similar to those observed in this sample; thus the presence of manganese sulfides cannot be used as an indicator of a recent date.

Phosphorus concentrations are high in this sample as well, with a continuous matrix of steadite observed; the phosphorus content is estimated as well in excess of 1%. This is higher than most recent cast irons, and since it causes a high degree of brittleness it might be expected to suggest an early date. However, until quite recently high-phosphorus cast irons remained desirable for particular applications, because the presence of phosphorus enhances the fluidity of the liquid iron thereby permitting thinner walled castings (in the present case the dimensions of the fragment show that it was not a part of a thin-walled casting). Phosphorus also enhances abrasion resistance, as shown by the sampling difficulty. This cast iron therefore is consistent with Elizabethan cast iron but also with more recent cast irons. It is of interest that in Elizabethan times, the vast majority of iron castings were used for military purposes, such as cannons and cannonballs, with only minor exploitation for pots, firebacks, grave slabs, and perhaps, some tools.

It is important to note that this piece of iron is not a bloom fragment. Blooms invariably and by definition consist of iron that has been reduced by a solid-state process (no melting) and the structure incorporates porosity, large amounts of slag, and sometimes charcoal as well as the iron matrix. This object is in the as-cast condition, and a material such as this could not· have been mechanically worked.

Discussion

As shown above, the arrowhead and wedge have compositions and microstructures that neither ascribe them to nor exclude them from the Elizabethan period. Both artifacts are consistent with Elizabethan iron products, but are also comparable with more recent irons, and in the case of the arrowhead, with much older irons as well. Thus, they can neither be dated on the basis of the preliminary results presented in this paper, nor can they be proven to be contact artifacts.

The ambiguity of the metallurgical analyses in dating the artifacts and the lack of smelting remains

discovered during a survey of the sites of Frobisher occupation in the Countess of Warwick Sound during August 1990 demand that further research be performed in an attempt to clarify whether these are contact artifacts. Two potential avenues for further research should be pursued. The possible sources of the iron in the artifacts should be sought by comparing their minor element concentrations with other Frobisher artifacts and European objects, and the potential origin and date of the arrowhead should be resolved by comparing its typology and microstructure with similar artifacts from other regions and time periods.

MINOR ELEMENT ANALYSES

The quantity of phosphorus contained in the arrowhead and wedge is relevant because of its similarity to the Frobisher iron blooms previously recovered from Kodlunarn island. The iron blooms are also phosphorus-rich (Unglik, this volume). Thus, it is possible, albeit improbable, that the metal for all of these artifacts could have been smelted from the same ore sources. This is not to imply that the arrowhead was produced from the blooms, but that the metal for the artifacts could have had similar origins.

Not all iron ores contain sufficient phosphorus to have produced the blooms, arrowhead, and wedge. Whereas the ore sources of the Scandinavian countries and the Labrador Trough are predominantly low in impurities, Britain has two major sources of phosphoric iron ore: the Jurassic Ridge and the Coal Measures of Wales. Thus, although the artifacts cannot be dated, their high phosphorus contents and similarity to the Elizabethan blooms might suggest that they originated in Britain and were transported to Kodlunarn Island by the Frobisher expeditions.

Before definite conclusions can be drawn, however, further comparative analyses must be performed. Iron artifacts from a range of regions and time periods should be examined for the compilation of comparative databases. Iron artifacts from Norse sites, Frobisher sites, and Elizabethan Britain should be sampled and metallurgically examined in a manner similar to that described above to determine whether the artifacts recovered from the Countess of Warwick Sound region could have been imported from either Britain or Norse settlements in North America or Greenland.

The arrowhead is an important find because it currently is the only identifiable iron artifact to be recovered. Unfortunately, the artifact appears to fit neither Inuit nor Elizabethan traditions. First, the artifact was not cold worked. As stated above, the Inuit were not aware of hot forging, and thus, the artifact should show signs of cold working if it were fabricated by the local population. However, the metallurgical results could conceivably have been skewed by the loss of the artifact's surface due to corrosion.

Second, the arrowhead resembles neither the hunting nor the military types of 15th–16th-century Britain (Tylecote and Gilmour 1986:109–110). Military arrowheads were usually short and daggerlike. The edges were carburized and heat-treated to permit them to pierce chain-mail and plate armor. Hunting arrowheads were usually smaller with barbs and sockets. Advanced heat-treatments were not used on this type since it did not have to penetrate armor. Archers were present on the Frobisher expeditions, so some British arrowheads might still be extant in the region. Although the shape of the Kodlunarn arrowhead fits neither of the two main types, it could still have been a hunting arrowhead forged in Britain or by Frobisher blacksmiths. Simple arrowheads may have been produced because the chances of recovery in such a region was unlikely.

The importance of the arrowhead as the only intact iron object recovered demands that further research be undertaken. Arrowheads from Norse sites (since the possibility also exists that this is a Norse artifact), Inuit sites, and Elizabethan Britain should be metallurgically examined for comparison to clarify the probable origin of the Kodlunarn artifact.

Summary

The lack of smelting remains discovered during survey of the sites of Frobisher occupation in the Countess of Warwick Sound during August 1990 (Ehrenreich, this volume) and the ambiguity of the results of the metallurgical examination of the artifacts have reemphasized the need for further excavation, artifact collection, and artifact analysis. Excavation of blacksmithing sites, further survey of outlying islands, and analysis of ironwork and ironworking residues is required to confirm that smelting was not performed, to identify the metalworking techniques used on the sites, to determine the sophistication of the metalsmiths working on the sites, and to identify the type of iron used by the Frobisher expedition. Further examination of Norse artifacts and Elizabethan British artifacts in the new and old worlds is necessary for the compilation of comparative databases to identify both the potential sources of the iron artifacts and the possible fabricators.

13

An Evaluation of the Frobisher Iron Blooms: A Cautionary Tale

ROBERT M. EHRENREICH

The origins of the four iron blooms discovered within the archeological remains of the Frobisher sites on Kodlunarn Island and the one bloom found within an Inuit tentring on Lookout Island are a mystery. The two extreme radiocarbon dates for these artifacts are A.D. 640–760 and A.D. 1250–1440 (Harbottle et al., this volume), placing their production to at least 135 years prior to the Frobisher voyages. If the dates for these blooms are accurate, then how did they enter the archeological record of these islands and what purpose did they serve? The possible uses and origins of the blooms will be discussed in this article using (1) the analysis of the metalworking residues recovered from the region during the 1981 and 1990 field seasons to determine whether iron was produced there, (2) the historical records of the expeditions to ascertain whether sufficient need ever existed for iron to have been smelted on the island, (3) the archeological context of the artifacts to ascertain their possible uses, and (4) the physical characteristics of the blooms to clarify their potential origins.

Metallurgical Evidence

The iron smelting process will be analyzed in this section to determine both the energy investments required to smelt the four blooms previously discovered and the metalworking debris that should have been produced. The results of this analysis will then be compared with the metalworking residues recovered during extensive surveying of the region in 1981 and 1990 to ascertain whether iron was smelted during Frobisher's expeditions. This analysis does not include the bloom discovered during the 1990 field season.

SMELTING OF IRON BLOOMS

Previous metallurgical analyses of the blooms have shown that they were produced in a hand-bellowed, charcoal-burning furnace of either slag tapping or non-slag tapping form (Unglik, this volume). A non-slag tapping furnace provides no exit for the gangue and impurities (i.e., slag) that are extracted from the ore during smelting. This type of furnace will reduce iron only until the quantity of slag collected in the bottom of the structure smothers the fire. A more efficient furnace would provide an exit for the slag, allowing it to be periodically removed, or tapped, before it chokes the fire.

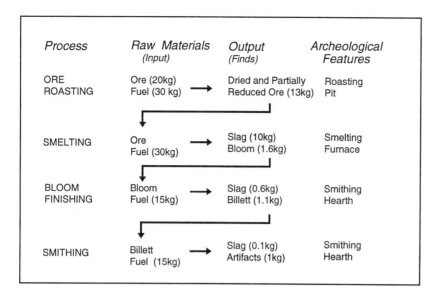

Process	Raw Materials (Input)	Output (Finds)	Archeological Features
ORE ROASTING	Ore (20kg) Fuel (30 kg)	Dried and Partially Reduced Ore (13kg)	Roasting Pit
SMELTING	Ore Fuel (30kg)	Slag (10kg) Bloom (1.6kg)	Smelting Furnace
BLOOM FINISHING	Bloom Fuel (15kg)	Slag (0.6kg) Billett (1.1kg)	Smithing Hearth
SMITHING	Billett Fuel (15kg)	Slag (0.1kg) Artifacts (1kg)	Smithing Hearth

Fig. 13.1. Summary of the iron production cycle for a basic hand-bellowed, charcoal-burning furnace system (after Salter and Ehrenreich 1984: fig.10.1).

A generic model of the raw materials and procedures required to construct a basic, hand-bellowed, charcoal-burning furnace and smelt the approximately 21 kg[1] of iron contained within four of the five blooms is discussed below (fig. 13.1). Analyzing a model of the smelting process potentially used to manufacture the blooms would help to determine the quantity and type of waste that should have been produced, the expertise that would have been required to manufacture these artifacts, and the time and energy investments that would have been needed to produce the blooms. Smelting iron requires six distinct steps: fuel production, mining, roasting, furnace construction, smelting, and finishing.

FUEL PRODUCTION.   Fuel production pervades all aspects of the preparation and smelting of iron ore. The roasting and smelting of sufficient ore to produce 21 kg of iron would have required roughly 1,260 kg of charcoal (fig. 13.1). Charcoal is manu-

factured by slowly burning wood for a number of days in a covered pit to expel the moisture and impurities contained in the material (Bealer 1984:34–35). The production of 1,260 kg of charcoal would have required the processing of 8,820 kg of wood, or 1,063 m³ of high-density trees (Cleere 1976:240). The collection of this extensive quantity of wood in a barren region such as Kodlunarn Island would have proved a monumental endeavor. Inventory lists from the final Frobisher expedition state that 10 tons of charcoal were brought to the island. Thus, sufficient charcoal was available on the island to produce four of the blooms, but smelting of just these four artifacts would have required approximately 14% of the entire store of the expedition, and analyses of charcoal samples from the blooms and the site suggest that the charcoal used to smelt the iron was not the same as that brought by the expedition (Laeyendecker, this volume). A structure containing large quantities of charcoal was discovered on the island, but charcoal was predominantly produced in pits or piles during the 16th century (Biringuccio 1942). Thus, this structure was probably a storage facility.

MINING.   Approximately 420 kg of ore would have been required to produce the estimated 21 kg of iron discovered on Kodlunarn Island alone (fig. 13.1). Since the hard-rock mining of both gold and iron ore are comparable procedurally, references in Best's memoirs to the rate of gold mining during Frobisher's second voyage can be used to estimate

---

1. The mass of iron contained within bloom 2 was very roughly estimated using its approximate dimensions (diameter at base, 17 cm; diameter at top, 12 cm; height, 9 cm) to determine its volume (1500 cm³). Analyses revealed that 30% of the volume of the bloom was slag with an average specific gravity of 5 (Unglik, this volume). Using these approximations, the mass of the slag contained within the bloom was calculated to be 2.3 kg. Since the bloom weighed 5.4 kg, the resulting weight of the iron should be 3.1 kg. The ratio of iron to total bloom weight determined for bloom 2 was then used to estimate the quantity of iron in the other three blooms: 7.3 kg for bloom 1, 6.2 kg for bloom 3, and 4.4 kg for the Smithsonian bloom. Thus, the total mass of iron contained within all four blooms was estimated to be 21 kg.

the amount of time that would have been required to collect 420 kg of iron ore. Best states that "having onely with five poore miners, and the helpe of a fewe gentlemen and souldiers, [we] brought aboorde almost twoo hundreth tunne of golde ore, in the space of twentie dayes" (Best 1875:152). If the number of men actually mining the ore and the number of hours of mining per day are both assumed to be ten for Best's quote, the collection of 420 kg of either gold or iron ore would have required roughly five man-hours.

ROASTING.   Iron ore is roasted prior to smelting for two reasons: it fractures the ore, making it easier to grind to a size suitable for smelting, and it removes many of the impurities in iron ore, increasing the efficiency of the furnace and producing a purer metal. Roasting would have required approximately half of the 1,260 kg of charcoal needed for the production of the iron blooms. Fuel and ore would have been mixed in a heap measuring approximately 2.5 m high and 4–18 m wide (fig. 13.2). The length of the heap would vary depending upon the supplies available and the quantity to be produced (Marechal 1985:37). The heap would be covered with a layer of dirt, ignited, and allowed to burn from 2 to 16 weeks depending upon the size of the pile (Marechal 1985:37). Once the roasting process was complete, the ore would then have been crushed to 4–6-cm cubes (fig. 13.3) and screened to remove any dust that would inhibit air flow within the furnace and reduce its efficiency (Tylecote 1986: 131).

FURNACE CONSTRUCTION AND SMELTING.   The furnace used to produce the blooms would have been constructed from a fine clay with grass or straw temper and probably had a shaft of approximately 1 m in height and 0.5 m in diameter. The completion of the furnace would have required either one month for full air-drying or 4–8 hours with extensive pre-heating (Avery et al. 1988:271–273). Pre-heating a furnace is conducted by allowing the structure to air-dry for several hours, burning wood within its interior to increase its temperature slowly, and then burning charcoal to achieve a smelting heat (Nosek 1985:168). Once the furnace had attained a proper temperature, 2-kg loads of ore and charcoal in the ratio of approximately 1:2 would have been poured into the shaft of the furnace every 15 to 20 minutes for 12 to 124 hours, depending upon the

Fig. 13.3. Illustration of the 16th century procedure for crushing ore (Agricola 1950:272).

voids in the Frobisher blooms indicate that these objects were only partially finished.

ESTIMATE OF TIME REQUIRED TO SMELT FOUR BLOOMS. Although the description of the iron smelting process above is a simplified working model for an elementary European furnace and is not meant to be a complete and accurate assessment of each of the steps performed by the individuals responsible for smelting the blooms recovered from the island, all of the procedures presented had to be executed in one manner or another. Depending upon the expertise, equipment, and supplies available, the production of just four of the five blooms would have demanded between approximately 4 and 13 weeks. It should be noted that one additional bloom

size of the structure (Nosek 1985:168; Avery et al. 1988:271). Once the supplies of ore and charcoal had been exhausted or the quantity of slag produced had choked the fire, the furnace would have been allowed to cool to a temperature permissible for the removal of the raw bloom. If an exit were not initially incorporated into the side of the structure, the removal of the bloom would have required the destruction of the furnace. A new furnace would then have had to have been built for each successive run. If an exit were present in the furnace, then the bloom could have been removed without damaging the structure and the interior of the furnace would have been quickly raked and prepared for the next smelting run before excessive heat was dissipated. It should be noted that no clays suitable for the construction of furnaces were located during surveying in the 1990 field season.

FINISHING. Since the iron formed in a non-slag tapping furnace is never molten, the separation of iron and slag is incomplete and a slag-rich bloom is produced. The slag in the bloom must be expelled from the metal and the resulting voids have to be welded shut by repeatedly heating and hammering the artifact (fig. 13.4). Blooms not finished in this manner are not usable. The quantity of slag and

Fig. 13.4. Cleaning of an iron bloom through repeated heating and hammering (Agricola 1950:422).

was also found by Hall and that more blooms were mentioned by Fenton in his memoirs (Harbottle et al., this volume). Thus, the time and materials requirements outlined are only minimum estimates.

METALWORKING REMAINS

Roughly 575 g of slag and cinders were recovered from Kodlunarn Island during preliminary surveying and excavation of the site in 1981. The discovery of slag on a site does not prove that iron was smelted there, however. Slag can be manufactured by many processes: fuel ash slag is produced when fuel ash reacts with furnace linings at high temperatures and oxidizing conditions (McDonnell 1984:48); plano-convex slag lumps can be formed when the slag inclusions in iron melt while the piece is being heated in a forge, eventually collecting in the bottom of the hearth; or slaggy materials are produced when iron falls into a forge and burns. Cinders are also formed during blacksmithing by the reaction of slag with fuel ash and hearth linings (ibid.:48). To maintain the efficiency of the hearth, blacksmiths must periodically clean out forges and dispose of the slag and cinders.

The metalworking residues recovered from the Frobisher site during preliminary surveying and excavation were analyzed in the hope of determining whether it was smithing or smelting residue. Unfortunately, the distinction between these two forms of slag is negligible (ibid.:52). In the future, a method may be devised to distinguish these slag types using a range of chemical, physical, mineralogical, and morphological attributes (ibid.:52), but no reliable system currently exists.

The source of the slag discovered on a site can occasionally be inferred from the quantity recovered. Since roughly 10.7 kg of slag is produced by the manufacture of 1 kg of iron (fig. 13.1), the quantity of slag that should have been produced by the smelting of the estimated 21 kg of iron within four of the blooms should have been approximately 224.7 kg, or 4.5 m³. Slag is an extremely durable substance and usually does not erode. The preliminary surveying and excavation of the site in 1981 produced only 19.6 kg of slag on the island (575 g recovered from the archeological remains and 19 kg contained in the blooms themselves), and the extensive surveying conducted during the 1990 field season also did not locate any slag heaps. Thus, an additional 205.1 kg of slag, or 4.1 m³, is still outstanding. Also, since

most of the slag produced by a non-slag tapping furnace collects in the bottom of the pyrotechnological structure, a large mass of slag weighing up to 25 kg is usually formed (Tylecote 1986:137). No such smelting byproducts were found on the island during either the 1981 or 1990 field seasons.

CONCLUSIONS BASED ON METALWORKING REMAINS

The comparison of the expected metalworking debris from the smelting of the four blooms with the remains recovered from Kodlunarn Island during surveying and preliminary excavation in 1981 and 1990 suggests that iron was not produced on the site for two reasons. First, the quantity of metalworking remains so far recovered from Kodlunarn Island was insufficient for smelting. If iron had been produced on the site, large furnace bottoms and roughly ten times the quantity of metalworking residues should have been found. The quantity and location of the slag discovered is also more indicative of blacksmithing activities, especially since the metalworking residues were predominantly found near the smithy. Thus, the small quantity of slag, the total absence of furnace bottoms, and the location of the metalworking residues recovered from the site would currently imply that only blacksmithing was performed on Kodlunarn Island.

Second, the incomplete state and the location of the blooms would suggest that iron was not in sufficient demand during Frobisher's occupation of the island to warrant their production. The expertise required to produce the blooms may have been present on the island, but suitable ore and clay sources, at least 14% of their charcoal store, and 4–13 weeks would have been demanded. If such an urgent need for iron had existed during Frobisher's inhabitation of the site, then the blooms should have been finished by continuing to expel the large quantities of slag contained through the repeated heating and hammering of the metal, and the artifacts should have been stored in the vicinity of the blacksmith's forge. Since the metal in the artifacts was not usable and the artifacts were discovered far from the blacksmith's forge, the iron content of the blooms must not have been vital to the expedition. Thus, it appears that insufficient need for iron existed on Kodlunarn Island to warrant the extensive investment in time and energy required for iron to have been smelted there.

Historical Records Suggesting that Iron Was Not Smelted on the Site

The memoirs of the crew would also imply that iron was probably not smelted on Kodlunarn Island during the voyages. First, the historical records never mention a need to produce iron. Second, a specific iron stock was deficient on only one occasion during the expeditions, and the situation was remedied without having to smelt new metal. Best states that the ships *Anne Francis, Thomas* of Ipswich, *Moon, Thomas Allen,* and *Gabriel* were initially blocked from entering the sound by ice during the third voyage (Best 1875:260–270). In order to clear the passage and guide the ships safely to Kodlunarn Island, a pinnace was built from the stores of the *Thomas.* Due to a lack of iron stock of suitable size for the manufacture of nails, the sailors were forced to cannibalize some of the ships' tools:

> . . . having by chance a smythe amongst them (and yet unfurnished of his necessarie tooles to worke and make nayles withall), they were faine of a gunne chamber to make an anvil to worke upon, and to use a pickaxe instead of a sledge to beat withall, and also to occupy two small bellows insteede of one payre of greater smyths bellow. And for lack of small iron, for the easier making of the nayles, were forced to break their tongs, grydiern, and fiershovell in pieces (Best 1875:266).

This quote implies that the reason for the scavenging of tools to make nails was not because of a lack of iron stock, but rather because the supplies available were not suitable for the manufacture of nails. Thus, the memoirs would suggest that the smelting of iron on the island was probably not required. Any need for iron on the expedition always seemed to have been remediable through either the use of the ships' stores or the cannibalization of other metalwork.

An Alternative Use for the Kodlunarn Blooms

If iron was not sufficiently scarce to warrant the production of iron during the voyages, then why were the blooms on Kodlunarn Island left in the ship's trench and caches? In this section, the Kodlunarn Island blooms, the "Winters fornace" blooms mentioned by Captain Fenton in his memoirs (Harbottle et al., this volume), and the Lookout Island bloom will be discussed in the context of Elizabethan ship building and Inuit trade.

THE KODLUNARN IRON BLOOMS

The context in which the blooms were discovered would suggest that they were on Kodlunarn Island for reasons other than their iron content. Best (1875:273) states in his memoirs that on the "thirtith of August the Anne Frances was brought aground, and had viij great leakes mended, whiche she had received by means of the rocks and ise." The archeological evidence contained in the ship's trench corroborates Best's statement. The ship's trench produced two iron blooms, wood shavings, and an iron nail. During the Elizabethan period, planking was attached to hulls with both treenails (wooden dowels) and clinched nails (Salisbury and Anderson 1958:5). Clinched nails were early forms of rivets and affixed using a four-step process (Davis 1918:57–59). First, holes were drilled through the frame of the ship and the planks of wood to be joined. Second, a nail was hammered through the hole from the exterior of the hull. Third, a roove (an iron washer) was placed over the end of the nail. Fourth, the protruding point of the nail was hammered over the roove, securing the nail. To prevent the nail from being loosened during the deformation of its point, the head was backed by a dolly (a heavy weight).

The dimensions, archeological context, and surface morphology of the blooms suggest that they could be dollies (Fitzhugh, this volume, p. 78). First, the blooms were of sufficient size, shape, and weight to support a nail during clenching. Second, the two blooms found in the ship's trench were discovered in conjunction with wood shavings. Shavings would have been produced during the drilling into the ship for insertion of the nails. After the ship was repaired and returned to the water, two of the blooms were presumably left where they lay and two others were probably placed in the caches for use by future expeditions.

THE "WINTERS FORNACE" BLOOMS

Captain Fenton states in his memoirs that he found a series of "osmondes" on the island of "Winters fornace," and Harbottle (Harbottle et al., this volume) has concluded that these "osmondes" were further examples of small iron blooms. As stated above, a pinnace was built during Frobisher's third expedition when the *Anne Francis, Thomas* of Ipswich, *Moon, Thomas Allen,* and *Gabriel* were initially unable to enter the sound owing to ice. The nails scavenged from the ships and used to build the pinnace should also have been clinched, thus requiring the use of dollies. If iron blooms were the standard weights employed in the clinching of nails, then the blooms referred to by Fenton could have been dollies, used to build the pinnace. Before any definite conclusions can be drawn, however, additional research must be performed to determine whether "Winters fornace" was the island on which the pinnace was built.

THE LOOKOUT ISLAND BLOOM

The discovery of a bloom within the context of an Inuit tentring on Lookout Island during the 1990 field season is important for two reasons. First, the deposition of European artifacts within Inuit sites confirms that the local population were scouring Frobisher sites. This proves that evidence of cultural contact is detectable within the archeological record of this region and reemphasizes the need for further excavation to determine the extent and effects of the contact.

Second, the state in which the bloom was abandoned shows that it was of neither use nor value to the indigenous population. The artifact was discovered half-buried within the tentring with one edge protruding from the ground. The exposed end of the bloom had been hammered before abandonment and parts of the bloom were scattered about the artifact. It may be concluded from the state of the artifact that the individuals who scavenged it were incapable of working the material successfully and, on realizing this, abandoned the bloom as useless. Thus, the theory that the blooms were brought to the island originally by the indigenous population would seem implausible since the artifacts appear to have been of no significance to the local inhabitants.

Potential Origin of the Blooms

Although the metallurgical and archeological evidence presented above would suggest that the blooms were brought to the island by the Frobisher expedition as part of the equipment required for the repair of ships, the sources of the blooms remain unknown. Discussion in this section of possible dates and origins of the blooms is based on their physical attributes and elemental concentrations.

POSSIBLE DATES OF BLOOMS BASED ON TYPE

The Frobisher artifacts are typical of the blooms produced prior to the 16th century. Before 1500, British blooms had remained relatively constant in size for over a millennium (Tylecote 1986:211). The introduction of two technological advances dramatically changed iron production during this period, however: the water-powered bellows system, which allowed larger furnaces to be run efficiently and blooms weighing over 100 kg to be produced (ibid.: 211), and the blast furnace, which allowed cast ingots to be produced for the first time in Britain. Thus, these two techniques should have caused the complete displacement of hand-powered furnaces and smaller blooms by the time of the Frobisher voyages.

Historical evidence shows that the previous iron smelting processes and smaller blooms were not totally displaced, however. In Scandinavia, blooms of roughly the same size as the Frobisher examples were being manufactured well into the 19th century (ibid.:209–210). Réaumur states in 1722 that steel was commonly being produced in France and Germany by smelting small blooms in non-slag tapping furnaces (Sisco 1956:20–21). In Britain, furnaces with hand-powered bellows systems were being built as late as the 1530s (Schubert 1957:146). Thus, hand-bellowed furnaces were being used in the 16th century and smaller iron blooms were probably still available during the time of the Frobisher expeditions.

The reference to "osmondes" in the memoirs of Captain Fenton also supports the hypothesis that smaller iron blooms were available during the Elizabethan period (Harbottle et al., this volume). If the iron production systems used to make these blooms were completely obsolesced during the early and middle 16th century, one might expect that Fenton should either have had greater difficulty in identifying these blooms, or perhaps have made some mention of their archaic character. His comments, however, sound as if he were totally familiar with the objects, implying that small blooms must still have been available throughout Europe in the 16th century and perhaps even part of the inventory of the Frobisher expeditions.

POSSIBLE SOURCES OF BLOOMS BASED ON ELEMENTAL CONCENTRATIONS

Although trace element analysis has not yet been proven to be reliable for the exact sourcing of iron, the minor elemental concentrations of iron can occasionally reveal whether an artifact could have been produced from the ores of a particular region or country. The Jurassic Ridge and the Coal Measures of Britain both contain iron ore that is unusually high in phosphorus, causing the resultant metal produced from these ores to be atypically phosphorus-rich (i.e., concentrations in excess of 0.05%; Groves 1952:3). Scandinavian iron was coveted throughout history for its incredible purity, however.

The iron in bloom 2 contained a phosphorus concentration of 0.1 to 0.25% (Unglik, this volume), placing it well within the range of high-phosphorus iron. Although it cannot be proven beyond a doubt that bloom 2 was produced from the Jurassic Ridge or Coal Measures ore sources, there is no reason to suspect that the blooms were smelted anywhere other than Britain based on their minor element concentrations. Thus, if not for the dilemma caused by the radiocarbon dates of the blooms, the typology and minor element concentrations of the artifact sampled would also tentatively support the hypothesis that the blooms were produced in Great Britain and brought to the site by the Frobisher expedition.

Conclusions

The evidence presented in this article would suggest that the iron blooms were brought to Kodlunarn Island by the Frobisher expedition as part of the carpenter's assemblage for the repair of ships. The blooms, or dollies, were used in the mending of the *Anne Francis* and were left with other supplies on the island for the benefit of future expeditions. On the basis of minor element analysis, there is no reason to suspect that the blooms were smelted anywhere but Britain.

The enigma of the radiocarbon dates of the blooms still remains, however. There are three possible explanations for these dates. First, dollies probably had a lengthy life span since their function as heavy weights for the clinching of nails would rarely have resulted in their destruction. Thus, the blooms could have been traded as dollies for long periods of time prior to the expedition. Second, blooms periodically appear in early British slag heaps. For exam-

ple, a local antiquary at the Isle of Portland recently identified two "spitzbarren" ingots, circa 100 B.C., being used as doorstops at a neighbor's house (Ehrenreich 1985:113). Thus, the blooms found at Kodlunarn Island could have been remnants of the earlier British ironworking industry and used as dollies because they were not worthy of finishing. Third, the blooms could have actually been made in the 16th century, but the radiocarbon dates are inaccurate. The dates obtained from the iron and the pieces of charcoal contained within the bloom vary over a considerable time period: A.D. 640–760 to A.D. 1250–1440. It is true that the radiocarbon dating of iron should be reliable since charcoal made from young trees is predominantly used in the smelting and forging of metal (Harbottle et al., this volume), but the use of any sources of old or "dead" carbon (e.g., driftwood, aged charcoal, coal, calcium carbonate fluxes) during smelting or forging would cause the dates of the artifacts to be inaccurate.

Although the hypothesis that the blooms were dollies brought to Kodlunarn Island by the Frobisher expedition seems logical, more research is required before the origins and ages of the blooms can be absolutely concluded. First, the archeological record of the entire region of Frobisher Bay should be more thoroughly examined and excavated to determine the range and types of ironworking remains currently extant, the total number of blooms left behind, and the other potential uses for the blooms. Second, the historical records from the Frobisher expeditions should be scrutinized to discover whether the blooms were logged under an alias. Finally, a coherent research strategy for sampling British and other European blooms and artifacts should be devised to provide additional data for comparison with results of examination of the Frobisher blooms.

Acknowledgments

I would like to express my appreciation to William Fitzhugh of the Department of Anthropology, Smithsonian Institution, Jacqueline Olin of the Conservation Analytical Laboratory, Smithsonian Institution, and Michael Wayman of the Department of Mining, Metallurgical and Petroleum Engineering, University of Alberta, for their assistance in the completion of this article. I would like to thank Klaus M. Zwilsky of the National Materials Advisory Board, National Research Council, and Carmel McGill of The British Council for their advice and support.

TAKING STOCK

Fig. 14.1. Dosia Laeyendecker mapping Structure A7 tentring at Tikkoon, where a small wedge-shaped piece of cast iron was excavated in 1990. New excavations here failed to produce more iron or any other possible Frobisher material culture. In the background is the gull rookery described to Hall by his Inuit friends as the "place where a mast is put up" (Rowley, this volume). It is here, according to Inuit tradition, that a group of sailors, abandoned by Frobisher, stepped a mast into a boat they had built and sailed away, but died of cold in the ice.

PREVIOUS PAGE: Animal resources, such as this polar bear photographed in Jackman Sound in 1991, are vivid reminders of continuities between the Frobisher era and the present. Other evidence of ties with the past include Inuit oral history of the Frobisher expeditions, continuing Inuit lifeways and traditions, and a long sequence of archeological sites and remains.

14

Questions Remain

WILLIAM W. FITZHUGH

At the conclusion of this preliminary stage of Frobisher research it is useful to assess what has been learned, what can be confidently concluded, and what remains uncertain or even completely mysterious and worthy of further study.

Kodlunarn Island Sites

One of the most basic issues is the identity of the Kodlunarn Island sites. Are they the remains of Martin Frobisher's basecamp and mines, or could they be of Inuit, Norse, or other European origin? Our work, like Kenyon's in 1974, supports Hall's conclusions that these sites are indeed the remains of Frobisher's camps, industrial workplaces, and mines. Corroborating data to this effect include the evidence of the Frobisher records, which closely match the archeological evidence on the ground, and Inuit oral history, which is quite specific about the number of ships in the Frobisher expeditions and their activities ashore. These could hardly be confused with other European exploring or whaling ventures. Although less specific in nature, various archeological evidence also links the Kodlunarn sites with Frobisher: the inventory of European species of wood and charcoal, mid-16th-century radiocarbon dates from site structures and features, presence of industrial ceramics (cupels, crucibles, muffles) not generally found in other 16th-century sites in the New World, and presence of coal dumps with English flint inclusions associated with mining sites. It would be difficult indeed to conceive of any other European venture that could have left this particular assemblage of remains and whose presence agrees so closely with written and oral historical accounts.

The Lost Sailors

A second issue, one that remains a considerable problem for future research, is the question of the identity of the lost sailors. As noted, Frobisher's accounts describe the loss of five men and a ship's boat on his first voyage, 1576, whose tattered and arrow-holed belongings were found in York Sound Inuit camps upon his return in 1577. No other sign of the lost men was found by Frobisher, whose own personal experience (having narrowly escaped capture himself) led him to conclude they had been killed for their weapons and boat. Yet Inuit accounts about what can hardly be other than Frobisher encounters tell of a group of five men being abandoned, spending a difficult winter on Kodlunarn Island, building a boat and trying to sail away. Do these stories refer to the same group of lost sailors or to different groups, one in 1576 and another in 1578? Or do these events, as reported, represent an amalgam with imprecise content and chronology (see Rowley, this volume)? For instance, Frobisher's men in 1578 assembled a prefabricated pinnace on Kodlunarn Island (Best, in Stefansson and McCaskill 1938, 1:112). Was this the event remembered by Inuit but ascribed to another group of "abandoned" sailors? The possibility that the Inuit story refers to 1578 and not to the 1576 voyage rests on the fact that Frobisher did not discover Kodlunarn Island until 1577, and had his lost sailors lived on Kodlunarn in 1576 Frobisher would have noted the remains of their winter camp when he discovered the site in 1577.

Iron Blooms

A third issue concerns the origin of the iron blooms—who made them? when, how and why were they made? and what function did they serve? Although associated with demonstrable Frobisher remains, their radiocarbon dates, size, and composition continue to indicate a pre-Elizabethan origin. Two of the blooms have been found to contain coniferous or birch/alder charcoal that might suggest local rather than English production; but on the other hand, Kodlunarn Island has not yet produced remains of smelters or smelting, nor does it seem possible that sufficient driftwood was available to supply the charcoal required to smelt the six blooms that have been found already in the Frobisher Bay region. A related problem involves the association of the blooms with the Frobisher site. Were these artifacts brought to Kodlunarn from England by Frobisher, or by other, perhaps Norse, visitors and later became associated with the Frobisher remains?

As it happens, not only the bloom dates, but many of the wood and charcoal dates run on the Kodlunarn Island samples do not correspond to the date of the Frobisher voyages (tables 5.3, 9.2, 10.1). In addition, none of the blooms recovered fits what is currently known of the typological pattern for 16th-century English iron technology; further, their small size and high phosphorus content are more typical of bloomery iron of the early medieval period than of Elizabethan iron. All these indications support the "Norse" attribution originally proposed

by Sayre et al. (1982) and supported here by Harbottle et al. and Unglik. To complicate matters even more, Henry Unglik, analyzing materials from the Frobisher smithy test pit, discovered bloom fragments, slag, and a lump of cinder that radiocarbondated to 25,640 ± 220 B.P. (Unglik, this volume). The circumstances of these finds were unusual:

> The metallurgical implications of the lumps of slag and cinder must indicate that some sort of iron working was taking place at the Frobisher site. The bloom fragments and the lumps of slag and cinder most likely resulted from a smelting operation in which the same type of ore and fuel were used. This was a low-phosphorus and practically manganese-free iron ore, not as rich and pure as the ore used for making the bloom. Coal not charcoal was used as fuel. No attempt has been made to deliberately add lime as a flux. The furnace was likely lined with siliceous stone and operated at temperatures of 1150–1200°C. The bloom fragments and the lumps of slag and cinder are a product of an unsuccessful attempt at smelting with coal, rather than that of a regular iron smelting operation. . . . In fact, if the Frobisher crew attempted to smelt any iron at the site, the small bloom fragments and the lumps of slag, both made with coal, would be most likely the products of their toil (Unglik, this volume).

One wonders who would have tried to smelt or rework iron with coal. Certainly not Frobisher's experienced blacksmiths, who had enough iron anyway and must have known that coal, the chief fuel of the expedition's smithies and forges, could not be used to smelt useful iron. Likewise why would coal be used when the expedition had brought huge quantities of English charcoal for their assay furnaces?

Several possible bloom origins are worth consideration.

LOCAL INUIT OR AMATEUR EUROPEAN IRON PRODUCTION. The possibility that a bloom, let alone the six blooms now known, might have been manufactured by Inuit seems too remote to consider seriously. Certainly the kinds of contact noted in the records could not have resulted in Inuit acquiring the knowledge and procuring the large amount of charcoal needed to smelt iron.

On the other hand, could the blooms have been produced by a group of English amateurs? The Frobisher accounts, which are quite detailed regarding activities on Kodlunarn Island, make no mention of smelting. Yet the primitive nature of the Kodlunarn blooms and their local types of charcoal inclusions argues against their being ancient heirlooms or specialized artifacts brought from England. But why, if they were produced locally, were these precious artifacts abandoned in a useless, semirefined state in the vicinity of the ship's trench? Could the early bloom dates result from attempts at coal-fired smelting or forging by a desperate group of men unaware that coal-fired bloom production produces brittle, worthless iron?

BLOOMS AS SHIPWRIGHT IMPLEMENTS. In this connection we may also consider the possibility that the blooms, four of which have been found in or near the ship's trench, may actually be considered as tools rather than as iron production stock, which, in their unrefined state, they are not. The concentration of blooms in an area said to have been used for building a ship—and which we found to contain remains of oak timbers and shavings—suggests a possible ship-building role for these artifacts. Their most likely function is for "dolly" hammers used to clench nails against and to provide a heavy weight behind timbers when they are being spiked, nailed, or dowelled. The abandonment of such implements might be expected following completion of a vessel and departure of its crew. This hypothesis does not explain where the blooms originated, how they got to Kodlunarn, their pre-Frobisher dates, or how fragile charcoal remains survived as adherents on exterior bloom surfaces, but it does makes some sense of the bloom find locations, the carpentry remains in the trench, and the Inuit accounts. (See the Addendum for another possible source of the blooms.)

NORSE CONTACTS. We can probably disregard the possibility that the Inuit stories and Kodlunarn remains resulted from a post-Frobisher party of abandoned sailors. Henry Hudson was set adrift far away in Hudson Bay, and post-Frobisher European remains, while a possibility, have yet to be identified on Kodlunarn Island. We then are left with the idea that prompted the dating of the Smithsonian bloom in the first place—the Norse connection. Most of the authors who worked on the Smithsonian bloom project (Washburn, Olin, Sayre, Stoenner, and Harbottle) believe that the dates from the new round of analyses on blooms 1 and 2 support their earlier conclusions of a Norse origin for these specimens. Justifiably, these scholars have faith in their dating procedures. No doubt, the dating is accurate; the

problem is that we cannot yet be sure of the origin of the carbon or charcoal being dated. The major problem with a Norse attribution is that it does not explain how six (or more) partially refined blooms, and blooms only, were abandoned by iron-hungry Norse to become part of the archeological record of a 16th-century English mining site. It is almost inconceivable that Norse abandoned so much iron in one place, and that all the blooms should become associated with the Frobisher sites, either directly in deposits or by Inuit removal from the island.

Perhaps some clue to this puzzle may be found in the Frobisher expedition's visit to "Freesland" (West Greenland) early in the 1578 season. There expedition members found recently abandoned settlements, implements, and a box of iron nails. If these were Norse, the latter is a peculiar find in an iron-starved land. If not the remains of some of the last Greenland Norse (for whom such an iron cache seems unlikely), could they have been left by an undocumented 14th-or 15th-century colony or camp of Brest or other European voyagers? Whatever the case, we can expect that some of the objects found would have been collected by Frobisher expedition members.

The continuing mystery of the Frobisher iron is only one of many problems highlighted in this volume. Others raised here include the explanation of late radiocarbon dates received from the smithy; questions of Elizabethan assaying, smelting, and smithing methodology; the possibility of local iron production; interpretation of the many new structures found; locating European sources of Frobisher ceramics and flints; and the nature and significance of Frobisher contact materials found at various Frobisher Bay Thule sites.

The issues noted above cannot be seen as isolated research problems; in fact it seems certain that resolution of the many problems still surrounding the Frobisher voyages will require extended study and collaboration by specialists in many fields. Obviously work on the Frobisher sites has not progressed to the point where one can offer final conclusions. Nor does it seem wise to try to resolve in this early stage of investigations differences arising from preliminary study. Still, it must be said that consideration of Hall's data, Inuit stories, analysis of the Smithsonian bloom and finds (blooms, charcoal, ceramics, and other data) from the 1981 and most recently from the 1990 regional surveys continue to support Hall's original interpretation of a single Elizabethan occupation by the Frobisher expeditions. If there were earlier visitors on Kodlunarn Island, perhaps Norse, their traces have not yet been identified. One can hardly imagine Norsemen leaving six blooms in the Kodlunarn Island vicinity with nothing else to record their presence. More likely, the peculiarities of the blooms may be resolved in some manner concordant with a Frobisher agency—heirlooms, ballast, primitive Elizabethan "backyard" iron production, or contamination by early carbon sources like coal or arctic driftwood.

Rather than trying to resolve such questions at this time we see the results of work to date as demonstrating potential for future interdisciplinary Frobisher-related studies in the Kodlunarn area and in the larger regional setting of southeast Baffin Island.

Epilogue: Evidence of a Pinnace Lost in 1578 and Its Possible Relationship to the Frobisher Blooms

As the mystery of the Frobisher blooms deepened during the course of this analysis, I kept returning to the same basic conclusion—that the Kodlunarn Island sites make sense archeologically only as the remains of Frobisher's mining ventures and not as the remains of Native American, Norse, or other European visitors. The concordance between archeological evidence and historical data is too great to allow any other interpretation. Many specifically identifiable archeological features, such as the layout of the Kodlunarn Island sites, Fenton's mortared watchtower at the summit of the island, locations of mines, coal dumps, and Best's Bulwark ("redoubt"), and other details, all agree precisely with Frobisher's historical record. Even what we know of the ceramic finds—industrial slag-coated crucibles—could hardly be expected in any other New World location. And while there is a considerable spread in the radiocarbon dates from the site, the non-bloom samples are compatible with an Elizabethan origin if the two-sigma ranges are valued and if the oak plank wood from the carpentry remains in the ship's trench are seen as derived from remains of older vessels or old treewood at time of cutting in 1576–78.

In fact, the only complication in interpreting the remains of this site is the evidence of the iron blooms. These dates are too early to be explained away; their small size is not compatible with 16th-century English blooms but is in the range of medieval bloom production; the coniferous and birch/alder charcoal identified in both blooms 1 and 2 suggests a northern (if not local Kodlunarn) production rather than English production; both blooms had fragile chunks of charcoal adhering to their cortices in a way that seems incompatible with longterm bloom curation or use as dollies; and finally, bloom fragments from the smithy have been found with a high concentration of phosphorus, suggesting coal-fired production or reworking. This list of anomalies should include also the possibility that the S13 feature might possibly be the remains of a bloom furnace, suggesting an activity not recorded in any of the Frobisher accounts, which are otherwise quite explicit with regard to pyrotechnics, especially Fenton's journal (Kenyon 1980/81). How could these two apparently irreconcilable sets of conditions be joined? How do primitive, possibly locally produced, early-dating iron blooms appear in the archeological context of a 16th-century English mining and exploration site in Frobisher Bay?

The fact that Inuit oral tradition as recorded by C. F. Hall (1865a, b) explicitly noted the abandonment of a group of Frobisher's men in Countess of Warwick Sound has always seemed inexplicable given the historical facts as they have been recounted. Frobisher's account of his first voyage clearly reports the loss of his pinnace—his only ship's boat and means of getting ashore—and its crew to a supposed Inuit attack (see fig. 1.2). (Although this attack was never verified, in 1577 Frobisher found evidence that it had occurred in the form of English clothing and material remains in the hands of Inuits.) This attack occurred soon after Frobisher's arrival on his first voyage, in 1576, and it provoked his premature departure for England, because thereafter he had no means of reaching shore to continue his exploration. If the Inuit story was correct and a group of Frobisher's men had been abandoned and remained in the Kodlunarn Island region during the winter of 1576–77 and had assembled a larger vessel (the pinnace being too small for ocean voyaging) and had departed in spring, "to die in the ice" as the Inuit account tells, why was this overwintering tragedy not discovered from material remains left by the struggling crew when Frobisher returned and commenced mining here in the summer of 1577? Further, in 1576 Frobisher remained in Frobisher Bay several days after the loss of the pinnace, hoping his lost men would return. They did not; quite the contrary, during this time Inuit made ever more bold appearances. Finally, Frobisher, on his first voyage in 1576 did not carry extra materials that could have been left behind on Kodlunarn Island or elsewhere in caches. The 1576 operation was a spartan venture and there were no cached materials from which the men could have built a larger vessel, even if Frobisher had had a boat to transfer goods ashore. Further, if such an attempt had been made by the lost 1576 crew, Frobisher would have immediately noted the evidence of their winter quarters and ship building activities when he returned in 1577. In fact, no such remains were found. It seems unlikely that evidence of a lost crew would have been concealed from others if it had been noted; and there is no logical reason for concealment, as Frobisher took pains to locate the crew or discover news of them from the Inuit in 1577.

While searching for additional clues to unravel these mysteries, I was struck by a passage in Captain Edward Fenton's journal written on the 2nd of September, 1578, the day of the fleet's final departure for England. Here, on the last page of his accounts for Frobisher Bay, Fenton recorded extreme hardships due to severe storm conditions and noted the destruction that day of his two pinnaces and a ship's boat that swamped and smashed to pieces by careening into his own ship while being towed in high seas. George Best's account provides an even broader view of the confusion and damage wrought by this storm (Stefansson and McCaskill 1938). Fenton's report, however, has the intriguing details:

> 2 [September] . . . Thus having lost ii pynnasses and our boote (not without daunger of the loosse of our shipp) abowt 4 or v of the clock in the afternoone we cam to the Quenes foreland, and there founde the Gabriell and the Generall aborde her, being commed that daie from Beares sownde with a Pynnasse and 26 men in her like to be caste awaie; there was also in view iii other shipps, viz., the Michaell the Anne ffraunces, and the Moone, who for that she seemed to make saile awaie from the rest, the Generall sente his Pynnasse to will her staie, but she paste the faster awaie so that there was daunger to loose the Pynnasse and men in her, wherupon the Generall willed us to make sail to save theim (if it were possible) which we willinge performed. But they being iii leagues before us (and the night drawing on) were forced to leave theim sailing nigh to the Moone (as we immagyned) not farr from whom we might descrie v sailes more passing on there course to Englande: and so we reatorned backe again to the Generall lying of an on of the Quenes foreland, at-

tending for Thayde and Thomas Allin, which we supposed to be behind, spente all the night in this sorte before we mett with him

> 3 Wedensdaie the iiide daie of September. We mett with the Generall erlie in the morninge, and told him what we had donne, he sente unto us from the Gabriell a xi men which we receaved, becawse the Barke was neather hable to victuall nor conteyne theim, being over charged with other men besides her coplemente And afterwardes we bare into the straits againe to see if we could meete the Ayde or any other of the shipps (which failing of) the Generall determyned to passe home in the Gabriell willing me, that if I mett with the Thayde to entre into her and to take the charge of her; and in the meane time to passe home wardes (if we failed that night of the shipps,) the winde was in the morning at northwest and in the afternoone at southwest. We spente the daie of an on of the quenes forelande according to his appointmente, and abowt vi of the clock in the afternoone it grew foggie with snowe good store, we caste abowte making our course southest and by south est [identified by Kenyon as an error as the course is southeast by south] from the quenes forelande, and so did also the Gabriell and Anne ffrauces, who in casting abowt were on the sterne of us, which was the best course we colde holde for 200 leagues to passe into warmer climate.

> *Margin note:* ayds that if we had not receaved in a xi of theire companie & as manie into the anne ffraunces Bothe the Generall & reste in the ii Barks had perished for wante of victuall (Fenton, in Kenyon 1980/81:202–203)

Thus, reading between the lines in a report probably phrased to obscure possible legal culpability, we might conclude that on this last day of his stay in Frobisher Bay, a pinnace sent from the *Gabriell* to overtake the *Moone* may not have reached its destination. Further, even with the loss of these men, we discover Frobisher's *Gabriell* was still so overcharged that Frobisher was compelled to transfer 11 more men to Fenton's vessel the next morning to avoid starving his crew on the homeward voyage. By this we may assume that food stocks on all the vessels were extremely low, a fact treated in some detail in Best's account and blamed on poor casking, on wanton drinking aboard the "beare" cargo ships, and on breakage during the stormy spring crossing. Under these conditions, fleet ships would have been extremely reluctant to take on any more men—especially miners and other non-seamen—than they already had on board.

So what became of the lost pinnace? who were these men? and were they ever accounted for? The records tell us little of their fate, probably because the confusion of the stormy departure was so extreme that the losses of small boats and men (32 boats and about 30 men in Best's account) for the whole fleet was never precisely tallied. From Fenton's account we surmise that the *Moone* departed prematurely to avoid having to accept, at Frobisher's orders, more men than they already had, and did not want to feed, for if Frobisher's flagship was low on food we may expect other vessels to have been in a similar condition. Frobisher and Fenton seem to have assumed the pinnace was picked up by the *Moone* or others of the larger fleet. But his concern was so great about the possible loss of a pinnace full of men that he took the precaution of remaining at the "Queen's Foreland" (southwest entrance of Frobisher Bay), endangering his vessels and men to the extreme during a raging gale, until 6 pm of the following day (3 September) when fog and snow made their position untenable (and in any case invisible to a lost pinnace crew) before finally departing for England. Frobisher could not have known the fate of the missing pinnace—if he ever did—until arrival in England, where much more shocking news of worthless ore, courts-martial, and impending bankruptcy awaited him.

The possible loss of a pinnace and crew on the eve of Frobisher's final departure from Countess of Warwick Sound in 1578 is a clue that may resolve discrepancies between the archeological, archeometric, and historical records and provides a possible solution to the mystery of the Frobisher blooms. In this scenario, after having failed to make contact with any of the departing vessels, the pinnace crew would have returned to their only source of hope for survival, the stone house and stash of lumber, iron, and other goods Fenton cached on Kodlunarn Island in anticipation of the fleet's return to continue mining and explorations in 1579. It is to the succeeding events that the Inuit stories recorded by Charles Francis Hall refer, including the privations expected of a group abandoned with only the clothes on their backs, without suitable implements or means of survival, let alone knowledge of shipbuilding, iron making, and necessary materials and tools for surviving a winter and constructing a vessel under arctic conditions. We may expect that their efforts would have included smithing activity, using the abundant stores of coal dumped by Frobisher on

Neoontilik (Newland) Island and elsewhere to manufacture iron fastenings—nails, bolts, pins, and straps—and possibly new attempts to augment the limited stock of cached iron by forging new iron from the existing iron blooms brought as ballast or for use as dolly hammers. Caches of English charcoal or coal would have been available for this forging activity. Alternatively, new charcoal could have been produced from local driftwood. Forging new iron would have been more difficult and would have entailed location of a suitable iron ore and production of new charcoal if cached supplies were not in sufficient supply. The latter course—smelting new iron—seems an unlikely outcome because quantities of English charcoal were present in the archeological finds in 1981 and because there is no evidence for the presence of smelting slags or smelting furnaces on Kodlunarn Island (consideration, however, should be given to the pit feature noted south of the smithy). Nevertheless, if smelting did occur it could account for the presence of coniferous charcoal, high phosphorus, small size, and early radiocarbon dates that might have resulted if a mixture of charcoal and coal was used in the smelting process. Attempting to smelt iron with coal itself argues for primitive conditions and lack of metallurgical knowledge (as might be expected of a group of desperate, abandoned sailors), because the presence of sulfur in coal renders coal-smelted iron brittle and technologically useless.

Recent Developments

In keeping with the rapidly unfolding nature of the Frobisher research program, as this volume goes to press an important new consideration has come to light through the continuing collaboration among our team of historians, archeologists, and archeometrists. After hearing a discussion of the bloom problem at a seminar held in April 1992 at the Smithsonian, Ivor Noël Hume recalled a reference to an entry in the Frobisher inventory records noting purchase in the spring of 1576 of "v. of yronstones of Russia at iiij. pece beinge vj tones for balliste for the Gabriell bought of master Patrik & Hopton" at a price of "li 8.6.8" (McDermott 1984:144). As Hume (pers. comm. 22 May 1992) notes, this description may relate to the mysterious iron blooms:

One mustn't lose sight of the fact that ironstone was geologically available in England and much used, regionally, as building material in the medieval and post-medieval centuries. Consequently, if all "Master Patrik & R. Hopton" were supplying was rock, Russia would not have been specified, and the invoice would have been in the singular (e.g. yrone stone . . . for balliste) and not in the plural. You ask why should Lok have bought the blooms rather than rock when the weights would have been similar. I have two answers, the first being that the blooms would have been more readily placed in the ship (and more importantly, more easily off-loaded) than would rock of differing and awkward shapes. The second relates to the place where the *Gabriell* was built. I have not done the research needed to establish this, but the spikes, nails, bolts, etc. for the construction were purchased from Leryges Smythe of Ratcliff on the Thames, and this was a major ship outfitting area in the 16th and 17th centuries. Frobisher's voyages began there. It was also a major landing place for incoming vessels. I suggest, therefore, that the blooms had been used aboard a vessel of the Hanseatic League and had been off-loaded before exports were taken aboard. They were simply available, manageable, and maybe had some metallurgical potential. I would add that shops were built at Ratcliff as early as the 14th century, and it is quite possible that bloom ballast had been coming and going for centuries—possible, but in this case not likely. Otherwise, Lok would not have known that the "yronstones" came from Russia.

This hypothesis seems to have more merit than the theory noted in Harbottle et al. (this volume) that the blooms might be identified in the accounts as the "osmunds" mentioned in Fenton's journal. If in fact the blooms are "yronstones of Russia," many of their anomalous features noted above might be resolved. Russian technology might be expected to have been less advanced than Elizabethan methods, resulting in smaller blooms, and boreal forest production in Russia, as in northern Scandinavia, would quite likely include smelting with coniferous rather than temperate European hardwood charcoal. Use of iron as ballast might also explain the abandonment of blooms in the ship's trench area, where the loading of iron ore on pinnaces and other ships took place. If so, we might expect to find many more of these unusual artifacts around Kodlunarn and possibly in the waters offshore, near the ship's trench. Although the use of iron as ballast seems extravagant when flint nodules and barrels of water were the most common materials used for this purpose, Russian iron blooms may have been considered obsolete as potential iron sources in terms of Elizabethan English iron production, but still may have been an effective, economical option for ballasting small vessels that could less easily accommodate the more common option of barrels of water used on larger ships.

While Hume's explanation seems to make better account of the available historical, archeological, and physical evidence regarding the blooms and their function, it should be considered only as one other in a series of hypotheses advanced in the course of ongoing studies of the archeological evidence of the Frobisher voyages. This hypothesis, like the possibility that a group of abandoned sailors may have resided on Kodlunarn Island during the winter of 1978–79, as suggested by Inuit accounts, calls for new research on the Frobisher records, sites, and physical remains, as well as on Inuit sites and records. Future research at Kodlunarn Island and other sites, combined with archival and Inuit oral historical study, promises to provide a rich source of new knowledge that will significantly augment, and perhaps revise, the current historical record of the earliest English enterprise and native contacts in the New World.

Recent field work in Baffin Island during the late summer of 1992 has resulted in some new material, new photographs, and clarification of previous research, and some changes and additions since the volume went to press should be noted.

About people: On the steering committee of the Meta Incognita Project (footnote page 104), Donald Clark has replaced Roger Marois, and Douglas Stenton has replaced Tommy Owlijoot. The acknowledgments on page 134 should include Bert Rose and Lynn Maas of Arctic College.

We have discovered another bloom in the mineral collection of the American Museum of Natural History, where it was deposited by Admiral Richard Peary. Peary acquired it, indirectly, from an Inuit in Baffin Island and believed it was the lost Frobisher anvil described by Hall (see page 87). Upon investigation, it is a bloom, not an anvil.

A pale-blue bead dating to the 16th century was recently recovered in a test pit in one of the houses from the Imilik sod-house village site (KiDk-9), reported as not yet tested on page 122.

It should be emphasized, especially for climatic interpretations (see pages 95–96), that the Frobisher accounts are set in the Julian calendar, so that the entries in Fenton's journal for September 2 and 3 (page 235) are actually ten days later, September 12 and 13 in our Gregorian calendar.

About illustrations: Hall did not identify the following keyed locations on figure 2.2: *A*, Countess of Warwick Sound; *B*, Beare Sound; *C*, Chapell Inlet; *D–G*, Resolution, Edgell, and Lower Savage islands; *H*, York Sound; *I*, Jackman Sound. In figure 5.7, the view is to the west; in figure 5.11, to the south, in figure 5.13, to the west. Figure 5.36 should be credited to W. Fitzhugh. Figure 5.45 should be credited to R. Auger/Laval University. The scale shown in figure 6.3 applies to the bi-lobed two-family house used in the 14th–19th centuries (*b*) and the rectangular longhouse (*c*); the diameter of the small single-family house (*a*) is 4 m. The Anvil Cove 1 site shown in figure 6.13 has been designated as locality KeDe-13. The site shown in figure 6.23 was excavated by L. Gullason and A. Henshaw in 1992. In figure 6.50, House 4 is to the right. Unless otherwise credited, photographs in this book were taken by William W. Fitzhugh, except for those in chapter 8, which were taken by R. Auger.

APPENDICES
GLOSSARY
BIBLIOGRAPHY
INDEX

APPENDIX 1. Personnel, ship assignments, and duties in the three voyages of Martin Frobischer

Name	Ship	Duty
1st voyage, 1576		
Aldaye, James		sailor
Becket [Bocket], Phillip	G	surgeon
Bolde, Thomas		master bondsman
Bormane [Burman[, Thomas	M	master's mate
Brackenbury, Francis	G	gentleman
Bucher [Burche], John	G	carpenter
Chancelor, Nicholas	G	purser
Clother, Edward	M	cooper & cook
Colbrooke, Joseph[a]		sailor
Cominge, John	M	gunner
Creake, Alexander	M	sailor
Crespe, Renold[a]		sailor
Dean, William	G	sailor
Frobisher, Martin	G	captain & general
Frynd, Richard	G	boatswain
Garret, Robert	G	sailor; captured by Inuit Aug. 20
Gryffen, Owen	M	master
Hall, Christopher	G	master
Hamond, John	P	sailor, d. July 1
Hollowaye, Roger	M	carpenter
Jacob, John	M	gunner & smith
Kindersley, Mathew	M	captain
Millar, Richard	G	sailor
Mogare, Peter[a]		carpenter & tailor
Nemet, William[a]		sailor
Parkines, Edward	M	sailor
Peele, John	M	sailor
Peke, Thomas[a]		sailor
Priar, William	G	sailor
Purdye [Purder], Richard	G	trumpeteer
Slight, Richard	G	master gunner
Smythe, John	G	cook
Thomson, William	M	sailor
Westone, Robert	M	sailor
Whitere [Whithed], Paul	M	boatswain
Wilmot, John	G	sailor
2nd voyage, 1577		
Amorey, John	M	sailor & cook
Ardington, John	A	sailor boy
Armshow, William	A	gentleman
Bartley [Bartlet], Andrew	A	sailor
Beare, James	M	master
Beare, Samuel	M	gunner
Bell, Thomas	M	trumpeter
Best, George	A	gentleman
Bishoppe, Thomas	M	sailor
Bona, Gregory	A	assayer
Boyden, Thomas	A	gunner
Boyer, Richard	A	sailor
Boyse, Stephen	A	sailor
Brackenbury, Francis	A	soldier
Brewen [Bruene], John	A	soldier
Bridges, Brian	G	sailor
Browne, John	G	trumpeter
Bull, Bartholemew	G	master's mate
Bynes, William	A	soldier
Cane [Came], Anthony	A	sailor
Carew, Henry	A	gentleman
Chamberlyne, Thomas	M	gentleman

a. Pay-list data suggest these men may have died during the voyage.

Abbreviations of ships: A, *Ayde;* B, *Bear Leicester;* D, *Bark Dennis;* F, *Francis* of Fowey; G, *Gabriel;* H, *Hopewell;* J, *Judith;* M, *Michael;* P, pinnace; S, *Salomon* of Weymouth; AE, *Armonell* of Exmouth; AF, *Ann Francis;* EB, *Emanuel* of Bridgwater; MF, *Mone* of Fowey; TA, *Thomas Allen;* TI, *Thomas* of Ipswich.

APPENDIX 1—Continued next page

Name	Ship	Duty
2nd voyage, 1577 *cont.*		
Chancelor, Nicholas	A	purser
Coltermane, Christophere	M	master's mate
Cominge, John	A	sailor
Conger, Nicholas	A	soldier
Conney, William	A	sailor
Cooley, Edward	A	surgeon
Corbett, Owen	A	boatswain's mate
Cowley, Richard	G	sailor
Cox, Richard	A	trumpeter
Coxe, Richard	A	master gunner
Creake, Alexander	A	sailor
Cullen, James	A	gunner's mate
Cut, Timothy	A	sailor
Cutter, John	A	cooper
Denham, Robert	A	assayer
Diare [Dyer], Andrew	A	pilot & master's mate
Drap [Draper], Esdras	A	sailor
Edwards, John	A	sailor boy
Edwards, William	M	surgeon
Englishe, Edmond	A	soldier
Englishe, John		trumpeter
Estwood, Christopher	M	soldier
Fardar [Forder], Francis	A	gentleman
Fenton, Edward	G	captain
Fisheborne, Richard	A	sailor boy
Frebodye, John	A	soldier
Frenche, George	A	sailor & carpenter
Frobisher, Martin	A	general
Fysher, Anthony	A	trumpeter & baker
Gore, John	A	sailor
Gostellowe, Phillip	A	cook
Hall, Christopher	A	master
Harvye, Edward	A	gentleman
Hawle, John	A	sailor boy
Hebbes, Robert	A	sailor
Hewes, Anthony	A	soldier
Heywod, John	A	miner
Hope [Hoope], John	A	sailor
Hopkines, Robert	A	gunsmith
Houlte [Hault], Peter	G	sailor
How, Hew	A	boatswain
Jackelyne, James	G	sailor
Jackman, Charles	A	master's mate
Jackson, Christopher	A	trumpeter
Jacob, John	A	smith
Jenkynes, Thomas	A	pumpmaker
Jonas, Paul	A	sailor
Kent, Henry	A	soldier
Kerkeman [Kirkman], Henry	A	soldier
Kindersley, Mathew	A	gentleman
Kindersley, Robert	A	gentleman
Lawse [Lanse], Cuthbert	A	carpenter
Ledger [Lydger], George	M	carpenter
Lee, John	A	gentleman
Lintz [Lyns], Gabriel [= Linche, Abraham?]	A	gentleman
Littlestone, Roger	A	soldier
Longe, Nicholas	A	sailor
Luce, William	A	sailor
Lunt, John	A	sailor
Lyle, Richard	A	soldier

Abbreviations of ships: A, *Ayde;* B, *Bear Leicester;* D, *Bark Dennis;* F, *Francis* of Fowey; G, *Gabriel;* H, *Hopewell;* J, *Judith;* M, *Michael;* P, pinnace; S, *Salomon* of Weymouth; AE, *Armonell* of Exmouth; AF, *Ann Francis;* EB, *Emanuel* of Bridgwater; MF, *Mone* of Fowey; TA, *Thomas Allen;* TI, *Thomas* of Ipswich.

APPENDIX 1—Continued next page

Name	Ship	Duty
2nd voyage, 1577 *cont.*		
Marsh, Thomas	A	merchant
Mathew, Simon	A	gunner
Merifeld, Hewe	A	sailor
Morgan, John	A	miner
Morise, William	M	sailor
Morley, William	G	sailor
Myllett, William	A	soldier
Nethercylste, John	G	surgeon
Okeley, John	A	
Ormeshawe, William	A	soldier
Pavie [Parye], Edward	A	sailor boy
Peale [Peddell], Henry	G	sailor
Pelle, John	A	sailor
Phillpot, Richard	A	ensigne
Pinder [Pynder], Richard	A	sailor
Powell, John	M	sailor
Price, Thomas	A	soldier
Pryne, James	A	gunner
Richards, Nicholas	A	sailor
Rise, Thomas	A	soldier
Robinson, Edward	A	sailor
Robinson, Tobias	A	sailor
Roke, John	A	miner
Rumbridge [Rambridge], Anthony	A	instrument maker
Seely, William	A	steward
Sellman, Edward	A	merchant
Settle, Dionites	A	soldier
Sherloke, William	A	gunner
Shutz, Jonas	A	assayer
Simones, Sebastian	A	sailor & cooper
Smithe, William	G	master; d. Sept.
Sparrow, John	A	soldier
Stafford, Edmond	A	gentleman
Stanley, John	A	soldier & miner
Stanton, Thomas	A	sailor
Stevensone, Peter	G	sailor
Stoker, Henry	A	carpenter
Streate, Walter	A	sailor
Stubberne, Henry	A	sailor
Tanfield, William	A	gentleman
Taylor, Richard	A	miner
Taylor, William	A	miner
Terrey, Nicholas	A	soldier
Thompson, Anthonty	A	surgeon's boy
Todar [Tether], Robert	A	smith
Turner, John	A	soldier
Utye, James	G	sailor
Wade, Thomas	A	sailor
Wallis, Giles	A	gunner; wounded by Inuit
Webb, John	A	sailor
Weddal, William	M	sailor
Whitson, William	A	miner
Whittingham, Anthony	M	sailor
Wilcox, Robert	A	miner
Wiley, Robert	A	soldier & tailor
Williams, Thomas	A	carpenter
Wilmot, Henry	A	sailor
Wines, James	A	gunner

Abbreviations of ships: A, *Ayde;* B, *Bear Leicester;* D, *Bark Dennis;* F, *Francis* of Fowey; G, *Gabriel;* H, *Hopewell;* J, *Judith;* M, *Michael;* P, pinnace; S, *Salomon* of Weymouth; AE, *Armonell* of Exmouth; AF, *Ann Francis;* EB, *Emanuel* of Bridgwater; MF, *Mone* of Fowey; TA, *Thomas Allen;* TI, *Thomas* of Ipswich.

APPENDIX 1—Continued next page

Name	Ship	Duty
2nd voyage, 1577 *cont.*		
Woode, Richard	A	sailor
Wright, John	A	sailor
Wyars, Thomas	M	boatswain
York, Gilbert	M	captain
Yugen [Jugeyn], John	A	miner
3rd voyage, 1578		
Abraham, William	TA	miner
(Afferton, Henry see Offerton, Harry)		
Aldredge, Thomas	A	sailor
Allyn, William	S	miner
Anderson, Thomas	M	cook
Anthony, John	AE	master
Ardington, John	J	sailor boy
Austen, Francis	A	sailor
Awle [Hall], Robert	J	sailor
Ayvie [Ivye], John	TI	minister & miner
Badcock, George	J	carpenter
Banester, John	S	miner
Baraball, John	MF	miner
Barret, James	A	sailor
Barter, Nicholas	J	sailor
Bartlet, Andrew [al. Lyger]	A	sailor
Batterbie, Harry	A	gunner
Batterick [Batterby], Thomas	A	sailor; d. Sept. 6
Battesfield, John	H	miner
(Beale, Walter, see Kelley, Walter)		
Beane, Robert	TA	miner
Beare, James	AF	master
Beare, Samuel	MF	pilot
Bellowes, John	A	miner
Bendall, Harry	A	sailor
Bennes, William	M	master's mate
Bennet, Christopher	D	miner & piper
Best, George	AF	captain & lieutenant
Beton, ____	TI	surgeon
Blake [Black], Thomas	AE	miner
Boddie, Henry	AF	miner
Bogar [Banger], Roger	A	sailor
Bona, Gregory	A	assayer
Bond, Harry	H	miner
Bower [Bowrey], William	A	carpenter
Bowge, Michael [= Bowgle, William]	A	sailor
Bowryn, John	F	miner
Boyes [Boyse], Stephen	A	sailor
Brackenbury, Francis	A	gentleman
Bradeberye, John		gentleman
Brock, Robert	H	miner
Brook, Roger	H	miner
Brooke, ____		gentleman
Brown, John	EB	miner
Bryan, Nicholas	A	sailor
Bull, Bartholemew	M	master
Burnit, Richard	J	gunner
Bushe, Edmund [Edward]	TI	miner
Caine [Came], Anthony	A	sailor
Cara, John	AF	purser
Carew, Henry	H	captain
Catesbie, Thomas	A	miner
Chamberes, Richard		soldier
Chamberlynde, Thomas	A	soldier
Champion, Walter	AF	miner

Abbreviations of ships: A, *Ayde;* B, *Bear Leicester;* D, *Bark Dennis;* F, *Francis* of Fowey; G, *Gabriel;* H, *Hopewell;* J, *Judith;* M, *Michael;* P, pinnace; S, *Salomon* of Weymouth; AE, *Armonell* of Exmouth; AF, *Ann Francis;* EB, *Emanuel* of Bridgwater; MF, *Mone* of Fowey; TA, *Thomas Allen;* TI, *Thomas* of Ipswich.

APPENDIX 1—Continued next page

Name	Ship	Duty
3rd voyage, 1578 *cont.*		
Chatterton, Alden	TI	miner
Chauncellor, Nicholas	J	purser
Chaynalse, Reynold	H	miner & purser
Clickers, Thomas	F	miner
Clytherall, Robert	A	soldier
Cock, Pearse	D	miner
Cole, Thomas	A	miner
Cole, William ["Sea"]		
Collines, Walter	A	gunner
Cominge, John	A	sailor & purser
Conger, Nicholas		soldier
Cooke, John	A	miner
Cooke, John	G	soldier & sailor
Cooke [Cock], Nicholas	S	miner
Cooke, Richard		tailor & soldier
Corbett, Owen	G	sailor
Cornishe, John	A	sailor
Cotton, John	A	sailor
Courtney [Courtenay], Thomas	AE	captain
Cowley, Richard	G	sailor
(Cowe, John see Towe, John)		
Coxe, Richard	TI	pilot
Cracknell, Lionel		labourer
Creake, Alexander	A	boatswain
Crosse, John	TI	miner
Cundie [Condye], John	H	miner
Cunningham, Thomas	A	sailor; d. Sept. 25
Cutter, John	A	cooper
Dabnay, ____	D	master
Dardes, Roger		labourer
Davie, Richard	AF	miner
Davis [Davies], Harry	A	sailor
Davis [Davy], Robert	A	master
Davis, Roger	A	soldier
Davis, William	A	miner
Davis [Davies], William	A	sailor
Debois, John	A	master gunner
Denham, Robert	A	chief assayer
Dennys, John	A	sailor
Diare [Dyer], Andrew	H	master & pilot
Dod, William	J	sailor
Dowde, John	F	miner
Dragford [Drayford], Thomas	A	sailor & baker
Draper [Drap], Esdras	A	sailor
Edgill, Phillip	TI	miner
Edwards, Alexander	A	miner
Edwards, Christopher	TA	miner
Ellarde, Phillip	A	charge of apparel; d. Aug. 16
Ellis, John	A	sailor
Ellis [Ellyer], Richard	A	miner
English, William	A	sailor
Erelease, Thomas	A	sailor
Essex, Cipio		gentleman
Estwood, Christopher	TA	miner
Evans, Davis	G	soldier & baker
Evans, Davy		baker
Evans, Edward	A	miner
Evans, Robert	A	miner
Facie, Arthur	MF	miner
Fairweather, Richard, Jr.	B	master

Abbreviations of ships: A, *Ayde;* B, *Bear Leicester;* D, *Bark Dennis;* F, *Francis* of Fowey; G, *Gabriel;* H, *Hopewell;* J, *Judith;* M, *Michael;* P, pinnace; S, *Salomon* of Weymouth; AE, *Armonell* of Exmouth; AF, *Ann Francis;* EB, *Emanuel* of Bridgwater; MF, *Mone* of Fowey; TA, *Thomas Allen;* TI, *Thomas* of Ipswich.

APPENDIX 1—Continued next page

Name	Ship	Duty
3rd voyage, 1578 *cont.*		
Fenton, Edward	J	lieutenant general & captain
Fishborne, Richard	J	sailor
Fisher, Anthony	A	sailor & trumpeter
Flowen, Christopher	J	fisherman
Fowcat, Richard	AF	miner
Frebodie, Randoll	TA	miner
Frethye, Walter	H	smith
Frobisher, Martin	A	admiral & general
Frobisher, Thomas	A	
Frye, John	A	sailor
Gamaige, John	J	fisherman & sailor
Gardiner, Richard	S	miner
Garland, John [William?]	TI	miner
George [Jorye], James	F	miner
Gibbes, ____	TA	master
Gower, John	H	miner
Graves, Thomas	J	sailor
Gray [Greg], John	AF	master's mate
Greene, Richard		soldier
Greye, William	TI	miner
Griffen, Pears	TI	miner
Griffeth, Peter	A	soldier
Gryffin, Manas	G	sailor
Hake [Hawkes], William	A	steward
Hall, Christopher	A	chief pilot
Hall, John	A	sailor boy
Hancoke, Thomas	EB	sailor
Hapton, Charles	A	sailor
Harberd, Richard	J	sailor
Harris, John	AE	miner
Harrison, Phillip	A	sailor
Hartgill, John	S	geometrician
Harvey, Edward	G	lieutenant & captain
Harwood [Horwood], John	A	sailor & surgeon
Hawke, Nicholas	H	miner
(Hawkes, William see Hake, William)		
Hayson, Robert	J	gunner
Hayzens, Harry	TA	miner
Heale, Edward	A	miner; d. Sept.
Heale, Roger	A	miner
Hegs, Richard	A	miner
Hellard, John	A	gentleman(?)
Herd, Robert [Richard]	EB	miner
Hetherington, John	EB	miner
Hewes, James	AF	miner
Hewes, Tege	G	sailor
Hews, Anthony		soldier
Heywood, James [John]	TI	miner & cook
Hill, Edmund	F	miner
Hill, John	F	miner
Hills [Hille], John	A	sailor
Hilpe, John	A	sailor boy
Hilton, Richard	TA	miner
Hind, Robert	M	surgeon
Hitchcocke, John	A	sailor
Hodges, Richard	A	miner
Hodgys, John		smith
Hogg [Hoge], Robert	AE	miner
Hollyland, John	EB	miner
Holmes, Walter	A	sailor

Abbreviations of ships: A, *Ayde;* B, *Bear Leicester;* D, *Bark Dennis;* F, *Francis* of Fowey; G, *Gabriel;* H, *Hopewell;* J, *Judith;* M, *Michael;* P, pinnace; S, *Salomon* of Weymouth; AE, *Armonell* of Exmouth; AF, *Ann Francis;* EB, *Emanuel* of Bridgwater; MF, *Mone* of Fowey; TA, *Thomas Allen;* TI, *Thomas* of Ipswich

APPENDIX 1—Continued next page

Name	Ship	Duty
3rd voyage, 1578 *cont.*		
Holt, Adam	J	shipwright
Hopton, Charles	A	sailor
Hornebrok, Roger	AE	miner
Horsey, Edmond		labourer
Hudson, ___	S	master
Humphrey, William, Jr.	A	assayer
Hunt [Lunt], John	G	master's mate & pilot
Hutchen, John	F	miner
Hutchens [Huggens], Saunder	AF	miner
Hutchens, Thomas	D	miner
Incent [Juncent], John	G	sailor
Jacklin, James	G	boatswain
Jackman, Charles	J	master
Jackson, Christopher	A	sailor & trumpeter
James, William	TA	miner
James, WIlliam John	AF	miner
Jenkins, Harry [Henry?]	A	sailor
Jenkins, Thomas	A	pumpmaker
Jennynges, Thomas		smith
John, Baltazar	D	miner
John, Harry	H	miner
John, Richard	A	miner
John, Robert	H	miner
Johnson, Godfrey		shoemaker & soldier
Johnson, John		soldier
Jonas, Paul	A	sailor
Jones, Hewe	A	sailor & gunner
Jones, Nicholas	J	sailor
Jones, William	D	Capt. Kendall's man
Joyner, William		miner
(Juncent, John see Incent, John)		
Kelley [Beale], Walter	A	carpenter & sailor; d. Sept. 24
Kendall, ___	D	captain
Kent, Harry	A	soldier
Kindersley, Matthew	M	captain
Kindersley, Robert		gentleman
King, John	AF	miner
Kirkman, Harry		ensign
Kletara, Robert	A	
Laborne, William	M	sailor
Lambell, John	J	asayer
Lamberton, Bennet	H	miner
Landam, Titus		labourer
Lane, William	G	gunner
Lang, John	AE	miner
Larkin, Ralph	J	sailor
Larman, George	J	sailor
Larrance, Nicholas		labourer
Laton, Thomas	M	sailor
Lawson, John	M	sailor
Layne [Lane], Richard	S	miner
Lee, John		lieutenant
Leeche, James	EB	master's mate (?)
Leonard, Dominic	J	sailor
Letherbye, John	S	miner
Lewis, Tege	A	sailor
Littlestone, Roger	A	Frobisher's servant; d. Aug. 28
Loe, John		sailor & cooper
Long, William	S	miner
Lowring, John	J	sailor

Abbreviations of ships: A, *Ayde;* B, *Bear Leicester;* D, *Bark Dennis;* F, *Francis* of Fowey; G, *Gabriel;* H, *Hopewell;* J, *Judith;* M, *Michael;* P, pinnace; S, *Salomon* of Weymouth; AE, *Armonell* of Exmouth; AF, *Ann Francis;* EB, *Emanuel* of Bridgwater; MF, *Mone* of Fowey; TA, *Thomas Allen;* TI, *Thomas* of Ipswich

APPENDIX 1—Continued next page

Name	Ship	Duty
3rd voyage, 1578 *cont.*		
Luce, Richard	A	sailor
Luce, William	F	pilot
(Lunt, John see Hunt, John)		
Lydiet, William		soldier
Lydger, George	J	shipwright
(Lyger, see Bartlet, Andrew)		
Mannering, William	A	sailor
Martine [Marten], William	AE	miner
Mather, Brian	A	sailor
Mathew, Edward	M	sailor
Maye, Harry	H	miner
Merifield [Meryfeelde], Hewe	A	sailor & gunner
Modye, Thomas	F	grocer
Molton, Peter	G	shipwright
Morrys, Clement	AF	miner
Morrys [Morris], Thomas	F	master
Moyle[s], Henry	F	captain
Mundaye, John	F	miner
Mychaell, Harry	A	sailor; d. Sept.
Nancarne, Stephen, J. sailor		
Newton, Richard	EB	captain & owner
Newton, Thomas	AF	miner
Newton, William	EB	miner
Nicholas, Thomas	A	sailor
Nicholls, Francis	TI	miner; d. Sept. 18
Nickyns, John	TI	miner
Norton, John	M	sailor boy
Offerton [Overton], Harry	A	sailor
Oliver, William	S	miner
Onyon, John	G	sailor
Organ, Richard	A	miner
Ormeshawe [Armshow], William		soldier
Page, John	G	miner
Paradice, John	J	surgeon
Parsons [Persons], William	A	miner
Pascowe [Paskall], Warne	AF	miner
Pavie, Edward	A	sailor boy
Payne, William	J	carpenter
Peacock, Robert	A	assayer
Peacocke, John	A	sailor
Pearse, Harry	TI	miner
(Pearse, Thomas see Price, Thomas)		
Pearse, Walter	A	miner
Peaseley, William	TI	miner
Pemberton, Robert	EB	miner
Pepowell, Timothy	A	soldier
Peterfield, John	AF	miner
Phillpott, Richard	B	captain & ensign
Phillippes, Thomas	G	sailor (?)
Pillion, Thomas	J	sailor
Piper, Arthur	MF	miner
Pope, John	F	sailor; d. Aug. 19
Price, John		baker
Price, John	G	soldier & baker
Price [Pearse], Thomas	G	master
Price, Thomas	A	sailor
Pynchyn [Pinchin], John	A	miner
Randall, Hewe	S	captain & owner
Richard, Oliver [Allen]	MF	miner
Riche, Cornelius	A	sailor; d. Sept. 27

Abbreviations of ships: A, *Ayde;* B, *Bear Leicester;* D, *Bark Dennis;* F, *Francis* of Fowey; G, *Gabriel;* H, *Hopewell;* J, *Judith;* M, *Michael;* P, pinnace; S, *Salomon* of Weymouth; AE, *Armonell* of Exmouth; AF, *Ann Francis;* EB, *Emanuel* of Bridgwater; MF, *Mone* of Fowey; TA, *Thomas Allen;* TI, *Thomas* of Ipswich

APPENDIX 1—Continued next page

Name	Ship	Duty
3rd voyage, 1578 *cont.*		
Ridesden, Nicholas	A	
Ridisdaile, Stephen	A	minister
Rigbie, Edward	A	miner
Riland, Edward	TA	miner
Rise, John	A	miner
Risse [Ryse], John	AF	miner
Roade [Rade], Harry	F	miner
Robartes, Davie	TI	miner
Roberts, William	F	miner
Robinson, Edward	A	sailor
Robinson, Peter	J	sailor
Roper, George		soldier
Rowse, Roger	MF	miner
Russell, Thomas	TI	miner
Salt, Richard		miner
Sampson, John	A	sailor
Sane, Anthony	A	sailor
Sargent, Thomas	D	miner
Saunders, John	A	sailor
Saunders, William	A	sailor
Saverie, John	H	miner
Seely, William	J	steward
Sellman, Edward	A	merchant & registrar
Settell, James		gentleman
Shefeelde, Abraham	G	soldier
Sisse [Syse], Roger	MF	miner
Skrevener, John	A	gentleman
Skypwith, Lionel	J	pilot
Sleyton [Sleaton], Nicholas	EB	miner
Smithe, John	EB	master
Smithe, William	AE	miner
Smithton, Edward		labourer
Sparrow, Anthony	A	sailor & quartermaster; d. Aug. 31
Sparrow, John	AE	miner
Sprage, Harry	M	shipwright
Sprake [Sparrche], George	A	miner
Stafford, Edmond	A	gentleman & assayer
Stanley, John	G	soldier
Stanton, Thomas	A	sailor
Staunton, William		gentleman
Stawker, George		carpenter
Stoberne, Harry	G	sailor
Streat, Walter	A	sailor
Stubble, Thomas	M	sailor
Syllebin, Giles	M	boatswain
Syllins, Thomas	G	sailor
Symon, Thomas	H	miner
Symondes, Sebastian		cooper
Syncke, Christopher	TI	miner
Tanfield, WIlliam	TI	captain
Tarte [Thorte, Tort], Thomas	A	sailor; d. Sept. 24
Tatoricke, Thomas	A	sailor
Taylor, John	A	sailor boy
Taylor, Richard		miner
Taylor, William		shoemaker
Teag [Teage], Roger	A	miner
Tedder, Robert		smith
Thorne, John	A	sailor boy
Thorne, John	AE	miner
Thorneton, Thomas	A	purser

Abbreviations of ships: A, *Ayde;* B, *Bear Leicester;* D, *Bark Dennis;* F, *Francis* of Fowey; G, *Gabriel;* H, *Hopewell;* J, *Judith;* M, *Michael;* P, pinnace; S, *Salomon* of Weymouth; AE, *Armonell* of Exmouth; AF, *Ann Francis;* EB, *Emanuel* of Bridgwater; MF, *Mone* of Fowey; TA, *Thomas Allen;* TI, *Thomas* of Ipswich

APPENDIX 1—Continued next page

Name	Ship	Duty
3rd voyage, 1578 *cont.*		
Towe [Cowe], John	A	miner
Tregarton, John	AF	miner
Threherne, George	MF	miner
Trelagan, WIlliam	MF	purser
Trelease [Trelos], Thomas	D	sailor; d. Aug. 16
Treliver [Treviller?], James	A	sailor
Trethewen [Tredew], Richard	D	miner
Trewick, Raulf	H	miner
Truscot, Walter [al. Richards]	D	miner
Trybe, Robert	J	sailor
Upcot	MF	captain
Utey, James		soldier
Vincent, Peter		gentleman
Wallis, James [John]	G	master's mate
Walter, James	A	sailor
Ward, Luke	A	gentleman
Ward, WIlliam	J	master's mate
Warrin, Nicholas	A	carpenter
Waters, George	MF	miner
Watson, Richard	A	sailor
Webbe, William	AE	miner
Webber, Adam	AE	miner
Welder, Thomas	A	soldier
Wharton, Philemon	A	miner & "musician"
Wheatley, Richard	A	sailor
Whit [White], Guy	J	sailor
Wiars, Thomas	EB	passenger
Wilcoke, Richard	F	miner
Wilcoke [Wilcox], Robert	A	miner
William, Henry	AF	miner
William [Williams], John	H	miner
William, John [al. Trevorian]	H	miner
William, Raulf	H	miner
Williams, Hewe	S	miner
Williams, John	AE	miner
Williams, John	A	master's mate
Williams [Willins], Martin	J	sailor
Wilmater, Robert	A	sailor
Wilmot, John	A	sailor; d. Sept. 28
Wilmot, Nicholas	A	miner
Wilson, John	J	sailor
Wilye, Robert	TA	miner
Wollock [Woodcocke], Penticost	MF	miner
Woolfall [Wolfall], Robert	J	minister
Workman, John	H	miner
Wyllins, John	A	sailor
Yeles, John	TA	miner
Yorke, Gilbert	A	captain
Young, George [al. Whet]	A	miner; d. Sept. 17
Young [Younge], John	A	miner

Abbreviations of ships: A, *Ayde;* B, *Bear Leicester;* D, *Bark Dennis;* F, *Francis* of Fowey; G, *Gabriel;* H, *Hopewell;* J, *Judith;* M, *Michael;* P, pinnace; S, *Salomon* of Weymouth; AE, *Armonell* of Exmouth; AF, *Ann Francis;* EB, *Emanuel* of Bridgwater; MF, *Mone* of Fowey; TA, *Thomas Allen;* TI, *Thomas* of Ipswich

APPENDIX 2. Summary of ships and personnel of the three voyages of Martin Frobisher

Ships	Captain	Master	Master's mate(s)	Master gunner	Boatswain & mate	Shipwright(s)	Pilot	Surgeon	Purser(s)	Tonnage	Ship's company*	Owner(s)
FIRST VOYAGE (1576): M. Frobisher, general												
Michael	M. Kindersley	O. Gryffen	T. Bormane		P. Whithed				N. Chancellor	25	13	venturers
Gabriel	M. Frobisher	C. Hall		R. Slight	R. Frynd			P. Becket		20	15	venturers
Pinnace										7	4	venturers
SECOND VOYAGE (1577): M. Frobisher, general; R. Phillpot, ensign												
Ayde	M. Frobisher	C. Hall	C. Jackson	R. Coxe	H. Howe & O. Corbett		A. Diare	E. Cooley	N. Chancellor	200	116	Cathay Co.
Michael	G. Yorke	J. Beare	C. Coltemane		T. Wiars			W. Edwards		25	16	Cathay Co.
Gabriel	E. Fenton	W. Smithe	B. Bull		H. Peale (?)			J. Netherclyfte		20	13	Cathay Co.
THIRD VOYAGE (1578): M. Frobisher, general; E. Fenton, lieutenant general; G. Best, E. Harvey, J. Lee, lieutenants; H. Kirkman, R. Philpot, ensigns												
Company's ships												
Ayde	M. Frobisher	R. Davis	J. Williams & J. Treliver	J. Debois	A. Creake		C. Hall	J. Harwood	T. Thorneton & J. Cominge	200	134	Cathay Co.
Judith	E. Fenton	C. Jackman	W. Ward	R. Burnit		A. Holt & G. Lydger	L. Skypwith	J. Paradice	N. Chancellor	100	38	Cathay Co.
Michael	M. Kindersley	B. Bull	W. Bennes		G. Syllebin	H. Sprage		R. Hind		25	13	Cathay Co.
Gabriel	E. Harvey	T. Pearse	J. Wallis	W. Lane	J. Jacklin	P. Molton	J. Hunt			20	22	Cathay Co.
Commissioned ships												
Thomas Allen	G. Yorke	W. Gibbes								160	13	T. Allen
Hopewell	H. Carew						A. Diare		R. Chaynalse	150	22	R. How
Anne Francis	G. Best	J. Beare	J. Gray						J. Cara	130	18	F. Lee
Thomas of Ipswich	W. Tanfield						R. Coxe			130	20	T. Bonham
Francis of Fowey	H. Moyle	T. Morrys					W. Luce	– Beton		130	15	J. Rashley
Mone of Fowey	– Upcot	J. Lakes					S. Beare			100	13	W. Mone
Beare Leicester	R. Phillpot	R. Fairweather							W. Trelagan	100	30	R. Fairweather, Sr., & M. Lok
Noncommissioned ships												
Salomon	H. Randall	– Hudson					J. Lunt			120	12	H. Randall
Emanuel	R. Newton	J. Smithe (?) J. Leeche (?)								100	12	R. Newton
Armonell	T. Courtenay	J. Anthony								100	14	T. Courtenay
Bark Dennis	– Kendall	– Dabnay								100	11	N. Dennys

*Minimum numbers. In the first voyage, six persons cannot be placed; five are presumed lost during the voyage. One of these, John Hammond, is known to have gone down with the pinnace.

Cat. No.	Culture	Type	Material	Condition	Joins	Remarks
Site Name: Kodlunarn Island-1; Borden No.: KeDe-1						
Surface collection, Area 3						
1	Dorset	core	chert	chunk		
2	Dorset	microblade	other	whole		
3	Historic	bullet	lead	fragment		
Surface collection, Area 8						
4	Historic	tile	ceramic	fragment		
Surface collection, Area 12						
5	Historic	cartridge	brass	whole		
Excavation, Structure 2, test pit 1						
6-68	Historic	crucible	ceramic	fragment		
Surface collection, pond adjacent to Structure 1						
69	Historic	crucible	ceramic	fragment	1	
70	Historic	crucible	ceramic	fragment	4	
71	Historic	crucible	ceramic	fragment	7	
72	Historic	crucible	ceramic	fragment	10	
Excavation, Structure 1, test pit 1						
73	Historic	tile	ceramic	fragment	4	
74	Historic	tile	ceramic	fragment	1	
75	Historic	tile	ceramic	fragment	21	
76	Historic	tile	ceramic	fragment	14	
77	Historic	tile	ceramic	fragment	16	
78	Historic	tile	ceramic	fragment	20	
79	Historic	fish can key	metal	whole		
80	Historic	nail	iron	fragment		
81-86	Historic	crucible	ceramic	fragment		
Excavation, Ship's Trench, test pit 1						
87	Historic	bloom	iron	whole	88	bloom 2
Excavation, Ship's Trench, test pit 2						
89	Historic	dowel	wood	fragment		at base of bloom 3
90	Historic	bloom	iron	whole		bloom 3
91	Historic	bloom	iron	whole		bloom 1
Site Name: Willows Island-1; Borden No.: KeDe-2						
Surface collection, upper rill (Locus 1)						
1	Hist.Inuit	pipe	ceramic	stem fragment		
2	Hist.Inuit	walrus tooth	enamel	whole		
Surface collection, lower rill (Locus 2)						
3	Pre-Dorset	utilized flake	grey chert			
4	Pre-Dorset	biface	grey chert	proximal		
5	Pre-Dorset	utilized flake	quartz	whole		
6	Pre-Dorset	biface	grey chert	medial		
7	Pre-Dorset	burin spall	grey chert	whole		
8	Pre-Dorset	microblade	grey chert	whole		
9	Hist.Inuit	harpoon endblade	slate	whole		
Site Name: Tikkoon Point; Borden No.: KeDe-4						
Surface collection, Locus 1 (furnace)						
1	Historic	wire nail	iron	fragment		
2	Historic	sheet	iron	fragment		
3	Historic	wire nail	iron	fragment		
4	Historic	sheet	iron	fragment		
5	Historic	wire nail	iron	fragment		
6	Historic	nail	iron	fragment		
7	Historic	bag	burlap	fragment		
8	Historic	nail	iron	fragment		
Excavation, Locus 2, test pit						
9	Dorset	S/N biface	grey chert	whole		

Note: Artifacts are stored at the Prince of Wales Northern Heritage Centre, Yellowknife, Northwest Territories.

Sample No.	Field No.	Yellowknife No.	Material
Site Name: Kodlunarn Island–1; Borden No.: KeDe–1			
Surface collection, Structure 1 pond:			
41	–	981.42.42i	charcoal, coal
42	2	" .42h	cinder
43	3	" .42j	cinder
44	5	" .42d	coal
45	6	" .42c	slag
46	8	" .42e	slag
47	9	" .42g	slag
94	–	" .69a,b,c	tile
95	–	" .69a,b,c	chert
96	–	" .69a,b,c	coal
97	–	" .69a,b,c	slag
98	–	" .69a,b,c	cinder
Test pit, Structure 1:			
48	–	*	charred wood
49	–	*	charcoal
50	–	*	brick
51	–	*	tile
52	–	*	soil
53	–	*	slag
54	–	*	cinder
55	–	*	coal
56	–	*	flint
57	–	*	misc. rocks
58	–	*	iron lump
59	–	981.42.47	brick
60	–	" .48e	yellow clay
61	–	" .48f	charcoal
62	–	" .48b	brick
63	–	" .48e	brick
Test pit 1, Structure 2 (55.80S/5.80W):			
13	–	981.42.6	brick, tile
14	–	" .6	iron ore
15	–	" .6	cinder
16	–	" .6	soil
Test pit north of Structure 2 (45.6–45.1S/5.0–5.5W):			
17	–	981.421	charcoal
18	–	" .32	charcoal
22	–	" .6b	charcoal
Test pit 1, Structure 3 (40.40S/8.00E):			
19	–	981.44,42k	charcoal
20	–	" .44	coal
21	–	" .44	rock
23	–	" .44	cinder
Test pit 1, Structure 7:			
24	–	981.50	charcoal
25	–	" .50a	wood
26	–	" .56b	coal?
27	–	" .56c	tile
Test pit 2, Structure 7:			
28	–	981.54	tile
Test pit 3, Structure 7:			
29	–	981.57a	tile, cinder
30	–	" .57b	charcoal
Unidentified test pit, Structure 7:			
31	–	981.1	tile, cinder, charcoal
Surface collection, Structure 7:			
32	–	981.9	–
Surface collection, Structure 8:			
33	–	981.51	chert, tile
34	–	" .55	general mortar sample
35	1	" .23	tile
36	2	" .30	mortar
37	3	" .41	ivory
38	4	" .24	tile
39	5	" .25	mortar, chert
40	6	" .27	mortar, tile
Structure 11:			
89	–	981.42.42n	coal, slag, chert
90	–	" .42o	coal, slag, chert
91		.42p	coal, slag, chert
92		.42m	coal, slag, chert

*Samples are in various bags with Yellowknife inventory numbers: 70, 48g, 7, 68, 48c, 28, 62, 65, 58, 60 and 6.

APPENDIX 4—Continued next page

Sample No.	Field No.	Yellowknife No.	Material
Site Name: Kodlunarn Island–1; Borden No.: KeDe-1 *cont.*			
Test pit 1, Structure 12:			
64	–	981.66a	amorphous carbon
65	–	" .67a	amorphous carbon
66	–	" .66b	brick, tile
67	–	" .37	tile
68	–	" .8b	charcoal, carbon
69	–	" .8c	charcoal, carbon
70	–	" .8a	charcoal, carbon
71	–	" .46a	wood
72	–	" .46b	wood
Test pit 2, Structure 12:			
73	–	981.39	wood
74	–	" .38	wood-mush
75	–	" .72	wood-mush
76	–	" .11	wood
77	–	" .10	wood or bark
78	–	" .34	tile, brick
79	–	" .78	rust
80	–	" .71	soil
Test pit 3, Structure 12:			
81	–	–	rust
Surface collection, Structure 12:			
82	–	981.26	coal
102	–	" .80	geological sample
Bloom 1:			
83	–	–	charcoal
84	–	–	rust
85	–	–	rust
86	–	–	soil, rust
Top of Ship's Trench, east side:			
87	–	981.42.33	tile
41 m north of cairn:			
93	–	981.42.40	tile
Site Name: Tikkoon Point; Borden No.: KeDe-4			
Furnace:			
1	1	981.42.76h	charcoal, cement
2	2	" .73	hearth rock
3	3	" .76i	bone
4	4	" .77a	charcoal
5	5	" .77b	cement
6	6	" .77c	tar(?)
7	–	" .77j	charcoal, tar
Bog, north 60°W (mag.):			
8	1	981.42.74a	peat
9	2	" .74b	peat
10	3	" .74c	peat
11	4	" .74d	peat
12	5	" .74e	peat
General wood sample:			
106	–	981.42.81b	wood
W. Kenyon's camp:			
107	–	981.42.81b	metal
Site Name: Willows Island (Opingivik); Borden No.: KeDe-2			
99	–	981.42.5a–g	iron ore
100	–	" .4	powdered ore
103	2	" .12a–g	wood
104	–	" .16a–d	wood
105	1	" .81c	wood
110	–	" .20,21	clam shell, jaw bone
111	–	" .82	bone
112	–	" .82	geological sample
Site Name: Countess of Warwick Sound; Borden No.: KeDe-5			
108	–	981.42.35	wood
109	–	"	driftwood

Note: Samples stored at Prince of Wales Northern Heritage Centre, Yellowknife, Northwest Territories.

Glossary

bloom: a partially processed mass of smelted iron

cupel: a small vessel used in refining gold or silver, similar in function to a crucible but made from pulverized bones mixed with ashes from the previous smelts

HBC: Hudson's Bay Company

Inuit, Innuit, plural of Inuk: previously known as the Eskimo. Inuit is their name for themselves and means "people"

Inuk: person

Inuktitut: the language of the Inuit

Iqaluit: administrative center of the Eastern Canadian Arctic, meaning "place of char fishing"

kablunat, kadlunat, kodlunar, kodlunat, qallunat: variant spellings of the Inuktitut word for Europeans and Americans

kia: Hall's spelling of the word "kayak"

Kinggamiut: Inuit inhabitants of the western coast of Cumberland Sound

Kodlunarn: the name given by Inuit to the island formerly used by "white people;" from the Inuktitut word "kodlunat"

miksanut: Inuit word meaning "about," "concerning"

muffles: clay objects which act as protective covering for scorifiers containing ores being assayed

nauluk: harpoon head used by Inuit for seal, walrus, and formerly whale hunting

Nepouetiesupbing: Inuktitut for "place where mast is put up," a bluff at Tikkoon

Nugumiut: Inuit inhabitants of Frobisher Bay

oomien: Hall's spelling of umiak, a large slim boat sometimes known as the "woman's boat"

osmund, osmunde: Swedish term for a small, highly refined lump of iron from which tools were forged

pinnace: a light sailing ship, especially one used as a tender. Small pinnaces were frequently carried in pieces on larger ships for assembly when reaching a destination requiring a smaller vessel

qallunat: see kablunat

qarmat: a subrectangular low sod- and rock-walled tent probably used during the fall or early winter

sea coal: an old British synonym of bituminous coal, named after coal washed ashore and used for fuel; the name was extended to mined coal, as well

scorifier: a shallow fireclay vessel used in assaying

Sikosuilarmiut: Inuit inhabitants of Cape Dorset area

Skraeling: Norse term for native inhabitants of the North American Arctic

supunyers: beads

tood-noo: caribou back fat

took-too: variant of tuktu, Inuit word for caribou

Bibliography

Aa, P. van der
1706   *Naakeurige Versameling der gedenk waardig-*
        ste zee en land Reysen na Oost en West-Indi-
        en, 17(3). Leyden: Pieter van der Aa.

Agricola, G.
1561   *De re metallica, Libri XII.* 2d Latin edition.
        Basle: Froben.
1912   *Georgius Agricola. De re metallica.* Translated
        by H. C. Hoover and L. H. Hoover from the
        1st edition of 1556. London: The Mining
        Magazine.
1950   *Georgius Agricola. De re metallica.* Translated
        by H. C. Hoover and L. H. Hoover from the
        1st edition of 1556. New York: Dover Publica-
        tions Inc.

Aitchison, L.
1960   *A History of Metals.* London: MacDonald and
        Evans Ltd.

Anonymous
1576   Ships newly built since the beginning of ye
        year 1571. MS in Public Record Office, SP
        12/107/68. Mar. 10 1576.
1577   Names of ships throughout the realm . . . . MS
        in Public Record Office, SP 12/96. Feb. 6
        1577.
1616   *Ursprung und Ordnungen der Bergwerge inn*
        Königreich Böheim. Leipzig: Inn Vorlegung H.
        Grossen des Jugern.
1983   Iron blooms in the north-west passage. *Jour.*
        Hist. Metall. Soc. 17:50.

Arrhenius, O.
1959   Die Grundlagen unserer ûlteren Eisenherstel-
        lung. *Antikvariskt Arkiv* 13, KVHAA, Stock-
        holm.
1967   Ore, iron, artefacts and corrosion. *Sveriges*
        Geologiska Undersökning, sec. C (626), 61
        (11), Stockholm.

Avery, D. H., N. J. van der Merwe, and S. Saitowitz
1988   The metallurgy of the iron bloomery in Africa.
        In *The Beginning of the Use of Metals and Al-*
        loys, R. Maddin, ed., pp. 261–282. Cam-
        bridge: MIT Press.

Baillie, M. G. L.
1982   *Tree-Ring Dating and Archaeology.* Chicago:
        University of Chicago Press.

Barkham, S.
1980   A note on the Strait of Belle Isle during the pe-
        riod of Basque contact with Indians and Inuit.
        Etudes/Inuit/Studies 4(1–2):51–58.

Barrow, J.
1818   *A Chronological History of Voyages into the*
        Arctic Regions. London: John Murray.

Bartholin, T. S.
1979   The Picea-Larix problem. *IAWA Bulletin* 1:
        7–10

Bartholin, T. S., and C. Hjort

1987   Dendrochronological studies of recent drift-wood on Svalbard. In *Methods of Dendrochronology I,* L. Kairukstis, Z. Bednarz, and E. Feliksik, eds., pp. 207–219. Polish Academy of Sciences Systems Research Institute.

Bealer, A. W.

1984   *The Art of Blacksmithing,* 3d edition. New York: Harper & Row.

Bell, H.

1912   Notes on a bloom of Roman iron found at Corstopitum (Corbridge). *Jour. Iron Steel Inst.* 85(1):118–135.

Bennett, C. L., R. P. Beukens, M. R. Clover, D. Elmore, H. E. Gove, L. Kilius, A. E. Litherland, and K. H. Purser

1978   Radiocarbon dating with electrostatic accelerators: Dating of milligram samples. *Science* 201:345–47.

Bennett, C. L., R. P. Beukens, M. R. Clover, H. E. Gove, R. B. Liebert, A. E. Litherland, K. H. Purser, and W. E. Sondheim

1977   Radiocarbon dating using electrostatic accelerators: Negative ions provide the key. *Science* 198:508–10.

Best, George

1578   *A true discourse of the late voyages of discoverie, for the finding of a passage to Cathaya, by the northweast, under the conduct of Martin Frobisher generall....* London. Reprinted in Stefansson and McCaskill 1938.

1875   *The Three Voyages of Martin Frobisher.* London: T. Richards.

Beukens, R. P., D. M. Gurfinkel, and H. W. Lee

1986   Progress at the IsoTrace Radiocarbon Facility. *Radiocarbon* 28:229–236.

Biringuccio, V.

1942   *The Pirotechnia of Vannoccio Biringuccio, 1540.* Translated by C. S. Smith and M. T. Gnudi. New York: American Institute of Mining and Metallurgical Engineers.

Blackadar, R. G.

1967   Geological reconnaissance, southern Baffin Island, District of Franklin. *Geological Survey of Canada Paper* 66-47.

Blake, W., Jr.

1961   Radiocarbon dating of raised beaches in Nordaustlandet Spitsbergen. In *Geology of the Arctic,* G. O. Raasch, ed., pp. 133–146.

1972   Climatic implications of radiocarbon dated driftwood in the Queen Elisabeth Islands, Arctic Canada. *In* Climatic Changes in Arctic Areas during the Last 10,000 Years, Y. Vasari, H. Hyvarinen, and S. Higgs, eds., pp. 77–104. *Acta Universitatis Ouluensis, ser. A, Geologica* no. 1.

1975   Radiocarbon age determination and post glacial emergence at Cape Storm, Southern Ellesmere Island, Arctic Canada. *Geografiska Annaler 57* A (1–2).

Boas, F.

1888   *The Central Eskimo.* Sixth annual report of the Bureau of American Ethnology. Washington: Smithsonian Institution.

Boyle, R. W.

1979   The geochemistry of gold and its deposits (together with a chapter of geochemical prospecting for the element). *Geological Survey of Canada Bulletin* 280.

Brimble, L. J. F.

1946   *Trees in Britain.* London: McMillan and Co.

Brøndsted, J.

1965   *The Vikings.* Translated by Kalle Skov. Hammondsworth: Penguin Books.

Brown, G. T.

1964   Roman bloom from Cranbrook, Kent. *Jour. Iron Steel Inst.* 202(6):502–504.

1970   The examination of two samples of bloomery iron. *Bull. Hist. Metall. Group.* 5(1):29–32.

Cheshire, N., T. Waldron, A. Quinn, and D. Quinn

1980   Frobisher's Eskimos in England. *Archivaria* 10:23–50.

Cleere, H. F.

1976   Some operating parameters for Roman ironworks. *Bulletin of the Institute of Archaeology, London* 13:233–246.

Coghlan, H. H.

1977   Notes on Prehistoric and Early Iron in the Old World. *Pitt Rivers Museum Occasional Papers on Technology* No. 8, Oxford.

Collins, H. B.

1950   Excavations at Frobisher Bay, Baffin Island, Northwest Territories (preliminary report). Annual Report of the National Museum of Canada for the years 1948-49. *National Museum of Canada Bulletin* 118:18-43. Ottawa.

Collinson, R. (ed.)

1867   The three voyages of Martin Frobisher, in search of a passage to Cathaia and India by the north-west, A.D. 1576–8. *Hakluyt Soc. Works,* [1st ser.], vol. 38.

Cresswell, R.

1987   Radio-carbon dating of iron using accelerator mass spectrometry. M. Sc. thesis, University of Toronto.

1991a   Report to Meta Incognita Steering Committee. Manuscript on file, Arctic Studies Center, Smithsonian Institution.

1991b   The radiocarbon dating of iron artefacts using accelerator mass spectrometry. *Jour. Hist. Metall.* 25(2):78–85.

Davis, C. G.
1918   *The Building of a Wooden Ship*. Philadelphia: United States Shipping Board Emergency Fleet Corporation.

Davis, R., Jr.
1978   Brookhaven National Laboratory Report 24674.

Dyke, A. S., and T. F. Morris
1990   Postglacial history of the Bowhead whale and of driftwood penetration; implications for paleoclimate, central Canadian Arctic. *Geological Survey of Canada Paper 89-24*.

Eber, D. H.
1989   *When the Whalers Were up North: Inuit Memories from the Eastern Arctic*. McGill-Queen's University Press.

Eggertsson, O.
1991   Driftwood in the Arctic, a dendrochronological study. *Lundqua Reports*. Department of Quarternary Geology, University of Lund, Sweden.

Ehrenreich, R. M.
1985   Trade, Technology, and the Ironworking Community of Southern Britain in the Iron Age. *BAR British Series 144*. Oxford.

Ehrenreich, R. M., and M. L. Wayman
1991   Metallurgical examination of iron objects from the Eastern Arctic: Preliminary analysis. Report to the Meta Incognita Steering Committee. Ottawa. October 1991.

Ellis, H.
1816   Sir Martin Frobisher's instructions when going on a voyage to the North-west Parts and Cathay, in the time of Queen Elizabeth. *Archaeologia: or Miscellaneous Tracts Relating to Antiquity* 18:287–290.

Ellis, T.
1578   *A true report of the third and last voyage into Meta incognita: achieved by the worthie Capteine, M. Martine Frobisher esquire, Anno 1578* (London 1578). Reprinted in Stefansson and McCaskill 1938.

Ercker, L.
1951   *Lazarus Ercker's treatise on ores and assaying*. Translated by A. G. Sisco and C. S. Smith. Chicago: University of Chicago Press.

Eurola, S.
1971   The driftwoods of the Arctic Ocean. *Rep. Kevo Subarctic Stat.* 7: 74-80

Evans, E. E.
1948   Strange iron objects from Co. Fermanagh. *Ulster Jour. Arch.* 11:58–64.

Fenton, E.
1578   Journal [of the *Judith*]. MS in Pepys Library, Magdalene College, Cambridge, MS PL 2133, ff. 5-74.

Field Museum
1928   Kodlunarn Island note. *Field Museum of Natural History Reports*. 7(3):417–423.

Fitzhugh, W. W.
1985a   Early contacts north of Newfoundland before A.D. 1600: A review. In *Cultures in Contact*, W. W. Fitzhugh, ed., pp. 23-43. Washington: Smithsonian Institution Press.

1985b   (editor) *Cultures in Contact: The Impact of European Contacts on Native American Cultural Institutions, A.D. 1000–1800*. Washington: Smithsonian Instutition Press.

1987   Archeological ethnicity and the prehistory of Labrador: a reappraisal. In *Ethnicity and Culture*, R. Auger, M. F. Glass, S. MacEachern, and P. McCartney, eds., pp. 141–153. Calgary: Chacmool Archaeological Association, University of Calgary.

1990   Archeology of the Frobisher Voyages: Field report for 1990. 1 October 1990. Report to Prince of Wales Northern Heritage Centre, Yellowknife, NWT, Canada.

1991   Archeology of the Frobisher Voyages and European-Inuit contact: 1991 field and research report. 10 October 1991. Report to Meta Incognita Steering Committee, Canada Museum of Civilization.

Fitzhugh, W. W., and H. Lamb
1984   Vegetation history and culture change in Labrador prehistory. *Arctic and Alpine Research* 17(4):357–370.

Forbes, A.
1953   *Quest for a Northern Air Route*. Cambridge: Harvard University Press.

Forbes, R. J.
1972   The Early Story of Iron. In *Studies in Ancient Technology*, vol. 9, chap. 3, pp. 187–305. Leiden: E. J. Brill.

Frobisher, G.
n.d.   The Frobisher story. Unpubl. MS. Carnforth, Lancashire, England.

Gad, F.
1971   *The History of Greenland*, vol. 1, *Earliest Times to 1700*. Translated from Danish by E. Dupont. Montreal: McGill-Queen's University Press.

Giddings, J. L.
1941   Dendrochronology in Northern Alaska. *University of Arizona Bulletin* 12(4). *Laboratory of Tree-Ring Research Bulletin* No.1.

1952   Driftwood and problems of Arctic sea currents. *Proceedings of the American Philosophical Society* 96(2):129–142

1954   Tree-ring dating in the American Arctic. *Tree-Ring Bulletin* 20(3/4):23–25.

Gilles, J. W.

1936 Die Grabungen auf vorgeschichtlichen Eisen-
hüttenplätzen des Siegerlandes ihre Bedeutung
und die hüttentechnischen Erfahrungen im
Vergleich mit anderen Funden. *Stahl und Eisen*
56(9):252–263.

1957 25 Jahre Siegerlander Vorgeschichtsforschung
durch Grabungen if alten Eisenhüttenplatzen.
Arch. Eisenhütten. 28(4):179–185.

Goldring, P.

1985–88 Southeast Baffin Island Historical Reports.
Manuscripts on file, National Historic Sites
Directorate, Parks Canada, Ottawa, K1A 0H3.

Gordon, R. B.

1983 Materials for manufacturing: The response of
the Connecticut iron industry to technological
change and limited resources. *Technology and
Culture* 24(4):602–634.

1988 Strength and structure of wrought iron.
Archeomaterials 2(2):109–137.

Graves, H. S.

1919 The use of wood for fuel. *US Dept. of Agricul-
ture Bulletin* No. 753.

Greguss, P.

1955 *Identification of Living Gymnosperms on the
Basis of Xylotomy.* Budapest: Académiai Kiadó.

1959 *Holzanatomie der europäischen Laubhölzer
und Sträucher.* Budapest: Académiai Kiadó.

Groves, A. W.

1952 Wartime Investigations into the Haematite and
Manganese Ore Resources of Great Britain
and Northern Ireland. *Ministry of Supply Permanent Record of Research and Development
Monograph* 20-703, London.

Gullason, L.

1991 Archaeological investigations of Kuyait (KfDf-
2) and Kamaiyuk (KfDe-5), Frobisher Bay,
Baffin Island, N.W.T. Report to the Meta
Incognita Steering Committee. Ottawa. October 1991.

Gulløv, H. C.

1985 Whales, whalers, and Eskimos. The impact of
European whaling on the demography and
economy of Eskimo society in West Greenland.
In *Cultures in Contact,* W. W. Fitzhugh, ed.,
pp. 71–96. Washington: Smithsonian Institution Press.

Gulløv, H. C., and H. Kapel

1979 Haabetz Colonie 1721–1728. A historical-ar-
chaeological investigation of the Danish-Nor-
wegian colonization of Greenland. *National
Museum of Denmark Ethnographical Series*
16, Copenhagen.

Haggblom, A.

1982 Driftwood in Svalbard as an indicator of sea
ice conditions. *Geografiska Annaler* 64 A
(1–2):81–94.

Hakluyt, R.

1598–1600 *The Principall Navigations, Voiages, Traf-
fiques and Discoveries of the English Nation,* 3
vols. London: George Bishop, Ralph Newberie
and Robert Barker.

Hall, C. F.

1864 *Life with the Esquimaux,* 2 vols. London:
Sampson Low, Son, and Marston.

1865a *Arctic Researches and Life Among the Esquimaux.* New York: Harper and Brothers.

1865b *Life with the Esquimaux: A Narrative of Arctic Experience in Search of Survivors of Sir
John Franklin's Expedition.* Popular edition,
with maps, coloured illustrations, and one
hundred wood cuts. London: Samson Low,
Son, and Marston.

1880 *Deux ans chez les Esquimaux, voyage de dé-
couvertes et d'aventures.* Abridged by H. Lore-
au. Paris: Hachette. [Reprinted in 1882, 1884,
1888, 1892, 1896, 1899, 1902, 1906.]

Harbottle, G., E. V. Sayre, and R. W. Stoenner

1979 Carbon-14 dating of small samples by proportional counting. *Science* 206:683–5.

Harp, E.

1974/75 A late Dorset amulet from Southeastern Hudson Bay. *Folk* 16–17:33–44.

Hickey, C. G.

1984 An examination of processes of cultural chang-
er among Nineteenth Century Copper Inuit.
Etudes/Inuit/Studies 8(1):13–36.

Hogarth, D. D.

1985 Petrology of Martin Frobisher's "black ore"
from Frobisher Bay, N.W.T. *Geological Association of Canada, Mineralogical Association of
Canada. Program with Abstracts* 10: A 28.

1989 The *Emanuel* of Bridgewater and discovery of
Martin Frobisher's "black ore" in Ireland. *The
American Neptune* 49:14–20.

1990 Field investigations of Martin Frobisher's
mines and furnace sites in SE Baffin Island,
August 7–12, 1990. Field report to Arctic
Studies Program, Smithsonian Institution.

1991 Geological observations 1991 of some Frobisher mines, Baffin Island, and suggestions
for future research. Report to the Meta Incognita Steering Committee. Ottawa. October
1991.

Hogarth, D. D., and W. A. Gibbins

1984 Martin Frobisher's "gold mines" on Kodlunarn Island and adjacent Baffin Island, Frobisher Bay, NWT. *Contributions to the Geology of the Northwest Territories* 1:69–77.

Hogarth, D. D., and J. Loop
1986   Precious metals in Martin Frobisher's "black ores" in Frobisher Bay, Northwest Territories. *Canadian Mineralogist* 24:259–263.

Hogarth, D. D., J. Loop, and W. A. Gibbins
1985   Frobisher's gold on Kodlunarn Island–fact or fable? *Canadian Institute of Mining and Metallurgy, Bulletin* 78:75–79.

Hogarth, D. D., and J. C. Roddick
1989   Discovery of Martin Frobisher's Baffin Island "ore" in Ireland. *Canadian Journal of Earth Sciences* 26:1053–1060.

Hulton, P. H.
1961   John White's drawings of Esquimos. *The Beaver,* Summer 1961:16–20.

Hume, M. A. S., ed.
1894   *Calendar of Letters and State Papers Relating to English Affairs, Preserved in the Archives of Simancas. Elizabeth,* vol. 2, 1568–1579. London: Her Majesty's Stationery Office.

Ingstad, A. S.
1977   *The Discovery of a Norse Settlement in America,* vol. 1, *Excavations at L'Anse aux Meadows, Newfoundland 1961–1968.* Oslo: Universitetsforlaget.

Ingstad, H.
1969   *Westward to Vinland.* New York: St. Martin's Press.

Ingvarson, F.
1910   Die Treibholzer auf dem Ellesmereland. *Sec. Arct. Exp. Fram.* 1898–1902. No. 24.

Jacobs, J. D.
1985   Environment and prehistory, Baffin Island. In *Quaternary Environments: Eastern Canadian Arctic, Baffin Bay and Western Greenland,* J. T. Andrews, ed., pp. 719–740. Boston, London, Sydney: Allen & Unwin.

Jacobs, J. D., W. N. Mode, C. A. Squires, and G. H. Miller
1985   Holocene environmental change in the Frobisher Bay area, Baffin Island, N.W.T.: deglaciation, emergence, and the sequence of vegetation and climate. *Geographie physique et Quaternaire* 39(2):151–162.

Jacobs, J. D., and G. Sabo III
1978   Environments and adaptations of the Thule culture on the Davis Strait coast of Baffin Island. *Arctic and Alpine Research* 10(3):595–615.

Jacobs, J. D., and D. R. Stenton
1985   Environment, resources, and prehistoric settlement in upper Frobisher Bay, Baffin Island. *Arctic Anthropology* 22(2):59–76.

Jane, F. W.
1956   *The Structure of Wood.* New York: The MacMillan Co.

Jones, G.
1968   *A History of the Vikings.* London, New York: Oxford University Press.

Jordan, R. H.
1978   Archaeological investigations of the Hamilton Inlet Labrador Eskimo: Social and economic responses to European contact. *Arctic Anthropology* 15(2):175–185.

Jordan, R. H., and S. A. Kaplan
1980   An archaeological view of the Inuit-European contact in central Labrador. *Etudes/Inuit/Studies* 4(1–2):35–45.

Kaplan, S. A.
1983   Economic and social change in Labrador Neo-Eskimo culture. Ph.D. dissertation, Department of Anthropology, Bryn Mawr University, Bryn Mawr, Pennsylvania.

1985   European goods and socio-economic change in early Labrador Inuit society. In *Cultures in Contact,* W. W. Fitzhugh, ed., pp. 45–69. Washington: Smithsonian Institution Press.

Kenyon, W. A.
1975a   All is not golde that shineth. *The Beaver* Summer, 1975:40–46.

1975b   (editor) *Tokens of Possession. The Northern Voyages of Martin Frobisher.* Toronto: Royal Ontario Museum.

1980   The Reverend Robert Wolfall in arctic Canada: "A watry pilgrimage" of 1578. *Rotunda* 13(1):6–11.

1980/81   (editor) The Canadian Arctic journal of Capt. Edward Fenton, 1578. *Archivaria* 11:171–203.

1986   The history of James Bay 1610–1686. A study in historical archaeology. *Archaeology Monograph* 10. Royal Ontario Museum.

Kieser, W. E., R. P. Beukens, L. R. Kilius, H. W. Lee, and A. E. Litherland
1986   IsoTrace Radiocarbon Analysis—Equipment and Procedures. *Nuclear Institutes and Methods* B15:718–721.

Killick, D. J., and R. B. Gordon
1988   The mechanism of iron production in the bloomery furnace. In *Proceedings of the 26th International Archaeometry Symposium, Toronto 1988,* R. M. Farquhar, R. G. V. Hancock, and L. A. Pavlish, eds., pp. 120–123. Toronto: Archaeometry Laboratory, University of Toronto.

Kindle, E. M.
1921   Mackenzie River driftwood. *Geographical Review* 11:50–53.

Klingelhofer, E.
1976   Three lost ceramic artifacts from Frobisher's colony, 1578. *Historical Archaeology* 10:131–134.

Kolchin, B. A.

1953   Chernaya metallurgia i metalobrabotka v drev-
        ney Rusi. *Materialy i Issledovania po Arkhe-
        ologi* 32. Moscow: Akademia Nauk SSR.

Kummer, F. H., R. W. Stoenner, and Davis, R., Jr.

1972   Brookhaven National Laboratory Report
        16972.

Laeyendecker, D.

1987   Wood and charcoal identification of an early
        European mining and exploration outpost in
        Frobisher Bay, NWT, Canada. Society for His-
        torical Archaeology Conference, Savannah,
        Georgia (unpublished).

1991   Conservation, wood, and charcoal sampling,
        and driftwood collection: 1991 field season in
        Frobisher Bay. Report to the Meta Incognita
        Steering Committee. Ottawa.

n.d.   Report on file in the Smithsonian Institution.

Lankford, W. T., et al., eds.

1985   *The Making, Shaping and Treating of Steel*,
        10th ed. [Pittsburgh, Pa.]: United States Steel,
        Association of Iron and Steel Engineers.

Levin, E. M., H. F. McMurdie, and F. P. Hall

1956   *Phase Diagrams for Ceramists.* Columbus,
        Ohio: American Ceramic Society.

Lok, M.

1578a   Report to the Commissioners of the Cathay
        Company. Account Book. MS in Huntington
        Library, San Marino. HM 715.

1578b   Lok, M. to Lord Burghley. Hatfield House MS,
        161, No. 71.

ca.1581 The doynges of Captayn Furbusher Amongest
        the Companyes busyness. MS in British Li-
        brary, attributed to M. Lok. Lansdowne
        100/1.

Lok, M., Frobisher, M., et al.

1576–78 Report to the Commissioners of the Cathay
        Company. Account Books. MS in Public
        Record Office, London. E 164/35.

Lok, M., Sellman, E., et al.

1578–81 Report to the Commissioners of the Cathay
        Company. Account Books. MS in Public
        Record Office, London. E 164/36.

Loomis, C.

1971   *Weird and Tragic Shores.* New York: Alfred A.
        Knopf.

Magnusson, M., and H. Palsson

1965   Introduction. In *The Vinland Sagas. The Norse
        Discovery of America,* pp. 7–43. Ham-
        mondsworth: Penguin Books.

Marechal, J. P

1985   Methods of ore roasting and the furnaces used.
        In Furnaces and Smelting Technology in An-
        tiquity, P. T. Craddock and M. J. Hughes, eds.
        British Museum Occasional Paper No. 48.

Markham, A. H., ed.

1880   The Voyages and Works of John Davis the
        Navigator. *Hakluyt Society Works,* [1st ser.],
        vol. 59.

Martens, I.

1988   Jernvinna pa Mosstrond i Telemark. En studie
        i teknikk, bosetning ag okonomi. *Kjemiske og
        Mineraligiske undersökelser, Norsk Oldfunn*
        XIII. Oslo: Universitetets Oldsaksamling.

Maugh, T. H. II

1978   Radiodating: Direct detection extends range of
        the technique. *Science* 200:635–637.

Maxwell, M.

1976   Archaeology of the Lake Harbor District,
        Baffin Island, Canada. *National Museum of
        Man, Mercury Series, Archaeological Survey of
        Canada Paper* 6. Ottawa.

1985   *Prehistory of the Eastern Arctic.* Orlando:
        Academic Press.

1988   The Crystal II site: the Dorset component. Fro-
        bisher Bay, Baffin Island, N.W.T., Canada.
        Manuscript.

McCartney, A. P., and D. J. Mack

1973   Iron utilization by Thule eskimos of central
        Canada. *American Antiquity* 38(3):328–339.

McDermott, J.

1984   The account books of Michael Lok . . . relat-
        ing to the northwest voyages of Martin Fro-
        bisher, 1576–1578: text and analysis. M. Phil.
        thesis, University of Hull.

McDonnell, J. G.

1984   The study of early iron smithing residues. In
        The Crafts of the Blacksmith, B. G. Scott and
        H. Cleere, eds., pp. 47–52. Symposium of the
        UISPP Comité pour la Sidérurgie Ancienne,
        Belfast, September 1984. Belfast: Ulster
        Museum.

McFee, W.

1928   *The Life of Sir Martin Frobisher.* New York:
        Harper and Brothers.

McGhee, R.

1984   Thule Prehistory of Canada. In *Handbook of
        North American Arctic,* D. Damas, ed., pp.
        369–378. Washington: Government Printing
        Office.

McGovern, T. H.

1984   *Sandnes Archaeological Rescue Project.* Initial
        Field Report. Hunter College

Merwe, van der, N. J.

1965   Carbon-14 dating of iron: A new archaeologi-
        cal tool. *Current Anthropology* 6:475.

1969   *The Carbon-14 Dating of Iron.* Chicago: Uni-
        versity of Chicago Press.

Michael, H. N., and E. K. Ralph, eds.
1971   *Dating Techniques for the Archaeologist.* Cambridge: MIT Press.

Miller, G.
1980   Late Foxe glaciation of southern Baffin Island, N.W.T., Canada. *Geological Society of America Bulletin* 91(7):399–405.

Morison, S. E.
1971   *The European Discovery of America: The Northern Voyages, A.D. 500–1600.* New York: Oxford University Press.

Morton, G. R., and J. Wingrove
1969a   Constitution of bloomery slags: Part I: Roman. *Jour. Iron Steel Inst.* 207(12):1556–1564.
1969b   Slag, cinder and bear. *Bull. Hist. Metall. Group* 3(2):55–61.
1969c   The efficiency of the bloomery process. *Bull. Hist. Metall. Group* 3(2):66–67.
1972   Constitution of bloomery slags: Part II: Medieval. *Jour. Iron Steel Inst.* 210(7):478–488.

Neumann, B.
1954   Die ältesten Verfahren der Erzeugung technischen Eisens. *Freiberger Forschungshefte* D6:7–65. Kultur und technik, Berlin.

Nielsen, N.
1930   Evidence on the extraction of iron in Greenland by the Norsemen. *Meddeleser om Grøenland* BC 76:193–212.

Nosek, E. M.
1985   The Polish smelting experiments in furnaces with slag pits. *In* Furnaces and Smelting Technology in Antiquity, P. T. Craddock and M. J. Hughes, eds. *British Museum Occasional Paper* No. 48.

O'Neil. H. E., and G. T. Brown
1966   Metallurgical investigation of an iron object of Roman origin from Lower Slaughter, Glos. *Bull. Hist. Metall. Group* 7(1):30–34.

Oelsen, W., and Schürmann, E.
1954   Untersuchungsergebnisse alter Rennfeuerschlacken. *Arch. Eisenhütten.* 25(11/12):507–514.

Osann, B.
1959   Eisenhüttenmännische Aussagen der Rennofen-Rennstahl-und Rennschlackenfunde von Salzgitter-Lobmachtersen. *Stahl und Eisen* 79(17):1206–1211.

Panshin, A. J., and C.de Zeeuw
1970   *Textbook of Wood Technology,* vol. 1. 3d ed. New York: McGraw-Hill Book Co.

Pastore, Ralph
1987   Fishermen, furriers, and Beothuks: The economy of extinction. *Man in the Northeast* 33:47–62.

Patterson, T.T.
1939   Anthropogenic studies in Greenland. *Jour. Royal Anthropological Inst. of Great Britain and Ireland* 69:45–76.

Pearson, B.
1966   Cathay revisited. *Nord* 13(3):1–11. Ottawa: Department of Northern Affairs and National Resources.

Percy, J.
1864   *Metallurgy: Iron and Steel.* London: John Murray.

Perlin, John
1989   *A Forest Journey: The Role of Wood in the Development of Civilization.* New York, London: W. W. Norton & Co.

Petersen, R.
1974/75 Some considerations concerning the Greenland longhouse. *Folk* 16–17:171–188.

Phillips, E. W. J.
1948   The identification of coniferous woods by their microscopic structure. *Forest Prod. Res. Bull.* 22. London.

Piaskowski, J.
1961   Metallographic investigations of ancient iron objects from the territory between the Oder and the basin of the Vistula River. *Jour. Iron Steel Inst.* 198(3):263–281.
1964   The method of determination of the origin of ancient iron objects based on metallographic investigations. *Archaeologia Polona* 6:124–160.
1970   The achievements of research carried out in Poland on the history of early technology of iron. *Archaeologia Polona* 12:187–215.
1972   Metaloznawcze badania wczesnosredniowiecznych przedmiotów aazelaznych i próbek żużla z Górnego Śláska. *Sprawozdania Archaeologiczne* 24:439–453.
1973   Technologia żelaza na Pomorzu zachodnim w starozytności, II w.p.n.e. do II w.n.e. *Wiadomości Hutnicze* 7/8:260–265.
1981   Hipotetyczne wyprowadzenie cech żelaza wytapianego w staroźytnym ośrodku mazowieckim i ocena tego ośrodka. *Kwart Hist. Kult. Mater.* 29(4):433–450.
1989   Phosphorus in iron ore and slag, and in bloomery iron. *Archeomaterials* 3(1):47–59.

Pleiner, R.
1958   Základy slovanské zelezárského hutnictvi v ceskych ziemich. *Monumenta Archaeologica* 6, Prague.
1968   Problem of direct steel production in early ferrous metallurgy. *Steel Times* 196:312–318.
1969   Experimental smelting of steel in early medieval furnaces. *Pamatky Archeologické* 60(2):458–487.

Pope, P. E.

1986   Ceramics from Seventeenth Century Ferryland, Newfoundland (CgAf-2, Locus B). Unpublished Master thesis, Department of Anthropology, Memorial University of Newfoundland.

Postlethwaite, J.

1976   *Postlethwaite's mines and mining in the English Lake District with a new biographical sketch of the author by E.H. Shackleton, F.G.S.* 3d ed. Ilkley, Yorkshire, England: The Moxon Press.

Purser, K. H., R. B. Liebert, A. E. Litherland, R. P. Beukens, H. E. Gove, C. L. Bennett, M. R. Clover, and W. E. Sondheim

1977   An attempt to detect stable N- ions from a sputter ion source and some implications of the results for the design of tandems for ultra-sensitive carbon analysis. *Rev. Phys. Appl.* 12:1437–1492.

Quinn, D. B.

1979   *New American World: A Documentary History of North America to 1612,* vol. 4. New York: Arno-Press.

Rackham, O.

1980   *Ancient Woodland, Its History, Vegetation and Uses in England.* London: Edward Arnold.

1986   *History of the Countryside.* London: Dent.

Raistrick, A., and B. Jennings

1983   *A History of Lead Mining in the Pennines.* 2d ed. Littleborough, England: Davis Books Ltd., Newcastle-upon-Tyne and George Kelsall, Publishers.

Rhodes, D.

1976   *La Poterie: Terres et Glacures.* Paris: Dessain et Tolra.

Rickard, T. A.

1934   Drift iron, a fortuitous factor in primitive culture. *Geographical Review* 24(4):525–543.

Rowley, S.

1985   The Significance of Migration for the Understanding of Inuit Cultural Development in the Canadian Arctic. Ph.D. thesis, University of Cambridge.

Ross, G.

1975   Whaling and Eskimos: Hudson Bay 1860–1915. *National Museum of Man Publications in Ethnology,* 10. Ottawa.

1980   Whaling, Inuit, and the Arctic islands. In *A Century of Canada's Arctic Islands,* M. Zaslow, ed., pp. 33–50. Ottawa: Royal Society of Canada.

Rostoker, W., and J. R. Dvorak

1986   Additional studies on the Smithsonian iron bloom. In *Proceedings of the 24th International Archaeometry Symposium,* J. S. Olin and M. J. Blackman, eds., pp. 279–289. Washington: Smithsonian Institution Press.

Roy, S. K.

1937   The history and petrography of Frobisher's "gold ore". *[Chicago] Field Museum of Natural History. Geol. ser.* 7(2):21–38.

Sabo, D., and Sabo, G.

1978   A possible Thule carving of a Viking from Baffin Island, NWT. *Canadian Journal of Archaeology* 2:33–42.

Sabo, G.

1981   Thule culture adaptations on the south coast of Baffin Island, N.W.T. Ph.D. dissertation, Department of Anthropology, Michigan State University.

1991   *Long Term Adaptations among Arctic Hunter-Gatherers: A Case Study from Southern Baffin Island.* New York: Garland Press.

Salisbury, W., and R. C. Anderson

1958   *A Treatise on Shipbuilding and a Treatise on Rigging Written About 1620–1625.* London: The Society of Nautical Research.

Salter, C., and R. M. Ehrenreich

1984   Iron age iron metallurgy in central southern Britain. *In* Aspects of the Iron Age in Wessex, B. Cunliffe and D. Miles, eds. *Oxford Archaeology Monograph 2.*

Savelle, J. M.

1985   Effects of nineteenth century European exploration on the development of the Netsilik Inuit culture. *In* The Franklin Era in Canadian Arctic History, P. D. Sutherland, ed., pp. 192–214. *National Museum of Man, Archaeological Survey of Canada Paper* 131. Ottawa.

Sayre, E. V., G. Harbottle, R. W. Stoenner, R. L. Otlet, and G. V. Evans

1981   The use of the small gas proportional counters for the carbon-14 measurement of very small samples. In *Proceedings of an International Symposium on Methods of Low-level Counting and Spectrometry.* Intl. Atomic Energy Agency, Berlin, 6–10 April 1981. Paper IAEA-SM-252/20.

Sayre E. V., G. Harbottle, R. W. Stoenner, W. Washburn, J. S. Olin, and W. W. Fitzhugh

1982   The carbon-14 dating of an iron bloom associated with the voyages of Martin Frobisher. *In* Nuclear and Chemical Dating Techniques, Lloyd Currie, ed., pp. 441–451. *ACS Symposium Ser.* 176. Washington: American Chemical Society.

Schenck, C. A.

1904   *Forest Utilization.* Syllabus of instruction given at the Biltmore Forest School. Biltmore, North Carolina: Biltmore Forest School.

Schledermann, P.

1975 Thule Eskimo prehistory of Cumberland Sound, Baffin Island. *National Museum of Man, Mercury Series. Archaeological Survey of Canada Paper* 38. Ottawa.

1976 The effect of climatic/ecological changes on the style of Thule culture winter dwellings. *Arctic and Alpine Research* 8(1):37–47.

1980 Notes on Norse finds from the east coast of Ellesmere Island, N.W.T. *Arctic* 33:454–463.

Schubert, H. R.

1957 *History of the British Iron and Steel Industry from c.450 B.C. to A.D. 1775.* London: Routledge and Kegan Paul.

Schürmann, E.

1958 Die Reduktion des Eisens im Rennfeur. *Stahl und Eisen* 78(19):1207–1308.

Schweingruber, F. H.

1976 Prähistorisches Holz, die Bedeutung von Holzfunden aus Mitteleuropa für die Lösung archäologischer und vegetationskundlicher Probleme. *Academica Helvetica* 2. Bern: Verlag Paul Haupt.

1978 *Microscopic Wood Anatomy* (in German, French, and English). Birmensdorff: Swiss Federal Institute of Forestry Research.

1989 *Tree Rings: Basics and Applications of Dendrochronology.* English edition. Durdrecht/Boston/London: Kluwer Academic Publishers.

1990 *Anatomy of European Woods* (in German and English). Bern and Stuttgart: Paul Haupt.

Scott, B. G.

1990 *Early Irish Ironworking.* Belfast: Ulster Museum.

Sellman, E.

1578 Journal of the third voyage to Meta Incognita [contains marginal notes not present in the published version]. MS in British Library, Harley 167, ff. 165–180.

Serning, I.

1973 Forhistorik järnhantering i Dalarna. *Jernkontorets Forskning.* Ser. H., No. 2. Stockholm.

Settle, D.

1577 *A true reporte of the laste voyage into the west and northwest regions, etc. 1577, worthily achieved by Capteine Frobisher of the sayde voyage, the finder and generall.* London. Reprinted in Stefansson and McCaskill 1938.

Shammas, C.

1975 The invisible merchant and property rights. The misadventures of an Elizabethan joint stock company. *Business History* 17:95–108.

Shaw, W. T.

1975 *Mining in the Lake Counties,* 3d ed. Clapham, England: Dalesman Publishing Co.

Sisco, A. G.

1956 *Réaumur's Memoirs on Steel and Iron.* Chicago: University of Chicago Press.

Skelton, R. A., T. Marston, and G. D. Painter

1965 *The Vinland Map and the Tartar Relation.* New Haven and London: Yale University Press.

Smith, C. S.

1967 Metallurgy in the seventeenth and eighteenth centuries. In *Technology in Western Civilization,* vol. 1, M. Kranzberg and C. W. Pursell, eds., pp. 142–167. New York: Oxford University Press.

Smith, C. S., and R. J. Forbes

1957 Metallurgy and assaying. In *A History of Technology,* vol. 3, *(c.1500–c.1750),* C. Singer et al., eds., pp. 27–71. Oxford: Clarendon University Press.

Smithsonian Institution

1873 [Report on Charles Francis Hall research] Report of the Secretary. In *Smithsonian Institution Annual Report for 1871,* p. 32.

Smythe, J. A.

1936/37 Ancient Sussex iron blooms: A metallographic examination. *Trans. Newc. Soc.* 17:197–203.

Sokolov, A. L.

1966 Drift of ice in the Arctic Basin and changes in ice conditions over the Northern sea route. *Problems of the Arctic and Antarctic, Collection of Articles,* no. 11, pp. J1–J20. Arct. Inst. North America. [Translation of Dreif l'dov v arkticheskom basseine i izmenenie ledovykh uslovii na trasse severnogo morskogo puti. *Problemy Arktiki i Antartiki Sbornik statei,* 1962, vyp. 11:81–89.]

Sperl, G. J.

1979 Vergleichende Untersuchungen an frühgeschichtlichen Eisenschlacken. *Berg-und Hüttenmannische Monatshefte* 124(3):79–84.

Stead, J. E.

1918 Iron, carbon and phosphorus. *Jour. Iron Steel Inst.* 97:389–415.

Stefansson, V., and E. McCaskill, eds.

1938 *The Three Voyages of Martin Frobisher In search of a passage to Cathay and India by the North-West, A.D. 1576-8. From the original 1578 Text of George Best,* 2 vols. London: The Argonaut Press.

Stenton, D.

1987 Recent archaeological investigations in Frobisher Bay, Baffin Island, N.W.T. *Canadian Journal of Archaeology* 11:13–48.

1991 Caribou population dynamics and Thule Culture adaptations on southern Baffin Island, N.W.T. *Arctic Anthropology* 28(2):15–43.

Story, G. M., ed.

1982   *Early European Settlement and Exploitation in Atlantic Canada.* Selected Papers from a symposium. St. John's: Memorial University of Newfoundland.

Straube, H.

1964   Beitrage zur Geschichte des Eisens im alpenlandischen Raum. VI. Erzreductionsversuche im Schachtöfen norischer Bauart am Magdalensberg. *Arch. Eisenhütten.* 35(9):932–940.

Strong, D.

1927–29 Rawson-MacMillan expedition field notes, Aug. 23-4, 1927. National Anthropological Archives, Smithsonian Institution.

1927   The Rawson-MacMillan arctic expedition of Field Museum. *Science* 66:295, Sept. 30.

1929   [report of Duncan Strong concerning Kodlunarn Island and Labrador research]. *In* Annual Report of the Director for Year 1928. *Field Museum Natural History Bulletin* 7(3):417–423.

Stuiver, M., and G. W. Pearson

1986   High-precision calibration of the radiocarbon time scale, A.D. 1950–500 B.C. *Radiocarbon* 28(2b):805–838.

Sturtevant, W. C., and A. B. Quinn

1987   This new prey: Eskimos in Europe in 1567, 1576, and 1577. In *Indians and Europe: An Interdisciplinary Collection of Essays*, Christian Feest, ed., pp. 61–140. Aachen: Rader Verlag.

Sutherland, P. D., ed.

1985   The Franklin Era in Canadian Arctic History. *National Museum of Man, Archaeological Survey of Canada Paper* 131. Ottawa.

Taylor, E. G. R.

1930   *Tudor Geography, 1485–1583.* London: Methuen & Co., Ltd.

1959   The Troublesome Voyage of Captain Edward Fenton 1582–1583. *Hakluyt Society Works,* 2d ser., vol. 113.

Todd, J., and J. A. Charles

1978   Ethiopian bloomery iron and the significance of inclusion analysis in iron studies. *Jour. Historical Metallurgy Soc.* 12(2):63–87.

Trigger, B. G.

1982   Response of Native peoples to European Contact. In *Early European Settlement and Exploitation in Atlantic Canada*, G. M. Story, ed., pp. 139–155. St. John's: Memorial University of Newfoundland.

Tuck, J. A.

1981   Basque whalers in southern Labrador, Canada. In *Early European Exploitation of the North-ern Atlantic 800-1700,* A. G. F. van Holk, ed., pp. 69–78. Groningen: Arctic Centre, University of Groningen, Netherlands.

1982   A sixteenth century whaling station at Red Bay, Labrador. In *Early European Settlement and Exploitation in Atlantic Canada,* G. M. Story, ed., pp. 41–52. St. John's: Memorial University of Newfoundland.

1985   Unearthing Red Bay's Whaling History. *National Geographic* 168(1):50–57.

Tylecote, R. F.

1962   *Metallurgy in Archaeology.* London: Edward Arnold (Publishers) Ltd.

1965   The development of iron smelting techniques in Great Britain. *Organon* 2:155–178.

1986   *The Prehistory of Metallurgy in the British Isles.* London: The Institute of Metals.

1992   *A History of Metallurgy,* 2d ed. London: The Institute of Metals.

Tylecote, R. F., J. N. Austin, and A. E. Wraith

1971   The mechanism of the bloomery process in shaft furnaces. *Jour. Iron Steel Inst.* 209(5):342–363.

Tylecote, R. F., and B. J. J. Gilmour

1986   *The Metallography of Early Ferrous Edge Tools and Edged Weapons.* Oxford: BAR British Series 155.

Unglik, H.

1986   Copper alloy objects, iron objects and slag from Carthage, fifth to seventh centuries A.D.: A metallurgical study. Manuscript on file, National Historic Parks and Sites, Environment Canada—Parks, Ottawa.

Unglik, H., and J. Stewart

1979   Metallurgical investigation of archaeological material of Norse origin from L'Anse aux Meadows, Newfoundland. Manuscript on file, National Historic Parks and Sites, Environment Canada—Parks, Ottawa.

Wagenfuhr, R.

1984   *Anatomie des Holzes.* Leipzig: VEB Fachbuchverlag.

Wallace, B.

1977   The Norse in Newfoundland. *Conservation Canada* 3(2):2–7. National Historic Parks and Sites, Environment Canada—Parks, Ottawa.

Ward, B. M.

1926   Martin Frobisher and Dr. Dee. *The Mariners Mirror* 12:453–455.

Wayman, M.

1991   Metallurgical examination of iron objects from the Eastern Arctic. Report of 26 June 1991 on file at Arctic Studies Center, Smithsonian Institution.

Weeks, W. F.
    1978   Sea ice conditions in the arctic. *Inst. Arct. Alp. Res. Glacial Data Rep.* GD-2:1–14.

Wingrove, J.
    1970   Identification of iron oxides. *Jour. Iron Steel Inst.* 208(3):258–264.

Wynne, E. J., and R. F. Tylecote
    1958   An experimental investigation into primitive iron-smelting technique. *Jour. Iron Steel Inst.* 190:339–348.

Index

Page numbers in italic indicate illustrations or tables.

accelerator mass spectrometer (AMS), 175, 209

Anne Francis, 138, 226, 227, 228, 235. *See also* ships *under* Frobisher

anvil, 18, 33, 34, 87, 113. *See also* relics *under* Frobisher

Anvil Cove, 108, 110

Anvil Cove 1, 91, *106, 107,* 110. *See also* sites *under* Inuit

archeology, 59f, 99f, 158

archeological
  context, 221, 234
  sites, features, 66–82, 104–131, *106, 107,* 222, 234. *See also* structures *under* Frobisher, sites *under* Inuit
  survey, 25, 61, 102–131, *103,* 147
    Countess of Warwick Sound, 104f, 213
    Cyrus Field Bay, 125f
    Kingait coast, 123f

Armonell, 15, 16, *138,* 141, *251. See also* ships *under* Frobisher

arrowhead, 6, 87, 214–216. *See also* finds *under* iron

assayers ("goldfiners"), 138
  John Baptista Agnello, 45
  Robert Denham, 138, 142, 144, *242, 245*

assaying, 143f, *145,* 148f

assay
  furnace, 141, 143f, 150
  office, 13, 25, 68, *69,* 150, 160. *See also* structures *under* Frobisher

Ayde, 11, *14, 138,* 142, 235, *251. See also* ships *under* Frobisher

Baffin Island, *2,* 16, 133

ballast, 92, 108, 234, 236
  "yronstone," 236–237

Bark Dennis, 138, 251. See also ships *under* Frobisher

Barrow's Chronological History of Arctic Discovery, 29, 40

Beare Leicester, 15, *138, 251. See also* ships *under* Frobisher

Best, George, *xvi, 2,* 12, 15, 35, *95, 98,* 109, 121, 162, 163, 179, 222–223, 226, 235, *241, 243, 251*

Best's Bulwark, 22, *58, 63, 65,* 79, 93, 155, 234. *See also* structures *under* Frobisher

bills of lading, *142*

Boas, Franz, 2, 4, 21, 120

blooms, 4–6, *18,* 31, 83–87, 161, 165f, 173, 226, 232f. *See also* bloom *under* Lookout Island, bloom *under* Smithsonian
  analysis of, 181–196
  dating of, 174f, *176*
  manufacture of, 204–207
  origin of, 207–210, 227, 236
  smelting of, 53, 221–225
  structure of, 202–204

brick, 91, 150

Bristol, 12, 45

Brookhaven National Laboratory, 5, 49, 52, 94, 161, 165, 175, 209

cache pits, 25, 71. *See also* structures *under* Frobisher

cairn, 75. *See also* structures *under* Frobisher

Cape Haven Whaling Station, *106, 107,* 130f

Cape Sarah, *2,* 61, 116

Cape Sarah Neck 1, *106, 107,* 116. *See also* sites *under* Inuit

Cathay Company, 11, 14, 16, 43, 45, 137

ceramics, *5,* 88, 147–151
  refractory, 149

charcoal, *5,* 24, 91, 155–172, 222, 234
  store, 25, 70, 160. *See also* structures *under* Frobisher

cinder, 91, 196f, 225

climate (Little Ice Age), 95

coal, 19, 34, 81, 142, 236
    dump 19, 104–110
Collins, Henry, 4, 22
conservation (site), 93, 110
Conservation Analytical Laboratory, 24, 49, 52, 209
contact, European-Inuit, 7, 40, 99f, 121, 151, 213, 227, 233
Countess of Sussex mine, 104, 141. *See also* mines *under*
        Frobisher
Countess of Warwick
    Island, *10, 12, 20, 22. See also* Kodlunarn Island
    mine, 104, 139. *See also* mines *under* Frobisher
    Sound, *2, 20, 25,* 60, 104f, 123
crucible, 88f, *147,* 148
Cumberland Sound, 2, 22, 35, 37, 96, 100, 116
cupel, *147,* 149
Cyrus Field Bay, *2,* 16, 17, 28, 125f
    1, *106, 107,* 126. *See also* sites *under* Inuit
    2, *106, 107,* 126. *See also* sites *under* Inuit

dam, 25, 70. *See also* structures *under* Frobisher
dating
    carbon-14, 49f, *85, 94f, 167, 174f*
    of iron samples, 177
    of non-iron samples, 176
Davis, John, 2, 34, 100
Denham, Robert. *See* assayers
Denham's Mount, 104, *138,* 142. *See also* mines *under* Frobisher
dolly, 78, 226, 233
Dorset, 112f, 126, 132. *See also* culture history *under* Inuit
Drake, Sir Francis, 42
driftwood, 24, 53, 92, 94, *154, 162f, 164,* 165

Elizabeth I, 11, 14, 43
Elizabethan
    alley, 61, *64,* 65
    structures. *See* structures *under* Frobisher
Emanuel, 15, *138, 251. See also* ships *under* Frobisher
England, 1, 52, 166
ethnography, 59

Fenton, Edward, 15, 73, *138,* 141, 144, 173, 174, 225, 226, 227,
        234, 235, 236, *242, 246, 251*
Fenton's
    Fortune, 117, *138, 139,* 142. *See also* mines *under* Frobisher
    watchtower (stone house), 13, 25, 36, 45, 63, 73–75, 92, 156,
        234. *See also* structures *under* Frobisher
flint (English), 34, 92, 108
Francis, 138, 251. See also ships *under* Frobisher
Franklin, Sir John, 16, 17, 27
Frobisher, Martin, 1f, 11f, 29, *42, 43f, 231f, 241, 242, 246, 251*
    basecamp, 19, 49, 65, 231. *See also* Kodlunarn Island
    Bay (Strait, Streights), *2, 10,* 13, *14, 17,* 28, 29, 38, 59f, 102,
        133, 165
    mines, 5, 23, 36, 75, 77, 93, 104, 110, *136, 138,* 139f
    ore (black rock), 1, 11, 23, 45, 79, *105, 138,* 139–145
    relics, *18, 19, 34, 35f,* 41, *46f*
    ships, 15f, *138, 249*
    structures, 19, 35f, 61–80, *63, 64,* 231
    voyages, 1–4, 11–13, 21, 41, 43, 99
furnace, 35f, 76, 150, 204f, 217, 221f

Gabriel, 11, *138,* 235, 237, *251. See also* ships *under* Frobisher
geography, 59
George Henry, 16, 26, 27, 28
gold, 2, 11, 23, 45, 46, 137, 140, 141, 143, 145, 222
gravestone, 79. *See also* structures *under* Frobisher

Greenwich Hospital Museum, 23
Gull Rock, *13. See also* Nepouetiesupbing

Hall, Charles Francis, 4, 16–21, 23, 27–40, 45f, 87, 137, 139,
        144
Halford Island Narrows, *106, 107,* 125
Hall Peninsula 1 (Kussegeerarkjuan), 34, *106, 107,* 117
Hanseatic League, 237
Hopewell, 138, 251. See also ships *under* Frobisher
historical records, 226, 234
hostage, *3,* 12
Hudson, Henry, 38, 233
Hudson's Bay Company (HBC), 27, 38, 39, 46
Hume, Ivor Noël, 236

Idlaulitoo outpost camp, 122, *123*
Imilik, *106, 107,* 122
Inook, Ltd., 22
Inuit, 2, *3,* 11, 12, 17f, 27f, 60, 100
    culture history, 132f
    dwelling styles, *31, 101, 123, 134*
    sites, 80–82, 110–132, *106, 107*
iron
    finds, *23.* 87, 213. *See also* blooms
        dating of, 50, 177
        metallurgy of, 213
    ore, 93, 222
    wedge, 116, *214,* 216–218
Island 95, *106, 107,* 128. *See also* sites *under* Inuit
IsoTrace Laboratory, 5, 175f
Itilikjuak, *106, 107,* 126. *See also* sites *under* Inuit
Iqaluit, 22, 45, 60

Jackman Sound, *106, 107,* 125. *See also* sites *under* Inuit
    mine, 108f, 109. *See also* mines *under* Frobisher
James Bay, 38
Judith, 138, 142, *251. See also* ships *under* Frobisher

kadlunat (qallunat), 18, 21, 29, 30, 31, 35–39 *passim,* 60
Kamaiyuk, *106, 107,* 120. *See also* sites *under* Inuit
Kendall Strait, *106,* 125
Kenyon, Walter, 4, 22, 23, 66, 76, 86, 90, 93, 96, 101, 104, 114,
        115, 117, 139, 160, 173, 231
Kingait coast, 38, 123
Kodlunarn Island, *2,* 4, 12, 18–25, 28, 36, 59–97. *See also*
        Countess of Warwick Island
Koojesse, 28, 29
Kuyait 1, *106, 107,* 118. *See also* sites *under* Inuit

Lefferts Island, *106, 107, 108,* 165. *See also* sites *under* Inuit
    (Beare Sound) mine, 108, *109, 138. See also* mines *under*
        Frobisher
Lok, Michael, 1, 11, 15, 43, 45
longhouse, 25, *63,* 72, 160. *See also* structures *under* Frobisher
Lookout Island, 34, 126, 213
    bloom, 34, 86, 126, *128,* 227
Lyon, Captain, 2, 27, 38–39

MacMillan, Donald, 21–22, 74, *75,* 114
Merwe, van der, N. J., 50, 174
Meta Incognita, *2*
    Committee, 7, 104
metallurgy, 5, 181f, 213f, 221. *See also* blooms, iron, slag
metal detector, 54, 61
Michael, 11, *138,* 235, *251. See also* ships *under* Frobisher
mine pit, *63,* 79. *See also* structures *under* Frobisher

mines. *See* mines *under* Frobisher
miners (colony of 100), 12, 13, 73, 156
mining, 137f
   methods, 142
   tools, 142f
Minguktoo, *106, 107,* 122. *See also* sites *under* Inuit
missing (lost) sailors, 11, 12, 29f, 37, 80, 124, 231, 234
monument (to Frobisher?), 35, *37*
Moon, 138, 226, 235, 236, *251. See also* ships *under* Frobisher
mortar, 92
muffle, 150

National Historic Sites and Monuments of Canada, 22
Neoeskimo, 132. *See also* culture history *under* Inuit
Nepouetiesupbing ("place where a mast is put up"), 28, 37f, *230*
Newland Island. *See* Winter's Furnace
Norse (Viking), 5, 24, 60, 162, 179f, 211, 233
Northwest Passage, 1, 11, 27, 45

Ookijoxy Ninoo, 29, 30, 31, 35, 36, *37,* 38, 39
oral history (oral tradition), 5, 29–40, 234
osmunde, 24, 83, 174, 227

Paleoeskimo, 132. *See also* culture history *under* Inuit
Parks Canada, 5, 24, 84, 85, 176, 177
Parry, Captain, 2, 27, 38–39
pinnace, 226, 234f, *249. See also* ships *under* Frobisher
pit feature, *63,* 76. *See also* structures *under* Frobisher
Pitsiulak (research vessel), 86, 102, 103, 104, 134, 135
Pre-Dorset, 132. *See also* culture history *under* Inuit

Raleigh, Sir Walter, 42
reservoir (mine), 36, 61, *63,* 75, 140. *See also* structures *under* Frobisher
Roy, Sharat, 21, 22, 23
Royal Geographic Society, 23, 46, 86, 87, 155, 175
Royal Ontario Museum, 4, 22

Salomon, 15, *138, 251. See also* ships *under* Frobisher
ship's trench, 18, 36, *63,* 77f, 140, 160f. *See also* structures *under* Frobisher
silver mine. *See* Jackman Sound mine
Skraeling, 2

slag, 91f, *203*
   metallurgy of, 191–202 *passim*
small-volume counter, 5, 52
Smithes Island, 109
Smithsonian
   bloom, 5, 23–24, 45–47, *48,* 49–55, 83, 86, 87, 94, 95, 96, 114, 155, 162, 165, 166, 173–179 *passim,* 209, 210, 211, 222
   Institution, 4, 5, 24, 45, 46, 47, 49, 50, 102, 155, 158, 175, 181
smithy, *63,* 66f, 160. *See also* structures *under* Frobisher
Stefansson, Vilhjalmur, 46
stone house. *See* Fenton's watchtower
Strong, Duncan, 21–22, 74
Sumner Island 2, *106, 107,* 120. *See also* sites *under* Inuit
Sussex Island (Beare Sound) mine, 108, *138. See also* mines *under* Frobisher

Thomas, 138, 251. See also ships *under* Frobisher
Thomas Allen, 138, 251. See also ships *under* Frobisher
Thule, 132. *See also* culture history *under* Inuit
Tikkoon, 18, 37, 87, 213, *230*
   Point 1, *106, 107,* 114f
Tookoolitoo, 30
tile, *34,* 90, 150. *See also* relics *under* Frobisher
"tokens of possession," 1, 11, 45
Tylecote, R., 52

Viking. *See* Norse

Weasel Point 1, *106, 107,* 125. *See also* sites *under* Inuit
wedge. *See under* iron
well, *63,* 79. *See also* structures *under* Frobisher
Weymouth, 38
White, John, *12,* 16
Willows Island (Oopungnewing, Opingivik), 33, *106, 107,* 108, 111–114. *See also* sites *under* Inuit
Winter's Furnace, 104, *105, 138, 139,* 141–142, 174, 227. *See also* mines *under* Frobisher
wood, *34,* 78, 91, 155f
   photomicrographs of, *168–172*

York Sound 1, *106, 107,* 124. *See also* sites *under* Inuit
"yronstones of Russia." *See under* ballast